17$\underline{95}$

# California

## AN ILLUSTRATED HISTORY

# California

## AN ILLUSTRATED HISTORY

### Updated

by T. H. Watkins

The Great West Series

AMERICAN LEGACY PRESS    NEW YORK

*Sacramento City in 1851, when the gold rush and all that went with it helped
shape the character and quality of California's American life.*

*This book is dedicated to the memory of my two grandfathers:
both Californians by choice, both gone, both well remembered
by those who loved them.*

Copyright © MCMLXXIII by American West Publishing Company
All rights reserved.
This 1983 edition is published by American Legacy Press,
distributed by Crown Publishers, Inc., by arrangement with
T. H. Watkins

Manufactured in Hong Kong

**Library of Congress Cataloging in Publication Data**

Watkins, T. H. (Tom H.), 1936–
    California: an illustrated history.
    Reprint. Originally published: New York: Weathervane
Books, c1973. (The Great West series)
    Includes bibliographical references and index.
    1. California—History.   I. Title.   II. Series: Great
West series.
[F861.W35   1983]     979.4     82-16292

ISBN: 0-517-187809

h g f e d c b

*Preceding page: A view of San Francisco, painted
by August Ferran in about 1850.*

# CONTENTS

*Mount Shasta, Northern California — "Lonely as God and white as a winter moon."*

# PART ONE
# 1540–1900

*The California coast, from the edge of the sea: a view of the meeting of land and water at Point Lobos.*

# PROLOGUE
# The Land, Waiting

Out of the seas of time, a land was born, a land as diverse and self-contained geographically as it was later to be socially, economically, and polit-ically. It is axiomatic that the history of any region is shaped largely by its geography, but in few other places on earth has the maxim been illustrated more clearly than in California.

Water, air, fire, and ice: the forces of time molded California as they molded the rest of the cooling cinder called Earth—but in the process created something unique. Over a period of perhaps four hundred million years—from the beginning to the end of the Paleozoic Era—most of California was periodically inundated by

*The California coast, from 579 miles up: an infrared satellite photograph of Monterey Bay, the Coast Range, and the Salinas and San Joaquin valleys.*

ancient seas. About 180 million years ago, under the pressure of millions of years of sedimental deposits, the earth's crust began to buckle and warp, creating the great wall of the Sierra Nevada on the east. The sea continued to advance and retreat; wind and rain wore away at the exposed rocks of the new mountains, depositing ever more sediments; and the Coast Range of the west, the Transverse Ranges of the south, and the Cascade-Siskiyou Range of the north lifted above the sea, which now occupied a vast trough a hundred miles

in width and nearly six hundred long in the center of California, as well as a large expanse in the southern portions of the state.

Still the earth continued to rise, slowly lifting until the sea made its final retreat. Sputtering volcanoes formed, particularly in the north, where such fiery pyramids as Mount Lassen (not quite dead even today) and Mount Shasta scattered volcanic ash, rock, and lava over hundreds of square miles; the Sierra Nevada and Cascade-Siskiyou ranges thrust upward once again;

the huge plates of the earth's surface ground inexorably against each other, leaving a bewildering network of faults in the sedimental rocks along the western length of California, the largest and most unstable of which was the San Andreas, slicing diagonally across the state from Point Arena north of San Francisco Bay to Baja California.

And then the ice came, beginning about two million years ago, creeping down from the Arctic Circle in grinding sheets; four or five times the ice came and went, splitting and pulverizing and polishing the immense scarps of the Sierra Nevada, gouging out the glorious trench called Yosemite Valley. When the last of the ice retreated, perhaps ten thousand years ago, it left behind the California known to history, one of the most varied and spectacular geographic provinces on earth; it was, in fact, several geographic provinces.

The western portion of the southern one-third of the state—neatly separated from the northern part by the crescent of the Tehachapi Mountains—was a region of coastal basins and valleys, watered by the Santa Clara, San Gabriel, Santa Ana, and Los Angeles rivers. On the north and northeast, it was separated from desert country by the Santa Ynez, San Gabriel, and San Bernardino mountains, and farther south by the Santa Ana and San Jacinto ranges, some of whose peaks rose above ten thousand feet. Like most of the rest of California, it was a region of summer drought and winter rains, though generally semi-arid, since its annual rainfall averaged less than twenty inches.

The eastern part of California's southern third was a large desert triangle. In the extreme northeasterly point of the triangle, between the Panamint Range on the east and the Amargosa Range on the west, lay Death Valley. One hundred and thirty miles long and from 6 to 14 wide, Death Valley was the very manifestation of a medieval Hell, a stygian inferno whose bottom elevation of 276 feet below sea level was the lowest point on the North American continent. Some forty miles to the northwest, across the sawtoothed mountains, was the high desert country of the Owens Valley beneath the steep eastern escarpment of the Sierra Nevada. South of the Owens Valley lay the Mojave Desert, an expanse of dry lake bottoms, short rocky mountains, and large sandy valleys; and to the east of the Mojave was the Colorado Desert, which paralleled the Colorado

River to culmination in the deep sedimental sink of the Imperial Valley.

The largest geographic fact in the northern two-thirds of the state was the Sierra Nevada range, which joined the Tehachapi Mountains in the southeast and spread some six hundred miles to the north, until its trailing spurs mingled with those of the Cascade-Siskiyou Range. The Sierra Nevada, whose highest peak (Mount Whitney) topped fourteen thousand feet, trapped much of the state's annual precipitation out of moisture-laden air from the Pacific, condensing it as snow, which was stored during the winter and released each spring down the dancing tributaries of the range's western slope.

The California coast, constantly eroded by the working of the sea and bent by the warps and inclinations of the continental shelf, extended nearly twelve hundred miles in actual shoreline from north to south, beset along much of its length by thick summer fogs and possessed of only three harbors of any significance: San Diego Bay in the south, San Francisco Bay in the center, and Humboldt Bay in the north. Above most of this shore loomed the mountains of the Coast Range. North of San Francisco Bay, the range gradually spread out in a tangled mass of mountainous rain forest, with a maximum annual precipitation of eighty inches, and then joined with the northwesterly jumble of the Cascade-Siskiyou Range. Its full-bodied rivers—the Klamath, the Trinity, the Scott, the Mad, the Eel, and the Russian—drained quickly into the ocean. South of San Francisco Bay, the range narrowed and became progressively less moist and less impenetrable, enfolding soft valleys behind a harsh facade that often plunged straight down to the edge of the sea. Even its rivers—the Carmel, the Salinas, the Santa Maria, and the Santa Ynez—were gentler.

Between the Coast Range and the Sierra Nevada lay the Central Valley, an enormous elongated bowl filled with the sedimental deposits of whole geologic epochs. In reality it was two valleys: its northern section was watered by the Sacramento River, which coursed south fattened by six major tributaries—the Pit and the Mc-Cloud in the north, and the Feather, Indian, Yuba, and American rivers from the slopes of the northern Sierra Nevada; its southern section was watered by the north-ward-flowing San Joaquin River and its southern Sierra

*On the Northern California coast, geography and history met to re-create*
*New England in the old lumber-port town of Mendocino.*

Nevada tributaries—the Fresno, Merced, Tuolomne, Stanislaus, Calaveras, Mokelumne, and Consumnes rivers. At about midpoint in the Central Valley, the Sacramento and the San Joaquin joined in a deltaic triangle whose waters were funneled westward through the Carquinez Straits to San Francisco Bay and thence to the ocean.

The sheer variety of this California landscape bred an abundance for the future's sake. Great stands of *Sequoia sempervirens,* the sturdy coast redwood, crowded the mountains of the Coast Range from Humboldt Bay to the Santa Lucias south of the Carmel River, and equally dense growths of yellow pine and sugar pine populated the western slopes of the Sierra Nevada. In the coastal and interior valleys, rich soil ached for a plow and millions of acres of grasslands stood ready for the herd.

Beneath the organic shales laid down millions of years before lay thick pools of oil ready for the tapping. And in the streambanks and riverbeds, gulches and gullies of the Sierra Nevada, placer gold lay strewn like largesse from the gods, detritus that wind and rain and time had conspired to carry down from veins in the exposed granitic outcroppings of the mountains.

This was the land waiting as the first Indians wandered into California from the mountains of the north and the deserts of the Southwest....

This was the land waiting as Francis Drake and his crew careened the *Golden Hind* into an unknown northern bay in 1579....

This was the land waiting as the first group of Spanish colonizers stumbled ashore at San Diego Bay in 1769....

This was the land, waiting.

*Looking toward Mount Rose across Donner Lake in the Sierra Nevada,
where geography met history in 1846 — and geography won.*

*Overleaf: Dante's View of Death Valley*
*National Monument — California's definitive desert.*

# SECTION ONE

# *The Island*

Know ye that on the right hand of the Indies there is an island called California, very near the Terrestrial Paradise and inhabited by black women without a single man among them and living in the manner of Amazons. They are robust of body, strong and passionate in heart, and of great valor. Their island is one of the most rugged in the world with bold rocks and crags. Their arms are all of gold, as is the harness of the wild beasts which, after taming, they ride. In all the island there is no other metal. . . .

In this island called California, with the great roughness of the land and the multitude of wild animals, are many griffins the like of which are not found in any other part of the world. In the season when the griffins give birth to their young, these women cover themselves with thick hides and go out to snare the little griffins, taking them to their caves where they raise them. And being quite a match for these griffins, they feed them the men taken as prisoners and the males to which they have given birth. All this is done with such skill that the griffins become thoroughly accustomed to them and do them no harm. Any male who comes to the island is killed and eaten by the griffins. . . .

—Garcí Rodríguez Ordóñez de Montalvo
(*Las Sergas de Esplandián,* ca. 1510)

*Water, wind, and earth — the essential elements of the California coast are joined at Big Sur.*

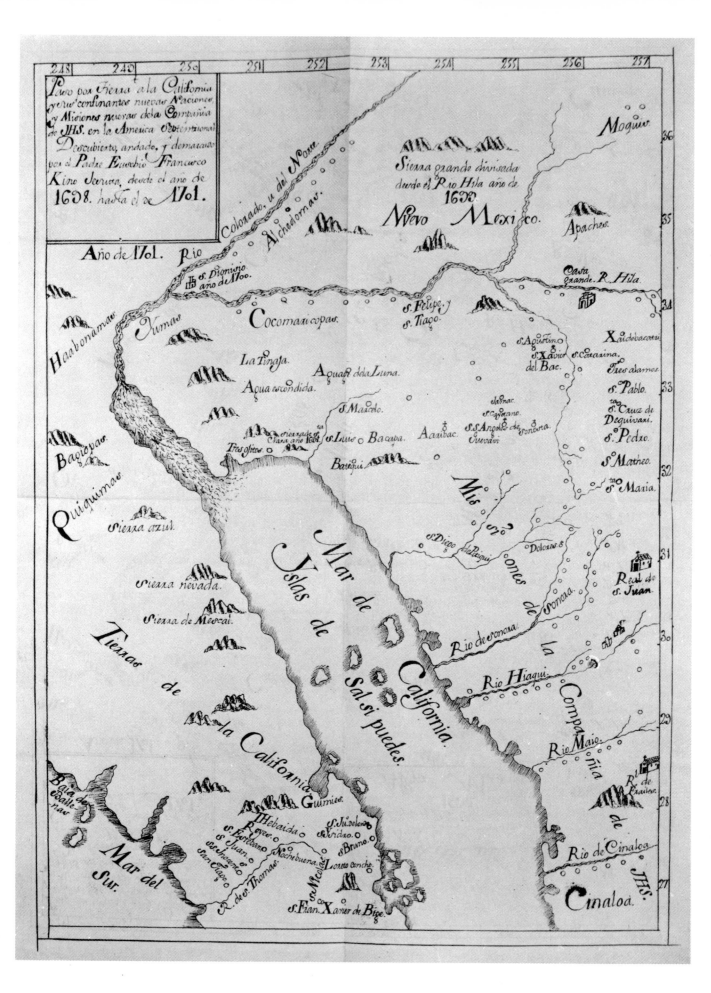

# CHAPTER 1

# A LAND OF GOLD AND GRIFFINS

*A two-hundred-and-fifty-year journey from myth to reality, from an*

*unknown land to a flyspeck outpost of Spanish empire*

O N ONE REMARKABLE DAY in April 1536, Capt. Melchior Díaz met his future, even though this hardheaded, frontier soldier might have scoffed at portents; he had spent too much time dealing with the solid and sometimes cruel realities of life in New Spain. The year before, he had played a major part in the grimly efficient pillage of Nuevo Galicia under the leadership of its governor, Nuño de Guzmán, a conquistador with a mind like an axe and an affection for spilling blood. Thousands of Indians had been killed or enslaved, scores of villages destroyed and their crops obliterated, in one of the most ferocious campaigns in the history of the conquest of Mexico. And now Díaz was commander of the military post of San Miguel de Culiacán, the northernmost extension of Spanish empire in the New World, a primitive garrison town that sat like a scab on the plain of Mexico's northwest littoral beneath the sawtooth wilderness of the Sierra Madre Occidental. From here, he sent his men out into the surrounding land to hunt for more slaves.

Characterized by a professional soldier's pragmatic toughness and as much casual brutality as most Spaniards in that time and place, Díaz nonetheless must have been shaken the April day his men brought back, not slaves, but specters whose presence in that rock-ribbed land was impossible: four nearly naked, half-starved men, three of them Spaniards and one a Moorish black man. The Spaniards were Alvar Nuñez Cabeza de Vaca, Alonso del Castillo Maldonado, and Andrés Dorantes de Carranca, who owned the black man, a slave called Estebánico. Their tale was an epic that had no parallel in its own time and place, and has had none since.

They were the only survivors of the three-hundred-man exploring expedition under Pánfilo de Narváez that had landed on the west coast of Florida in 1528. After months spent blindly fighting its way through the swamps and tangles of west Florida, the expedition had built crude boats and desperately set out into the Gulf of Mexico. Only eighty men stepped alive on the shores of east Texas to begin the long march back to the valley of Mexico, and one by one these died or were enslaved by Indians. Cabeza de Vaca and his companions broke free sometime in 1534 and began a wandering journey, sometimes befriended, sometimes worshipped, and sometimes enslaved again, by the Indians they encountered. It was a journey that took them up into the valley of the Rio Grande, west across what is now Texas, New Mexico, and Arizona, south through the deserts of Sonora, and finally to their encounter with Culiacán's slave-hunting soldiers in the northern reaches of Nuevo Galicia. It was a cosmic journey and European man's first blind thrust into land that would become the American Southwest.

Their survival alone was a miracle of stamina and determination, and the narrative of its accomplishment a tale worth any man's attention. But there was more—so much more that Díaz sent the emaciated men to Nuño de Guzmán for a re-telling. For they had heard and seen things, these four: they had seen shells of pearl-bearing oysters and arrowheads chipped out of emeralds; they had heard, Cabeza de Vaca said, that "on the coast of the South Sea are pearls and great

*Fray Eusebio Francisco Kino's 1701 map of the Gulf of California — cartography as myth-destroyer.*

riches, and the best and all the most opulent countries are near there." In these countries, he said, were "populous towns and very large houses." Guzmán listened, entranced, and listened again. Then he sent the travelers across the mountains to the City of Mexico and Viceroy Don Antonio de Mendoza, who also listened—and listened.

Their words were like wind on a long-burning ember. They fired hopes that had risen, and fallen, then risen again periodically ever since Columbus first sighted the green islands of the Caribbean. The lands of the New World were largely unknown and therefore magical, filled with all the yeasty possibilities fervent imaginations could provide. Those imaginations peopled the unknown with a nightmare's population—man-eating griffins; black, one-breasted Amazons; men with mouths where their stomachs ought to be—and gilded it with all the dreams of treasure Western man had dreamed since Ser Marco Polo; golden islands in the South Sea; El Dorado, the Gilded Man; the land of Gran Quivira, whose trees were hung with golden bells; the island of Antillia, whose seven great cities were laced by streets paved with gold . . .

For a time, it seemed that all such dreams were true. Shortly after landing at Vera Cruz on the east coast of Mexico in 1519, Hernán Cortes reported that it was "a land very rich in gold." Two years later, he conquered the Aztec city of Tenochtitlán and looted it of treasure so great that news of it vibrated in all the European capitals. From Tenochtitlán (now Mexico City), Cortes sent men in all directions in search of more treasure; they found little, but in 1533, Francisco Pizarro looted the Inca empire of Peru, with its rooms full of gold and silver, and the dream revived. Earlier, Cortes had dispatched explorers in search of the Great South Sea, "for everybody who has any knowledge and experience of navigation in the Indies is certain that the discovery of the South Sea would lead to the discovery of many islands rich in gold, pearls, precious stones, spices, and other unknown and wonderful things." What they found was the Gulf of California, which they named the Red Sea of Cortes; but in the year of Pizarro's success, the conqueror sent men in search of those treasure-filled islands that must lie somewhere to the west. They found the arid peninsula of Baja California, where twenty of the explorers died

in battle with Indians who were neither Amazons nor griffins. It was an island, they supposed, and they named it Santa Cruz.

Crippled by barren experience, the dream yet survived. Guzmán himself had encountered stories of seven rich tribes living in seven caves or cities somewhere to the north of his Nuevo Galicia . . . perhaps Antillia? He did not survive in the New World long enough to find out. Shortly after he sent the four dream-carriers to Mexico City, he was called back to Old Spain to account for himself and ended his life in prison.

So it was that Mendoza, viceregal successor to Cortes, listened intently to the tales recounted by Cabeza de Vaca and his companions. He listened and made his plans, slowly and carefully. Obviously, the discovery and conquest of the great cities of the north would require a major expedition, perhaps the largest the New World had yet seen. By 1539 he had decided that it should be a two-pronged affair: a land expedition under the command of Francisco Vásquez de Coronado, the new governor of Nuevo Galicia, and a sea force under the captaincy of Hernán de Alarcón designed to sail up the west coast of Mexico and make connection with Coronado in the north. Before proceeding, however, Mendoza determined to double-check his information by sending the slave Estebánico north as a guide for Marcos de Niza, a priest whose honesty was presumed unquestionable; if the stories were true, he above all others would know. De Niza returned alone to the City of Mexico three months later. The slave had been killed by Indians, but the good father had seen, from a safe distance, the first of the Seven Cities of what was now called Cíbola; it was a city of stone, he said, perhaps larger than the City of Mexico—and Indians had told him that it was the smallest of them all. What is more, he had heard further stories of gold and other treasures.

That was enough, more than enough, and early in 1540 the ambitious venture got under way. Alarcón left the west coast in command of three ships, bound for the great blank of the northern regions, while Coronado assembled his land forces at San Miguel de Culiacán. It was a most grand agglomeration, this expedition: it included 230 *caballeros* recruited from the greedy nobility of New Spain, nearly a thousand Indian servants, five friars to carry the word of God, more than fifteen hundred horses, mules, and beef cattle, and a hundred-man military escort under the command of Capt. Melchior Díaz, he who had greeted those four ghosts from the desert in the spring of 1536. In late February, after a review by Viceroy Mendoza, the massive party headed north for the country of myth.

Coronado soon separated himself and the military arm from the slow-moving main force, which inched painfully across the Sierra Madre Occidental. Even so, they did not reach the deserts of southern Arizona until mid-June, and then it was one long, dry march after another through the arid, tumbling-down country of the Colorado Plateau before they found the first of the Seven Cities of Cíbola—Hawíkuh, the adobe city-state of the Zuñi Indians, an earthen city that must have glistened tantalizingly in that wavering, mirage-ridden desert air. After putting down a brief and useless flurry of resistance on July 7, the expedition found food and water—but no more. There were no rooms filled with gold and silver, nothing at all to justify the effort and expense of six months. Frustrated almost beyond endurance, yet still hopeful of finding the treasures of Cíbola, Coronado sent bits and pieces of the expedition off on forays into the ragged land. In September, Melchior Díaz and twenty-five of his men were sent west with instructions to make contact with Alarcón and his three ships, which carried badly needed supplies.

Alarcón had done all he could. In late August, his command had reached the head of the Gulf of California and the mouth of the Colorado River, "a very mighty river, which ran with so great fury of a storm, that we could hardly sail against it." With desperate effort, they towed ships' boats up the river to the mouth of the Gila, then another hundred miles beyond that. They waited, but no word of the Coronado expedition came; and when their own supplies threatened to give out, they cached some letters beneath a tree, returned to their ships at the mouth of the Colorado, and sailed back to New Spain.

In October, Díaz and his men arrived at the Colorado, and friendly Cocopah Indians guided them to the spot where the Alarcón expedition had buried letters. "He [Díaz] dug up the letters," Pedro de Casteñeda, the expedition's chronicler, recalled some years later, "and learned from them how long Alarcón had waited for news of the army and that he had gone back with

Drake's 1579 plate of brass.

The question of Francis Drake's California anchorage remains open. The consensus among historians up to now has held that he landed in Drake's Bay (Estero) north of San Francisco Bay; this consensus, however, is little more than a set of agreed-upon assumptions, since there is little hard evidence to support that (or any other) claim. One bit of intriguing evidence that seems to point to San Francisco Bay is the *Portus Novae Albionis* (Port of New Albion) shown below, published as part of a commemorative world map drawn in 1589 by the Flemish cartographer Jodocus Hondius, whose friend was Thomas Talbot, Clerk of Records in the Tower of London and a man possibly privy to the records of the Drake voyage. The map is intriguing because it bears an uncanny resemblance to the part of San Francisco Bay that includes the Tiburon Peninsula and Belvedere Island, and none whatever to Drake's Bay.

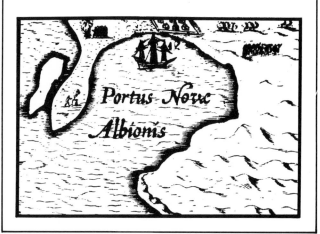

the ships to New Spain, because he was unable to proceed further, since this sea was a bay, which was formed by the Isle of the Marquis [Baja California], which is called California, and it was explained that California was not an island, but a point of the mainland forming the other side of that gulf."* There were no supplies, but the Indians were tractable and there was land yet to be explored. They crossed the Colorado on brush rafts and continued vaguely west, perhaps as far as the Salton Sink. There was little in this blistering land of spindly creosote bush, Joshua trees, alkaline flats, and brown, bubbling, sulphuric potholes that distinguished it from the living incarnation of a medieval hell, and Díaz decided to return to Cíbola.

On the way, the explorers killed rabbits for food, chasing after the fast, leather-tough little desert creatures on their horses, spearing them at full gallop with their lances. They were consummate horsemen, these soldiers, and years of Indian-chasing had given them a precise skill with the lance. (Passed on from generation to generation, both skills would come to fruition in the Battle of San Pascual more than three hundred years later—a battle that may have taken place less than one hundred miles from where they were.) But chasing rabbits at full tilt was a chancy business, a matter of inches. On one such gallop, Díaz miscalculated, probably by no more than a hair; the blade of his lance sliced into the earth and its butt caught him in the belly, impaling him. He was soon dead, and not pleasantly.

The somewhat ludicrous death of the Indian-fighting commander of San Miguel de Culiacán was a singularly apt footnote to the entire star-crossed Coronado expedition, which finally came to an end on the plains of Kansas, in 1542, still following myths of gold and finding only great herds of "hunch-back cattle." Yet, we must give the memory of Díaz its due, for his life-blood spilled in the acrid, unwelcoming country of the Colorado Desert was a first mark in the European discovery of California—even if the reality of what he found there had sent him skittering back toward Cíbola and the more familiar landscape of fantasy.

---

*In spite of this evidence, cartographers and explorers alike continued to see Baja as an island, a myth not fully discredited until the explorations of Father Eusebio Francisco Kino near the end of the seventeenth century.

OUT OF SUCH VAGUE COMBINATIONS of myth and memory, California entered the annals of Spanish empire in the New World. Even her name was derived from romance, lifted from a popular episodic novel written by one Garcí Rodríguez Ordóñez de Montalvo and published around 1510: *Las Sergas de Espandián.* "Know ye," the many-named novelist had written, "that on the right hand of the Indies there is an island called California, very near the Terrestrial Paradise. . . ." It was a land of Amazons, of gold, of "bold rocks and crags," and—as usual—of those obscure, nightmarish creatures sixteenth-century imaginations called griffins. No one knows precisely when the name was first applied to Baja California, but it is certain that it was in common use by the early 1540s, and given the forbidding nature of much of that desert land, its use was particularly apt. If ever there was a country that harbored griffins, this might well have been it.

At any rate, California was a name carried north in 1542 by João Rodrigues Cabrillo,* a Portuguese explorer in the employ of Viceroy Mendoza. Cabrillo, too, was chasing a myth, this one called the Straits of Anián, the magical sea passage through the North American continent that obsessed European explorers for more than two centuries. He found nothing of the sort, of course, but in his journey he made the first discovery and exploration of the coast of Upper California—beginning in September 1542, with San Diego Bay (which he named San Miguel), then San Pedro Bay, Santa Monica Bay, Point Conception, Catalina Island, San Miguel Island, and finally Monterey Bay (which he named "La Baya de los Pinos") in October. During a winter layover on San Miguel Island, Cabrillo died, but his men continued exploring, reaching as far north as the southern Oregon coast before returning to Mexico.

Cabrillo's mission had been a massive effort, bringing a vast new territory into the Spanish ken, yet his discoveries were received in Mexico City with hardly more enthusiasm than those of Melchior Díaz. What Viceroy Mendoza had wanted was the Straits of Anián; or failing that, at least news of a land rich in gold and silver, another Golconda for the plundering. What

---

*The Spanish "Cabrillo" is a corruption of the original Portuguese spelling, "Cabrilho."

Cabrillo had found was apparently little more than another Baja, a profitless locality with a rock-ribbed coast, only one harbor (San Diego) worth mentioning, and the whole thing populated by belligerent Indians. Reports of the Cabrillo expedition were filed away and all but forgotten.

Nearly forty years passed before California again entered the annals of exploration. Again, it was partly the result of myth-chasing, but this time it was an English freebooter who figured. Armed with a commission from Queen Elizabeth I, Francis Drake set out in 1578 to circumnavigate the globe, search for a Northwest Passage (the English version of the Straits of Anián), open up British trade in the Pacific, and last—but most definitely not least—garner what Spanish treasure he could as a privateer. In 1579 his *Golden Hind* entered Spanish trade lanes in the Pacific and soon captured the *Cacafuego*, a Spanish treasure ship carrying 1,300 bars of silver and fourteen chests of silver coin, gold, jewelry, and plate. The weight of this precious cargo was almost too much for the *Golden Hind,* whose seams began to bulge alarmingly, so when he reached the California coast, Drake determined to find a safe harbor to careen and reinforce the ship. Although it has long been supposed that the anchorage he chose was in what is now called Drake's Bay, just north of San Francisco, there is other evidence which suggests that it actually was a cove near Point San Quentin on San Francisco Bay (see side panel)—nearly two hundred years before any Spaniard set eyes on California's greatest natural harbor.

Wherever he landed, Drake spent more time in California than anyone before him and many of those who followed; for five weeks the *Golden Hind* remained in the harbor, and those not working on the ship spent much of their time exploring the country, building a crude base camp on shore, and consorting with the local Indians (the Coast Miwok, most likely), who they fondly supposed cheerfully relinquished all claim and title to this land to Her Gracious Majesty, Queen Elizabeth. Drake called the country Nova Albion, because the white cliffs that annotate much of the shoreline north of San Francisco Bay reminded him of the cliffs of Dover. Before leaving to continue his circumnavigation, he fixed a brass plate to a post, claiming "Nova Albion" for England. (The brass plate, discovered in Marin County in 1937, is now on display at the Bancroft Library, University of California at Berkeley.) Even though England never seriously followed up on his claim, Drake's little ritual was the first formal claim to the territory of Upper California.

If the English displayed no particular interest in California after Drake, neither did the New World Spanish, who had just about given up myth-chasing as a vocation. There were other things to be considered by then, among them the Philippine trade, which was real, tangible, and immensely profitable. In 1565, Miguel López de Legaspi had conquered these islands, providing New Spain with a trade outlet to the coasts of Asia and giving rise to the great voyages of the massive galleons between Manila and Acapulco on the west coast of Mexico. In that same year, Andrés de Urdañeta established the "great circle" route that followed the winds and currents of the Pacific from Manila to California's Cape Mendocino, then south to Acapulco; it was this trade and this route that inspired the next Spanish examination of California. The galleons, crammed to the scuppers with luxury goods on the return voyage, were floating horrors to the men who served in them, great wallowing death ships rampant with scurvy, dysentery, starvation, and thirst. Moreover, they were easy prey for English freebooters in smaller, faster ships. It was supposed that both problems would be solved if a good port of call could be established somewhere on the north coast of California; water and food could be taken on, and a military vessel provided for escort on the remainder of the journey.

To this end, Pedro de Unamuno sailed in a galleon from Manila in 1587 with instructions to locate a suitable harbor. He landed at Morro Bay, an inadequate scoop out of the coastline one hundred miles south of Monterey Bay, and penetrated inland for a few miles before hostile Indians drove him and his men back to their ship. Eight years later, Sebastián Rodríguez Cermeño was given a similar assignment in the galleon *San Augustin;* he landed at Drake's Bay, and after a southeast gale pounded the ship to pieces on the beach, he and seventy men crowded into a small launch and in a remarkable journey back to Acapulco managed to accomplish the first detailed survey of the California coast from 41 degrees North latitude to 30 degrees— although he managed to miss the entrance to San Francisco Bay.* But he found no decent harbor, and in 1602, Sebastián Vizcaíno, a merchant-adventurer who had been promised command of a galleon for his services, launched yet another exploration and found, by his own self-serving account, what they all had been looking for: a "noble harbor . . . the best port that could be desired, for besides being sheltered from all the winds, it has many pines for masts and yards, and live oaks and white oaks, and water in great quantity, all near the shore." He named this remarkable bay after the viceroy who had authorized the voyage, the Conde de Monterey, then continued his exploration as far north as Cape Mendocino before returning to Mexico, with nearly half his crew dead or dying.

During this expedition, Vizcaíno gave the California coast most of the names it bears today, but that accomplishment was thoroughly overshadowed by the sheer mischief he caused with his overdrawn description of Monterey Bay. This bay was not a "noble harbor . . . sheltered from all the winds," it was an open roadstead susceptible to all the whims of wind and weather. Fortunately for the galleons, Viceroy Monterey was succeeded by the Marqués de Montesclaros, who was unimpressed both with Vizcaíno and with the need for a California port of call, pointing out that by the time the ships reached the northern coast, prevailing southerly winds brought them to Mexico quickly. Even so, Vizcaíno's luminous rendition of the harbor of Monterey persisted, gaining luster as the years passed, until it glimmered as the Seven Cities of Cíbola had once glimmered.

F OR DECADES AFTER VIZCAÍNO, California was a neglected foundling whose only apparent value was that it possessed the splendid harbor of Monterey—should the occasion arise when a splendid harbor might be needed. In the meantime, New World officialdom proceeded to ignore both Californias, except for an occasional venture into the upper gulf in search of pearls. The silver mines and Indian troubles of northern Mexico, southern Arizona, and New Mexico occu-

*With the possible exception of Drake, all of the coast's early explorers missed the Golden Gate—most likely because of the prevailing fogs that shroud the coast in this region, particularly in the summer months.

pied the attention of Mexico City, and Spain herself was too busy protecting her weakening position in the arenas of European power to think of expanding a New World empire that she could no longer afford.

Expansion was left to the "Black Robes," the militant, profoundly courageous, and ambitious Jesuits, who saw in the wilderness of New Spain a treasure trove far richer and more significant than the lunatic dreams of the conquistadors—a storehouse of souls. With the cheerful dedication of prospective martyrs and the organizational skill of Vatican politicians, they carried their version of civilization into nearly all the wilderness valleys of western Mexico, from Culiacán to Pimería Alta (the northernmost extent of what would later be the state of Sonora). Among them was Father Eusebio Francisco Kino, a transplanted Austrian who came to Mexico in 1681 at the age of thirty-six. In 1687 he was assigned to the northern country of the Pima Indians (Pimería Alta), and in a little over ten years this energetic man had established functioning missions as far north as the Gila River. He had aided his superior, Fray Juan María Salvatierra, to found the Pious Fund, a system of providing finances for mission work that would be used for another century. One of the first uses to which this fund was put was the establishment of the first of twenty-three missions in Baja California in 1697.

Since Baja was still imagined to be an island, all communication with the missions there was by the turbulent waters of the Gulf of California, an unreliable and occasionally disastrous undertaking. But Kino, who had seen "blue shells" (probably abalone) traded among the Indians of his Pimería Alta, was convinced that Baja was a peninsula and that a land route could be established from Mexico. In 1701, he set out to prove his contention by rafting across the Colorado River and walking west until he encountered Indians who informed him that the great "South Sea" itself was a journey of but a few days farther. He returned to Pimería Alta, drew a map that stood for decades as the authoritative depiction of the region, and wrote to Fray Salvatierra: "I . . . am of the opinion that this California near the new land passage recently discovered might be called Alta California, just as the preceding region . . . as far as 30 degrees of north latitude, might be called California Baja." Having linked the two Californias for the first time since Alarcón in 1540, he went on in an excess of enthusiasm: "For with the favor of Heaven, if your Reverence and his Majesty . . . will give us workers and missionaries, all in good time they must go forward until they reach perhaps as far as Gran China, and nearly to Japan. . . . And perhaps to the north of these our lands we may be able to find a shorter road to Europe, partly through these lands and partly by way of the North Sea."

A century or more sooner, such words might have inspired expeditions in the grand manner of Coronado —but Spain was bleeding now, wasting her energy in the War of the Spanish Succession, the first of the eighteenth-century wars that would cripple her forever. Kino did not receive his missionaries, nor did those Jesuits who followed him after his death in 1711; and in 1767 the Jesuits themselves, the "soldiers of God," pushed too far in their militant righteousness and Charles III expelled them from New Spain. Ironically, it was also in 1767 that events ponderously began to shape California's future along the lines Kino and the Jesuits had long advocated.

VISITOR-GENERAL JOSÉ DE GALVEZ of His Majesty's Supreme Council of the Indies had been in Mexico for two years. Gálvez was a vain, ambitious man with a number of severe personality flaws and occasional mental lapses (among other quirks, he once seriously advocated importing 600 Guatemalan apes, dressing them in uniforms, and using them to put down rebellious Indians); yet he also was an able, sometimes superbly effective, administrator. His ambition, however selfish, was the immediate cause of the first European settlement of California. His official mission was the investigation and reorganization of New Spain's administrative and financial structure, and the expulsion of the Jesuits, replacing them with members of the more tractable Franciscan order. But Gálvez had larger ideas —much larger. He advocated the consolidation and development of all of New Spain's northwestern region, including both Californias, reasoning (not without justification) that such moving and shaking would enhance Spain's international image and as an attractive byproduct sweeten the prospects of his own career.

In this last, he was entirely correct; he ultimately became Minister of the Indies, the single most powerful position in the Spanish New World.

But Gálvez needed better reasons to force official Spain, exhausted by the recent Seven Years War, to act. He found it in rumors of a growing Russian interest in the coastal regions of the Pacific Northwest. Spain was in a suitably paranoid frame of mind to react predictably to such rumors. The 1763 Treaty of Paris, ending the Seven Years War, had left most of North America in the hands of the British, and Spain felt the weight of England's power pressing down on her Mexican lands; her position was more insecure than ever.

In 1767, Gálvez dutifully recorded the rumors of Russian activity, together with whatever additional rumors he could lay hands on, and sent a report to the Marqués de Grimaldi, Spain's first minister of state. Early in 1768, he had the distinct satisfaction of seeing his own words come back to him in the form of a letter from Grimaldi to the viceroy of New Spain, the Marqués de Croix: "The Russians have several times made attempts to open a route to America and have recently carried out their intention through navigating in the northern part of the Pacific. We are certain they have succeeded and that they have reached the mainland. . . . The King has ordered me to inform Your Grace of the danger so that the governor named for California can be made alert and be given instructions with regard to the watchfulness and concern he should exercise in observing the attempts the Russians are able to make there, thwarting them however possible and providing immediate information of everything to Your Grace for His Majesty."

Interpreted loosely enough, Grimaldi's letter stood as *carte blanche* for Gálvez's ambitions—and that was exactly how he proceeded. In May 1768, he organized a junta to lay out precise plans for California's settlement. Of first importance was a sea expedition from San Blás to Monterey for the establishment of a presidio (military garrison); but Gálvez also felt that an overland force would be useful, as he noted in his subsequent report to Grimaldi: "At the same time it was also agreed that it would be most important to undertake an entry or search by land . . . from the missions to the north of California, so that both expeditions might unite at the same harbor of Monterrey *[sic]*, and by means of the observations made by one and the other they might acquire once and for all complete knowledge and in this wise aid greatly the founding of a presidio and settlement at that place which is truly the most advantageous for protecting the entire west coast of California and the other coasts of the southern part of this continent, against any attempts by the Russians or any northern nation."*

Originally, the enterprise was scheduled to begin in the summer of 1768, but Indian uprisings in the northern regions that summer (brought on, at least in part, by the unsettled state of affairs after the expulsion of the Jesuits) took most of Gálvez's time and attention until winter, when he was finally able to begin assembling the necessary elements. The sea-borne arm of the expedition was to precede the land force and was divided among three ships, the *San Carlos* (the expedition's flagship under the command of Captain Vicente Vila, chief pilot of New Spain's Pacific ships, including the galleons), the *San Antonio,* and the *San José.* Those assigned to the *San Carlos* in addition to the regular crew were Lt. Pedro Fages and twenty-five Catalan soldiers, military engineer and cartographer Miguel Costansó, and former French army surgeon Pedro Prat. These ships were to sail to San Diego, establish a presidio as a way station, then proceed to Monterey. The land expedition was to be similarly divided into two companies, the first under Capt. Fernando Rivera y Moncada with twenty-seven "leather-jacket" soldiers (who were also to drive a large herd of cattle, horses, and mules), and the other under Gaspar de Portolá, governor of Baja California, who was appointed by Gálvez as the supreme commander of the entire expedition and who would be the governor of Upper California until settlements were firmly established.

The settlement of California was a military venture whose only real justification was to protect New Spain's northern frontier. Yet nearly two hundred years of experience in the wilds of Mexico had taught the coun-

try well that the value of the mission as a civilizing and stabilizing influence on the course of settlement was great, indeed incalculable. So it was that Fray Junípero Serra, Franciscan father-president of the Baja California missions after the expulsion of the Jesuits, was assigned to the land expedition to supervise the establishment of a mission system in Upper California —first at San Diego, then at Monterey, and then at other points where the Church's presence might be useful. It should be pointed out that, however indispensable the establishment of missions was, it was still only a part of the whole expedition; contrary to much popular history, the venture was not considered a "sacred expedition" by anyone but Serra and his Franciscan assistants, and Portolá was in full command, not Serra.

The two arms of the overland division would not be ready to leave Loreto in central Baja until the spring of 1769. In the meantime, the three ships were made ready for the voyage. All had been built to the somewhat primitive standards of Mexico's west-coast artisans and arrived in Baja California shipping water badly. Careening and repair took several weeks, and after that, more time was taken to load church furniture, chalices, vestments, and other religious equipment, and food (nearly all of this stripped from the older Baja missions, as was the custom). Finally on January 9, 1769, the first ship, the *San Carlos,* put to sea from La Paz. It was a moment of some significance in the annals of New Spain, a fact noted grandiloquently by Miguel Costansó in his diary: "This enterprise, desired for so many years, begun many times with great preparations and expenses, will undoubtedly be pleasing to the august Monarch of Spain, whose magnanimous spirit and religious piety, Heaven rewards, by raising in his kingdom great and illustrious men, in every station, Ecclesiastical, Military, and Politick; who contend equally in executing the great charges committed to their eminent capacity and talents...."

It had been a two-hundred-and-fifty-year journey from myth to reality, from a land of gold and griffins to a flyspeck outpost of Spanish empire on the very rim of Christendom.

---

*It is significant that Gálvez's report mentions no other California place name but Monterey; the legend of Vizcaíno's "noble harbor" was still going strong in 1768—and would play hob with the land expedition's efforts to find it in 1769 (see chapter 2).

*A Mojave Indian mother and child.*

# California Mirror:
# The Children of Light

No one knows precisely when they came, although speculation has it that at least some of them wandered down from Asia via the Bering Strait and Alaska when the last Ice Age began its retreat something over ten thousand years ago. At about the same time, it is believed, others meandered out of the Southwest and northern Mexico into the southern portions of California. However and whenever they came, it is known that there were well over one hundred thousand Indians in California at the time of the first European contact. Exactly how many over is open to debate. An early estimate by anthropologist A. L. Kroeber placed the number at 133,000, while later investigators have maintained that there may have been as many as 275,000. Even the lowest figure, however, establishes the fact that there were more Indians in California than in any other of the United States; at the very least, her Indian population comprised nearly 15 percent of the total

native population in what is now the United States.

As numerous as they were, California's Indians shared certain cultural traits. With the exception of a few bands of Mojave and Yuma in the extreme southeast corner of the state, they practiced no agriculture; they were hunters and gatherers and fishers, living off the California bounty. They gathered acorns and mesquite pods, grinding them into a high-caloric meal; with baskets, nets, and sharpened poles, they fished for salmon and trout in the northern streams; in the mountains of the Coast Range and the foothills of the Sierra Nevada, they hunted deer, in many cases simply running the animals down with relay teams until they fell from exhaustion; they hunted rabbits in the Paiute fashion, rounding them up by the hundreds, then clubbing them to death, and using every part of the animal's body—meat, tendon, hide, and bone—to serve their needs, much as the Plains Indians used the buffalo; on the coast they gath-

*Hostages to an uncertain future, a group of burro-riding Mojave Indian children gravely contemplate a man and his camera, 1900.*

*The serenity in the face of this Pomo Indian speaks for the
pride and assurance a man could find in a closeness with the earth.*

ered shellfish, particularly abalone, whose iridescent shells were often used as a medium of exchange.

They had little in the way of technology and even less of art, although their basketmaking was the finest in the world, in terms of both utility and design. Their weapons, when they had them, were simple bows and arrows, spears, and clubs. Many tribes of the north coast, however, developed a high degree of skill in the construction of dugout canoes, and the Chumash of the Santa Barbara Channel devised a dependable plank canoe. A common social institution among them was the **temescal**, or sweat house, reserved almost exclusively for the male members of a tribe, and having some of the therapeutic value of a modern neighborhood tavern.

Their religion was simple and totemistic, concerned less with elaborate ritual than with individual, day-to-day, hour-to-hour observance, much of it spent in propitiating the gods of disaster. Among many, however, the rites of puberty and death were observed with appropriate ceremony. With the exception of some tribes of the north and northwest, who frequently fought to capture slaves, warfare was a very rare occurrence, and when it did occur, it was more likely to be between individual families than between whole tribes. Because most California Indians had neither territorial nor acquisitive ambitions, there was little to fight about.

For all their common heritage, the California Indians were astonishingly diverse in their groupings and languages, and extremely localized geographically. Most lived in communities of no more—and usually less—than one thousand people, most of them related in one way or another, whose location was dictated strictly by the availability of food. So long as that food remained available, they did not move. This geographic isolation and provincialism was reinforced by extraordinary linguistic diversity. There were five main language stocks among the California Indians; the stocks were divided into twenty one language families, which were in turn divided into at least 135 individual dialects—most of which, as historian Walton Bean has put it, "were mutually unintelligible."

Divided into isolated, Stone Age bands and unaccustomed to organized warfare, the Indians were no

*Mercedes Nolasquez, a basket maker of the Agua Caliente Indians of Southern California.*

*A 1903 portrait of Cibimoat, a tribal leader of the Agua Caliente.*

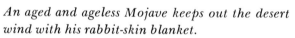

*An aged and ageless Mojave keeps out the desert wind with his rabbit-skin blanket.*

match for the people of the Iron Age. In design, the mission system of the Spanish was meant to help the Indians adapt to an advanced society. In reality, it helped to destroy them. First, it deprived them of the only cultural security they had ever known; in their own world they had been the children of light, who found definition of themselves in the serene assurance of the earth, but in the world of the missions they were the smallest cogs in the machinery of a civilization beyond their comprehension. Second, they were destroyed by disease; of the more than eighty thousand Indians who were converted and/or coerced to embrace Catholicism and the regimented life of the missions during the Spanish and Mexican periods, more than sixty thousand died.

The Spanish at least considered the Indian as a soul to be saved, a potentially useful member of society. To most Americans, as we shall see in chapter 7, he was something to be ignored, used, or dispatched. The resulting cultural degradation was often appalling, as the **Los Angeles Semi-Weekly News** described it in 1869: "For years past it has been the practice of those . . . engaged in the cultivation of the soil, to hang around the Mayor's court on Monday morning and advance the degraded Indian a few dollars with which to pay his nominal fine for having been dragged through the streets to the station house in a state of beastly intoxication . . . and on Saturday night, after deducting the sum advanced, pay him a couple of dollars, which insures him a place in the station house on the following Monday, should he not lose his miserable life in a drunken brawl before that time—and thus the process goes on."

Such scenes were all too common in the years when the photographs on these pages were taken. It is good to know that we have such records, for the photographs document with a clarity beyond words the grace that existed in a vanished world—the world of the first Californians.

*A string ensemble of Mission Indian girls (possibly Gabrieleños) from the Pala Indian School, 1900. The dog appears unimpressed.*

# CHAPTER 2

# THE TWILIGHT OF EMPIRE

*In an atmosphere of suffering, death, and internal friction, Spanish civilization is implanted on the land called California*

THE NOBLE EXPERIMENT of New Spain's settlement of California was crippled at the outset by a series of mishaps that came near to aborting the entire project. On April 11, 1769, the Mexican-built brigantine *San Antonio* hove to and anchored in San Diego Bay after an uncommonly speedy fifty-four-day journey from the southern tip of Baja California. But the bay was empty of the ship that should have been there waiting—the flagship *San Carlos,* with Captain Vicente Vila, his officers and crew, and Lieutenant Pedro Fages with his twenty-five Catalan soldiers. Juan Pérez, the *San Antonio*'s captain, was understandably nervous; the *San Carlos* had sailed from La Paz in Baja more than a month before his own ship left Cabo San Lucas—it should have been in San Diego weeks before.

The *San Antonio* was without soldiers, and Pérez dared not risk going ashore to face Indians who had more than once demonstrated a certain belligerence. So for nearly three weeks the ship lay at anchor, waiting. Finally on April 29, the *San Carlos* wallowed into the bay. She was a mess. She had spent weeks drifting in the dismal, almost windless regions of the "horse latitudes"; her water casks had leaked and scurvy had sickened her crew; and to top it off, Vizcaíno's ancient charts (the only guides the expedition had) had led the ship all the way up to the Santa Barbara Channel before Vila realized their inaccuracies. Most of those on board had to be carried ashore and placed in makeshift hospital tents; soon, many of the *San Antonio*'s

crew were stricken, and the expedition's main concern for weeks was the simple matter of staying alive.*

By the time the two overland divisions arrived—Fernando Rivera y Moncada on May 14 and Gaspar de Portolá, the expedition's commander, on June 29 (Fray Junípero Serra, hampered by a suppurating foot sore that would torment him for the rest of his life, did not arrive until July 1)—the entire venture was near the point of collapse. Within a few months, almost half the expedition had died in the flyblown tents of the San Diego camp. However desperate the situation, Portolá was determined to get on with the march to find Vizcaíno's "noble harbor" of Monterey, and two weeks after his arrival set off with Rivera, Fages, Costansó, Fray Juan Crespí, and anyone else who could still move.

Roughly following the route of what is now Highway 101, they crossed the Santa Ana River, where a massive earthquake threw them to the ground; entered the Los Angeles plain, where they found and named the Río de Porciúncula (later the site of the pueblo of Los Angeles); crossed a spur of the San Gabriel Mountains and followed the coast north to the site of San Luis Obispo; then with great effort crossed the Santa Lucia

---

*They might have hoped for relief from the expedition's third vessel, the *San Jose,* but it was futile: after sundry delays, she did not sail until June—and then promptly disappeared for three months, eventually turning up dismasted in Loreto. She sailed again for San Diego in May 1770 and was never seen again.

*Fray Junípero Serra, a saint in the eyes of many but a holy terror in the opinion of California's several military governors.*

Range and entered the valley of the Salinas River, following the river to its mouth in Monterey Bay.

The mission was accomplished—except that they did not know it. In no way did Monterey Bay fit the lambent description given it by Vizcaíno in 1602. Fray Crespí articulated their frustration when he noted in his diary that "we have to say that it is not found after the most careful efforts made at cost of much sweat and fatigue. . . . At Pt. Pinos there is no port, nor have we seen in all our journey a country more desolate than this . . . Sebastián Vizcaíno to the contrary notwithstanding. . . ." The port had to be *somewhere* ahead, so they moved on, finally stumbling upon San Francisco Bay early in November; it is probably a comment upon the persistence of myth that Portolá looked upon this magnificent bay and saw it only as one more obstacle in his search for Monterey. The expedition had "found nothing," he noted disconsolately in his own diary, "leaving us in doubt as to whether we could find anything further on." (Crespí was less glum: "This port . . . is very large and without doubt . . . could contain not only all the armadas of our Catholic Monarch but also all those of Europe.")

Discouraged and low on rations, the expedition turned back to San Diego, arriving there (after eating twelve of its mules) on January 24, 1770. In their absence, Serra had founded the first of the California missions, San Diego de Alcalá, on July 16, but it was so far without a single convert. Little else had changed —men were still sick and dying, food was all but exhausted, and the enterprise still wore failure like a hairshirt. In February, Portolá sent the *San Antonio* back to Baja for provisions; when it returned on March 19, he dispatched Serra, Costansó, and Fages to Monterey in the *San Carlos* and set out with twelve men to try once more to find the harbor by land.

This time he succeeded, finally accepting the fact that what he saw at Monterey was all there was to see. Costansó supervised the construction of an earthen-walled presidio, and Serra oversaw the erection of his second mission, San Carlos Borroméo; both were formally dedicated on June 3, 1770. His duty done at last, Portolá placed the governorship of Alta California in the hands of Pedro Fages and returned to Mexico. Fages and Serra fell to bickering almost immediately, and in 1771 Serra moved San Carlos Borroméo across the hills to the Carmel River in order to remove the few neophytes he had painstakingly gathered from the corrupting influence of Fages' soldiers.

I**N AN ATMOSPHERE OF SUFFERING**, death, and internal friction, Spanish civilization had finally been implanted on the land called California—two little pinpricks of settlement more than four hundred miles apart, inadequately garrisoned, poorly equipped, surrounded by Indians notably reluctant to accept the word of God and the supremacy of His Catholic Majesty's will, and weeks removed even from the primitive villages of Baja, much less the seat of government at Mexico City.

The situation was a long time improving. Portolá's report upon his return to Mexico was a masterpiece of pessimism; among other things he maintained that if Russia really wanted California, Spain should let her have it. Visitor-General Gálvez, the architect of California's settlement, returned to Spain in 1771, and the loss of his direct support was painfully felt in California. For the next four years, the government of New Spain regarded her northern provinces with indifference, a maddening situation for those attempting to function on the thin edge of a frontier.

In spite of all this, as well as the constant friction with Fages (which soon achieved the level of an open feud), the determined Serra managed to establish five more missions, including San Gabriel in the San Fernando Valley, and kept up a steady stream of correspondence with Mexico, begging for supplies and equipment and priests, and demanding the immediate removal of Fages. In 1773 Serra took his complaints to Mexico City personally, gaining the ear and the sympathy of Viceroy Antonio de Bucareli. Fages was removed and replaced by Rivera y Moncada.* Moreover, Serra's influence prompted Bucareli to listen carefully to the propositions put forth by Capt.

---

*It was a phyrric victory, for Serra was soon having his troubles with Rivera, who continued the Spanish policy of maintaining the supremacy of military rule over the religious—a policy which Serra was never able to accept with any enthusiasm. In fact, the testy priest did not get on well with *any* governor from the time of his arrival in 1769 to his death in 1784, and his successors continued the tradition.

Juan Bautista de Anza, a soldier with long experience in the wastelands of northwestern Mexico. It was Anza's contention (as it had been Fray Kino's contention three-quarters of a century before) that a "land bridge" to Alta California could be established from Sonora, setting up the first reliable communication with the new settlements.

Bucareli agreed, and more: Anza should not only open such a route, he should go on to the Bay of San Francisco and establish a presidio and mission there in order to discourage foreign interest in the region—particularly by the British, who were being seen plying the waters of the Pacific more and more frequently in the mid-1770s. Consequently, in 1774 Anza led a small party of men from Tubac, in southern Arizona, to the Colorado River, where they made a necessary peace with the Yuma Indians by exchanging presents and other expressions of good will, then blazed a desert trail to Mission San Gabriel, arriving in March. With the route established and the Yumas pacified, Anza then returned to Sonora and began piecing together the elements of a major *entrada* for the next year.

To the bulk of Mexico's population, California was still a perilous unknown, and settlers could only be induced to travel there by promises of substantial aid in clothing, food, equipment, and supplies—and even with such inducements, Anza could persuade only thirty-four families to make the trek. It was better than nothing, and in September 1775 the expedition set out from Horcasitas, Sonora, with the families, Fray Pedro Font, and a large herd of cattle and horses. In January 1776 they had arrived at Mission San Gabriel and by March had made their way to Monterey. Anza left the main expedition there and traveled on to San Francisco Bay, where he selected sites for a mission and presidio. In the summer the rest of the expedition followed, and by October both the presidio and Mission San Francisco de Asís (later popularly called Mission Dolores) had been established. Fray Serra had not been present for the founding, but he did arrive in October in time to give the enterprises his blessing. "Thanks be to God," he is said to have remarked. "Now our father St. Francis, the crossbearer in the procession of missions, has come to the final point of the mainland of California."

Not quite. Two more missions would be established

*Captain Juan Bautista de Anza, who opened the short-lived "land bridge" to California.*

even farther north—one at San Rafael in 1817 and one at Sonoma in 1823 (the only mission established during the Mexican era)—but in a very real sense his words were true: the presidio and the mission, the first two legs of what historian W. H. Hutchinson has called the "Spanish Tripod of Settlement," were now firmly established, and the outlines of California's life for the next half-century nearly complete. Only the third leg, the pueblo (or civilian town), remained, and when Filipe de Neve replaced Rivera y Moncada as California's governor in 1777, he created two agricultural villages to supply the military and civilian population of the province (the missions needed, or at least wanted, their own products for themselves and their Indian charges). In November 1777 he established fourteen families from Monterey and San Francisco in the pueblo of San José de Guadalupe in the Santa Clara Valley, and in 1781 sent twelve families from Sinaloa, Mexico, to a new pueblo on the banks of the Río de Porciúncula in southern California; they called the town *El Pueblo de Nuestra Señora la Reina de los Angeles del Río de Porciúncula* (the Town of Our Lady the Queen of the Angels by the Porciúncula River). Sixteen years later, the pueblo of Branciforte was established near Mission Santa Cruz on Monterey Bay and settled by a number of ex-convicts (few others would voluntarily go to California by then). Branciforte soon withered and died, unsurprisingly, and only the pueblos of San Jose and Nuestra Señora la Reina de los Angeles del Río de Porciúncula remained to sink roots and survive. Today, the many-named pueblo is called Los Angeles, among other things.

SUCH WERE THE BEGINNINGS of California's Spanish life—and very nearly all that there would ever be. For California was not so much settled by the Spanish as loosely tacked down along her western edge. That action represented the last major thrust of Spanish empire, but it was the reflexive, almost instinctive gesture of a dream dying. When it was done there was little energy left for more, and California floundered in a backwash of time. Only a little over three hundred soldiers, whose duty was the defense of a coastline 1,150 miles in length, were ever assigned to California by the authorities of New Spain. The first blush of civilian colonization was soon reduced to a thin and intermittent trickle, and by 1820 there were only about 3,750 non-Indians in the province (a significant number of whom had been *born* there). Even the mission system—which ultimately grew to twenty-one individual establishments, acquired more than twenty thousand Indian converts, and laid the foundation for California's agriculture and husbandry—was badly under-manned, underfinanced, and undersupplied for the duration.

Moreover, California was soon nearly as isolated as she had been when the first scurvy-ridden sailors were carried ashore at San Diego in 1769. In 1776 José de Gálvez, now minister of the Indies, was finally able to carry out his massive reorganization of New Spain's northern provinces (which included present Texas,

New Mexico, Arizona, and the two Californias) and appointed Teodore de Croix as commander-general. De Croix's main interest was the state of his budget; he refused to continue the bribery necessary to keep the Yuma Indians on a friendly basis and thus keep Anza's hard-won "land bridge" open. The Yumas, who had come to look upon regular gifts as one of their natural rights, took offense at this penny-pinching and in 1781 destroyed the two missions that had been established the year before near the Colorado River, killed the two priests in charge, and massacred a column of colonists that was being led to California by Rivera y Moncada to join the other settlers at the Los Angeles pueblo. The "land bridge" was not opened again until well into the nineteenth century, leaving only the sea and the long overland route from Loreto in Baja as the principal lines of communication between the California settlements and the other Mexican territories.

Caught in this vacuum of neglect and isolation, the inhabitants of California soon learned to define life in their own terms. Governors appointed by the City of Mexico came and went and were accorded a polite allegiance; the customary proclamations, *reglamentos,* and orders issued by the central government were dutifully noted, and often obeyed; and news of developments in New and Old Spain were greeted with what amounted to mild surmise. But in less than a generation, the province's population began to identify almost completely with California—they were the *gente de razón,* the people of reason, the *Californios.* Most were of mixed blood—some Negro, some Indian, some Spanish—and of common experience and ambitions. California, they knew by now, would be the only life any of them would know, and they set about making the best of it.

They cheated—as people will cheerfully do when they feel they have no choice—on the brutal trade and mercantile restrictions placed on them by New Spain; smuggling became standard practice, for there was no other way to obtain the simple, manufactured necessities of life. When the Russian American Fur Company established Fort Ross on the Mendocino Coast in 1812 as a means of furnishing foodstuffs to its trapping enterprises in the Alaskan archipelago, the *Californios* (including the missionary fathers) blithely ignored regulations forbidding trade with the eastern heretics.

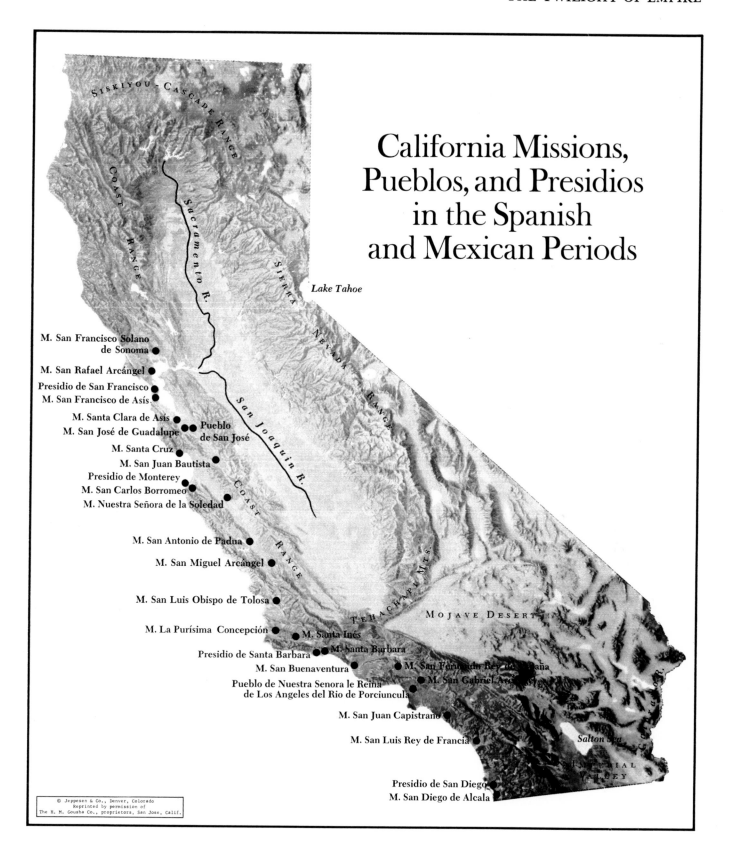

California Missions,
Pueblos, and Presidios
in the Spanish
and Mexican Periods

*Lake Tahoe*

M. San Francisco Solano
de Sonoma ●

M. San Rafael Arcángel ●

Presidio de San Francisco ●
M. San Francisco de Asís ●

M. Santa Clara de Asís ●
M. San José de Guadalupe ● Pueblo
de San José
M. Santa Cruz ●
M. San Juan Bautista ●
Presidio de Monterey ●
M. San Carlos Borromeo ●
M. Nuestra Señora de la Soledad ●

M. San Antonio de Padua ●

M. San Miguel Arcángel ●

M. San Luis Obispo de Tolosa ●

M. La Purísima Concepción ●
● M. Santa Inés
Presidio de Santa Barbara ●● M. Santa Barbara
M. San Buenaventura ●
Pueblo de Nuestra Senora le Reina
de Los Angeles del Rio de Porciuncula ●
M. San Juan Capistrano ●

M. San Luis Rey de Francia ●

*Salton Sea*

Presidio de San Diego ●
M. San Diego de Alcala ●

*MOJAVE DESERT*

M. San Fernando Rey de España ●
● M. San Gabriel Arcángel

Similarly, they traded with every foreign vessel that wandered to California with something of value.

When Spain's New World experiment began to crumble in the fits and starts of the Mexican Revolution between 1810 and 1821, the *Californios* viewed the change from colony to independent empire with pragmatic aplomb. Verbally loyal to Spain, California nonetheless pledged its fealty to the Mexican Empire in 1822 and, when the empire became a shaky republic in 1823, calmly went along with the situation. It was no better, and no worse, to be ignored by Republican Mexico than by Imperial Spain, and the *Californios* cheerfully went on working out their own destiny. The province's internal politics quickly evolved into an occasionally bitter and frequently farcical power struggle among the entrenched mission system (by now fat in land, cattle, and produce), some twenty or twenty-five family groups who had acquired a measure of prestige through grants of land and were about equally divided in their loyalties between the northern and southern regions of California, and the Mexican government, as represented by a series of governors who found themselves caught in the middle of a situation they never did learn to handle.

Between 1822 and 1845, three Mexican-appointed governors were forcibly expelled from California—Manuel Victoria in 1831, Nicolás Gutiérrez in 1838, and Manuel Micheltorena in 1845—and not even California-chosen governors could rest easy in their administrations (for more about this, see chapter 3). But the true loser in the continual struggle was the mission system—and its Indian charges.

Ideally, the ultimate secularization of mission lands was built into the system; these lands were to be held in trust for the Indians until they had acquired the skills necessary for survival on their own, at which point the land was to be divided among them and the missions converted into simple parish churches. As usual in the affairs of men, ideal and reality were some distance apart. The friars treated the Indians as retarded children, sometimes lovable, but nearly uneducable. As a result, the friars quite correctly held that few of the neophytes were ever ready for the civilized world. Almost none could read or write, most

had acquired only a primitive "horseback" Spanish, and they had been nurtured and controlled for so long that the mission compound provided them with the only stability and sense of community they had known since they left the lifeway of their ancestors. Moreover, there was an understandable reluctance on the part of the mission system to abandon voluntarily its own success, and the government of New Spain had never seen fit to enforce the ideal.

But one of the goals of the revolutionary government of Mexico was to dissipate the power of the Church, and one certain way of accomplishing this was to force secularization. It came to California in 1831, when Governor José María Echeandía issued a proclamation for the division of mission lands. The Church was granted a brief reprieve during the conservative administration of Manuel Victoria, but in 1833 Governor José Figueroa took office with specific orders from Mexico City: "It being a matter of the greatest necessity that the neophytes rise from the state of abasement to which they find themselves reduced, you will cause to be distributed to such as are fitted for it such fields of the mission lands as they may be capable of cultivating, in order that they may thus become fond of labor and may go on acquiring property." Figueroa, an able and compassionate man, did his best to protect the Indians, dividing half the land and livestock among neophytes and placing the rest under the administration of *Californios,* who were to use the income from the properties to finance welfare plans for the Indians.

In 1835 Figueroa died, and the administration of the mission lands became what Hubert Howe Bancroft called an "unfathomable pool of corruption." Most of the land designed to provide welfare income fell into private hands (often those of the administrators themselves); most of the Indians either sold their properties for liquor and worthless goods or simply abandoned them to whoever came first; mission lands were stripped of livestock; and the adobe buildings which had marked the final expression of Spanish empire in the New World began to flake and crumble. It was the pathetic end to a long dream—and the beginning of one of the largest pastoral societies the world has ever known.

*Roping a California steer, as rendered by August Ferran.*

# California Mirror:
# Kingdom of Grass

*"Ranchero," by James Walker.*

The secularization of the California missions in 1834 and the consequent availability of immense sweeps of land, coincided with the early stirrings of the industrial revolution in New England, which needed three things: cattle hides for the manufacture of leather goods, tallow for the making of soap and candles, and a reliable market for these and other manufactured goods. In Cali-

fornia, all three needs could be met—and were.

Beginning in the 1820s—after the stringent trade restrictions of the Spanish were eliminated by Mexican independence—American ships began trading for hides and tallow with increasing frequency, and in the 1830s the trade blossomed. Hides stripped from cattle all over the state were hauled to collecting points—chiefly San

*"Caballero," by James Walker.*

Diego—where they were cured and stored for delivery to the American traders. Similarly, tons of cattle fat were rendered into tallow, casked, and stored for pickup. No one knows precisely how many hides were traded during the Mexican era (estimates vary from 600,000 to 1,250,000); but some 80 percent of them were handled by one Boston firm, Bryant & Sturgis.

The life-style that the trade nurtured was one wedded to the horse for even the briefest sort of journey, and was marked by the qualities of indolent pride, physical grace, enormous hospitality, and a kind of innocent arrogance. In our own time, it has been made the stuff of romance, but contemporary observers viewed it somewhat more realistically.

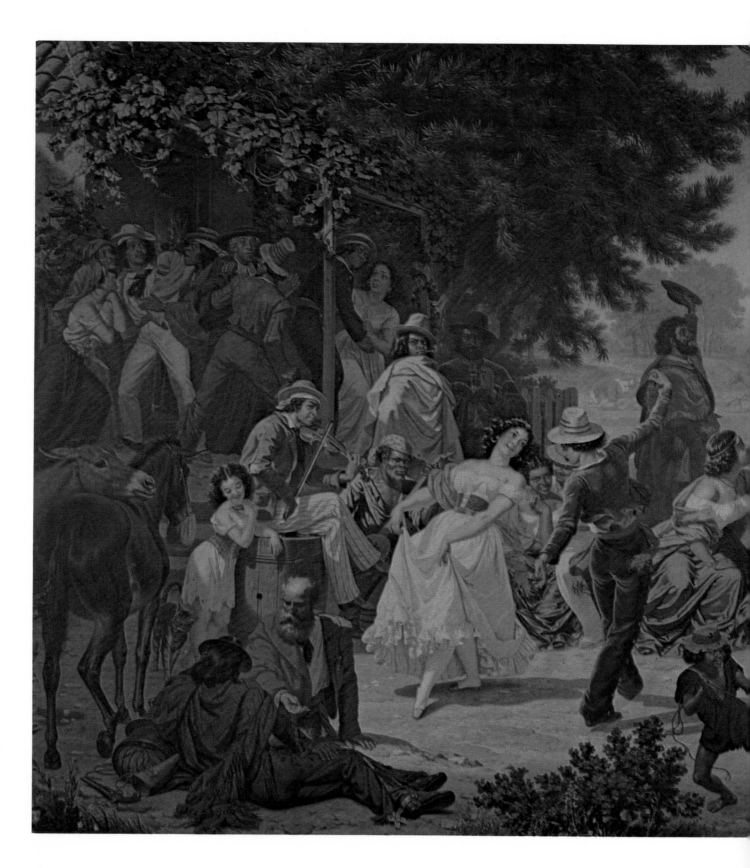

Charles Nahl, who was not above embellishing his paintings with a thick patina of romance, created the fandango scene at the left in about 1860. The buxom exuberance of the dancing maiden was apparently painted as an example of wishful thinking, at least if one is to believe the description of a fandango given by Richard Henry Dana in his **Two Years Before the Mast** (1842): "After supper the gig's crew were called, and we rowed ashore, dressed in our uniforms, beached the boat, and went up to the fandango. . . . As we drew near, we heard the accustomed sound of violins and guitars, and saw a great motion of the people within. Going in, we found nearly all the people of the town—men, women, and children—collected and crowded together, leaving barely room for the dancers; for on these occasions no invitations are given, but everyone is expected to come. . . . The music was lively, and among the tunes we recognized several of our popular airs, which we, without doubt, have taken from the Spanish. In the dancing I was much disappointed. The women stood upright, with their hands down by their sides, their eyes fixed upon the ground before them, and slid about without any perceptible means of motion; for their feet were invisible, the hem of their dresses forming a circle around them. . . . They looked as grave as though they were going through some religious ceremony, their faces as little excited as their limbs; and on the whole, instead of the spirited, fascinating Spanish dances which I had expected, I found the California fandango, on the part of the women, at least, a lifeless affair."

*"The Fandango," by Charles Nahl.*

Richard Henry Dana was disappointed in more than the fandango, for he found the **Californios** to be "an idle, thriftless people." Sir George Simpson, governor-in-chief of the Hudson's Bay Company, condemned the very lifestyle that later captured the imagination of the romantics in his **Narrative of a Journey Round the World** (1847): "The population of California in particular has been drawn from the most indolent variety of an indolent species, being composed of super-annuated troopers and retired office-holders and their descendents. . . . Such settlers . . . were not likely to toil for much more than what the cheap bounty of nature afforded them, horses to ride and beef to eat, with hides and tallow to exchange for such other supplies as they wanted. . . . As one might have expected, the children improved upon the example of the parents through the influence of a systematic education, an education which gave them the lasso as a toy in infancy and the horse as a companion in boyhood, which, in short, trained them from the cradle to be mounted bullock-hunters, and nothing else and if anything could aggravate their laziness, it was the circumstance that many of them dropped, as it were, into ready-made competency by sharing in the lands and cattle of the plundered missions."

*The luxuriance of natural grass on a thousand
rolling hills fed the nearly-wild cattle of
California's brief pastoral era.*

# CHAPTER 3

# PAPER WARS AND FOREIGN DEVILS

*Mexican Independence, California autonomy, and a bitter, bloodless*

*struggle for position and power among relatives*

LATE IN 1831, José María Echeandía (former governor of California), Pío Pico (a Los Angeles shopkeeper who had recently acquired title to a local rancho), and Juan Bandini (a ranchero of some years' standing) got together to issue the territory's first *pronunciamiento*, a political device that *Californios* would utilize repeatedly over the next decade. This one was aimed dead center at Lt. Col. Manuel Victoria, recently appointed governor, who was attempting to rule California strictly by the book of Mexican law. What is more, he was distinctly opposed to the secularization of mission lands, which appalled most landed or hoped-to-become-landed *Californios*.

"Mexican citizens residing in the upper territory of the Californias," the proclamation began grandly, "if the enterprise we undertake were intended to violate the provisions of the laws, if our acts in venturing to oppose the scandalous acts of the actual governor, D. Manuel Victoria, were guided by aims unworthy of patriotic sentiments, then should we not only fear but know the fatal results to which we must be condemned. Such, however, not being the case, we, guided in the path of justice, animated by love of our soil . . . find ourselves obliged, on account of the criminal abuse noted in the said chief, to adopt the measures here made known. We know that we proceed . . . against an individual who violates the fundamental bases of our system, or in truth against a tyrant. . . ."

Wrapped up in the singularly convoluted language of this splendid document is one significant implication: the *Californios* were determined to run things for

themselves, secure in the knowledge that the City of Mexico, caught up in an almost constant political boil itself, could do little more than appoint governors and hope for the best. That, at any rate, was how Echeandía and his cohorts proceeded. They gathered a volunteer army, marched in and took San Diego, then moved on to Los Angeles and captured it. When Governor Victoria responded by marching south from Monterey with a small force, the insurgents met him at Cahuenga Pass on December 4, 1831. The resulting "battle" was mainly a matter of artillery fire from safe distances, and while each side did lose one man and Victoria himself was wounded, the otherwise bloodless encounter was inconclusive. It did serve one useful function, however, at least from the point of view of the *Californios*: Mexico City, startled that blood had actually been shed, eventually recalled Victoria, and for almost a year Echeandía once again was allowed to play governor.*

When José Figueroa replaced Echeandía in 1833, he granted amnesty to all those who had taken part in the insurrection of 1831, and otherwise attempted to apply administrative bandages to the open wounds of California politics. For a time the effort succeeded,

---

*For the next fifteen years, California's political conflicts would kill very few people, although several horses and mules would meet their end. War among the *Californios* was largely a matter of florid proclamations and troop movements with many a flourish and threatening charge—more a matter of style than of blood and death. Given the widespread intermarriage of the *Californios*, this made good common sense; as historian Walton Bean has noted: "There was too much risk of killing a brother-in-law."

*Mission Santa Barbara today, one of the few surviving relics of the age of Spain in California.*

*Mariano G. Vallejo at ease in the yard of his Sonoma Valley home, years removed from paper wars and the flamboyant puzzlements of early California government.*

aided in no small part by the fact that he initiated and pushed through a program of secularization and judiciously appointed only *Californios* (such as Mariano G. Vallejo in the north or Pío Pico in the south) to administer the lands of each of the twenty-one missions. Upon his death in 1835, however, California soon fell into the old squabbling scramble for power.

In November 1836 Juan Bautista Alvarado marched upon his native Monterey, fired a cannon at the house of Governor Nicolas Gutiérrez, and graciously accepted the governor's immediate surrender. Gutiérrez and other Mexican officials were deported back to Mexico, and California was declared "a free and sovereign State" within the Mexican republic, with autonomy in its personal affairs. Alvarado proclaimed that Monterey

would remain the capital of California but placated the powers of southern California by allowing them to choose a subgovernor with headquarters in Los Angeles —evidence that the rift between north and south that had been brewing for several years had at last reached the point of open contention. Mariano G. Vallejo, Alvarado's uncle, was appointed military commander for the entire province. Official Mexico sputtered with outrage but was powerless to do much about Alvarado's actions; in 1837 he was officially confirmed as the governor of California.

For the next five years the *Californios* were allowed to go about their business (much of which had to do with the looting of mission lands) without interference from the mother republic. But in 1842 Mexico made one more effort to regain control over the intransigent territory, sending Manuel Micheltorena to San Diego with an army of three hundred *cholos* (ex-convicts employed as soldiers). Micheltorena announced his function as the new governor of California, then marched to Monterey. Hungry and unpaid, his *cholo* army committed repeated acts of pillage, plunder, and rape on the march, thoroughly destroying any chance Micheltorena might have had for a long-lived and peaceful administration. Vallejo, sick to death of five years of intrigue and argument (much of it with his nephew Alvarado), cheerfully relinquished his military post, and Alvarado gave up the governorship without a fight—but these were the only grace notes the amiable, but ineffective Micheltorena would enjoy in his term. In February 1845 Alvarado and José Castro, another native of Monterey, raised an army and met the forces of Micheltorena, again at Cahuenga Pass. The usual artillery fire was exchanged (killing two mules, but no one's relatives), and Micheltorena surrendered, removing himself and his raggle-taggle army to Mexico. Pío Pico, with headquarters in Los Angeles, was installed as the territory's governor, and José Castro, representing the interests of the north, became military commandant at Monterey. For the next year and a half, Castro and Pico constantly jostled each other for supremacy, but to no conclusion.

Mexico's rule over California, tenuous to the point of myth from the beginning, came to an end in a kind of de facto independence. Yet if the *Californios* were ready to congratulate themselves, they might also have been sobered by one discomforting fact: among those forces that had taken part in the troubles of both 1836 and 1845 had been a number of foreigners. And among these foreigners had been a number of Americans— only a few, but a few whose presence was like a shadow on the land.

THE AMERICAN GENIUS for foreign trade, held in check first by British colonial restrictions and then by the extended agony of the Revolutionary War, entered a new flowering in 1784, when the *Empress of China* sailed from New York to Canton and launched American participation in the China trade. A staple of that trade was fine furs—particularly the silky pelts of fur seals and sea otters. These were welcomed by the government of China—not as articles of vulgar trade (anathema to the life-styles of her rulers), mind you, but as gifts and articles of tribute. In exchange, of course, the Chinese would return presents for presents —teas and silks and spices and elegant ceramics—the whole business neatly accommodated by carefully placed bribes.

Most of the fur seals and sea otters were located on the coasts of southern Alaska, the Pacific Northwest, and California. The British discovered this happy fact when Captain James Cook visited Nootka Sound in 1778, but Britain was soon involved in the Napoleonic Wars, which prevented her from gaining much of a foothold. New Spain's Manila Company had a vigorous interest in the trade, but when Spain attempted to enforce her claims of discovery in the region in 1789, the British backed her down, forcing her to sign the Nootka Sound Treaty in 1790, in which Spain relinquished all exclusive claim to the territory. The Russians, who had pioneered the trade before the turn of the century, expanded by establishing the post of Sitka in the Alaskan archipelago in 1804 and Fort Ross and a small trading post at Bodega Bay in 1812, none of which were ever very successful.

However, it was American ships that soon dominated the trade—starting as early as 1788, when the *Lady Washington* and the *Columbia Rediviva* sailed into Nootka Sound and began bartering New England manufactured goods for seal and otter pelts from local Indians. In less than five years, regular trade lines were established, as ships from Boston and other New England ports sailed around Cape Horn to the Pacific Northwest, traded for furs, sailed to Hawaii for provisions and precious sandalwood, then to Canton to trade the furs and wood—and finally back to New England via the Sunda Strait, the Isle of France (Mauritania), Madagascar, and the Cape of Good Hope. Each journey took two years or longer; each was worth thousands of dollars in profits.

As a result, the sea otter and fur seal populations of the Northwest were nearly exterminated in a few years, and the hunters moved down to the coast of California, whose southern kelp beds harbored millions of the creatures. They soon learned that the *Californios* could be persuaded to take a somewhat casual attitude

*Thomas Oliver Larkin, the first and only American consul to Mexican California.*

toward Spanish trade restrictions, and before long American ships provided the inhabitants of California with most of their "luxury" goods—such things as ironware, tools, shoes, and other articles of clothing. The trade also gave America its first connection with California, as well as its first published account of the province: Captain William Shaler's "Journal of a Voyage Between China and the Northwest Coast of America . . .," an article in the *American Register, or General Repository of History* in 1808. Shaler had visited California in 1803 in the *Lelia Byrd;* at San Diego, he had encountered an uncommonly stubborn reluctance to trade, and after his first mate was arrested, managed to rescue him and fight his way to the open sea. This was all very exciting, but his observations on the political and military conditions of the province were more to the point. California, he said, was "in a situation to want nothing but a good government to rise rapidly to wealth and importance. The conquest of the country would be absolutely nothing; it would fall without an effort to the most inconsiderable force. . . . It would be

as easy to keep California in spite of the Spaniards as it would be to win it from them in the first place."

By the end of the Spanish period, then, New England mercantile interests had planted an image of California in the American consciousness—a vague, frequently distorted image, but one that inevitably appealed to go-ahead Yankee enterprise: it was a weak land unlettered in the mechanics of trade and industry, desperately in need of the accoutrements of civilization, and an easy mark for anyone with the gumption to step in and throw his expertise around—an image reinforced by the growth of the hide-and-tallow trade in the 1820s and 1830s (see "California Mirror: The Kingdoms of Grass"). After 1824, when a comparatively liberal Mexican Congress passed an act that promised security of person and property to foreigners settling in California and obeying its laws, a trickle of Americans detected the sweet smell of opportunity on the California coast and quickly established themselves. As anywhere else, money was power in California, and the Yankees knew how to handle both; men like William Richardson, Thomas Oliver Larkin, Jacob Leese, Abel Stearns, William A. Gale, Alfred Robinson, William Goodwin Dana, and John Warner soon achieved an importance that may have been unprecedented for foreigners in a foreign land. Traders, merchants, and middlemen, they were the *Californios'* only connection with the mysteries of commerce and finance; they provided liquid capital, a ready stock of goods, a credit system, and agencies through which the *Californios* could sell their few exportable goods. Most of them hard-shell Protestants, they embraced Roman Catholicism (leaving "their consciences at Cape Horn," according to one disapproving observer), became naturalized citizens of Mexico, married into prominent, landed *Californio* families, and by 1840 were a generally smooth-functioning part of the California scene.*

Other Americans found different opportunities in California—the rich beaver populations of the San

---

*Unlike most, Thomas Oliver Larkin retained his conscience. On his way to Monterey in 1832, this Massachusetts Yankee met a fellow Protestant passenger and later married the lady. He kept his faith and his undiluted citizenship, but there is nothing to indicate that this harmed his career in any way; with interests in lumber, manufactures, and land, he was reputed to be the richest man in California by the time of American occupation.

Joaquin and Sacramento valleys. Beaver pelts were as popular in America as sea otter fur was in China, and as early as the mid-1820s, these fat-tailed creatures had been stripped from many areas in the Rocky Mountains by trappers—"mountain men," they were called, the footloose, somewhat primitive entrepreneurs whose wanderings laid open vast areas of the West to exploration. Among them was Jedediah Strong Smith, a non-swearing, non-drinking young man with Calvinistic tendencies and a lust to see new country. In 1826 he purchased the Rocky Mountain Fur Company of St. Louis and with seventeen men went off in search of new beaver territory.

After traversing the wastelands of what is now southern Utah, Nevada, and Arizona, the Smith party made its way across the Mojave Desert, descended Cajon Pass in the San Bernardino Mountains, and wandered onto the Los Angeles plain, arriving at Mission San Gabriel at the end of November 1826. Governor Echeandía, imbued with the paranoid uncertainties common to California governors, believed they were spies and ordered Smith and his men out of the territory. He apparently did not specify a route, however, so the party went north, crossing the Tehachapi Range into the lower San Joaquin Valley, where beaver were found in abundance. The trappers worked their way up the valley, taking a small fortune in furs. In May 1827 Smith left the main party camped on the Stanislaus River while he and two of his men crossed the mountains and returned to Utah for more trappers—the first recorded crossing of the Sierra Nevada by white men. He returned later that summer, was again challenged by Echeandía, and again ordered out of the province. Still addicted to the roundabout, he took his party out of California in early 1828 by making the first known journey through the green tangle of California's northwest coast into Oregon, where Umpqua Indians killed all but Smith and two others. The survivors finally made it to the safety of the Hudson's Bay Company outpost of Fort Vancouver late in 1828. Three years later, Smith stopped a fatal Comanche arrow on the Santa Fe Trail.

Even before Smith left California, two more trappers entered—and had their own troubles with the authorities. Sylvester and James Ohio Pattie, a father-and-son team, had trapped down the Gila River to the Colorado until running out of food near the end of 1827. They straggled vaguely west into northern Baja and were finally rescued by mission priests—rescued, arrested, sent to San Diego, and put into jail, where Sylvester died. A smallpox epidemic was James Ohio's deliverance; he just happened to have a supply of vaccine on him and used it to vaccinate some twenty thousand grateful Californians and Christianized Indians, by his own count (it must have been quite a supply of vaccine). In return he was given his release. He wandered back to the United States, and with the help of Timothy Flint, a professional amanuensis who rarely let the facts interfere with a good story, set down the account of his travels in *The Personal Narrative of James O. Pattie,* published in 1831; it is the only "authority" we have for his story.

Pattie's adventures were largely apocryphal; those of Jedediah Smith were real and epic in scope and importance. He made the first American entry into California by land, and the desert trails he blazed were etched into the lexicon of the mountain men who followed him. There were quite a few: Ewing Young and William Wolfskill (and a young apprentice by the name of Christopher (Kit) Carson) in 1830 and 1831; Joseph Reddeford Walker, who made his own crossing of the Sierra Nevada in 1833; "Pegleg" Smith and James P. Beckwourth, who made a good thing of horse theft on a massive scale in the 1830s, crossing the Mojave Desert into southern California, cutting hundreds of horses from the thick herds of the *Californios,* and driving them back across the deserts to Utah and Colorado for sale; even the Hudson's Bay Company trappers were known to work their way down from the Columbia River into the Upper Sacramento Valley in the early 1830s.

The hope of forestalling such infiltrations gave luster to the schemes put forward by Capt. Johann August Suter (later called Sutter), a self-commissioned former officer in the Royal Swiss Guard of France who had arrived in Monterey in 1839 after sporadic and singularly unsuccessful careers as a storekeeper in his native Switzerland, a trader on the Santa Fe Trail, and a visionary everywhere. Sutter's ambition was simple: he wanted his own country, a place he could rule himself by his own lights and to his own aggrandizement. He liked the looks of the Sacramento Valley and wanted

*Captain Johann August Suter (Sutter), who dreamed of empire in the Sacramento Valley.*

to carve out his empire there and call it New Helvetia, after his homeland. With this in mind, he requested a huge land grant from Governor Juan Bautista Alvarado, who was no stranger to the technique of using foreigners to further his own ends. During the troubles of 1836, he had employed the services of a number of American ex-trappers under the leadership of Isaac Graham to oust Governor Nicolas Gutiérrez; the threat of their riflepower had been a distinct asset. Of course Graham and the others were now a bit of a nuisance, drunk most of the time, sullen and arrogant all of the time, engaged in God only knew what subversive schemes against his administration.* Still, Sutter might be a boon: his presence in the Sacramento Valley could block further incursions of trappers and help domesticate the Indians of the region; certainly his presence would dilute the power of Alvarado's uncle, Mariano

---

*Graham and his companions finally got their comeuppance in 1840, when Alvarado rounded them up and shipped them off to Mexico in chains. They were later released, but not until the "Graham Affair" had inspired an exchange of stiff diplomatic notes between the governments of the United States and Mexico.

Vallejo, who was exercising altogether too much influence from his headquarters in Sonoma. Sutter got his wish: a land grant of eleven square leagues near the confluence of the Sacramento and American rivers.

Sutter fell to with a will. With the help of Indian labor and an occasional passing American, he constructed Sutter's Fort in 1839, roughly the size of a modern football field, with walls eighteen feet high and two feet thick, corner bastions complete with cannon, a three-room headquarters building he called Casa Grande, together with a barracks, a bakery, a mill, a blanket factory, and sundry workshops. He built a road down to a little *embarcadero* on the Sacramento River and bought a small launch to take his goods down to San Francisco Bay. Out on the sweep of his land, he planted wheat and raised cattle and horses. By 1841 he had progressed so well that he felt tempted to branch out; when the Russians expressed a desire to sell the post of Fort Ross, he signed a note for $30,000, with a down payment of $2,000. New Helvetia was no longer a dream.

But Sutter was not alone in the Great Central Valley. Some fifty miles to the southwest of Sutter's Fort, "Doctor" John Marsh was erecting his own little empire beneath the grassy slopes of Mount Diablo, near the present-day town of Martinez. Marsh, a canny, hermitlike man who had parlayed a Latin-script bachelor of arts diploma from Harvard College into a full-fledged medical degree, had bought his land and settled on it in 1837, planting figs, pears, olives, and grapevines, and building himself a respectable herd of cattle by charging as many as fifty head for each house call, depending upon how far he had to travel. With an eye on the future, he also solicited immigration to California, writing glowing letters to the folks back east—particularly those in the Mississippi Valley. His letters would help to convert Sutter's hegemony, his little empire of New Helvetia, into no more than a way-station for Manifest Destiny.

B Y THE 1840s, the westering urge that had always marked the American story had reached a pitch of importance that required that it be given a name—and so it was: Manifest Destiny, the almost sacred conviction that America was destined to sweep from sea to shining sea. Those who believed it, believed it utterly, as one of them stated: "There is such a thing as a destiny for this American race . . . because we, the people of the United States, have spread, are spreading, and intend to spread, and should spread, and go on to spread . . . and this our destiny has now become so manifest that it cannot fail but by our own folly."

The land to which most Americans were spreading was Oregon, where hundreds, then thousands, of stolid, determined, land-hungry wagon-train pioneers challenged British domination by the sheer physical fact of their presence. For years men, women, and children lumbered up the Oregon Trail, a road that traveled up the valley of the Platte River, through Wyoming's South Pass, on to Fort Hall, then across the arid Snake River plains and the high desert of eastern Oregon, around the Cascade Range, and down into the lush valley of the Willamette River. But in 1841 a subtle, almost imperceptible shift took place, as John Bidwell, John Bartleson, and a train of about thirty people left the Oregon Trail before reaching Fort Hall, drawn away by tales of a golden land called California. They marched south and west, down the Humboldt River, across the Carson Sink, up the canyon of the Walker River, and across the Sierra Nevada into the San Joaquin Valley.

Thirty people . . . it was a small beginning, but a beginning. In 1842 no one came across the mountains, but in 1843 Joseph Chiles and Joseph Reddeford Walker led two individual parties overland, and in 1844 Elisha Stevens captained a train of forty-six people, who made the first wagon crossing of the central Sierra Nevada, clambering up the canyon of the Truckee River and double-teaming their wagons up the steep, rocky, incredibly difficult slopes of what would become known as Donner Pass, before rumbling into the Sacramento Valley and the heartening sight of Sutter's Fort. Sutter welcomed them, fed and supplied them generously; a naturally kind man, he was nevertheless not without self-interest: settlers meant laborers for his fields and shops, markets for his goods, potential buyers of his land, and allies when he threw his weight behind Governor Manuel Micheltorena during the conflict of 1845.

In the interim California had been visited by yet another American, the flamboyant Lt. John Charles Frémont of the U.S. Topographical Engineers, son-in-law of Senator Thomas Hart Benton of Missouri and an avidly ambitious young man possessed of a yen for far places and enough scientific discipline to mark those places down when he found them. His Exploring Expedition of 1843–44 took him and a complement of mountain men and Delaware scouts (including Kit Carson) up the Oregon Trail into Oregon, back down into Nevada, across the Sierra Nevada in the dead of winter, down the Central Valley into southern California, and back east via the Gila River and the deserts of Utah. With the aid of his wife, Jessie, he put together a detailed, exciting, informative, and generally accurate report, published in December 1844; it was an instant best seller and a valuable addition to any man's wagon if his goal was to cross the trans-Mississippi West to California.

There were about two hundred fifty of these remarkable people in 1845 (many of whom had succumbed to the proselytizing efforts of old Caleb Greenwood, a mountain man hired by Sutter to divert as much of the pioneering flood as possible to the direction of California), and in the spring of 1846, nearly a thousand more gathered on the banks of the Missouri River, making ready for the great trek. By the time they arrived, California was well on its way to becoming an outpost of the American republic—for even while the *Californios* engaged in their bickering squabbles, their family fights, their struggles for power and position, forces they could neither see nor comprehend were gathering to put an end to a world they may have thought would last forever.

# CHAPTER 4

# COMEDY AND CONQUEST

*America's continental urge gathers force, gives birth to a war, and
leads to the conquest of California*

ON MAY 10, 1849, there occurred in New York City one of those events which frequently color our definitions of an era—and one which effectively clarified a significant factor in the American acquisition of California. For months Charles Macready, a touring English actor, and Edwin Forrest, America's reigning thespian, had engaged in a sordid exchange of unpleasantries, featuring the temperamental vitriol at which actors are particularly adept. Forrest, in Macready's opinion, was "a blackguard, a thick-headed, thick-legged brute, an ignorant, uneducated man, burning with envy and rancor at my success," and he elaborated on the point by expressing the view that Forrest represented his fellow Americans, who were a race of hopeless clods. Forrest, for his part, called Macready a foul, aristocratic snob, a miserable actor, and a liar. Newspapers from Cincinnati to New York City followed the affair with undisguised relish, most of them siding with Forrest. As the weeks passed the whole business achieved the level of what the *New York Herald* called "a national question, and made to turn on national grounds."

In May both actors had engagements in New York, Macready at the Astor Place Opera House, Forrest at the Broadway Theatre. On his first night Macready was driven off the stage under a barrage of theatre chairs and such sentiments as "Down with the English hog!" Undaunted by this vulgar display, the British actor stiffened his lip and scheduled another performance for the night of the tenth. The five acts of *Macbeth* were completed that night, but not without genuine danger; a violent, caterwauling crowd gathered outside the opera house to bombard it with cobblestones, brickbats, and rocks throughout the performance, ultimately breaking every window on one side of the place. Members of the state militia, who had ringed the theater to protect the actor's continued existence, came in for their share of the fury, and what had to happen did: the militia opened fire, and a few minutes later twenty people had died.

If it seems incredible that national sentiment could have been raised to such a grotesque pitch over something so trifling as an actor's opinion of anything, it should be pointed out that the Astor Place Riot of May 10, 1849, was no aberration; in the context of its time, it was the perfectly logical climax to more than thirty years of fierce resentment. Great Britain was the *bête noire* of a young America. In 1840 there were thousands of people who could remember the sound of musketry during the Revolutionary War and several million who could remember when British soldiers had burned the national capitol during the War of 1812. Moreover, with a self-consciousness that suggested a certain insecurity, the adolescent republic officially and unofficially preened and blustered in an extraordinary fashion in these years, most of the posturing directed against her erstwhile parent. England, in turn, tended to view the antics of the United States with an unconcealed and frequently snide condescension, all of which simply nourished the flames of resentment.

The point is important, because the transcontinental movement that was already beginning to people the

*John Bidwell's hand-drawn diseño (map) of the Sacramento Valley, showing
land grants claimed by Americans. Most of the claims were fraudulent.*

Pacific Coast with Americans was markedly intensified by this emotional relationship with England. Chief among the country's paranoid anxieties was the fear that England was ready and willing to seize California for her own, should the chance arise. Some, like the old fire-eater, Senator Thomas Hart Benton of Missouri, were convinced that England's designs on California dated clear back to Drake's landing in 1579 and that Her Majesty's government was simply waiting for it to fall into her lap like one of the golden apples of the sun.

Superficially, at least (and, given this government's emotional conditioning, appearances were all that mattered), this was a distinct possibility. Mexico's influence on California's internal affairs degenerated steadily during the early 1840s. Had the government of the *Californios* been inclined to annex itself to, or ask the protection of, any other nation, Britain included, there would have been little that Mexico could have done about it. Exactly such a scheme had been unofficially promoted by one Britisher or another ever since the publication of George Vancouver's *A Voyage of Discovery to the North Pacific Ocean* in 1798, in which he took pains to describe the ludicrously inadequate defenses of the port of San Francisco (two three-pounders, one of them mounted on a log). Seizing upon similar evidences of Mexican neglect and pointing out the unsettled nature of the province's internal politics, such individuals as Alexander Forbes, a British merchant, and Sir George Simpson, governor of the Hudson's Bay Company, had publicly advocated the direct intervention of Great Britain in the 1830s and early 1840s.* But the English government was singularly uninterested in the whole idea. Quite correctly gauging the intensity of America's continental urge, Prime Minister Robert Peel and his foreign secretary, the Earl of Aberdeen, knew that any such move would propel the pugnacious young America to the brink of war—a war they were unwilling to undertake without a French alliance. And France, riven by internal strife, was too busy fighting herself to fight anyone else.

---

*Forbes' opinions were expressed in his *History of Upper and Lower California*, published in 1839; Simpson, who visited California in 1841, did not publish his views until 1847, in *Narrative of a Journey Round the World*. Nevertheless, he made no secret of them, and they were well known in the United States in the early 1840s.

The British government, however, was quite as good at concealing its true intentions as any other nation. As a consequence, what England thought, what it was *thought* she thought, what she did, what it was felt she *might* do, what she said, what it was *said* she said—all were factors which profoundly influenced the course of American involvement in California. Nothing more thoroughly typified this fact than the clownish incident involving the unfortunate Commo. Thomas ap Catesby Jones.

In September 1842, while the administration of President John Tyler engaged in some ticklish negotiations with the Mexican government for the sale of California —or at least the port of San Francisco—Commodore Jones and his Pacific squadron were anchored at Callao, Peru, nervously watching the movements of the British Pacific squadron as it prepared to depart for points unknown (under sealed orders, rumor had it). Shortly after the British squadron left, Jones received word that the United States and Mexico were at war and that Mexico had arranged to cede California to England in payment of her debts to that country. Jones instantly bent sail, weighed anchor, and raced for California, where he arrived in mid-October. At Monterey, he congratulated himself on beating the British squadron, demanded the surrender of the town and the province, raised the American flag, and issued a proclamation declaring the peaceful American occupation of the territory. One day later, when he examined letters and newspapers from Mexico City, he discovered that there was no war and no Mexican-English arrangement. With no little embarrassment he extended apologies to every official in sight, lowered the American flag, attended a dance given by the *Californios,* and removed himself from Monterey with as much grace as he could muster.

The *Californios* were far more entertained than outraged by this abortive conquest, but officialdom in Mexico City reacted with bleats of protest, eliminating whatever slim chance there had been for Tyler to arrange a peaceful cession of California to the United States. The idea was not revived until the presidency of James K. Polk, America's strongest president between Andrew Jackson and Abraham Lincoln, and a dour, secretive, utterly determined individual with the instincts of a professional poker player and the gall of a successful horse trader. Nurtured at the political knee

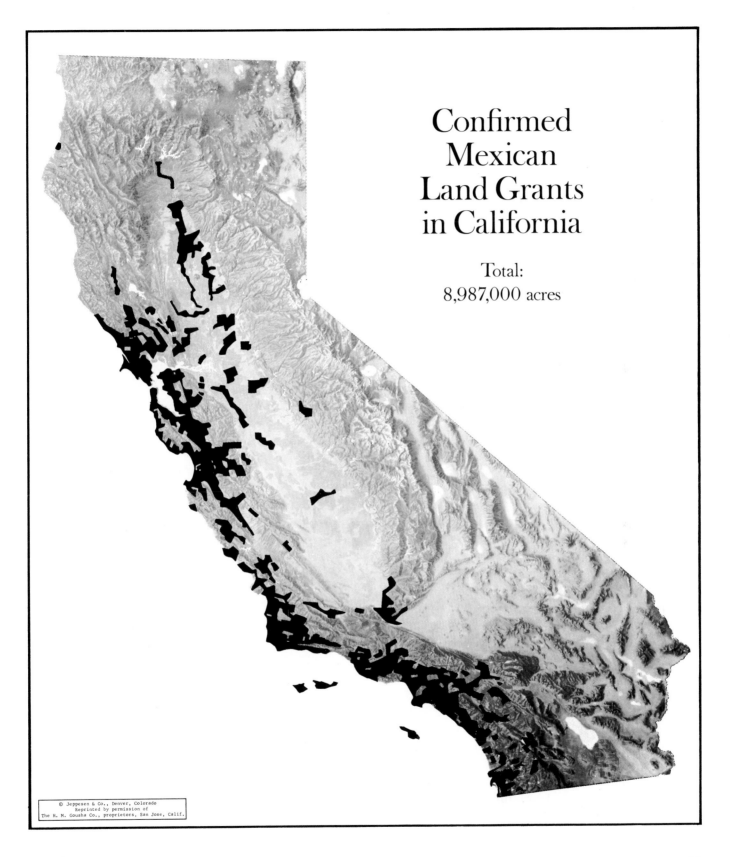

# Confirmed Mexican Land Grants in California

Total:
8,987,000 acres

of Jackson—who himself had tried to buy the San Francisco Bay region from Mexico in 1835 and who hated England with a passion born of the Revolution—Polk took office in March 1845, with a talent for muscular duplicity that had been forged by twenty-five years of experience in the particularly serpentine politics of ante-bellum Tennessee and the equally tangled affairs in the House of Representatives. He was fully primed to accept at face value any and all vague rumors concerning British intentions toward California. This psychic stew was an important factor in the achievement of the three major foreign policy goals that he brought to the office of president: the completed annexation of Texas, the settlement of the Oregon question with Great Britain, and the acquisition of California (later expanded to include New Mexico). Counting heavily on British reluctance to go to war, he managed in 1846 to reach an agreeable settlement on the Oregon question with a combination of bluff and compromise, extending America's Oregon territory to the 49th parallel and acquiring Puget Sound in the bargain. But his other two goals were not satisfied before one of the most complex wars in the history of the United States had ground to a bloody end in Mexico.

EVER SINCE the embryonic nation of Texas had won its independence from Mexico in 1836 (an independence, however, which the Mexican government steadfastly refused to recognize), there had been sentiment within the Lone Star republic and the United States for its annexation to the Union. On March 1, 1845, just three days before Polk's inauguration, President John Tyler signed a joint resolution of Congress which offered statehood to the republic. The act was greeted with joy by most southern Democratic politicians, who welcomed the addition of one more slave state to the fold, but opposed by most anti-slavery, anti-expansionist Whigs, who saw it, in the words of former President John Quincy Adams, as "the first step to the conquest of all Mexico, of the West India islands, of a maritime, colonizing, slave-tainted monarchy, and of extinguished freedom."

Polk had no visible interest in the West Indies at that time, or so far as we know, the creation of a monarchy—but he *was* a southerner, a Democrat, an expan-

sionist, and as full of schemes as a Borgia. He not only welcomed Texas for its own sake but immediately saw it as a possible key to his California ambitions. A disputed strip of territory between the Nueces River, the Texan boundary claimed by Mexico, and the Rio Grande, the boundary which the republic itself claimed, provided him with a framework for his plans. At about the same time he was judiciously allowing his political opponents to believe that the question of the final boundary was open to negotiation with Mexico once annexation was a fact, Polk wrote to his representative in Texas, "Of course, I would maintain the Texan title to the extent which she claims it to be, and not permit an invading enemy to occupy a foot of soil East of the Rio Grande."*

Shortly after the Texan Congress accepted the United States' offer of annexation in June 1845, he ordered Gen. Zachary Taylor and his army to occupy Corpus Christi, on the northern edge of the disputed territory, and had Secretary of the Navy George Bancroft instruct Commo. John D. Sloat, the new commander of the Pacific squadron, to "at once possess yourself of the port of San Francisco, and blockade or occupy such other ports as your force may permit," should war break out between Mexico and the United States.

However aggressive in tone, all this saber-rattling was at first designed to frighten Mexico into abandoning her claims to the country of the Rio Grande and negotiating for the outright sale of New Mexico and California; Polk had no particular desire for war—not in June, at any rate. But by November, when he sent John Slidell to Mexico City with the authority to offer as much as fifteen million dollars for New Mexico and another twenty-five million for California, he may well have changed his mind. Slidell's mission was hopeless.

---

*Polk's motives in making such a statement were typically convoluted. Among other purposes, by assuring Texas of its boundary claims, he hoped to head off a plot between anti-annexation forces in Texas, including her president, Anson Jones, and British diplomats, as unenthusiastic as ever at the prospect of an expanding America. These interests were attempting to obtain from the Mexican government an official recognition of the independence of Texas, theorizing that uncontested nationhood might stem the young country's drift toward the United States (they ultimately got the offer, but too late). Texan sentiment in favor of annexation was far too strong for any such manipulation to succeed—but, of course, Polk could not know that, and he was never one to leave a possibility uncovered.

The current government of Mexico, about as shaky as a government could be and still function, was in no position to bargain for the cession of so much territory; had it done so, the outcry of national protest would have obliterated it overnight. There is evidence to suggest that Polk was fully aware of this; a few months earlier Duff Green, a man familiar with the permutations of Mexican governance, had outlined the situation to him, and it is not impossible that Slidell's mission was meant simply to satisfy public opinion (and history) that Polk had done all in his power to avert open conflict.

By then, another avenue toward acquisition of California had come to his mind—one that appealed to his apparent love of intrigue and reflected his profound mistrust of England. For months the United States consul in California, Thomas O. Larkin, had been sending reports to Washington that communicated (and sometimes exaggerated) every wisp of rumor concerning British intentions and outlined his conviction that California's political leaders, such as they were, could be persuaded to declare independence from Mexico and follow the pattern of Texas by joining the United States. In his view, official as well as de facto independence was inevitable, and if the United States hoped to keep the province from joining Her Majesty's Empire (as a small but rabid number of Californians actually wished), she had better make official overtures to the *Californios* and make them soon. Polk took the bait, and on October 17, 1845—only a little over three weeks before he sent Slidell to Mexico City—he dispatched Commo. Robert F. Stockton from the Gulf of Mexico to Monterey via the Sandwich Islands (Hawaii) with orders from the secretary of state, James Buchanan, that made Larkin "confidential agent in California" (at six dollars a day) and gave him the authority to make it clear to the *Californios* that while the United States could not and would not actually encourage such a move, "if the People should desire to unite their destiny with ours, they would be received as brethren." Another copy of the order was carried overland through Mexico by Marine Lt. Archibald H. Gillespie, disguised as a merchant traveling for his health.

It might have worked. Larkin was well known and respected among many *Californios,* and his words carried weight—an influence in no way hindered by his role as one of the province's few "bankers," who extended credit and provided liquid capital. Besides, dissatisfaction with the Mexican government was intense, and many of California's leading spirits, particularly Sonoma's Don Mariano G. Vallejo, had already resigned themselves to eventual American dominance. In Monterey, Gen. Don José Castro, military *comandante* of California, was even then entertaining the notion of ousting Governor Pío Pico from Los Angeles, declaring California an independent republic (with guess-who as president), and proceeding from there to whatever development seemed most attractive. And Governor Pico, while publicly expressing his undying fealty to Mexico, dramatically stepped up his land grants to friends and relatives of the local government, possibly in anticipation of a rise in land values once the province changed hands. In the first few months of 1846 alone, Pico dispensed eighty-seven such grants, most of them of the maximum size of eleven square leagues (48,818 acres) and many of them in the northern part of the province—a fact which probably did not escape the notice of the Americans of the region, as we shall see.

In short, California trembled in a state of flux; given a little time to exercise his clout to its full potential, Larkin might well have been able to nudge the province into the welcoming arms of the United States. But even before Stockton or Gillespie could deliver their dispatches, circumstances rendered the scheme pointless. In December 1845 Congress formally accepted Texas into the Union and the Mexican government, just as formally, broke off diplomatic relations with the United States, refusing to receive John Slidell and expressing its indignation with military ruffles and flourishes. When word of this reaction reached Washington on January 12, 1846, Polk ordered Taylor's army to advance to the Rio Grande, where it arrived in late March. A few days later a Mexican force encamped across the river near the Mexican town of Matamoras, but for the next few weeks the two armies did nothing more than send out patrols and exchange belligerent proclamations.

By now, Polk was convinced that war was inevitable, but reluctant to be the first president in the country's history to actually start one. He waited for several weeks, hoping that Mexico would make the first move, either by declaring war openly or by attacking American forces, and he vaguely toyed with yet another scheme whereby a million dollars in immediate cash might buy him enough support in Mexico to put together a treaty. Finally, on Saturday, May 9, he decided he could wait no longer; the severance of diplomatic relations and Mexico's continuing refusal to talk to Slidell would have to do as an excuse for a declaration of war, which he determined to request when Capitol Hill opened for business Monday morning. But that night, he received word that on April 26 an American patrol had been attacked and captured by the Mexicans on "American" soil above the Rio Grande. He amended his message accordingly and delivered it the morning of the eleventh (Mexico, meanwhile, had already made its own declaration). One can sense the satisfaction and relief that must have accompanied his announcement that "now, after reiterated menaces, Mexico has passed the boundary of the United States, has invaded our territory, and shed American blood upon American soil," and that war existed "by the act of Mexico herself." After some frantic opposition by those who considered the whole business little better than territorial larceny, Congress gave the president what he asked for, and on Tuesday he signed it.

Mr. Polk's war of acquisition had begun.

THE GREAT BATTLES of the Mexican War were played out a long distance from both the city where war had been declared and the land for which it was fought. It was America's first major expeditionary war, and men struggled, marched, and sweated out the long agony of conflict in places with names unfamiliar to the American experience: Monterrey, Buena Vista, Vera Cruz, Resaca de la Palma, Chapultepec, the Hall of the Montezumas. It ground on for nearly two years, and at its end had killed 13,283 Americans (most by disease) and uncounted Mexicans, and had cost one hundred million dollars. California experienced few of those deaths and financed little of that cost; seen against the backdrop of the very real war going on in the valleys and plains of Mexico, where armies clashed by day and night in generous bloodshed, the California conflict appears as a parody of warfare. The irony of the comparison is heightened by the fact that this gray comedy was futile by any standards of military, political, or diplomatic necessity.

With all deference to the risks of historical speculation, there seems little reason to doubt that the province's inexorable drift toward the United States would simply have been accelerated once news of war reached its inhabitants. After all, for all their bluster and self-importance, the *Californio* leaders had always demonstrated a decent respect for the arts of survival and an ability to accept and adjust to the inevitable—providing that their honor could also be satisfied, by no means an impossible task. If American occupation had been entrusted to reasonable men, the chances were excellent that the transition would have been as slick and peaceful as anyone might have desired. As it turned out, a handful of small men who danced to the puppet-strings of their large ambitions managed to sabotage this possibility and create a bitter, pointless little farce which only an unjustifiably charitable view of history could dignify with the title of "conquest."

The meaningless character of the affair was established even before war broke out between the United States and Mexico. It began in December 1845 with the arrival of John C. Frémont and a force of sixty hand-picked, well-armed men, most of them weathered, hard-bitten veterans of sundry wilderness exploits. His ostensible mission was to expand and correct some of his previous explorations, but the mission he carried in his head went far beyond that prosaic, if necessary, task. He had competently accomplished some of the most extensive, well-reported, and useful exploring expeditions in the nineteenth century and had reaped more than a fair share of the country's official and unofficial gratitude (see chapter 3). But this was not glory enough for him. He was beginning to see himself as a Great Man, an image nourished by the artful prodding of his wife Jessie—who was herself beautiful, brilliant, ambitious, and trapped in a time and place that robbed her of any alternative way to make her mark in a world ruled by men. To both of them—and to Frémont's father-in-law, Senator Benton—California appeared as a potential arena for the further development of a young man's swelling career. One way or another, it seemed inevitable that the province would soon have to change flags—either design her own, accept that of Great Britain, or be given America's. The presence of a highly mobile force of sharpshooters on the scene might just sway circumstances. And as for the commander of such a troop—who knew what wonders might ensue?

So, armed with a headful of sugar-plum visions, Benton's fatherly encouragement, and his wife's vigorous support, Frémont entered California in December 1845 with a thirst for destiny. It got him into trouble almost immediately—and thoroughly crippled Larkin's patient efforts for a peaceful political transition. After making a verbal promise to Don José Castro in Monterey that he would sit out the winter in the San Joaquin Valley then proceed to Oregon (or to the Gila River in the south; he had not made up his mind) in the spring, Frémont loitered instead in the Santa Clara Valley until March 1846, soaking up rumors, speculations, grievances, and possibilities expressed by American settlers and traders. Then he set out—not east across the mountains, but south toward Monterey. When Castro demanded that he keep his word and remove himself and his party from the coast, Frémont's response was to compose a screed of high-toned outrage, send it to Castro, retire to Gavilan (now Fremont) Peak near Mission San Juan Bautista, erect a jerry-built fort of logs, whittle a pole, nail the American flag to it, plant it with appropriate ceremony, and vow to defend it to the last man. Castro's honor required that he pelt the region with belligerent circulars in the finest *Californio* style, round up a troop of volunteers, and maneuver them in various aggressive poses within range of American telescopes but not American rifles.

Larkin was aghast and worked frantically to prevent an exchange of gunfire that would start a war he considered neither necessary nor profitable. His intercession (coupled with a natural reluctance on Castro's part) kept the two forces apart long enough for the situation to cool. After three days the wind toppled Frémont's brave little banner. He announced that this was an omen to move on, and the party retired across the mountains and up the Central Valley, arriving at Sutter's Fort on March 21. His position was now ridiculous as well as profoundly illegal. Recognizing this, he decided at least to make a gesture toward reality and wandered north, apparently on his way to Oregon.

Behind him, Frémont left a well-roiled California. Larkin did his best to placate Castro and the other *Californio* authorities, while clusters of settlers, squatters, adventurers, and con men gathered in Yerba Buena, Monterey, and Sutter's Fort over glasses of brandy or wine and gossiped, feeding the flames of their insecurity.

On April 17 Lt. Archibald H. Gillespie arrived in Monterey, delivering the orders that appointed Thomas Larkin a confidential agent (Stockton was then at the Sandwich Islands, preparing to complete his journey to California). Gillespie also had news of the situation in Washington (as of the previous November, at any rate) and—perhaps most significant—of the Mexican government's refusal to receive Slidell in December and its military preparations. After meeting with Larkin, Gillespie almost immediately set out to find Frémont, for whom he had a packet of letters from Jessie and the senator. He discovered him on the shores of Klamath Lake early in May, desultorily surveying his route and preparing to cross the mountains. After an evening's discussion with Gillespie, Frémont decided to return to California. It appeared that another moment for the seizing might present itself after all—and, besides, how would it look to the folks back in Washington (including his wife) if he spent his time maundering about in the safety of Oregon while a war of conquest was going on behind his back?*

By the end of May the Frémont party was in camp at the Marysville Buttes, some fifty miles north of Sutter's Fort, and Frémont had sent Gillespie ahead to requisition 300 pounds of rifle lead, one keg of powder, and 8,000 percussion caps from the U.S.S. *Portsmouth*, which Commodore Sloat had sent from Mazatlán to

---

*This decision has inspired an incredible amount of historiographic ink, largely because of Frémont's later insistence that he was carrying out the secret wishes of his government—that, in fact, his entire expedition was a confidential mission undertaken with the full knowledge of the Polk administration. The "family cipher" contained in Benton's letter, he said, established this; the verbal instructions of Gillespie reinforced it. Frémont may actually have believed this later, but the fact remains that it was all glorification after the fact. There was no family cipher instructing him; there were no verbal orders; Frémont had been given no secret assignment of any kind. Polk not only had no such scheme in mind (perhaps uncharacteristically), he actually had to be reminded later by James Buchanan that Frémont was even *in* California. Frémont's decision to return to California was his own, one inspired by nothing more than a convenient blending of his own inclinations and the speculations of Gillespie.

San Francisco Bay in April for purposes of observation. It was not long before the camp was infested by restless Americans from all over the northern part of the territory who interpreted Frémont's return as a portent of one kind or another. Castro, who was then assembling a militia force for one more demonstration in his long, if inconclusive, feud with Governor Pío Pico, chose this unfortunate moment to send two officers and eight privates north to requisition horses from Don Mariano Vallejo in Sonoma. With the encouragement if not the active support of Frémont, the Americans milling about at Marysville Buttes elected to intercept the herd, and on June 10 a small group of adventurers captured it near the Cosumnes River and drove it back to Sutter's Fort, while Frémont broke camp and moved down to Bear Creek, much nearer the scene of action.

And action there was. The raw larceny of horse theft could be cleansed only by an act which raised the whole business to the level of at least semi-legitimate warfare. They had to capture something besides horses, so in the pre-dawn hours of June 14 a cadre of about thirty men launched an "assault" on the military garrison at Sonoma (again without Frémont's direct aid). This attack had its peculiar logic, in California terms at any rate: there was no garrison at Sonoma, and there had been none since the year before. What the midnight marauders captured were nine tiny cannon, some of which were actually mounted on carriages, 200 arthritic muskets, a small quantity of ammunition, two minor Mexican officers, and a sleepy-eyed but characteristically gracious Don Mariano Vallejo, who invited the party's leaders into his house to discuss the terms of capitulation over glasses of brandy and wine. That done and the agreement signed, the prisoners of war were shuttled off to Sutter's Fort, where Frémont ordered them imprisoned, and the leaders of the rebellion sat down and began to figure out exactly what it was they were doing.

What they were doing, they decided, was founding a new republic, so they had an election and a visionary Yankee schoolteacher by the name of William B. Ide was chosen commander in chief. A nation should have a flag, it was agreed, so the founding fathers extemporized one on a piece of cotton cloth, featuring a hand wrought picture of a grizzly bear under a star reminiscent of that on the flag of the Texas Republic; on the bottom of this ensign were lettered the words, "CALIFORNIA REPUBLIC" (a considerably improved version, of course, is now the state's official flag). Ide then issued a declaration that attempted to ape both the tone and the language of the one written by Thomas Jefferson in another time and place, and sent out a call for volunteers from the countryside.

Thus was born one of the strangest and shortest-lived republics in the history of the Americas.

IT IS TEMPTING to dismiss the creation of the Bear Flag Republic as either the singularly fey manifestation of a kind of crackpot patriotism or a somewhat cynical attempt to cover up what amounted to acts of banditry. There were elements of both factors involved, certainly, but the motives of those who engineered the revolt may well have been far more intricate than that.

The main reason for their action, they would later maintain, was that Castro had been about to drive them across the mountains; they said he had issued circulars ordering them out, that he was gathering an army to forcibly expel them if they did not go voluntarily, and that he had ordered the Indians to destroy their homes and fields, and even to massacre them. In his *History of California*, H. H. Bancroft discounted all of it: "General Castro did not issue the proclamations imputed to him; did not order the settlers to quit the country; did not organize an army with which to attack them; and did not instigate savages to destroy their crops. . . . The Americans of the Sacramento had nothing to fear from the Californians; and this must have been almost as well known to the leading spirits of the revolt as to us." A subsidiary reason offered was that they hoped to prevent an imminent British takeover, but again this makes little sense; if the British had been seriously interested in taking California with the built-in threat of instant war with the United States as a consequence, they would hardly have been dissuaded by the presence of a motley little republic—even one that had fearlessly captured nine tiny cannon. Doubtless, many of those who participated sincerely believed all or part of both justifications; just as certainly, as Bancroft notes, "The alleged motives, so far at least as the leaders were concerned, were assuredly not the real ones. They were but pretexts of designing men, used at the time to secure unanimity of action, and after success to justify that action."

What, then, were they after? The answer may lie buried in the middle of Ide's convoluted and sometimes incomprehensible proclamation of June 15. "The Commander in Chief of the Troops assembled at the Fortress of Sonoma," Ide wrote grandly, "solemnly declares his object to be First, to defend himself and companions in arms who were invited to this country [by whom?] by a promise of Lands on which to settle themselves . . . who, when having arrived in California were denied even the privilege of buying or renting Lands of their friends." It was also his intention "to overthrow a 'Government' which had seized upon the property of the Missions for its individual aggrandizement," and in a later version of the proclamation, he amended this sentence to read: "to overthrow a 'Government' which has robbed and despoiled the Missions and appropriated the property thereof for the individual aggrandizement of its favorites; which has violated good Faith by its treachery in the bestowment of Public Lands."

The capitalization of "Lands" in the above excerpts was not necessarily the result of Ide's typically slipshod composition. Land, the great common denominator of California history, may well have been at the root of the founding of the Bear Flag Republic, the one thing that could have inspired its leaders to risk everything in one wild throw of the dice. They were children of an age in which a man's material value was usually measured in terms of land, property, *real estate*—whether it was used for the purposes of production or simple speculation. The rumored availability of land was why most of them had ventured into California, and they had found little of it available. Given no other choice (but to leave), many had followed the fine old American tradition of squatting on land to which they had no reasonable expectation of title—hoping for the best while during the first months of 1846 Governor Pico gave away 372,792 acres of Sacramento and San Joaquin Valley land in eight individual grants, all of it to *Californios* or naturalized foreigners. Ide and his colleagues were have-nots who had hoped to get—and California was slipping away from them. To interrupt this giveaway may have been one workable reason for the revolt; indeed, it was mentioned later as one of several reasons, although far more emphasis was placed

on fear for their lives, patriotism, and a love of Republican Principles. Yet one of Ide's first acts as the leader of the minuscule nation was to promise at least one square league (4,438 acres) of land to every man who joined the enterprise and to declare that all mission lands (i.e., those lands already given away or being given away by the *Californio* authorities) were to become the public domain of the California Republic.

On one level, then, the Bear Flag Rebellion might accurately be characterized as the predecessor of the squatters' revolts that would punctuate the early 1850s. On another, it might be described as a genuine attempt to emulate the Texas republic, for the brief history of that land was common knowledge to most of the rebellion's participants, many of whom were refugees from the Mississippi Valley frontier and some, like William L. Todd (nephew of Mary Todd Lincoln and designer of the grizzly bear flag), from Texas itself. The one thing that would not have escaped the attention of land-hungry men was the fact that one of the main points agreed upon in the annexation negotiations between the Texas republic and the United States was that all public lands would remain in the control of Texas.* If the Republic of Texas could do it, Ide and his colleagues might have reasoned, why not the California Republic? If the shadow of a working government could be formed and maintained a sufficient length of time before open war between Mexico and the United States (and remember, they did not know that war had already begun), and if the United States government was forced to court California as it had courted Texas, it might well agree to honor the republic's appropriation of Mexican grant lands; not only would unavailable land become suddenly available, it would be land free of the $1.25 an acre charged for federal land under the provisions of the Pre-Emption Act of 1841, as well as that act's 160-acre limitation provisions—both matters of no small importance in a province used to measuring land in square leagues.

Altogether, it seems possible that the Bear Flag affair

---

*The Joint Resolution of Congress of March 1, 1845, read as follows: "Said State, when admitted into the Union . . . shall also retain all the vacant and unappropriated lands lying within its limits, to be applied to the payment of the debts and liabilities of said republic of Texas; and the residue of said lands, after discharging said debts and liabilities, to be disposed of as said State may direct."

was something more than a simple-minded excursion into the absurd. Moreover, had the timing not been off by several months, the scheme—if it was a scheme—could have worked. Within a week of the Sonoma conquest and Ide's declaration, the republic's "army" had grown to about 100 men; after a skirmish at Olompali, near San Rafael, in which some 20 Bear-Flaggers routed a 50-man force sent north by Castro, it swelled to 250, a force of respectable dimensions when it is remembered that the most Castro could put together at any one time was something less than 200 men. It grew even more respectable when John C. Frémont galloped into Sonoma at the end of June with his 60 men, bent on a "rescue" mission that might legitimize his active participation; when he assumed command of the entire force of more than 300 men (called the California Battalion) at their request on July 5, the movement acquired a genuine military leader, however limited his experience.* Had there been time enough to put together a decent campaign, there seems little reason to doubt that the Bear-Flaggers could have effectively controlled northern California—and that might have been enough to make the republic a reality.

But time had run out on them. Commodore Sloat first heard of the existence of war while at Mazatlán on May 17; old, sick, terrified of repeating Commodore Jones's mistake of 1842, and possessed, as H. H. Bancroft put it, of a "natural indecision of character," Sloat took three weeks to make up his mind to follow his instructions and depart for the occupation of San Francisco and Monterey. He finally arrived at Monterey on July 7, raised the flag, and issued a gentle proclamation: "I declare to the inhabitants of California that altho' I come in arms with a powerful force, I do not come among them as enemy to California; but on the contrary I come as their best friend." On July 9 Sonoma's Bear Flag was hauled down and replaced by the flag of the United States, and whatever dreams had been boiling in the heads of those who founded the Independent Republic of California were shredded like a tule fog in the wind.

---

*Frémont later maintained that he accepted command to prevent the affair from getting out of hand. Perhaps; but one wonders whether his thirst for destiny had not found a new attraction—leading the army of a free republic down the paths of glory. It was a heady image, and Frémont was vulnerable to such things.

ONE OF SLOAT'S first official acts was to relinquish his command, without any regrets (in fact, at his stated request), to his subordinate, Commo. Robert F. Stockton, whose career is worth a closer look. During the War of 1812, he had acquired the nickname of "Fighting Bob," less for his assaults upon the enemy than for his readiness to fight duels with his companions on the slightest provocation and his willingness to disobey orders when he disagreed with them; these same qualities caused the navy to remove him from command in 1821, whereupon he applied for—and quickly received—an extended leave. He requested foreign assignment in 1837, when his business interests necessitated a journey to England; once there, he commissioned John Ericcson (who would become one of the greatest mechanical engineers of the nineteenth century) to design and construct the U.S.S. *Princeton* for the navy. When completed, the *Princeton* was the first screw-propeller naval craft in history and featured, among other things, an enormous cannon capable of sending a 225-pound ball more than two miles, this also designed by Ericcson. Stockton sailed the ship to the United States and, over Ericcson's vigorous warnings, had an equally large cannon of his own design built. In February 1844 Stockton sailed the *Princeton* up the Potomac, billing himself as her designer, and invited President Tyler, his cabinet, and other Washington dignitaries on board for a demonstration of the ship's gunpower. During the festivities, Stockton's cannon disintegrated, killing the secretary of the navy, the secretary of state, and six other men, and injuring seventeen people, including Thomas Hart Benton, whose left eardrum was ruptured by the concussion of the explosion. Stockton promptly informed everyone that the cannon had been designed by "my assistant, an ingenious mechanic, named Ericcson." Not until a congressional investigation was Ericcson's name cleared—though Stockton himself received not so much as a reprimand. Finally, while stationed in the Gulf of Mexico in 1845, he gratuitously involved himself in a sordid and unsuccessful little intrigue designed to trick the Mexicans into attacking Texan or American troops—representing himself all the while as his government's official agent in the matter.

This was the man to whom the actual conquest of California was entrusted, and he went about it with a bombastic zeal calculated to enhance his image (it is no accident of history that Stockton, like Frémont, ultimately threw himself headlong into politics). Since Castro and what supporters he could find had fled Monterey for southern California shortly after Sloat's arrival, there were no military glories available in the northern part of the province; so Stockton mustered in Frémont's California Battalion, put it bag and baggage on board the *Cyane*, and sent it south to capture San Diego. The commodore then prepared to sail with 360 marines for San Pedro and the conquest of Los Angeles. Before leaving, he issued a proclamation, most of whose "information" was supplied by Frémont and Gillespie but whose tone and language were pure Stockton; blandly repeating every rumor and barefaced lie available, this "most extraordinary document," as Bancroft called it, completely annihilated whatever conciliatory effect Sloat's own proclamation had possessed. It cited, among other contortions of truth, "reports from the interior of scenes of rapine, blood, and murder," and "lawless depredations daily committed by Gen. Castro's men upon the persons and property of peaceful and unoffending inhabitants," then went on to announce that "I cannot, therefore, confine my operations to the quiet and undisturbed possession of the defenceless [*sic*] ports of Monterey and San Francisco, whilst the people elsewhere are suffering from lawless violence; but will immediately march against these boasting and abusive chiefs, who have not only violated every principle of national hospitality . . . but who, unless driven out, will, with the aid of hostile Indians, keep this beautiful country in a constant state of revolution and blood."

With this breathless scenario completed, Stockton sailed for San Pedro, where he arrived on August 6. The next morning two emissaries from Castro entered the camp with an offer to negotiate a peaceful settlement—providing Stockton advance no further. The commodore refused (a bloodless conquest was not on the agenda), and on the eleventh started toward Los Angeles; on the thirteenth he was joined by Frémont's California Battalion, which had occupied San Diego without resistance, and in the afternoon the two forces entered Los Angeles without a shot being fired, since Castro and Governor Pío Pico had circumspectly retreated to Mexico, littering the road to Sonora with proclamations all the way. Not much in the way of glory, but it would have to do.

And there it should have ended—except that a little over three weeks later, Stockton sailed north for Monterey and Frémont marched north to Sacramento, leaving Los Angeles in the hands of Lt. Archibald H. Gillespie and a garrison of fifty men. Gillespie, exercising fine American contempt for "greasers," so alienated the people of Los Angeles that by the end of September he found his little garrison surrounded by a guerrilla army under Juan Flores and Andrés Pico, brother of the governor. On October 2 he surrendered and was allowed to march away to San Pedro. Before surrendering, however, he had sent a messenger through the *Californio* lines, "Lean" John Brown, who streaked the distance to San Francisco in six days, delivering word of Gillespie's dilemma. Stockton was then making plans to appoint Frémont military governor of California and take himself, his sailors, and his marines to Mazatlán for a west coast assault on Mexico; events at Los Angeles interrupted these projects. After ordering Frémont and his battalion to sail to Santa Barbara, pick up horses, and march to join him in an assault on Los Angeles, the commodore sailed once again for San Pedro with his own forces. Once there, he found Gillespie and his men, and the combined forces immediately marched for Los Angeles—only to be driven back in the "Battle of the Old Woman's Gun" on October 8, an encounter that featured a horse-drawn antique cannon deployed brilliantly by the *Californios*. The landlocked American navy retreated to San Pedro and set about gathering supplies and horses to prepare for another attempt. Frémont, in the meantime, had received word from a passing ship that there were no horses at Santa Barbara; he returned to Monterey and began gathering them there.

While Stockton drilled his sailors and Frémont gathered horses, Gen. Stephen Watts Kearny was marching into California with one hundred dragoons from Santa Fe. He had originally started out with three hundred men but in August had encountered Kit Carson, who was carrying dispatches from Frémont and who reported that California was well under control; Kearny therefore sent two hundred men back to Santa Fe and resumed his march, employing Carson as guide. On the morning of December 6, Kearny's dragoons attacked a troop of insurgent horsemen under Andrés Pico near the little Indian village of San Pascual, some thirty miles northeast of San Diego. Exhausted from their long march and badly mounted, the dragoons were no match for the lances of the *Californios;* Kearny and his men held the field, but by the battle's end twenty-two Americans were dead and sixteen injured, including Kearny. Carson and another man were sent through the lines to San Diego to seek help from Stockton, who sent a relief force to escort Kearny's mutilated Army of the West to safety.

After Kearny and his men recovered and Stockton had completed his preparations, they launched a joint attack on Los Angeles on January 10, 1847. The assault was more of a protracted skirmish than a genuine battle, but it had the desired results; Los Angeles was recaptured. Juan Flores skittered off to Mexico, and Andrés Pico and the remnants of the insurgent army galloped north toward Cahuenga Pass. There they encountered Frémont's California Battalion. Frémont graciously accepted their surrender with the Capitulation of Cahuenga on January 13 and forever after billed himself as the Conqueror of California.

THE CONQUEST WAS ENDED, but the comedy lingered on. Kearny had marched into California with orders from the War Department to act as the military and civil governor of the conquered province. Stockton, who had no such orders, nevertheless considered himself to be in supreme command, presumably because he had arrived first. He ignored Kearny's authority and appointed Frémont (now lieutenant colonel) governor of California, a position the explorer accepted cheerfully. Stockton sailed for Mazatlán, and Frémont began his short reign as governor, issuing proclama-

tions, orders, and appointments. Patiently, Kearny pointed out that in spite of what Stockton had said, Frémont was utterly without authority in anything he did. He pointed this out several times, but Frémont very much wanted to be governor of California. He continued to defy Kearny, and in the end the general was forced to arrest him and escort him back to Washington in the summer of 1847. In Washington, Frémont was brought before a court-martial and in January 1848 was found guilty of disobedience of orders and dismissed from the army. President Polk remanded the dismissal, but Frémont's burgeoning pride had been assaulted; he huffily resigned his commission.

There is little in his short career of conquest to bring credit to Frémont's memory, but if most of his actions qualified him as the deserving butt of history, he did accomplish one thing in 1846 for which that history should thank him. He told it himself in his memoirs: "The Bay of San Francisco is separated from the sea by low mountain ranges. Looking from the peaks of the Sierra Nevada, the coast mountains present an apparently continuous line, with only a single gap, resembling a mountain pass. This is the entrance to the great bay, and is the only water communication from the coast to the interior country. Approaching from the sea, the coast presents a bold outline. On the south, the bordering mountains come down in a narrow ridge of broken hills, terminating in a precipitous point, against which the sea breaks heavily. On the northern side, the mountain presents a bold promontory, rising in a few miles to a height of two or three thousand feet. Between these points is the strait—about one mile broad in the narrowest part, and five miles long from the sea to the bay. To this gate I gave the name of *Chrysopolae*, or Golden Gate."

If nothing else, Frémont had given the future a name.

*Andrés Pico in elegant military attire.*

# California Mirror:
# The Californios

Governor Pío Pico with wife and nieces. After the war Pico attempted to reclaim the governorship.
"You will please inform him", Gen. William T. Sherman wrote, "that Upper California is now American territory".

The society of the **Californios,** like that of the Indians before them, succumbed with brutal swiftness to the pressures of a new age. Just as the Indian photographs reproduced on pages 27–33 document the living remnants of a time older than the memory of man, the daguerreotypes shown on these pages record the faces of yet another time—a time, one of them said, that held "a contented happiness which an alien race with different temperament can never understand." Thus, Andrés Pico perched like a fighting cock in his military finery, doubtless remembering that transient moment of glory when his lancers met the dragoons of General Stephen W. Kearny at San Pascual; thus, the Lugo family, all the generations of them, lined up with comely pride to display the grace of their physical beauty; thus, Mariano G. Vallejo gazing with irrepressible love into the face of

his granddaughter, secure in the knowledge that he would be one of the few whose patrimony would survive.

For, unlike that of the Indian, the society of the **Californios** would be destroyed not by death or disease but by litigation. It was land that had given them the framework for their lives, and it was land the Yankees wanted —and would have. It was not long after the American conquest that the first indications of what might happen could be seen, as American settlers—squatters, many of them—began demanding that the land grants of the Spanish and Mexican regimes be turned over to the United States government and opened to general settlement under the provisions of the Preemption Act of 1841.

The stakes were immense: 13,000,000 acres, embracing some of the richest land in California, had been given away in 809 individual grants. Most of these grants

*"The Yankees are a wonderful people,"* Mariano G. Vallejo *(above) once said.*
*"If they emigrated to hell itself, they would somehow manage to change the climate."*

had been dispensed during the Mexican era, most after the secularization of the missions in 1834, most during the five years preceding the American acquisition of the territory; and some, it was believed (and later proved), had in fact been given by Governor Pío Pico after his removal from office in the spring of 1846 and then antedated to give the impression that it had been granted before American control.

The **Californios,** together with those foreigners (including some Americans) who had obtained grants, held that the terms of the Treaty of Guadalupe Hidalgo, which stipulated that "property of every kind" would be "inviolably respected," guaranteed them the legal title

United States District Court and, if necessary, to the Supreme Court itself. Over the vigorous opposition of Senator Thomas Hart Benton, who considered the whole business to be "confiscatory," Gwin's bill passed the Senate and then the House, and was signed into law on March 3, 1851.

Proof, to most of the grantees, was indeed a burden, for under Mexican law grants had been given under the loosest sort of regulations and a vague disinclination to be precise as to the land's proper metes and bounds (there was so much land in California—who could bother with such trifles as a few hundred acres here and there?). The law required only that a petitioner for a

*Ignacio Coronel, ca. 1855.*

*Ignacio del Valle, ca. 1851.*

to their grant lands. But the political pressure brought to bear by the more numerous settlers and squatters was great, and in 1850 their champion, Senator William M. Gwin, introduced legislation that would create a board of land commissioners to determine the validity of land-grant claims. Under the board's operating rules, the burden of proof fell upon the grantees, not the government, although both parties had the right of appeal to the

grant describe it in his petition, that he submit a personally drawn **diseño,** or map, that he demonstrate his personal commitment to ownership by walking about on the piece of land before witnesses, "uprooting grass, scattering handfuls of earth, tearing twigs, and performing other acts and ceremonies of real possession," and that within one year he build a house on the land and occupy it.

72

The descriptions in the petitions offended the American fondness for precision in such matters, for they were riddled with such phrases as **poco más ó ménos** ("a little more or less"); and the hand-drawn **diseños**, although frequently charming as folk art, were ludicrously inexact and quite often indecipherable. Frequently, side-by-side claims overlapped each other in many places, sometimes to the point of merger. The stipulation regarding the building and occupation of a house was honored in the breach quite as often as in the observance, although under the casual Mexican government such omissions were generally ignored, as was the provision that any grant approved by a governor had to be passed on to the California Assembly for its approval before becoming legal (California's Mexican governors had a way of becoming a law unto themselves.)

With dogged persistence, attorneys for the United States zeroed in on such vagaries to challenge the validity of hundreds of claims, usually appealing any adverse decisions. The grantees fought back as best they could; in 1855 some of the largest of the **rancheros** banded together to issue a declaration to Congress: "In view of the doleful litigation proposed by the general Government against all the land owners in California in violation of the Treaty of Guadalupe Hidalgo and the law of nations, which year by year becomes more costly and intolerable, in view of the repeated falsehoods and calumnies circulated by the public press against the validation of our titles and the justice which supports us in this interminable litigation and which equally influences the tribunals of justice and prejudices our character and our dearest rights; in view of the injustices which have accumulated against us because of our patience in suffering and our silence in defending ourselves, we, the land owners in the state . . . mutually contract and agree to aid and support each other by every legal means as free men, which we are, to resist every effort made against us to carry out a general confiscation of our properties."

"Interminable litigation. . . ." It was time that the **Californios** were fighting, for time was costing them money. The land commission only held its hearings from January 1852 to March 1856, but case after case was dragged along the appeals route for years afterwards, sometimes for decades; the average length of time it took to secure a final decision was seventeen years. In

*Reginaldo del Valle, 1856.*

the meantime, legal fees ate into the finances of the landowners. When they tried to sell parts of their land to meet expenses, they had to accept prices far below any reasonable market value because title was not clear, and when they mortgaged the land, they were forced to absorb interest rates that ran as high as 8 percent per month.

Ultimately, out of the more than eight hundred claims submitted to the land commission, 604 were confirmed and 209 rejected. But for most of the original grantees, the final adjudication was irrelevant. Their money was gone, and with it the land that had given them, for a time, the taste of a baronial life. In the mid-1850s, Don Abel Stearns (who, as we shall see in chapter 12, was himself finally forced to relinquish his land to speculators) wrote to John C. Frémont: "The long lists of Sheriffs and mortgage sales in our newspapers, the depopulation of flourishing stock ranches, and the pauperism of Rancheros, but a short time since wealthy, all attest the disastrous consequences of too much litigation and of this unsettled state of titles." The lists grew longer as the years went by, and before the passing of another generation, one more of California's many civilizations had slipped into the dark of history.

*"The fecundity of the Californians is remarkable," Walter Colton wrote in 1850. At the left, the Lugo family lines up for a group portrait.*

# SECTION TWO

# *The Money Machine*

The scenes which I must try to depict for the reader will show a multitude of figures and many phases of passion. A host of adventurers flocking from the centers of civilization on the shores of the Atlantic, half across the world, to a remote corner on the coast of what was then the semi-barbarous Pacific. . . . At brief notice, they organized a state, complete in all its parts. As if by magic, their touch or their influence created magnificent cities; clipper ships, that cast the boasted India-men of England into disrepute; two railroads, connecting the Atlantic with the Pacific; a line of ocean steamers, connecting Asia with America, and a telegraph line from the Golden Gate to the Mississippi. . . . They saw in much of the state the savage retire before the cow-herd, who again retired before the wheat farmer. They saw the rise of a new horticulture which combines the energy of New England with the scientific training of Europe on a soil as fertile as that of Egypt, and in a climate as genial as that of Italy. They saw the development of a new mining industry, which lifted rivers from their beds, washed away the eternal hills, followed up and cleaned out the channels of the immense streams of an ancient geological era, and made topographical changes in the natural levels of the earth's surface so great that they may claim to exceed all that has ever been done elsewhere. . . .

The men who took part in most of these wonderful changes, and witnessed all of them, feel that California, and especially San Francisco, has an interest for them such as no other country or city could have acquired, in our age at least, nor do they lament that they did not live in some better time in the remote past. No golden era of romance or chivalry, no heroic period of Greece or Rome provokes their envy, or, in their conception, outshines the brilliancy of the scenes in which they have been actors. This is the very home of their souls.

—John S. Hittell
(*A History of the City of San Francisco. . .* , 1878)

*An 1851 daguerreotype of San Francisco's Sacramento Street—*
*one of the busiest blocks in the busiest town west of the Mississippi.*

# LE VOYAGE EN CALIFORNIE

ou

## LES CHERCHEURS D'OR

Actualité

Chantée par M<sup>r</sup> LEVASSOR au Th. de la Montansier

Paroles de

Musique de

# E. BOURGET     V. PARIZOT

Chansonnettes nouvelles

E. Bourget et Paul Henrion — la déclaration anglaise — le Bonnet d'Ane — La Fête du Pays

# CHAPTER 5

# THE FOOLS OF '49

*An itinerant carpenter finds "something shining" in a ditch, and a Mormon*

*entrepreneur cries "Gold! Gold from the American River!"*

FOR MORE THAN A YEAR following the Capitulation of Cahuenga, California was a kind of patchwork society, an uneasy and all but ungovernable mix of cultures. Aside from the resident population of about 9,000 *Californios* (not to mention some 85,000 uncivilized and 15,000 civilized Indians), the province's foreign population had steadily swelled to more than 4,000 by the end of summer 1847. That population alone was a distinctly uncommon mix. It included several "establishment" types like Abel Stearns of Los Angeles, Thomas Larkin of Monterey, and Jacob Leese of Sonoma, men who had long since put roots into California, who cheered her potential emergence as an American state and possessed an abiding interest in the orderly progress of enterprise—as well as an understandable interest in holding on to what they had acquired. It included a thousand land-seeking men, women, and children who had spilled across the mountains in the summer and early fall of 1846 and another four hundred in 1847—footsore, weary people in search of an elusive Eden, incredibly durable pioneers whose memory of the two-thousand-mile trek across rocks and hard places was haunted by the thought of those who had *not* endured—lost ones, like the forty members of the Donner Party who died in the winter drifts of the Sierra Nevada in 1846–47 and whose bodies provided food for many of that winter's survivors.

It included a band of rowdy settler-soldiers called the New York Volunteers, a regiment of 950 men under the command of Col. Jonathan D. Stevenson of New York City. Recruited in the summer of 1846, the Vol-unteers were to supplement Kearny's forces in California; their term of enlistment would expire with the end of the Mexican War, and it was desired that they remain in California. Arriving at San Francisco in March 1847 —too late to take part in the conquest—the regiment was split up into companies for garrison duty throughout California. In the way of occupation armies everywhere, a substantial number of the volunteers spent much of their time assaulting local maidens, making asses of themselves in various cantinas, and otherwise complicating Anglo-*Californio* relations. More than three hundred ultimately deserted.

This population included nearly six hundred Mormons in two separate contingents. The first was composed of colonizing families, 238 people who sailed from New York in February 1846 under the leadership of Elder Samuel Brannan (twenty-six years old), who dreamed of creating Zion on the shores of the Pacific. They arrived at San Francisco on July 31 and began the work of empire by hiring themselves out as laborers and by setting up a small agricultural colony called New Hope in the San Joaquin Valley. (To Brannan's everlasting disgust, however, Brigham Young, the spiritual and temporal leader of the Mormons, found Zion instead on the shores of the Great Salt Lake of Utah in the spring of 1847). The second contingent was made up of 350 soldiers of the Mormon Battalion, a group of Mexican War volunteers who had marched from Fort Leavenworth, Kansas, to San Diego, arriving in January 1847—like the New York Volunteers, too late for action. They, too, were used for garrison duty until

*The cry of "Gold!" was a matter for worldwide attention, including that of French songwriters, as this sheet-music cover suggests.*

*A somewhat misty overview of Sutter's mill and the Coloma Valley in 1849—"respectfully dedicated to Capt. John A. Sutter by his obedient servant John L. Little."*

war's end, and many of them remained in Southern California to establish Brigham Young's main communications link with the Pacific Coast.

Indians, *Californios,* traders, trappers, settlers, colonizers, entrepreneurs, military and naval men, drifters, and grifters . . . it was a fragmented structure on which to fasten the outlines of a new world. Even the military rule that might otherwise have created order out of chaos sported its own instability, as supreme commanders came and went like participants in some outlandish game: Commo. Robert F. Stockton was succeeded by Commo. W. Branford Shubrick, and Shubrick by Commo. James Biddle, all within the first three months of 1847; John C. Frémont's governorship, riddled with

uncertainty from the beginning, ended officially when Gen. Stephen Watts Kearny assumed it in the spring—and by the end of the summer, Kearny, in turn, had placed it in the hands of Col. Richard B. Mason. Add to this the arrival of Stevenson's New York Volunteers and the Mormon Battalion, and it is possible to sympathize with the feelings of one observer: "If you get all my letters you will see the changes we have had to contend with out here. Commodore Sloat, Commodore Stockton, Commodore Shubrick, and now Commodore Biddle, all in seven and a half months. . . . Then the farce of Frémont's governorship with General Kearny in the country. Then comes Colonel Stevenson anticipated by Colonel Mason. The Californians think that we cannot be much better than Mexico for they connect the appearance of every new commander-in-chief with the result of some new revolution."

Yet it began to function, this new world, sluggishly, vaguely, but with hints of an unseen future. In Monterey, *Alcalde* (Mayor) Walter Colton, who was first appointed, then later elected, to the post, joined with a young, seven-foot expatriate Kentuckian by the name of Robert ("Long Bob") Semple to issue the province's first newspaper, the *Californian*. The first edition of this little weekly, printed on a press Colton remarked in his diary was "old enough to be preserved as a curiosity," appeared on August 15, 1846, and produced "quite a little sensation." Its immediate success seemed to mirror the expectations Monterey's residents had for the prospects of the town itself. "All real estate has risen since our occupation of the territory," Colton wrote in September. "This tells what the community expects, in terms which none can mistake. A Californian told me today that he considered his lands worth forty thousand dollars more than they were before our flag was raised."

By May 1847, Semple had bought out Colton and moved the *Californian* to San Francisco, for it was obvious even then where the drift of the future lay.* The little village of Yerba Buena (population 459) had been graced with its new name in January, and it was beginning to stir. In March, General Kearny (with no authority for his action but with a sure instinct for what enterprising Americans considered right and proper) issued a decree which granted to the town 450 beach and water lots (those exposed at low tide) between Clark's Point and Rincon Point, the two bounds of what was then Yerba Buena Cove—and what would become the heart of the city's waterfront and financial districts. In July the lots were auctioned off for prices ranging from $50 to $600; about half of them were sold almost immediately. The town then expanded itself by some eight hundred landlocked acres, laid out more lots, and auctioned *them* off in August for between $16

---

*Semple, however, wanted that future to drift a little farther north—to Benicia across the Bay, a township that he helped to found and fully expected would outdistance San Francisco as the leading port of Northern California. It didn't, but Semple did find himself a wife, no small triumph for a seven-footer in a land short of women.

and $29 apiece; again, half of them went in a few hours. By this expedient, San Francisco's early residents (and a few nonresidents)—men like successive *alcaldes* Washington Bartlett, Edwin Bryant, and George Hyde—got their fingers in a speculative pie that neither they nor their posterity would regret.

Among them was Sam Brannan, the backsliding Mormon. One of the items he had brought with him in the Mormon's journey to California was a printing press and a font of type; in January 1847 he utilized these to start the *California Star,* San Francisco's first newspaper and California's second. During the August land auction he purchased a lot, erected a newspaper office, left the paper in the hands of E. P. Jones as editor, and traveled up to Sutter's Fort. Contemplating the anticipated stream of emigrants likely to pass through the region during the summer and fall of the next year and the happy fact that they would need any number of goods, the foresightful Brannan became co-owner of a general store at Sutterville, a tiny trading depot three miles below the fort.

Sutter himself was equally enterprising that summer and autumn of 1847. His empire had come through the uncertain months of the conquest generally unscathed; in April 1847 his fortress had been turned back to him, and he had been appointed Indian subagent for the northern territory by Governor Kearny. He was able to hire all the industrious Mormons he needed to do the work of his fields, mills, and other industries, and his prospects seemed altogether delightful, as he later recalled: "After the war, things went on prosperously with me. I found a good market, both in the newcomers and at the Bay. People from below came to me to buy leather, shoes, saddles, hats, spurs, bridle bits, and other articles. My manufactures increased. Good mechanics were plenty. I had large fields of grain and large herds of cattle, horses, and sheep."

In August he branched out by signing a contract with James Marshall to build a sawmill on the South Fork of the American River, about forty-five miles east-northeast of the fort. Marshall, the epitome of the American jack-of-all-trades, was a taciturn and somewhat moody individual, but a good worker; by January the mill itself was finished and digging of the race to supply it with water had begun. On the morning of January 24, Marshall inspected the section of the race his men had completed the day before and during his walk noticed flecks of something that winked and glittered in the red earth. He picked them up and fingered them reflectively. The next morning, he found more, and three days later, he knocked on the door of Sutter's office in the fort and stumbled in out of the rain in a highly agitated state. "He drew out a rag from his pocket," Sutter remembered. "Opening it carefully, he held it before me in his hand. It contained what might have been an ounce and a half of gold-dust—dust, flakes and grains. The biggest piece was not as large as a pea, and it varied from that down to less than a pinhead in size."

That tiny pile resting in the palm of Marshall's calloused carpenter's hand was more than gold—it was the stuff of dreams, Sutter's doom, and the history of California's next fifty years.

SUTTER WAS WORRIED, and with good reason. He needed a steady work force badly to keep his enterprises going and meet his heavy obligations. If his men started drifting off into the foothills after gold, it would cripple him. He might have consoled himself with the memory of California's first gold discovery in 1842, when it was found in a little canyon on the edge of Southern California's San Fernando Valley. A minor rush of miners from Sonora, Mexico, had infested the canyon for about a year, but the deposits had been shallow and quickly exhausted, and what excitement it had caused died swiftly. Marshall's discovery might be no more significant. Nevertheless, the cautious Sutter did what he could to protect himself. He offered the sawmill's workmen double wages to keep the discovery quiet, negotiated a treaty with an Indian tribelet in the area to get hold of the land, and sent this agreement to Governor Richard B. Mason for his approval.

It was useless. Mason, pointing out that Indians could not legally cede property, rejected the treaty. Sutter's employees, including Marshall, went loose at the mouth about gold, and even Sutter himself, perhaps weakened by too many of his customary nips at the bottle, could not resist prattling about it occasionally. Inexorably, one at a time, workmen put down their tools and wandered off. By May word had reached San Francisco, but with no immediate effect. Its citizens were too busy selling lots to one another; besides, Edward Kemble, the new editor of Brannan's *California Star,* called the whole thing a "sham" in the issue of May 20—as "supurb [*sic*] takein as was ever got up to guzzle the gullible."

Brannan himself was not so sure and left his Sutterville store for a trip to the site of the discovery. The gold was real, right enough, and he shrewdly calculated that if he could convince enough people of that fact, it would give his little store a bonanza in customers. He filled a bottle full of gold dust, took Sutter's launch down to San Francisco, and strode magnificently through the streets, waving the bottle over his head and shouting "Gold! Gold from the American River!" All day, he elaborated on the richness of the discovery, showed the heavy bottle to the town's citizens, let them heft it and rub its gold between their fingers.

His salesmanship had its desired effect. By the end of May scores of San Franciscans had abandoned their real estate and fled for what were already described as "the diggins." Hundreds more followed from Monterey, Santa Barbara, San Jose, and Los Angeles, as the news spread south. Soldiers stationed in garrisons from Sonoma to San Diego deserted; navy and merchant seamen jumped ship; servants disappeared, settlers left their crops, vaqueros left their cows, city officials abdicated, newspaper editors suspended publication, merchants and saloonkeepers locked their doors—it was a grand rout of almost all of that which had been pieced together as the new civilization in California. By July four thousand would-be miners had spread north and south of the original discovery, wandering into every convenient gully and gulch in a scramble for gold. As word fanned out from California to the Sandwich Islands, Oregon, Mexico, Peru, and Chile, they were joined by another six thousand.

What they found was incredible, a treasure western man had dreamed of for centuries, treasure that could be picked up out of the earth by *anyone,* with no more expertise required than a willingness to use a pick, pan, and shovel, and to sweat. Eons before, an accident of mountain-building and fracturing had deposited liquid gold in a great system of veins that extended some six hundred miles along the Sierra Nevada range; the deposits cooled and solidified, and during several

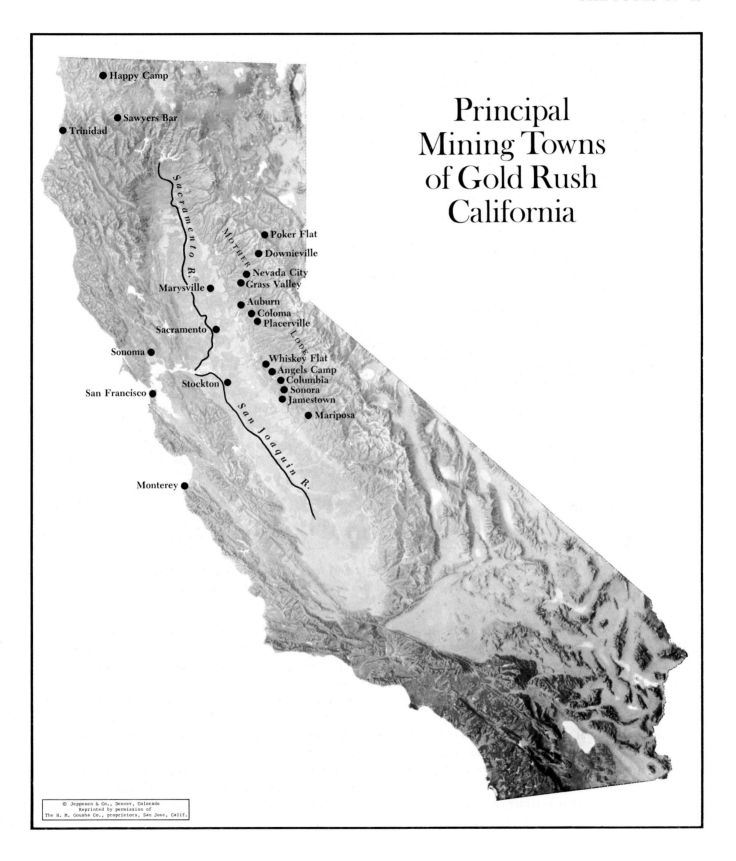

# Principal Mining Towns of Gold Rush California

● Happy Camp

● Sawyers Bar
● Trinidad

*Sacramento R.*

MOTHER

● Poker Flat
● Downieville
● Nevada City
● Grass Valley
Marysville ●
● Auburn
● Coloma
● Placerville

*LODE*

Sacramento ●

Sonoma ●

● Whiskey Flat
● Angels Camp
● Columbia
● Sonora
● Jamestown
● Mariposa

Stockton ●

San Francisco ●

*San Joaquin R.*

Monterey ●

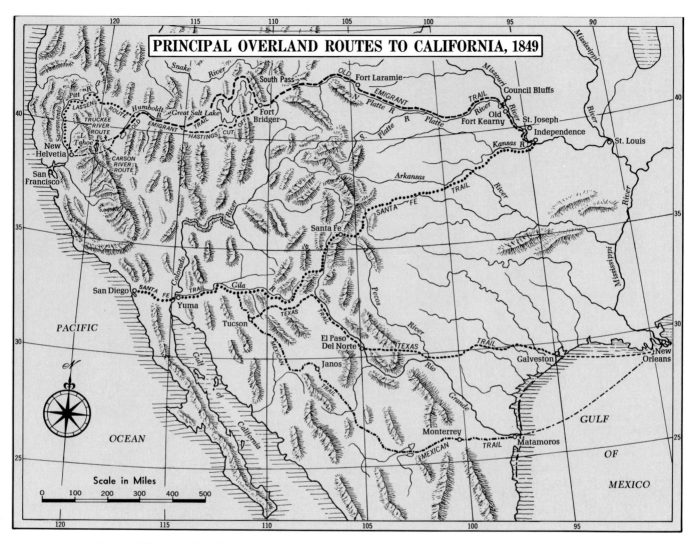

*Across the valleys of Mexico, the plains of Texas, the deserts of the Southwest, and the passes of the Rocky Mountains—over all the rocks and hard places of the West, the forty-niners scrambled.*

millennia of erosion were exposed and crumbled, washed by wind and water down the slopes of the mountains, coming to rest wherever their weight overcame the ability of the elements to move them. And that was where the fortunate seekers of 1848 found them, as dust, as flakes, as golden pebbles and fist-sized nuggets. The gold existed in such abundance that it was not so much mined as harvested, gathered with not much more effort required than if it had been sheaves of wheat.

At one spot near the canyon of the Middle Fork of the American River that summer, men took out $800 a day. On a sand bar in the Yuba River, another group harvested $75,000 in three months. At another spot, a man rode away with thirty pounds of gold from a single four-foot square of earth. A moderately successful effort might produce as much as $600 a week, and even "poor" ground yielded $10 or $15 a day—the maximum of which was at least five times the daily salary a working man could expect in the States. On the whole, it has been estimated that somewhere between $30,000 and $50,000 a day were being taken out of the ground in the summer and fall of 1848—and by year's end it had amounted to well over $6,000,000 and perhaps as much as $10,000,000.

Six million dollars was a great deal of money in 1848 —in modern terms, the equivalent of a good thirty million. This was news, big news, and the military commanders in California made haste to let Washington know what was happening. In July, Commo. Thomas ap Catesby Jones (who had been forgiven his blunder of 1842 and sent out to replace Biddle) sent Lt. Edward F. Beale across Mexico with descriptive, detailed reports and a small sample of California gold. In August, Governor Mason sent Lt. Lucien Loesser via Cape Horn with similar reports—and a tea caddy stuffed with 230 ounces of gold, worth about thirty-five hundred dollars.

SINCE LATE SUMMER, eastern newspapers had been picking up and printing stray letters from California that talked of gold, but they were read skeptically. By September, however, such letters had increased in frequency, and a thin murmur of excitement could be heard here and there—no mania, but tangible enough for the dour journalistic genius James Gordon Bennett to editorialize in the September 29 issue of his *New York Herald:* "No doubt the golden tales of these golden streams will excite the imaginations of many ardent and sanguine minds and lead them to think of packing up and removing off to regions where they may hope to become rich thus rapidly. To all such we would say beware of the mania of hasty money making; beware of seeking to become rich by sudden and extraordinary means; be assured that all the gold in the world will not make you happy; pursue, quietly and steadily, the sober path of regular industry; be thankful, contented, and act with honor and honesty, and then you will be happier in the enjoyment of a peaceful conscience and a peaceful life than all the gold of California can make its possessors."

Good, solid, American thinking, that—but no one, including James Gordon Bennett, yet realized the full power of what had been loosed that January morning in 1848. In early December, Lieutenant Beale arrived in Washington with the official reports from California; they were passed immediately to President James K. Polk, who must have received them gratefully. It had not been a good year for Polk. The treaty of Guadalupe-Hidalgo ending the Mexican War had been signed on

February 4 and ratified by the Senate on March 10, but not without more of the carping opposition that had plagued his administration. Many Whigs still called him a territorial bandit, and conversely, the more exciteable expansionists pilloried him for not demanding *all* of Mexico, instead of just California and New Mexico. Exhausted and sickened by four turbulent, demanding years, Polk decided not to run for reelection —and as a result saw the Whig Gen. Zachary Taylor elected as the next president of the United States in November, a development Polk quite sincerely believed was the first step in the ultimate ruin of America. But with the arrival of Lieutenant Beale came solid evidence that all the frustration and manipulation had been worth it, that he had seized the future and given into American hands a country more valuable than even he had hoped for. In his last State of the Union address on December 5, Polk articulated romance in his straightforward prose: "The accounts of the abundance of gold are of such an extraordinary character as would scarcely command belief were they not corroborated by the authentic reports of officers in the public service." A few days later, Lieutenant Loesser arrived in Washington with his tea caddy full of gold, which was quickly placed on public display in the War Department.

And there it was: the presidential seal of approval and more than fourteen pounds of genuine gold. Those who doubted did so no longer, and even the *New York Herald* could not restrain itself in the edition of December 9: "The gold region in California! Startling discoveries! The El Dorado of the old Spaniards is discovered at last. We now have the highest official authority for believing in the discovery of vast gold mines in California, and that the discovery is the greatest and most startling, not to say miraculous, that the history of the last five centuries can produce." Heady words, but they merely reflected the common pitch of agitation that followed the president's announcement. By January agitation had become hysteria, again as chronicled in the pages of the *Herald:* "All classes of our citizens appear to be under the influence of this extraordinary mania. . . . All are rushing towards that wonderful California which sets the public mind almost on the highway to insanity. . . . Every day men of property and means are advertising their possessions for sale in order

*James Marshall in his later years, when the gold of Coloma was only a memory.*

them captained by men as incompetent as their vessels and crewed by individuals with no more qualification for the job than a screaming desire to get their hands on gold. One way or another, more than eleven thousand of them left in 178 vessels during the first two months after Polk's address—left for an 18,000-mile voyage around Cape Horn through some of the meanest waters known to navigation, a voyage that would take anywhere from five to eight months, a voyage that would see near-mutinies, vicious squabbling, short rations, desperate thirst, and far too many bodies wrapped in canvas, ballasted, and slipped into the sea.

Thousands more had no patience for that journey. They chose instead to take passage on the steamers of the new, federally subsidized United States Mail Steamship Company's run to Chagres, on the east coast of the Isthmus of Panama. On paper, it was the quickest and least dangerous route, a simple matter of skipping across the Isthmus from Chagres to the west coast port of Panama, hopping aboard a steamer of the Pacific Mail Steamship Company (also subsidized by the government), and taking a quick run up to San Francisco. In fact, the route proved an emotional, physical, and financial disaster for most of those who chose it. One did not skip across the Isthmus—one was poled partway across in a native *bungoe,* when it could be found, while being assaulted by mosquitoes, heat, bad water and worse food; at Gorgona one then crawled aboard a mule (again if available) and entered a sweltering jungle on the muddy, cholera-ridden Gorgona Trail to Panama. Having survived this, one waited in Panama for passage . . . and waited, and waited. For this ancient, white-walled city, with its casinos and brothels and gambling hells and festering cholera, was crowded to the point of madness by many times more goldseekers than there were ships to take them to California. They rolled up in blankets and slept on the sand or beneath the ragged shelter of tents, watching for a boat, watching companions die, watching their money dribble away. And when a boat finally came and they were able to buy their way on board, it took most of what they had left, giving them almost nothing but their fragile wits to live on once they arrived in San Francisco.

Those were the two principal sea routes, but an equal number came overland in journeys hardly less demanding—some of them on the Santa Fe Trail, some on trails

to furnish themselves with means to reach that golden land. Every little city and town beyond the great sea ports is forming societies . . . and every day similar clubs of the young, educated and best classes of our population are leaving our shores. Poets, philosophers, lawyers, brokers, bankers, merchants, farmers, clergymen —all are feeling the impulse."

They were, indeed. They gutted their savings, borrowed from friends and relatives, or were subsidized for shares by those too old or timid to go; they formed gold mining companies, societies, associations, and brotherhoods, and crowded into eastern seaports from Charleston to Boston, clamoring for passage to California on anything that would float; when passage failed them, they bought fishing schooners and coastal barkentines and ancient square-riggers with rotten bottoms, ships that had no business on the open sea, many of

across Texas, New Mexico, and Arizona, perhaps fifteen thousand across Old Mexico, but most on the old Emigrant Trail, which in the previous ten years had been marked well with the blood and sweat of more than two thousand California-bound pioneers. As the argonauts had clustered in eastern seaports in the winter of 1848, thousands of overlanders from the Ohio and Mississippi valleys streamed into the prairie ports of Council Bluffs, Westport, St. Joseph, and Independence on the Missouri River in the early spring of 1849. Like the argonauts, most were organized into traveling companies and associations (many of which lasted only as long as it took to get to California, where they disintegrated into every-man-for-himself scrambles), but some came alone. However they came, they made rich men of the frontier merchants who outfitted them with wagons, horses, mules, oxen, guns, powder, salt pork, bacon, flour, sugar, tobacco, picks, pans, and shovels before pointing them toward the infinite prairie horizon.

Their lack of experience was appalling. They purchased thousands of guidebooks, the best of which were pieced together from Frémont's *Reports* and excerpts from the published letters of men like Thomas O. Larkin, and the worst of which were almost entirely fraudulent—promising rivers, streams, and springs where none had ever flowed, rich grasses where none had ever been known to grow, and easy mountain passes over nonexistent mountains. Fortunately, the Emigrant Trail was so thoroughly rutted that a man would have to work at it in order to get lost (a few did), but the guidebooks also stipulated the absolute necessity of taking along such things as India-rubber boats, alcohol stoves, sheet-iron stoves, fly traps, wading boots, air

M.r HEXEKIAH JEROLOMANS DEPARTURE FOR CALIFORNIA.

*Snide lithographers in Boston and New York made pocket money by lampooning the gold mania.*

BEST ROUTE TO CALIFORNIA.

R. PORTER & CO., (office, room No. 40 in the Sun Buildings,—entrance 128 Fulton-street, New-York,) are making active progress in the construction of an Aerial Transport, for the express purpose of carrying passengers between New York and California. This transport will have a capacity to carry from 50 to 100 passengers, at a speed of 60 to 100 miles per hour. It is expected to put this machine in operation about the 1st of April, 1849. It is proposed to carry a limited number of passengers—not exceeding 300—for $50, including board, and the transport is expected to make a trip to the gold region and back in seven days. The price of passage to California is fixed at $200, with the exception above mentioned. Upwards of 200 passage tickets at $50 each have been engaged prior to Feb. 1st. Books open for subscribers as above.

*The one route that nobody tried.*

mattresses, and massive gold-extraction machines (patent pending), as useless as they were difficult to haul. Then as now, Americans had an ungodly respect for books; if it was written, printed, bound, and published, it *had* to be true. Obediently, thousands of forty-niners overloaded their wagons with such items, only to end up littering the trailside with them when the weight threatened to cripple oxen, mules, or horses.

They drowned trying to ford streams, they straggled away to view the scenery and were picked off by an occasional Indian, they fell into gullies and canyons, and they shot themselves with startling regularity. If their own incompetence were not enemy enough, they also had to deal with cholera, whose deadly presence haunted all the land and sea trails of the gold rush. At least 750 people (and possibly as many as 5,000) died in the particularly agonizing throes of this ghastly disease even before they reached South Pass, and the trail was soon dotted with a string of crude wooden grave-markers, grim footnotes to a manic romance. And after four months of almost grassless plains, rocky defiles, deserts, bad water, heat, cold, and physical misery, when these greenhorns-become-veterans finally stumbled down the western foothills of the Sierra Nevada, most of them earnestly shared the sentiments of J. L. Stephens, of Marietta, Ohio: "The hardships of the overland route to California are beyond conception. Care and suspense, pained anxiety, fear of losing animals and leaving one to foot it and pack his 'duds' on his back, begging provisions, fear of being left in the mountains to starve and freeze to death, and a thousand other things which no one thinks of until on the way, are things of which I may write and you may read, but they are nothing to the reality."

How many of them were there? No one knows for certain, but in *The California Trail* historian George Stewart estimated that an "acceptable figure for the whole migration would be 22,500—certainly large enough!" Add to this the 15,000 who may have crossed Mexico, the 10,000 or so who took other trails, and the 40,000 or more who took the sea routes, and the California gold rush stands as one of the largest mass migrations in the history of western man.

B<small>Y LAND OR SEA</small>, some 90,000 people spilled into California during the spring, summer, and fall of 1849. It was only the beginning, for they kept coming: 36,000 in 1850, 27,000 in 1851, 87,000 in 1852, the year the gold rush can be said to have ended—simply because 23,000 people also *left* California that year. No region on earth had seen a population quite like it. Most were Americans, but thousands came from other civilized nations of the world, from England, France, Germany, Australia, Russia, Italy, Mexico, Chile, Peru —and 20,000 from China (a figure comprising nearly ten percent of the state's entire population). They were mostly men, for the gold rush was an adventure, not an exercise in pioneering (and most of the women who *were* present were not the sort of girls one wrote home about). They were young, few of them over thirty and many of them in their teens. Most came from relatively solid financial backgrounds, for it took money, quite a bit of money, to get to California, whether by land or by sea. They were generally well educated, and they wrote—thousands of letters and hundreds of journals and diaries (and in later years, hundreds of reminiscences); they documented the gold rush as few other events in American history have been documented.

They did not come to found a commonwealth, most of them, but to strip California of its gold and return as wealthy men to their homes and families in the East. They took little part in the formation of California's first government because they were too busy scrabbling after gold and because they had no intention of remaining long enough for government to have any relevance in their lives (see chapter 6). By the time it became obvious that circumstances were going to force most of them to remain whether they wanted to or not, they found that they had thrown away the last opportunity many of them would have to maintain some kind of control over their lives. Yet they were the materials out of which California's nineteenth-century life was structured, and it may be that many of them would have seconded the words of John S. Hittell, written twenty-five years later: "Whatever misfortunes have overtaken the individual citizens, they have the consolation of seeing that California has advanced with a swift and grand prosperity, and that they have participated in one of the most imposing pageants ever enacted on the stage of universal history."

Perhaps, but one wonders. . . . Many, too many, would have had better occasion to reflect on the implications of the ancient Hindu curse: "May you live in interesting times."

*A night scene in the gold country, date and artist unknown.*

# California Mirror:
# Pick, Pan, and Shovel

*"Gold Mining in California," as seen by the artists of Currier & Ives, 1849.*

Having survived the rigors of the overland trek or the briny dangers of the deep blue sea, the forty-niners were then forced to deal with the too often harsh realities of life in the California mines. One of the harshest, they found, was that mining for gold was work—grueling, backbreaking work, much of it performed while ankle-deep in the frequently chill, tumbling waters of Sierra Nevada streams, and all of it grimy and punishing.

The methods were simple enough, as one of the hundreds of proliferating 1849 guidebooks promised: "No capital is required to obtain this gold, as the laboring man wants nothing but his pick and shovel and tin pan,

begin a slow, steady, swirling motion designed to wash out the lighter materials gradually and leave a thin, heavy residue—or "drag"—that hopefully included gold. A good average for a hard-working former bank clerk was perhaps fifty such panfuls a day—no mean achievement.

But the more earth a man could handle in a day the better were his chances of obtaining more gold than the rare streak of dust in the drag of a pan. Yankee ingenuity came to the fore with the development of the rocker, a crude wooden device about the size and shape of a child's cradle. It was fitted with a screen at its upper end, to filter out the heavier pieces of rocks and gravel, and a slanting bottom that featured riffles, or cleats, behind which the gold could lodge as it was washed through. Rocking the gadget with one hand and pouring in alternate dipperfuls of water and earth with the other, a man could multiply his daily production several times over. When two men cooperated, even more earth could be run through the rocker.

A further, more sophisticated elaboration on the washing process was the sluice. In some cases this was no more than a ditch whose bottom was "cleated" with rocks, holes, and gravel riffle bars; more often, the sluice was in the form of a "Long Tom," a carpentered affair twenty feet long and a little less than two feet deep. Long Toms were built with a taper at one end so that a number of them could be fitted together to increase the amount of gold trapped behind the riffles—a procedure rendered even more efficient by pouring elongated pools of quicksilver behind each cleat, since this metal possessed an uncommon affinity for gold.

Such were the basics of small-scale placer mining (for large-scale operations, see "California Mirror: The Resource Economy"). Whatever the method chosen, all had one thing in common: toil. "This gold digging is no child's play," one confided to his journal, "but downright hard labor, and a man to make anything must work harder than any day laborer in the States."

with which to dig and wash the gravel." After digging out a pile of earth or gravel from the bank, the miner would deposit a small part of it in the bottom of a shallow pan about the size and configuration of a large frying pan (some in fact were frying pans), squat by the side of a stream, add a quantity of water to the pan, and

After two years of unsuccessful grubbing in the diggins, Englishman J. M. Hutchings made a fortune in 1853 by printing a letter-sheet called "The Miner's Ten Commandments," complete with the embellishment of lusty border sketches. More than one hundred thousand of the letter-sheets were sold, enough to finance him in the establishment of Hutchings California Magazine, one of the earliest in the state. The Englishman's letter-sheet was so popular, in fact, that it was quickly pirated by other printers, as in the example shown at the right. Color was frequently added, the title was changed, some of the pictures were redrawn, and some of the text altered, but the concept and much of the language remained unadulterated Hutchings. Over the next twenty years, similarly independent versions turned up all over the West.

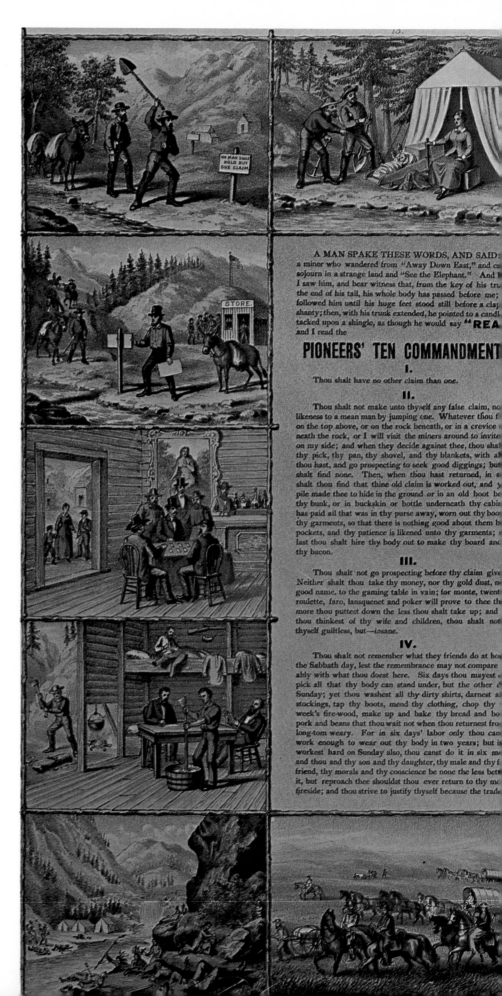

A MAN SPAKE THESE WORDS, AND SAID: a miner who wandered from "Away Down East," and c sojourn in a strange land and "See the Elephant." And I saw him, and bear witness that, from the key of his tru the end of his tail, his whole body has passed before me; followed him until his huge feet stood still before a clap shanty; then, with his trunk extended, he pointed to a candl tacked upon a shingle, as though he would say "**REA** and I read the

## PIONEERS' TEN COMMANDMENT

### I.
Thou shalt have no other claim than one.

### II.
Thou shalt not make unto thyself any false claim, no likeness to a mean man by jumping one. Whatever thou f on the top above, or on the rock beneath, or in a crevice neath the rock, or I will visit the miners around to invite on my side; and when they decide against thee, thou shal thy pick, thy pan, thy shovel, and thy blankets, with al thou hast, and go prospecting to seek good diggings; but shalt find none. Then, when thou hast returned, in s shalt thou find that thine old claim is worked out, and y pile made thee to hide in the ground or in an old boot be thy bunk, or in buckskin or bottle underneath thy cabir has paid all that was in thy purse away, worn out thy boo thy garments, so that there is nothing good about them b pockets, and thy patience is likened unto thy garments; last thou shalt hire thy body out to make thy board and thy bacon.

### III.
Thou shalt not go prospecting before thy claim giv Neither shalt thou take thy money, nor thy gold dust, n good name, to the gaming table in vain; for monte, twent roulette, faro, lansquenet and poker will prove to thee th more thou puttest down the less thou shalt take up; and thou thinkest of thy wife and children, thou shalt not thyself guiltless, but—insane.

### IV.
Thou shalt not remember what they friends do at hou the Sabbath day, lest the remembrance may not compare ably with what thou doest here. Six days thou mayest pick all that thy body can stand under, but the other d Sunday; yet thou washest all thy dirty shirts, darnest a stockings, tap thy boots, mend thy clothing, chop thy week's fire-wood, make up and bake thy bread and bo pork and beans that thou wait not when thou returnest fro long-tom weary. For in six days' labor only thou can work enough to wear out thy body in two years; but i workest hard on Sunday also, thou canst do it in six m and thou and thy son and thy daughter, thy male and thy f friend, thy morals and thy conscience be none the less bet it, but reproach thee shouldst thou ever return to thy mo fireside; and thou strive to justify thyself because the trade

blacksmith, the carpenter and the merchant, the tailors, ...ws and Buccaneers defy God and civilization by keeping not ...s Sabbath day, nor wish for a day of rest, such as memory ...youth and and home made hallowed.

### V.

Thou shalt not think more of all thy gold, nor how thou ...nst make it fastest, than how thou wilt enjoy it after thou hast ...dden rough-shod over thy good old parents' precepts and ex...mples, that thou mayest have nothing to reproach and sting ...ee when thou art left alone in the land where thy father's ...essing and thy mothers's love hath sent thee.

### VI.

Thou shalt not kill thy body by working in the rain, even ...ugh thou shalt make enough to buy physic and attendance ...h. Neither shalt thou kill thy neighbor's body in a duel, ...by keeping cool thou canst save his life and thy conscience. ...ither shalt thou destroy thyself by getting "*tight*," nor "*...ewed*," nor "*high*," nor "*corned*," nor "*half-seas over*," ..."*three sheets in the wind*," by drinking smoothly down ...*randy slings*," "*gin cock-tails*," "*whisky punches*," "*rum ...dies*" nor "*egg nogs*." Neither shalt thou suck "*mint-...eps*" nor "*sherry cobblers*" through a straw, nor gurgle from ...ottle the raw material, nor take it neat from a decanter, for ...ile thou art swallowing down thy purse and thy coat from ...thy back, thou art burning the coat from off thy stomach; ...d if thou couldst see the houses and lands, and gold dust, and ...me comforts already lying there—a huge pile—thou shouldst ...l a choking in thy throat; and when to that thou add'st thy ...ooked walking and hiccupping; of lodging in the gutter, of ...oiling in the sun, of prospect holes half full of water, and of ...afts and ditches from which thou hast emerged like a drown-...g rat, thou wilt feel disgusted with thyself, and inquire, "*Is ...y servant a dog that he doeth these things?*" Verily, I will ..., farewell old bottle; I will kiss thy gurgling lips no more; ...d thou, slings, cock-tails, punches, smashes, cobblers, nogs, ...ddies, sangarees and juleps, forever, farewell. Thy remem-...ance shames me; henceforth I will cut thy acquaintance; and ...adaches, tremblings, heart-burnings, blue-devils, and all the ...holy catalogue of evils which follow in thy train. My wife's ...iles and my children's merry-hearted laugh shall charm and ...ward me for having the manly firmness and courage to say: ...*o! I wish thee an eternal farewell!*"

### VII.

Thou shalt not grow discouraged, nor think of going home ...fore thou hast made thy "*pile*," because thou hast not ...*struck a lead*" nor found a rich "*crevice*" nor sunk a hole upon ..."*pocket*," lest in going home thou leave four dollars a day ...d go to work ashamed at fifty cents a day, and serve thee ...ght; for thou knowest by staying here thou mightest strike ...lead and fifty dollars a day, and keep thy manly self-respect, ...d then go home with enough to make thyself and others ...ppy.

### VIII.

Thou shalt not steal a pick, or a pan, or a shovel, from thy fellow miner, nor take away his tools without his leave; nor borrow those he cannot spare; nor return them broken; nor trouble him to fetch them back again; nor talk with him while his water rent is running on; nor remove his stake to enlarge thy claim; nor undermine his claim in following a lead; nor pan out gold from his riffle-box; nor wash the tailings from the mouth of his sluices. Neither shalt thou pick out specimens from the company's pan to put in thy mouth or in thy purse; nor cheat thy partner of his share; nor steal from thy cabin-mate his gold dust to add to thine, for he will be sure to discover what thou hast done, and will straightway call his fellow miners together, and if the law hinder them not they will hang thee, or give thee fifty lashes, or shave thy head and brand thee like a horse thief with "R" upon thy cheek, to be known and of all men Californians in particular.

### IX.

Thou shalt not tell any false tales about "*good diggings in the mountains*" to thy neighbor, that thou mayest benefit a friend who hath mules, and provisions, and tools, and blankets he cannot sell; lest in deceiving thy neighbor when he returns through the snow, with naught but his riffle, he present thee with the contents thereof, and like a dog thou shalt fall down and die.

### X.

Thou shalt not commit unsuitable matrimony, nor covet "*single blessedness*," nor forget absent maidens, nor neglect thy first love; but thou shalt consider how faithfully and patiently she waiteth thy return; yea, and covereth each epistle that thou sendeth with kisses of kindly welcome until she hath thyself. Neither shalt thou covet thy neighbor's wife, nor trifle with the affections of his daughter; yet, if thy heart be free, and thou love and covet each other, thou shalt "*pop the question*" like a man, lest another more manly than thou art should step in before thee, and thou lovest her in vain, and, in the anguish of thy heart's disappointment, thou shalt quote the language of the great, and say, "*sich is life*;" and thy future lot be that of a poor, lonely, despised and comfortless bachelor.

A new commandment give I unto you. If thou hast a wife and little ones, that thou lovest dearer than thy life, that thou keep them continually before you to cheer and urge thee onward until thou canst say, "*I have enough; God bless them; I will return.*" Then as thou journiest towards thy much loved home, with open arms, shall they come forth to welcome thee, and falling on thy neck, weep tears of unutterable joy that thou art come; then in the fullness of thy heart's gratitude thou shalt kneel before thy Heavenly Father together, to thank Him for thy safe return. Amen. So mote it be.

Another reality that faced the goldseeking wanderer to California was the quality of life in the mining regions— a quality that could best be described as barely organized chaos. The society that existed among the gulches, canyons, and stream banks of the Sierra Nevada foothills was atomistic, transient, and purely expedient. It could hardly have been otherwise, for it was populated by a milling horde of men, most of them young, whose only motivation for being there was the hope of getting gold and getting out, and who consequently "toiled and wrestled, and lived a fierce, riotous, wearing, fearfully exciting life," as one historian described it.

It was a society devoid of amenities—unless one could class alcohol, gaming tables, and a few prostitutes as amenities—devoid, in fact, of all but the very basic necessities of food and shelter: the one crude, simple, and expensive; the other quite frequently basic to the point of the primitive. Even the camps that survived long enough to become towns—the Jimtowns, Hangtowns, Shinbone Peaks, and You Bets—retained the raggle-taggle air of impermanence that had been theirs since birth: "What a contrast do these funny little villages present," one goldseeker wrote, "to the eye of one habituated to the sleepy agricultural towns of other countries; built of all kinds of possible materials, shapes, and sizes, and in any spot, no matter how inconvenient, where the first store-keeper chose to pitch himself. Sometimes they are found on a broad flat with no suburb visible, squeezed together as though the land had originally been purchased by the inch, the little streets so crooked and confined, a wheelbarrow could scarcely be made to go through them; sometimes again, they are made up of detached buildings, forming an extended village two or three miles long. . . . Some, too, are quite invisible until you discover them at your feet, buried in a deep chasm."

Government, what there was of it, was by compact, in

the finest American tradition, a form pared down to a skeleton of simple laws designed mainly to keep men from constantly robbing and murdering one another. The first concern of most miners was some way of regulating the size, ownership, and transfer of mining claims, and the method devised was a marvel of simplicity, as

*A curious blend of romanticism and realism, "Sunday Morning in the Mines"*
*was easily Charles Nahl's most popular painting.*

illustrated by the "By Laws of Washington Flat" (first published in Joseph Henry Jackson's **Anybody's Gold**):

"At a meeting of the miners upon Washington Flat, held April 6, 1850, Mr. H. D. Pierce was chosen Chairman and Mr. Thomas Day Secretary. The House being called to order, the Chairman stated the object of the meeting, which was to select an Alcalde and a Sheriff. Mr. J. P. Ward was elected by ballot to the office of Alcalde and Mr. J. Shores to the office of Sheriff. A motion was then made and carried that three men be chosen to draw up resolutions to regulate mining operations. Mr. J. F. Thompson, Mr. P. T. Williams, and Mr.

*Today, an abandoned gold dredge, the relic of a kind of mining that followed the days of '49, sprawls within sight of engine stands used for testing rocket fuel.*

Thomas Day were chosen as such committee. Agreeable to which, the committee reported Saturday eve, April 13, the following resolutions were adopted:

"1st Resolved:

That each individual be entitled to sixteen feet upon the River extending from bank to bank.

2nd Resolved:

That no claim shall be forfeited unless left for three consecutive days without tools, unless prevented by sickness or winter.

3rd Resolved:

That any Company designing to turn the River shall give at least one week's 'Public Notice' of their intentions in order to allow every person an opportunity of joining said Company. And said Company shall be entitled to all they improve.

4th Resolved:

That power to decide in questions of difficulties respecting claims or mining operations be vested in the Alcalde.

5th Resolved:

That these resolutions may be altered or amended by a vote of the majority of any Public Meeting duly notified."

And that was that. Such rules of procedure were far more complicated than the methods of keeping good order in the camp, which were simple to the point of being primitive: only such serious crimes as murder, theft, or reasonless assault were dealt with; once an alleged malefactor was apprehended, he was given the form of a trial by a "miners' jury," which might be either twelve good men and true or the entire community; defense and prosecution arguments were presented by extemporaneous appointees; once a verdict was reached, punishment was swift and to the point: since there were usually no jails (who had time to build jails?), the convicted was either executed, branded, flogged, or banished from the camp, depending upon the seriousness of his crime or the mood of the jury.

At its best, "miners' law" was an imperfect form of justice; it was the child of expedience, and vulnerable to charges of unseemly haste, gross miscarriages, and the taint of lynch law—but it was all they had.

*Two views of the forty-niner: above, an elegant dandy; below, a group of potential rowdies.*

The final reality every miner had to face was the question of whether it had all been worth it—all the long trudging across the deserts and mountains of the West or the months trapped in an ocean-going hell, the grim, demanding work, and the semi-bestial living conditions of the mining country. Most would have answered in the negative, for there simply were too many people scrambling after too little gold. "I do not believe," A. M. Williams wrote to his father in 1850, "that the average amount to the hand, exclusive of expenses, taken from the mines, will exceed two fifty or three dollars per day; while a great many are not doing that well. I know miners who came out last season that are not now able to lay in their winter's supply of provisions." The following year, a "Boone Emigrant" substantiated that view in a letter to the folks back home in Missouri: "A miner's life is one of hardships, toil, and exposure. There is no safe or easy way for him to obtain the precious metal, he must come right down to his work. . . . No man should think of coming to California to make his thousands or his fortune in a short time. This idea is utterly foolish and if he does not think so, let him come and learn in the school that all fools have to learn in."

Millions of dollars in gold had been extracted from the reluctant mountains, and millions more would be taken in the years to come—but by and for the few, not the many, as is usual in the affairs of men. Like the millions who would follow them, the "fools of '49" had discovered that the promise and the reality of California were not necessarily synonymous.

*Some of the sweat, drudgery, and*
*primitive living of the California mines*
*is suggested in this 1850 daguerreotype.*

*For some, gold was not all: A San Francisco tinsmith, ca. 1851.*

# CHAPTER 6

# THE DAYS OF OLD, THE DAYS OF GOLD

*Propelled by men who scramble after the main chance, a new
civilization is created on the shores of the Pacific*

THEY CALLED IT the Golden Era, and for those who lived and remembered it, this time was, as John S. Hittell wrote in 1878, "the very home of their souls." It lasted no more than ten years, yet the force of its life began shaping the state's society, laws, culture, industry, and politics into identifiable patterns that have lasted down all the generations.

To understand this era, we must first consider the quality of its population. There were roughly 100,000 people in California in 1850. By 1860, when the Golden Era is generally conceded to have run its course, the figure had risen to 380,000. Of these, 162,855 were men between the ages of twenty and fifty, whereas less than 50,000 were women of the same age. It was a society dominated by male adults, in most of whom the juices of life still ran strong—and largely untapped. It may be an exaggeration to suggest that the remarkable energy displayed by this male society was no more or less than plain sublimation, but it cannot be denied that the words of literary historian Franklin Walker ring at least partly true: "The dynamite of California," he said, "was composed of one part vigor and one part unsatisfied passion."*

---

*It is possible to argue that these men could have engaged the services of those several thousand women whom Hittell described as "neither maidens, wives, nor widows," and of course many did. Yet the middle of the nineteenth century was an era in which male virginity and chastity were looked upon as virtues, rather than evidence of a crippled libido, and for every one that kept the girls going on a Saturday night, there must have been ten who read the Bible or Byron's *Childe Harold* and took a great many cold baths. Whether such men went on to become giants of industry, commerce, and enterprise is a moot question.

Another volatile ingredient was the startling international flavor of California's population. It mixed nationalities, cultures, styles, and languages in a social montage that was unmatched in its own or any other time: there were 146,528 foreigners in California in 1860—34,935 Chinese, 33,147 Irish, 21,646 Germans, 12,227 English, 9,150 Mexicans, 8,462 Frenchmen, 5,438 Canadians, 3,670 Scots, 2,805 Italians, and 2,250 South Americans. Stirred together with—or at least in proximity to—233,466 Americans from every state in the Union, this agglomeration added its own measure of dreams to the hopes, fears, and ambitions of the state.

Foreign or American, California's population in the Golden Era was uncommonly well educated. There were many who spoke English with an uncertain tongue, but there were few who could not read and write, at least in their own language—and apparently fewer who did not want to do both. In the mid-1850s the city of San Francisco published more books than the rest of the civilized West (what there was of it) put together, and it could boast (and often did) that it possessed more newspapers than London. Libraries and literary societies blossomed. "California," Hittell wrote, "rose as if at one bound from the stagnation of semi-barbarous pastoral life to the varied arts and restless activity of a refined civilization." "Refined" may not be precisely the right word, but it definitely was restless—and literate.

Yet even more important than all of these qualities to the peculiar psychology of the Golden Era was gold itself—or rather, the human response to it. Of all the resources of the earth, useful or merely ornamental, none has had so much power to absolutely warp the

*Judge Peter H. Burnett, a transplant from Oregon and a critic of California government.*

mind of man as gold. The lust for it has haunted Western civilization since Jason trapped it out of Balkan rivers with sheepskins. As we have seen, it shaped the Spanish conquest of the New World, and not even the colonists of America's eastern seaboard were immune to its promise. (Among the several duties of the Jamestown settlers in 1607 was to search for gold under the direction of Capt. John Smith.) Finally, in California, a land as little known to most of the world as the plains of Afghanistan, all the dreaming after gold that had built empires, started wars, deposed kings, and annihilated whole peoples was distilled into one incandescent ray of hope.

That hope, become many more things than gold, shone undiminished for more than a century. Touched with it, California became fully as magical and myth-ridden as it was in the days when it was no more than a name in a third-rate Spanish romance. Broadcast

over the plains and deserts and mountains of America and all the oceans of the world, the call to California was a clarion of opportunity, of possibility, of new beginnings and great expectations. Not all the bald, sober facts or negative reports in the world—and there were plenty, even in the 1850s—could dilute the strength of that message, and those who came to California came with the light of tomorrow in their eyes.

Such was the conditioning that California gold inspired. Great expectations—and the inevitable corollary of great disappointment—were the warp and woof, the very fabric of American California's early life. Like some kind of hallucinogen, it heightened, distorted, and accelerated reality, propelling it in spurts, bursts, and great, explosive movements. The chronicle of the years that followed the gold rush is not so much a history as the record of a seismograph.

EARLY IN 1849 Judge Peter H. Burnett, who had deserted a career in Oregon Territory in order to move on to bigger and better things in California, outlined the new Golconda's basic problem: "The discovery of the rich and exhaustless gold mines of California produced a singular state of things in this community, unparalleled, perhaps, in the annals of mankind. We have here in our midst a mixed mass of human beings from every part of the wide earth, of different habits, manners, customs, and opinions, all, however, impelled onward by the same feverish desire of fortune-making. But, perfectly anomalous as may be the state of our population, the state of our government is still more unprecedented and alarming. *We are in fact without government*—a commercial, civilized, and wealthy people, without law, order, or system."

They were not entirely without law, order, or system, but it was a singularly makeshift arrangement. While "Miners' Law" could function adequately enough up in the mining camps of the Sierra Nevada, where the only compelling need was to keep outright anarchy at bay, the more settled regions were desperately in need of a generally sophisticated working government. For nearly two years after the end of the Mexican War, California's general government remained an unhappy compromise between military rule and the remnants of Spanish and Mexican colonial law. *Alcaldes* approved by the military were the closest approximation of civilian leaders in the province, and their power, according to one of them—Walter Colton of Monterey—was positively undemocratic: "There is not a judge on the bench in England or the United States whose power is so absolute as that of the *alcalde* of Monterey." The military governors could not be blamed for the situation, for they were caught in the middle of a circumstance never before encountered in the United States, as Richard B. Mason lamented: "To throw off upon . . . the people at large the civil management and control of the country, would most probably lead to endess confusion, if not to absolute anarchy; and yet what right or authority have I to exercise civil control in time of peace in a territory of the United States?"

The culprit was the Congress of the United States, dragging its collective feet over the question of what to do about California. Normally the process would have been simple: under the provisions of the Northwest Ordinance of 1787, the region would have been declared a territory, a governor would have been appointed, and a territorial legislature elected and approved; in the due course of time, California would draft a state constitution, apply for membership in the union, and be approved or not approved by Congress, depending upon how it felt at the time. Oregon had been so organized in 1848.

But the question of slavery—Thomas Jefferson's "firebell in the night"—was now clanging vigorously in the halls of Congress. Oregon had posed no problem, for it was well to the north of the Missouri Compromise Line of 1832, that line which divided slave states from free. But California, quite simply, was too big and too rich, and the Compromise Line neatly bisected her in the region of Monterey, a state of affairs that threw the august members of Congress into a monumental tizzy from which they were incapable of extracting themselves. They adjourned in the spring of 1848 without resolving the question, and in the spring of 1849 once again walked away from the responsibility, leaving California in a tangle of uncertainty.

At this juncture Bennett H. Riley, successor to Richard B. Mason, agreed that it was time for California to cut through the gelatinous mass of congressional inaction and force the issue. In June 1849 he issued a call for the election of delegates to attend a constitutional convention, hammer out a constitution for the state of California, set up elections, apply for admission to the United States, and hope that a *fait accompli* could be forced down the throat of Congress. On September 1, forty-eight delegates gathered at Colton Hall in Monterey. Among them were such familiar names as Robert "Long Bob" Semple, promoter of Benicia; Capt. John Sutter, who could still delude himself that his empire was intact; and Mariano Vallejo, patriarch of Sonoma and one of eight native Californians elected to the convention, together with such newcomers as William M. Gwin, a Tennessee Democrat with the announced intention of becoming one of California's first senators, and Peter H. Burnett, lately of the Supreme Court of Oregon Territory.

*Brown's Express Co., like many another delivery company, engaged in an early form of banking.*

*David C. Broderick, who learned his political lessons in New York but practiced the trade in California.*

Surprisingly, one of the questions most easily settled was whether California would declare herself a free or a slave state: the unanimous decision was that she should be free. The chief reason for this, of course, was that the Californians feared the use of Negro slaves as laborers in the mines, opening up the possibility of monopoly and—perhaps even worse—demeaning labor that had acquired dignity because it was performed by God-fearing, white Americans. The sectional antagonism that was ripping the rest of the country apart simply disintegrated in the face of plain economic good sense and the hard-won calluses of former bank clerks and newspaper editors who had learned the nobility of sweat. Besides, California was the land of new beginnings, no proper arena for perpetuating ancient legacies.

The assembly was less forthright in confronting the problem of whether or not to grant full citizenship to the former Mexican citizens of California. The Treaty of Guadalupe-Hidalgo had guaranteed full rights to

such individuals, and while the convention generally deplored such a travesty of the mid-nineteenth-century version of democracy, it was reluctant to antagonize Congress. The delegates finally compromised by authorizing the state legislature to grant the right to vote to former Mexican citizens, should it ever want to do such an outlandish thing. More to its credit, the convention drafted a proposal for the separate property of women, allowing a woman to hold claim to any property she owned before marriage (possibly a device to lure potential brides to California); resisted the temptation to extend the state's boundaries clear to Utah, settling instead for approximately the present limits; seriously considered a ban on duelling (not passed); and accepted Washington's so-far unextended offer of land grants to finance an educational system.

Amid a welter of similar stipulations, the convention managed to put together a working constitution. After it was rendered into splendid calligraphy on parchment by one Lieutenant Hamilton (paid $500 for the service), the delegates signed it on October 13, while naval guns boomed out a salute and Capt. John Sutter stood up, waved an arm in a vaguely triumphant fashion, and exclaimed, "Gentlemen, this is the happiest day of my life. It makes me glad to hear those cannon: they remind me of the time when I was a soldier. Yes, I am glad to hear them—this is a great day for California!"

On November 13, 1849, the constitution was ratified, a legislature chosen, and a slate of officers elected: Peter H. Burnett as governor, John McDougal as lieutenant governor, and William H. Gwin (ambition satisfied) and John Charles Frémont as senators.* Frémont and Gwin took the Constitution to Washington and presented it to Congress, most of whose members looked

---

*Frémont's star, as erratic as a thistle in a windstorm, was on the rise again. Before leaving California in 1847, he had given Thomas Oliver Larkin $3,000 to purchase a good tract of land, using his best judgment. Larkin had bought the Mariposa Grant, a stretch of land in the southern Sierra Nevada foothills. When he returned, Frémont was furious—but not for long. His mountain grant was thick with placer gold, and before the end of 1849 he was a millionaire—perhaps the only miner in California who was taking gold off his own land. In the middle of the nineteenth century, millionaires were, by definition, virtuous men, and the somewhat sordid details of his earlier California life had faded against the glitter of all that gold.

upon it without enthusiasm. Yet they could not ignore California's direct petition, as Carey McWilliams has written: "The union is an exclusive body, but when a millionaire knocks on the door, you don't keep him waiting too long; you let him in." Henry Clay, the great moderator, gathered his fragile strength (he was then seventy-three years old and would die in two years) and once more forestalled a plunge into the abyss of Civil War by putting together the Compromise of 1850, in which California was admitted into the union as a free state in exchange for harsher laws enforcing the return of fugitive slaves and the eventual admission of the territories of Utah and New Mexico with no specific ban against slavery. On September 9, 1850, President Millard Fillmore signed the bill of admission, and news of the great event reached California on October 18, giving rise to much dancing in the streets of San Francisco and fulsome newspaper editorials, such as this in the October 19 edition of the *California Daily Courier*: "Every one seemed happy—and we do not believe that the news of a brilliant victory was ever received by a people with greater joy than was the news yesterday, that California is now one of the brightest stars in our glorious galaxy of states. Thanks to a tardy but patriotic Congress—thanks to our brethren of the Atlantic states—thanks to an Administration which has shown itself true to California, and true to the Union! Long may our heaven-blessed, united country be preserved for the glory of our times and the pride of unborn generations."

WHILE IT CANNOT BE DOUBTED that a certain joy was expressed by many Californians over the state's admission to the Union, it is equally true that at least as many greeted it with a thundering indifference—for apathy was the political life-style of most of her citizens. During the election of December 1849, only 12,872 votes were cast out of a total electorate of perhaps 50,000 or 60,000 (no precise figures can be calculated). Californians, for the most part, were simply too busy to care. Up in the foothills of the Sierra Nevada, thousands were still scrabbling from one gulch to another, one streambank to another, one sand island to another, dreaming of the fortune that would take them back to the States wealthy men. Why should they care whether

California was military district, province, territory, or state? And down in the flatlands, in the supply and service centers of San Francisco and Sacramento, entrepreneurs of every stripe were reserving most of their energies for the hustle of progress. So California was now a state? Fine, a good move. Now, let's get back to the heart of the matter—making money.

The number of ways in which this worthy ambition could be satisfied were astounding, for as gold fed the imaginations of men, it also nourished a bewilderingly complex economic life. Between 1849 and 1859, $583,000,000 in gold primed the pumps of enterprise—more hard capital gathered into one place in one ten-year period than at any time in the nation's history. It was a fluid, hard-money economy, and the opportunities to exploit it were limited only by the ability of men to stretch a good thing as far as it would go. The first five years or so following 1849 were to the entrepreneurs what the first six months after the discovery of gold were to the lucky goldseekers of 1848: in both cases, for a while, it seemed there was enough for everybody. The resulting air of speculation, manipulation, and downright chicanery forged a particularly virulent "boom-and-bust" psychology that seeped into every area of the young state's fiscal life. It was not a very stable economy—but rarely was it dull.

City lots in San Francisco and Sacramento* were a speculator's dream. Those who had purchased San Francisco lots in 1848 for $16, $29, or even $600, for example, found their properties taking a screaming leap in value during the early 1850s, reaching as high as $2,000 a front foot. Landlords calmly charged thousands of dollars a month for use of their property, and many a hotel, gambling saloon, or brothel paid it without a whimper. Even in an age of relatively high property taxes (4 percent of full valuation), the profits in all this were stunning, even for those who came a little late. For one example, John Parrott, a former merchant of Mazatlán, built the first granite building

---

*For five years after the Constitutional Convention of 1849, the location of the state capital was a matter of some uncertainty, "hawked about," as Walton Bean has said, "in a most undignified manner." It was first in San Jose, then moved to Vallejo; then it was moved back to San Jose, then back to Vallejo; from Vallejo to Sacramento and back to Vallejo; then from Vallejo to Benicia—and, finally, in 1854, to Sacramento where it stayed.

*William M. Gwin, the stern-jawed opponent of David C. Broderick's political machine.*

on Montgomery Street in 1852 for a total cost of $117,500 (including the sale price of the property), then rented it out for $3,000 a month; down on California Street, he erected the Iron Building for $23,000 and rented it out for $1,200; and on the northwest corner of Montgomery and Sacramento, he built three buildings for a cost of $120,750 and rented them for a total of $2,500 a month. Thus, in about four years he could look forward to a clear monthly profit of $6,700 —providing he never raised the rent—and ownership of property whose value could only increase geometrically through the years.

For those engaged in simple trade, it was a seller's market. Scarce items sometimes rose in value two or three hundred times their market price in the East, and nearly everything that was sold went at prices far above those in any other market. The temptation to speculate was powerful; one shipload of, say, tobacco, arriving at precisely the right time, could set a man up for life. But it was a speculation, and not without risks. A man might observe that tobacco was selling in San Francisco for two dollars a pound, put in his order for several tons of the stuff from Charleston or New Orleans, and in the six months or so it took for his order to arrive might see *fifteen* ships full of tobacco sail through the Golden Gate, glutting the market, plunging the price to an all-time low, and forcing him to auction off his own tobacco once it arrived—to men who had the wherewithal and the patience to store it and wait for prices to rise once again. Wasteful and risky, it was a gambler's game, but California was full of gamblers, and the potential profits were irresistible. Between 1850 and 1860 nearly three million tons of freight entered California by sea.

With interest rates as high as 10 percent a month, it was equally tempting to engage in plain money-changing. Although a generation of experience in the East had created a healthy resentment of banks by most Americans, and had caused the Constitutional Convention of California to forbid the legislature to "pass any act granting any charter for banking purposes," the very nature of California's swelling economy made the formation of savings, lending, and investment institutions inevitable. At first, banking was fairly primitive, a sideline of saloon-keepers and hardware dealers, but soon more or less sophisticated firms moved in to dominate the business—freightage, passenger, and express-mail companies like Wells, Fargo & Company or Adams & Company; branches of larger eastern banks, such as Page, Bacon & Company, Palmer, Cook & Company, or Lucas, Turner & Company (the last managed by none other than William Tecumseh Sherman, long before he marched through Georgia); together with a handful of purely local concerns. Speculation in one thing or another was as common among bankers as anyone else, and since the state legislature had chosen officially to ignore their existence, California's banks were almost completely unregulated, a state of affairs that would last with minor modifications well into the twentieth century—and would contribute to more than one panic.

If California's future had been dependent upon such enterprises, of course, it is not likely that she would have progressed beyond the level of an Arizona or New Mexico, limited in their resources. But California not only had gold in so-far unimaginable quantities, she was rich in the resources of timber and land, both of which gave her a foundation as solid as it was immediately exploitable. During the first few years of the Golden Era, California used up wood like a fool at a fire. In the foothills of the Mother Lode, yellow pine and sugar pine were chopped down and sawn into planks and timbers for saloons, brothels, houses, mine timbering, cradles, sluices, water flumes, and dams for the moving of rivers. San Francisco built up and burned down five times between 1849 and 1851, and Sacramento once; much of the lumber to rebuild them both was stripped from the stands of redwoods that clustered in the Coast Range, including the Santa Cruz Mountains above Monterey Bay, the hills behind Redwood City (which began life as a lumber-shipping port), and those behind Oakland (which began as a tiny lumbering settlement). There were even more redwoods in the region of the Northwest Coast, and from the little "doghole" port of Mendocino, "Honest Harry" Meiggs shipped enough cut lumber down to San Francisco to enhance his ambitions for a political career and enable him to construct a two-thousand-foot wharf running out from the North Beach area of the city, a section which he fondly believed would be the commercial heart of San Francisco. Again, the potential profits were staggering, as lumber prices went as high as four hundred dollars per thousand board-feet, and only infrequently fell below one hundred.

The land which had made the graceful life of the *ranchero* possible during California's Mexican era was another resource put to quick use. For a time, at least, one cow, however lean and stringy, was worth five hundred dollars in the Mother Lode, for the miners would pay whatever they had to for a piece of red meat. Thousands of cattle were driven north, and to supplement these herds, thousands more were driven from Texas and the Mississippi Valley to feed on the rich grasslands of California and breed with the native stock. Agriculture lagged somewhat behind husbandry —as it had ever since the secularization of the missions —but by 1854 the state had 135,000 acres under cultivation. Most of this land was planted in wheat, foreshadowing the day when California would quite seriously be called the "breadbasket of the world."

Heavily resource-oriented already and geared to a speculative psychology, which dictated quick profits on a massive scale with a small initial investment, there was little room in the economy of the Golden Era for the steadier, slower, more stable qualities of manufacture, and what there was of it was designed almost exclusively for local consumption. Even the Union Iron Works of the Donahue brothers, founded in 1850 and for years the closest thing to a major heavy-industry firm in the state, began with the manufacture of heating and cooking stoves. Industry was growth as it was known in the eastern states—and California was not growing, she was booming.

GIVEN SUCH A WELTER OF OPPORTUNITY, it should not be surprising to learn that most Californians regarded the mechanics of government with a cold unsympathetic eye; it was a necessary evil, but something to be concerned about only when it interfered, one way or another, with the scramble after the main chance. As a result, of course, the government was quickly dominated by as pretty a mess of scoundrels and mountebanks as one could have found outside the wards of New York City—some, in fact, were *from* the wards of New York City. At an early age, California and the city of San Francisco were brushed by the tail of the Tammany Tiger.

The antagonistic careers of William M. Gwin and David C. Broderick straddled the Golden Era like a pair of colossi—Gwin, the Tennessee sharper who had become a United States senator, and Broderick a second-

*The execution of two Sidney Ducks, McKenzie and Whittaker, by vigilante action, August 1851.*

*Honest voters versus ballot-box stuffers—an early cartoonist's view of California politics.*

rate politician from New York City who saw in California a small pond for large frogs. Gwin, with the lever of federal patronage, had been able to build up a strong Democratic machine in California, but Broderick, patient, devious, and smart enough to get along, had the support of Tammany-trained former soldiers from the regiment of New York Volunteers—and a consuming ambition. He entered the state senate in 1850 and wormed his way into enough power to control state patronage by 1853. Along the way he amassed a substantial fortune for himself through a partnership in a private minting firm* and San Francisco real estate

---

*It was not until 1854 that the United States Treasury established a branch mint in San Francisco. Until then, most of the gold coin in California was minted privately—with considerable more "face" value than real value (for example, a five-dollar coin might contain no more than three or four dollars' worth of gold).

speculations, including the infamous "Peter Smith" land sale of 1851, one of the most transparent and brilliantly successful land frauds in any state's history (see "California Mirror: Chrysopolis").

In 1854, Broderick challenged Gwin for the senatorship by attempting to browbeat the state legislature into electing him before Gwin's term had expired; this failed, but in 1855 he tried again, creating such a deadlock in the legislature that neither he, Gwin, nor anyone else went to Washington for two years. The impasse was broken in 1857, when both of them were elected, but not until Gwin, by now respectful of Broderick's power, made a deal: in exchange for Broderick's support, Gwin promised to let him have the lion's (or Tiger's) share of federal patronage. Unfortunately, Gwin had not cleared this offer with President James Buchanan, who rejected the whole idea and continued to dispense federal favors to Gwin and his friends.

Broderick was incensed at this breach of contract and for the next two years took every opportunity to vilify Gwin, his friends, relatives, and ancestors. Judge David Terry, a justice of the State Supreme Court and a warm—even hotheaded—advocate of Gwin, came in for his share of Broderick's vituperation and in response challenged the senator to a duel. They fought on September 13, 1859, and when it was over, Broderick was dead. So was Gwin's California machine, for appalled Democrats by the thousands fled such violence and joined the Republican Party, carrying the state for Abraham Lincoln in the elections of 1860.

The venality of the Broderick-Gwin machines, with their coercion of voters, ballot-box stuffing, personal assaults, threats, open bribery, and other tactical paraphernalia, filtered like ashes down to the bottom-most level of California's civic life in the Golden Era. Not even the "cow counties" of Southern California, sleeping in the sun and awaiting their day, were immune, as Harris Newmark noted in recalling the election process in his *Sixty Years in Southern California:* "Although it is true, of course, that many votes were legitimate, yet aliens such as Mexicans . . . were permitted to vote, while Indians and half-breeds, who were not eligible for citizenship at all, were regularly given the franchise. The story is told of an election in Los Angeles at which a whole tribe of Indians was voted; while on another occasion, the names of a steamer's passenger list were utilized by persons who had voted that very day, once or twice. Cutting off the hair, shaving one's beard or moustache, reclothing or otherwise transforming the appearance of the voter—these were some of the tricks then practiced."

The law, from the state legislature down to the lowliest justice of the peace, was literally for sale more often than not; and while go-ahead merchants, newspaper editors, and other men of responsibility could be heard deploring the situation from time to time, only the most extraordinary circumstance could take their minds off the exchange of commodities and real estate long enough to actually *do* something, as historian Roger Olmsted has pointed out: "When the most substantial citizens thought of nothing but buying and selling, when *'everyone* was making money', what difference did it make that petty bandits and barroom murderers went unapprehended; or if arrested, unindicted; or if indicted, swiftly acquitted; or if convicted, then pardoned, released, or assisted in escape? So it went ... until at some point the arrogance, the insolence of swaggering blackguards provoked a violent revulsion and dramatic overreaction. The populace would acquiesce in cases of flagrant miscarriage of justice, would suffer an active criminal element to operate almost unchecked, would ignore jobbery, bribery, and all kinds of civic chicanery—but it would not be *run over*."

Or burned up—for fire was the immediate cause of California's first "reform" movement, otherwise known as the San Francisco Committee of Vigilance of 1851. Throughout 1850 a solid and not unreasonable suspicion had grown among the good citizens of San Francisco that the city's criminal element—refugees from penal colonies in Australia and New Zealand, together with a generous helping of native American scoundrels gathered from all the dark corners of the country—had been behind at least one of the disastrous fires that had swept the city three times since 1849. And if that were not bad enough, in February 1851 a storekeeper had been robbed and assaulted *in his own store*—a nightmarish business indeed, and one that quickly inspired Sam Brannan, William T. Coleman, and other merchants to gather a group of like-minded citizens together and form a "People's Court" to assure the swift conviction of the culprits. Unfortunately, their own hand-picked jury failed to agree, and the robbers were

disposed of by the instituted authorities; the "People's Court" was forced to adjourn in frustration.

As May 4, the anniversary of the great fire of 1850, approached, rumors spread that another would be set to memorialize the day, and so, perhaps, it was: on May 3 a fire broke out in a paint shop, and by the next morning seven million dollars' worth of property had gone up in smoke. The editor of the *Alta California* spoke for a great many when he wrote: "It seems useless to write and talk to the people of San Francisco. They have lost all resentment. They love to be burned out. They seem to have set it down as one of their luxuries. It is something *recherche*. We look with apparent satisfaction upon the sprightly attempts of the recruits of penaldom to illuminate our city free gratis."

It was too much—more than too much—and Brannan, Coleman, and other leading spirits gathered their people once again, wrote up a constitution and a set of bylaws creating a Committee of Vigilance, and pro-

*Law and order as art: A membership certificate issued by the 1856 Committee of Vigilance.*

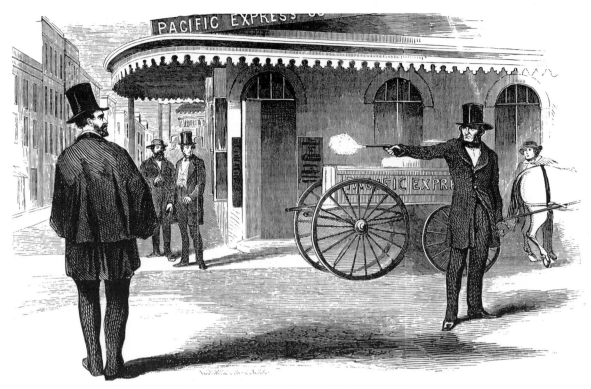

*The shooting of James King of William by James P. Casey, May 14, 1856.*

ceeded to become the judge, jury, courts, and law of San Francisco for the next three months. The committee's announced intention was to induce undesirables to "leave *this port*" (meaning California) by whatever means necessary, and while it did hang four men (none of them for the specific crime of murder) along the way, the committee never lost sight of that resolution: it made almost 90 arrests, whipped one man, deported 28, turned 15 over to the authorities, released 41, and simply frightened a good many more out of town. By September, membership had grown to six hundred, criminals and courts had been taught their lessons, and the committee adjourned itself, leaving behind the skeleton of an executive committee and a tradition of *ad hoc* justice that popped up periodically throughout the state, from Los Angeles to Downieville.

The members of the committee could—and frequently did—congratulate themselves on a job done with some dispatch, allowing them to return to business with no immediate probability of being robbed and beaten in

their own stores or burned out (although a fifth, and last, fire took place in June, this one presumably an accident). They were safe, perhaps, but not necessarily secure, for California was soon experiencing its first genuine recession; the big bubble of the boom was not going to burst, but it did sag a bit. By the end of 1853 gold production, the fuel that fed California's economy, began to fall off and by the end of 1854 had dropped from the high of $68,000,000 in 1853 to $64,000,000—a small decline on the face of it, but in an economy dependent upon the assurance of gold, gold, and more gold *ad infinitum,* it created a suddenly tight money market. Moreover, the decline continued throughout the 1850s, dropping as much as three, four, and even five million every year. The amount of tonnage entering the Golden Gate decreased by 25 percent in 1854; real estate and commodity prices dropped, and construction came to a near standstill; a growing agriculture undercut imported foodstuffs, and the lack of any substantial exports further hampered the activity of commission merchants. "California," the young banker

William T. Sherman wrote early in 1854, "is a perfect paradox, a mystery. The various ups and downs are enough to frighten any prudent person."

In October, Sherman and the rest of San Francisco's financial community were thoroughly frightened when "Honest Harry" Meiggs defaulted and fled for South America, owing something in the vicinity of eight hundred thousand dollars. Sherman called it "the great Meiggs failure, swindle, forgery and flight forming in all its details a perfect epic of crime . . . by far the most serious disaster that has befallen a community like ours. When confidence in men at best was small, now we suspect everybody for Meiggs was deemed incorruptible." Five months later he was forced to report another disaster to the home office of Lucas, Turner & Company, "the most terrible financial storm that has ever devastated any community."

Early in February 1855 the St. Louis home office of Page, Bacon & Company had gone bankrupt. When news of the failure reached San Francisco, there was an immediate run on the local branch, forcing it to default; and since popular reasoning had it that if one bank was in trouble *all* banks must be in trouble, the rest of the city's banks were subjected to runs. Adams and Company was ruined, and there were few banks that were not forced to close their doors at least temporarily. It would not be until gold and silver from the Comstock began flowing into California in 1860 that the state would fully recover from the trauma of 1855.

Suddenly it seemed "everyone was *not* making money," and when the citizens next turned their energies toward "cleaning up" San Francisco, it was with far more serious intent than when they had hanged a few muggers and thieves in 1851; the result was, as

*A popular revolution in action: Fort Vigilance calls out 4,000 armed men in 1856.*

Roger Olmsted has described it, "a popular revolution of such power, magnitude, and success that there are no clear parallels to be found for it." Political corruption—not incidental thievery or arson—was the target this time, brought into focus on May 14, 1856, when James P. Casey, a political thug whose specialty was ballot-box stuffing, shot down James King of William in the streets. King, a former banker, was the muckraking editor of the *Daily Evening Bulletin* and had exposed Casey's prison record; when Casey demanded a retraction, King refused and Casey, in the finest western tradition, did him in, afterwards retiring to the safety of his friends in the city jail.

Within days the Committee of Vigilance was reorganized under the stern administration of William T. Coleman, and there was little of the extemporaneous flavor that had marked the committee of 1851. It was carefully structured, with a board of executives, secrecy oaths, codes, and stiff regulations. Well-armed, grimly determined, and popular, ultimately achieving a membership of more than six thousand, it came down on the government of San Francisco with the weight of a monolith, to the dismay of California's governor J. Neely Johnson, who was powerless to do anything about it short of civil war, and of other law-and-order men, among them William T. Sherman, whose comments are downright poignant: "The Vigilance Committee are now in full possession of San Francisco and in a free American country where we pay taxes of four per cent on full valuation, we now are at the mercy of irresponsible masses."

The committee did its work efficiently; it hanged Casey and three other men, deported thirty of the better-known political poltroons, and as in 1851, simply frightened away a good many more. It also arrested Justice David Terry of the State Supreme Court for assaulting one of its officers with a bowie knife, an arrest that put the committee in a particularly uncomfortable position: if it released Terry, it would be an admission of weakness; if it tried, convicted, and executed him, it might force Governor Johnson to take direct action, with federal troops a distinct possibility.

The committee solved the dilemma by giving Terry a trial, convicting him—and, thanks to his victim's recovery, releasing him just before the leaders of Vigilance disbanded the organization for good, commemorating the occasion on August 18 with a massive, silent march of six thousand armed men through the streets of San Francisco. A few weeks later, a slate of clean committee-sponsored candidates won every office in the city government. But one of the proudest achievements of the new administration (and, in fact, the only measurable achievement) was the reduction of city expenses to only one-sixth those of the previous crowd, leading one to wonder if morality and money had once more gotten confused in this "most American of all the American states."

IN APRIL 1857, William T. Sherman was getting ready to pack up and leave, for Lucas, Turner & Company had decided to abandon the uncertain world of California finance. In one of his last letters from San Francisco, he penned an elegy to the best and the worst of the Golden Era he had experienced: "A wagon road may bring a different character of people, for the country has many advantages, mines of exhaustless gold, a large quantity of fertile land and a good healthful climate. The country is bound to become important and San Francisco is bound to become a great city, but both have got to pass through a severe ordeal. . . . I see no signs of moral reform in California, though some Vigilantes see it sticking out in every direction. My opinion is the very nature of the country begets speculation, extravagance, failures, and rascality. Everything is chance, everything is gambling, and I shall feel relieved when I am not dependent on the people of California for my repose."

Repose was not California's style, then, now, or at any other time, and the "days of old, the days of gold, the days of '49" drew to a close in an atmosphere of somewhat spurious moral fervor, genuine economic uncertainty, and a future as predictable as the fall of unloaded dice in a Pacific Street gambling hell.

VIEW OF SAN FRANCISCO, FORMERLY YERBA BUENA, IN 1846-7

BEFORE THE DISCOVERY OF GOLD

*Embryo of a city: Yerba Buena (San Francisco) in 1847.*

# California Mirror:
# Chrysopolis

In 1878 historian John S. Hittell dubbed San Francisco "Chrysopolis," the city of gold—an intriguing echo of the day in 1846 when John C. Frémont uncannily chose the name "Chrysopolae" to describe the entrance to the bay. Both descriptions—the one made by observation, the other by providential accident—were apt, but Hittell's was precise. San Francisco was indeed a city of gold—of gold, by gold, and for gold. The reality of it fed the machinery of her civilization, and the memory of it colored the city forever.

This is the city we remember as Will Irwin remembered it, the "gayest, lightest hearted, most pleasure loving city of the western continent, and in many ways the most interesting and romantic." Such a description was open to charges of sentimentality. What of the rank cribs and fetid alleys of Chinatown, the crowded shacks of Telegraph Hill, or the reek of municipal corruption that too often lingered in the air as much as the smell of fresh-baked bread on a North Beach street corner?

Such things were present in abundance, if one cared to look for them, but the sheer pace and exuberance of the city's life tended to obscure them, seducing belief even from one as sharp-eyed and frequently sour as Rudyard Kipling, who visited the city in 1889: "Recklessness is in the air. I can't explain where it comes from, but there it is. The roaring winds off the Pacific make you drunk to begin with. . . . The young men rejoice in the days of their youth. . . . At twenty they are experienced in business, and embark on vast enterprises, take partners as experienced as themselves, and go to pieces with as much splendour as their neighbors. Remember that the men who stocked California in the Fifties were physically, and as far as regards certain tough virtues, the pick of the earth. The inept or weakly died on route or went under in the days of construction. . . . It needs no little badge to mark the Native Son of the Golden West. . . . Him I love because he is devoid of fear, carries himself like a man, and has a heart as big as his boots."

*"Looking down California Street," a San Francisco scene of the 1880s (artist unknown).*

GREAT FIRE IN SAN FRANCISCO.

For the first few years one of San Francisco's main difficulties was staying built long enough to acquire an image. Between early 1849 and late 1851, most of the city's business district was swept by flames no less than six times. Currier & Ives captured a moment of burning fury during the "Great Fire" of May 1851 in the lithograph at the left, and Frank Marryat left us a spirited description of that same fire in his **Mountains and Molehills** (1855):

"On the 3d of May, at eleven in the evening, the fire-bell again startled us; but on this occasion the first glance at the lurid glare and heavy mass of smoke that rolled toward the bay evinced that the fire had already a firm grip on the city. The wind was unusually high, and the flames spread in a broad sheet over the town. All efforts to arrest them were useless. . . .

"No conception can be formed of the grandeur of the scene; for at one time the burning district was covered by one vast sheet of flame that extended half a mile in length. . . . The memory is confused in the recollection of the shouts of the excited populace—the crash of falling timbers—the yells of the burnt and injured—the hoarse orders delivered through speaking-trumpets—maddened horses released from burning livery-stables plunging through the streets—helpless patients being carried from some hospital, and dying on the spot, as the swaying crowd, forced back by the flames, tramples all before it—explosions of houses blown up by gunpowder—showers of burning splinters that fall around on every side—the thunder of brick buildings as they fall into a heap of ruin—the blinding glare of ignited spirits. Amidst the heat that scorches, let you go where you will . . . you throw your coat away and help to work the engine-brakes, as calls are made for more men.

"At daylight, you plod home, half-blind, half-drowned, half-scorched, half-stunned, and quite bewildered; and from that time you never care to recall one half of the horrors you have witnessed on the night of the conflagration of the 3d of May."

*Fire once again: San Francisco was completely or substantially destroyed more times than any other major American city.*

*Overleaf: The City of Gold—of all the bird's-eye views that proliferated in the nineteenth century, this 1877 lithograph may be the most spectacular.*

Unlike most American cities, whose architectural heritage tended to survive fire and other disasters only to succumb to the wrecking ball of progress, San Francisco retains an uncommonly flavorful sense of the past—as in this view of the distinctive "bay window" style of residential construction that is a legacy of the 1880s.

*Entrepreneurs: Jacob P. Leese, Talbot Green, Thomas O. Larkin,
Sam Brannan, and W. D. M. Howard.*

The city of gold was a city of fearfully busy entrepreneurs in whose veins opportunity ran like some sort of hallucinogenic drug. Economic mobility—upward as well as downward—obliterated the lines of class and caste, and efforts to re-create them out of whole cloth were often pretty ludicrous, as Samuel Williams illustrated in the July 1875 issue of **Scribner's Monthly:** "It is natural that in a community so largely made up of fortune-hunters, wealth should be a controlling social power; but it would be unjust to say that wealth is the sole standard of social position. Occupation, how one lives, and where one lives, have something to do with it. There is a story of a rich man . . . who some years ago gave a famous party. He had a large circle of acquaintances, but he could not invite everybody. 'We must draw the line somewhere, you know,' he said, and he drew it bravely between wholesale and retail. The man who sold soap and candles by the box was decreed to be within the 'sacred pale' of society's elect. The man who sold soap and candles by the pound was voted a social Philistine." The creation of "society" took time and leisure; in the golden era there was little of either.

How do you make a city? In San Francisco you began with parcels of land—the more lots the better, put down wherever there was room, and where there was not, you **made** room. "While adventurers continued to crowd in at the rate of several thousand every month," historian John S. Hittell wrote, "while the gold dust . . . was accumulating by millions, the people were not indifferent on the subject of town lots."

By the spring of 1849, most of the lots that had been surveyed in 1847 (see chapter 5) had been sold, and the city ordered another survey. On went the familiar town-lot grid—up the sides of hills, over rocks and gullies and sand dunes—and behind came the hodge-podge buildings. The cluttered nature of the town is suggested by the two daguerreotypes on the facing page. The top view shows the seaward side of Montgomery Street in early 1851, looking toward Telegraph Hill; most of that side of the street had been built on water lots covered with a singularly unengineered fill of sand, rocks, furniture, spoiled and unsold merchandise, empty bottles, garbage, and the rotting hulks of deserted ships. The bottom view shows the landward side of the street looking down toward Market Street—or what would have been Market Street had it not been for the massive sand dune that stood between the two streets, until it was dug away and used for fill.

Although nothing to compare with the "squatters' riots" of Sacramento in 1851, in which three men died, claim disputes and incidents of lot-jumping were not uncommon in San Francisco's early years. Even more notable were two rather splendid swindles. The first took place in 1852 when Peter Smith, a concessionaire at the city hospital, presented the city with a bill of $64,000. To satisfy the debt, the city announced an auction of municipally owned lots (including the site of the future city hall)—while word "escaped" that the sale might not be legal. Smart buyers consequently stayed away from the auction, and the land fell to a handful of those in the know, including political boss David C. Broderick and Peter Smith himself, who may have been fronting for those shy about revealing their names.

The second involved José Yves Limantour, a Frenchman living in Mexico, who in 1852 won approval from the California Land Commission of his Mexican grant claim to four square leagues in San Francisco. Before federal investigators were able to prove that his documents were forgeries, Limantour had collected a small fortune from his "tenants" in payments for quit-claim deeds; indicted, he jumped bail and disappeared, richer by an unknown amount.

San Franciscans were, indeed, "not indifferent on the subject of town lots."

*The Montgomery Street offices of Samuel Brannan's* Herald—*one of his many entrepreneurial schemes.*

*Two views of Montgomery Street, 1851.*

The state of the arts in the city of gold was not what one could call refined. At the right, a pair of sturdy minstrels; above, Lola Montez, courtesan of princes and a dancer who stirred the hearts of men. "Lola had scarcely appeared on the stage when some of the enthusiastic firemen who filled the Parquette threw their hats up on the stage," a critic wrote. "She danced with great grace, keeping time with the castanets." One would hope so.

San Francisco, the city of large events and a very serious passion for money-making, was also the city of inspired high jinks and a loving tolerance for the odd ones among us. If any one man came to symbolize both the promise and the foolishness of the city in this era, it was Joshua A. Norton, who was born in England in 1819, came to San Francisco as a young man with $40,000, ran his money up to more than a quarter of a million dollars, and then lost it all in an attempt to corner the rice market. He later declared himself Emperor of the United States and Protector of Mexico, and was described in 1875 by Samuel Williams as "a harmless creature who ... issues frequent pronunciamentos, exacts tribute ... spends his days walking about the streets, his evenings at the theatre, and his nights at a cheap lodging-house. ... appears on public occasions in tattered regalia ... calls at the newspaper offices to warn the conductors against the consequences of treasonable utterances—in short, is up early and late regulating the affairs of the world in general and the city and state in particular."

When the Emperor died in 1880, the city of gold buried him with great pomp and genuine regret.

*Emperor Norton, "monarch" of all he surveyed and the undisputed grandee of San Francisco eccentrics.*

# CHAPTER 7

# THE HYPHENATED CALIFORNIANS

*Indian-, Mexican-, Negro-, and Chinese-Americans—luckless*

*participants in the exercise of selective democracy*

THERE HAS ALWAYS BEEN a strong link between prejudice and money in the history of men's relations with their fellows. When all the clutter of chauvinism, xenophobia, deep racial hatreds, and the normal human fear of those who are visibly "different" is swept away, a sour little kernel of economic interest can nearly always be found—and this certainly was so in California. Men tend to do the things they do for *reasons,* however perverted the logic behind them; and if it is true, as one pair of after-the-facts critics tells us, that "no more sorry record exists in the Union of inhuman and uncivil treatment toward minority groups than in California," it is also true that the state's record documents something more complicated than a careless enthusiasm for discrimination, cruelty, and killing.

None of this, of course, makes that record any less sorry or less cruel. To read of it and to write of it is to despair at times that the human animal is capable of redemption. Yet the Californians had their reasons, or were convinced that they did, and it would be well to remember that the last half of the nineteenth century was an age in which most men could bend a fact to fit a preconception without feeling the twist, particularly when it came down to economic survival, as it often did. Before we rest too easily in the critical distance of a century, we had better be certain we are really that much different today.

The luckless California Indian, naturally divided and disorganized, and weakened by nearly eighty years of contact with Europeans, was so unprepared for the onslaught of the Iron Age in the form of thousands of American goldseekers that it is a kind of miracle that he did not go the way of the now-extinct Abenaki Indians of Maine almost immediately. His survival into our own time is far more of a tribute to his toughness and will to live than to any charitable instincts displayed by the dominant civilization. In 1846 there were about 98,000 Indians left out of an original population of some 250,000; twenty-five years later, there were about 30,000 left, and thirty years after that (in 1900) about 16,000.

As in the Spanish and Mexican periods, most of this population loss was due to disease—perhaps 60 percent succumbed to such afflictions as measles, diphtheria, whooping cough, smallpox, tuberculosis, and the venereal infections. Another 30 percent or so died of culture shock, starvation, and malnutrition, as the swelling American population drove them from their ancestral food-producing regions. The remaining 10 percent were killed outright.

With one exception—the Modoc conflict of 1873—there were no Indian "wars" as such in California, for few of the state's Indians were either able or willing to engage in the kind of warfare that took place in the plains and mountains of the trans-Mississippi West. What took place in California were isolated sorties of extermination. The latter term may seem incendiary, but there is no other way to describe the many instances

*The schoolhouse, teacher, and pupils of the Coahuilla Indian School at Martinez in about 1890.*

*A Charles Nahl view of Indian warfare for* Hutchings California Magazine, *1855.*

in which impromptu bands of settlers attempted to kill off entire tribelets—men, women, and children—throughout the 1850s and on into the 1860s.* By far the most virulent examples of such sorties took place in the northern and northwestern regions of the state —probably not because white settlers in these regions

*In an excess of delayed reaction, some historians and anthropologists have applied the word "genocide" to what happened to the California Indians. It is a poor use of the term, for it is defined as "the systematic, planned annihilation of a racial, political, or cultural group." Whatever else may be said of California's Indian-killing, it was neither particularly systematic nor planned, and certainly the extinction of the entire race of California Indians was at no time the official policy of the government—if it had been, there would have been *no* Indians left within a few years.

were any more inclined toward Indian-killing than those in other parts, but because the Indians themselves, untouched by the civilizing influence of the Spanish and Mexican eras, were less inclined to make room for their superiors. They had a way of defending themselves when put upon, and in several recorded instances initiated some killing themselves; what was more, and perhaps worse, they killed cattle, sometimes in retaliation but more often for food, since white hunters and settlers had driven off a good part of the game on which they lived. This kind of recalcitrance on the part of the "Diggers" (to most people *all* California Indians were Diggers) was, of course, infuriating; it also nourished a full-blown hallucination that the northern country was crawling with several thousand well-armed, well-organized Indians bent on wiping out American settlers, as the *Humboldt Times* of January 20, 1855, reported: "Indians of this vicinity, it is thought, are able to muster 3,500 warriors, armed with guns and six-shooters."

In such an atmosphere the response was predictable, if grisly. Proceeding on the traditional assumption that all Indians were entitled to an equal share of guilt, little bands of sufficiently aroused citizens made numerous quick and deadly raids on Indian camps and villages, killing everything in sight. The single most devastating such occurrence took place on February 26, 1860, when four undefended villages in the vicinity of Humboldt Bay were invaded, with the resulting death of 188 Indians, most of them women and children —a figure that compares well with the 450 killed at Sand Creek, Colorado, in 1864, and nearly matches the 200 killed at Wounded Knee, South Dakota, in 1890.

It is not to be supposed that such acts were condoned by the government; they were not. Maj. G. J. Raines, commander of Fort Humboldt, described what he saw at one of the villages attacked in February 1860 as "a scene of atrocity and horror unparalleled not only in our own country, but even in history . . . the murder of little innocent babes and women, from the breast to maturity, barbarously and I can't say brutally—for it is worse. . . ." His reaction would have been that of any decent man, and there were several decent men in both Washington and Sacramento. Yet the official stance of both the federal and state governments exuded such an air of fatalism that it could have been—and doubtless was—interpreted as a kind of tacit approval. Listen, for example, to Governor Peter H. Burnett in 1851: "That a war of extermination will continue to be waged between the two races until the Indian race becomes extinct, must be expected; while we cannot anticipate the result with but painful regret, the inevitable destiny of the race is beyond the power and wisdom of man to avert." Or Governor John Bigler in 1852: "The character and conduct of these Indians presents an additional illustration of the accuracy of observations repeatedly made—that Whites and Indians cannot live in close proximity in peace. . . ."

The state government, with absolutely no experience and almost no precedents on which to draw, faced a problem it was unequipped to handle; the simplest way out of the dilemma was to issue such vague pronouncements as those above, and to attempt to pass the buck, so to speak, to the federal government.* Unfortunately, the United States in the 1850s was a long distance away from any Indian policy more complicated than simply picking entire tribes up and moving them out of harm's way—as it had done with the Cherokee Nation in the 1830s. In 1852, Edward F. Beale— one of the men who took the news of gold east in 1848 and who was now commissioner of Indian affairs in California—made an attempt to fill the breach by suggesting a system of Indian reservations in the state to which the natives might be removed to be fed, cared for, and educated in the skills of survival in the modern world. Congress, having few ideas of its own to speak of, took his and in 1853 created five reservations in California to which Indians were invited (they were not supposed to be coerced, but in fact many were herded into reservations by soldiers). Beale was a solid, competent man, whose concern for the Indians was utterly sincere; had he remained in charge of the reservation system, it might have been given a chance. Unfortunately, Washington politics caused his removal in 1854, and the sole contribution of his successor T. J. Henley was a proposition that all California Indians be hauled off to a reservation east of the Sierra Nevada in order to "rid the state of this class of population." The reservation system soon degenerated into the kind of grotesque parody of ideals that characterized the similar reservations that were later set up all over the West.

On the legislative level, discrimination against Indians—by no means exclusive to California—was nearly absolute. They were not allowed to vote, hold office, own property, have a drink, carry a gun, attend public schools, testify in court in their own or anyone else's

---

*They almost had cause to regret it. In 1850 three federal Indian commissioners negotiated eighteen treaties with the California Indians; in exchange for relinquishing all their land claims, the Indians were promised a total of 8,518,000 acres to be set aside for their use forever. The Senate of the United States, reacting quickly to memorialized howls of outrage from California's legislature, rejected the treaties and placed them under a seal of secrecy. They were not exhumed until 1905, and not until 1944 was any restitution made to the descendants of the Indian signatories: five million dollars. In 1950 another award brought the total to something over ten million dollars.

*The Celestial menace: A Chinese family, complete with fidgeting toddler.*

behalf, serve on juries, or intermarry (in many of these stipulations, of course, they were no worse off than Chinese, blacks, and Mexicans). On top of these restrictions, the state legislature passed in 1850 an "Act for the Government and Protection of Indians," which established a system of indenture and apprenticeship of Indian children to any white citizen, providing the formal permission of the parents was obtained; if the parents were dead, a local justice of the peace could assign an orphan to indenture, effective until the child reached the legal age (for Indians) of twenty-five. The act was doubtless a sincere effort to provide respectable homes and education for Indian children; just as surely, it was so easily distorted through the connivance of cooperative justices of the peace that the kidnapping and sale of Indian children as servants and field hands

became quite common, the closest thing to a widespread system of slavery in California—however illegal. Periodically the government would seek to prosecute such incidents of kidnapping, but with little success inasmuch as the only competent witnesses were likely to be Indians, who, of course, could not testify against a white man.

In December 1861, Indian Commissioner G. M. Hanson issued a report to Washington whose substance is not only a comment on the practice of kidnapping but an eloquent testament to the careless brutality that was altogether too common: "In the month of October last I apprehended three kidnappers, about 14 miles from the city of Marysville, who had 9 Indian children, from 3 to 10 years of age, which they had taken from Eel River. . . . One of the three was discharged on a writ of *habeas corpus,* upon the testimony of the other two, who stated that 'he was not interested in the matter of taking the children'; after his discharge the two made an effort to get clear by introducing the third one as a witness, who testified that 'it was an act of charity on the part of the two to hunt up the children and then provide homes for them, because their parents had been killed, and the children would have perished with hunger.' My counsel inquired how he knew their parents had been killed? Because, he said, 'I killed some of them myself.'"

By modern times all such restrictive laws (including indenture) had been repealed, and it would be comforting to think that the century and more that has passed would have substantially altered the attitudes that gave them birth. Yet today the California Indian, surely the smallest and least threatening of all the state's minorities, is the poorest, least educated, most badly housed, and most neglected ethnic group in California. And there are small pockets in the state yet where the old prejudices hang on persistently, where the Indian is still described as an "animal," where he cannot get a drink (although it is illegal to refuse him), where he cannot buy or rent property providing he has the means (although it is illegal to deprive him of either right), where he is still marked by the ancient, inaccurate, contemptuous brand of "Digger."

F ROM THE BEGINNING most of those Americans who did not embrace the culture of the *Californios* cultivated an earnest contempt for it, a response that probably had its roots in the centuries of conflict between Spain and England, for it included not only *Californios* but all Spanish-speaking peoples—Mexicans, Peruvians, Chileans, or whatever. "The Spanish population of the Californias," William Shaler wrote in 1808, ". . . principally consists of a mixed breed. They are of an indolent, harmless disposition, and fond of spirituous liquors." In 1840, Richard Henry Dana called them "an idle, thriftless people," and Thomas J. Farnham was less than gallant that same year when he said "the Californians are an imbecile, pusillanimous race of men, and unfit to control the destinies of that beautiful country."

Their views were shared by the great bulk of those who came to California during the gold rush, but the line between verbal prejudice and active prejudice is sometimes broad, and it was not until American Californians began to feel pinched by circumstances that any significant contention developed. That it was inevitable, however, was indicated as early as January 1849, when the *Panama Star* editorialized in reaction to the refusal of 69 Peruvians to leave the steamer *California* to make room for American goldseekers: "If foreigners come, let them till the soil and make roads, or do any other work that may suit them . . . but the gold mines were reserved by nature for Americans only, who possess noble hearts."

In the spring, summer, and early fall of 1848, when there was "gold enough for all," Americans exhibited a remarkable tolerance for everyone, including some 1,300 Mexican miners from Sonora. By the middle of 1849 things had changed considerably; there were more than 40,000 people infesting the Sierra Nevada foothills, and it was perfectly clear that there was not gold enough for all—particularly not for the 10,000 Mexican miners then working in the southern mines of Calaveras, Tuolumne, and Mariposa counties. Verbal prejudice quickly found active form, as groups of American miners began harassing the Mexicans, running them off one claim after another. By the end of 1849 more than half of the Mexicans had given up and departed for Sonora; and when the state legislature passed the Foreign Miners Tax of 1850, which required a payment of $20 a month per man, most of the rest retreated from the suddenly hostile land of California. Too late those who had demanded the tax most loudly discovered that it was crippling enterprise by discouraging foreigners from coming to the mines and spreading their money around. The tax was repealed in 1851, and the *Alta California* issued a moving plea: "Let our Chilean friends and Mexican neighbors, the Gaul and the Briton, the Celestial and the Kanaka, hombres from the land of Pizarro and Mynheers from submarine Holland, let them all come and work with us, and become a part of us full of confidence that justice and policy will never again be so outraged as in that unfortunate law."

But the damage had been done. The energies of prejudice released upon genuinely foreign Mexicans were extended to anyone of Mexican or South Ameri-

*"Mongolian Miners Washing," a sketch of 1850.*

can descent, including native Californians, and the term "greaser" acquired a broad application—even a kind of perverted respectability when it was used by the state legislature in its 1855 Act to Punish Vagrants, Vagabonds and Dangerous and Suspicious Persons; in this law (later repealed), a vagrant was defined to include "all persons who are commonly known as 'Greasers' . . . who go armed and are not peaceable and quiet persons." All of this naturally encouraged a healthy resentment on the part of Mexican Californians, many of whom could remember when the state had been *their* country. The decade of the 1850s was one punctuated by repeated acts of banditry, pillage, and murder by numerous Mexican outlaws, the most famous of whom has come down to us in song, story, and Sunday-supplement historiography as Joaquin Murrieta.

Such antagonisms survived the next several generations (and in at least some respects are with us today), but in the 1880s a curious shift in the surface attitudes of American Californians took place as a vague neo-romanticism overcame the worlds of art, literature, and entertainment. It was an age when purple novels and trembling little poems spoke of gracious Spanish Dons and comely senoritas, when painters and architects discovered the beauty of the missions, a time when the dominant culture apparently could feel secure enough to sweetly memorialize the life-style it had overwhelmed.

As noted earlier (chapter 6), when California's Constitutional Convention of 1849 voted unanimously

to make California a free state, the action was in no way to be construed as a rejection of the *principle* of slavery—only slavery in California—nor was it evidence of any widespread desire to see black men walk free, particularly in California. In fact the convention debated for several days over a proposition introduced that would have forever prohibited *any* blacks, slave or free, from entering the state, and delegate Oliver Wozencraft spoke for the majority when he said, "I desire now to cast my vote in favor of the proposition . . . prohibiting the negro race from coming amongst us; and this I profess to do as a philanthropist, loving my kind, and rejoicing in their rapid march toward perfectability. . . . It would appear that the all-wise Creator has created the negro to serve the white race. We see evidence of this whenever they are brought in contact; we see the instinctive feeling of the negro is obedience to the white man. . . . If you would wish that all mankind should be free, do not bring the two extremes in the scale of organization together; do not bring the lowest in contact with the highest, for be assured the one will rule and the other must serve. I wish to cast my vote against the admission of blacks into this country, in order that I may thereby protect the citizens of California in one of their most inestimable rights—the right to labor."

Less pellucid orators pointed out that however regrettable it might be, if the convention banned free Negroes from the state it would be in violation of the Constitution of the United States and grounds for the Congress to reject California's application for admission to the Union. The proposition was not passed, but the sentiment behind it remained a viable force in the state until well after the Civil War. Even so, there were so few black people in California in the last half of the nineteenth century—about 1,000 in 1850, 7,000 in 1875, and only 14,000 in 1900—that antagonisms between the two races were reduced to a minimum. In the mines it was tacitly agreed that slave labor of any kind was not to be tolerated, and on the rare occasion when it was attempted (at least once with Indian labor), the offender and his minions were run out of camp. The usual laws prohibiting a Negro from voting, testifying against a white man, serving on a jury, or attending public schools were passed and continued in effect for several years; when most were repealed after the Civil

War, however, there was little of the hue and cry that attended such revisions in many other parts of the country. The "problem" was simply not large enough to generate much heat.

One notable exception to this was the case of Archy Lee and the Fugitive Slave Act of 1852, an act which affirmed the state's power to arrest, detain, and remove fugitive slaves from its borders. In 1857 one C. V. Stovall came to California with his slave, Archy. After a year of unsuccessful farming and the equally unsuccessful operation of a private school, Stovall decided to return to the South. Archy had other ideas, however, and ran away. Stovall had him arrested, but when Archy was brought before San Francisco County Court, the judge ruled that since the California constitution prohibited slavery and since Stovall could hardly be classed a transient visitor, Archy was therefore immune to the Fugitive Slave Act. Stovall had Archy arrested once more upon his release, and this time the case went to the State Supreme Court for adjudication, Justice Peter H. Burnett (California's first elected governor) presiding. Burnett, a strong pro-slavery man, took a close look at the law and came up with a decision few people could stomach even then: after affirming the rightness of the county court's decision to release Archy on strictly legal grounds, Burnett—with the concurrence of Justice David Terry—felt strongly that an exception should be made because Stovall was a young man and not feeling so well, and besides, "This is the first case and under the circumstances we are not disposed to rigidly enforce the rules for the first time."

Burnett's ruling met stiff derision in the public press, and when Stovall attempted to take Archy out of the state, he was arrested for kidnapping and the former slave was freed by a United States commissioner. California's black population—what there was of it—celebrated grandly that night, and well it might have: Archy's release was a rare grace note in the too often dismal chronicle of California's minority relations.

THE NEWS OF CALIFORNIA GOLD reached the coast of China later than most parts of the world, but by late 1849 and early 1850 it had spread throughout Toishan Province, about two hundred miles southwest of Hong Kong. Here, young men by the thousands in-

dentured themselves under the "credit-ticket" system, whereby their passage to California was paid by Chinese labor lords; in return, they sold their labor through Chinese subcontractors to various Chinese mining companies, which paid them wages. They were called *Gum Shan Hok*—"Guests of the Golden Mountain"—and their dream was the dream of every farm boy and shoe clerk who had left the eastern seaboard of the United States: to make enough money in California to return home for a life of ease and luxury. Most of the Chinese returned home only when their bones were packed in boxes for burial in the land of their ancestors.

By the end of 1851 there were more than twenty-five thousand Chinese in California, one-tenth the total population—a ratio that would hold true until the 1880s. It was not long before American gold diggers made it clear to the Chinese that they were not welcome to work alongside white men in most vicinities; that they were not even to hold claims in the *vicinity* of white men; and that any claim they made anywhere was subject to a white man's superior claim, legal or not. Incredibly stoical, the Chinese nevertheless hung in, patiently working every dry dust-hole they came upon and making it pay by sheer tenacity. The more quietly they succeeded, the more intense became American resentment of them. They worked in gangs for obscure Chinese companies and suggested an uncomfortable parallel to black slavery. Besides, they were strange—their food was strange, their language incomprehensible, their habits peculiar, their appearance outlandish—and their apparently serene indifference to the dominant culture was an affront to good Americans everywhere. In 1852, with the clear understanding that it was designed specifically for the Chinese, the Foreign Miners Tax was revived at three dollars a month per man, and later increased to four dollars. Perhaps to the chagrin of those who initiated the revival, the Chinese patiently paid it, and until its repeal in 1870, the revenues from this tax financed almost a quarter of the state's annual budget.

By the end of 1852 resentment reached a pitch of action, and so many assaults and lynchings took place in the Mother Lode that news of them substantially reduced immigration from China in 1853. Yet the Chinese kept coming, and in 1855 the legislature passed a law (later declared unconstitutional) that imposed a fifty-dollar head tax on every immigrant not eligible for citizenship. (Careful reasoning had already established the fact that since the Chinese came from Asia, and since the Indians were also presumed to come from Asia, they were blood relatives, which made the Chinese ineligible for citizenship.) Yet nothing stopped the flood; by 1860 there were 47,000 of them in the state.

When the American miners finally began falling back to the cities, convinced by now that the gold was gone for all but a few, the Chinese followed, gathering in city ghettoes (not yet an American word, but a reality) in San Francisco, Los Angeles, and other cities, competing for jobs, still dreaming of the day when they could leave the country.

Their numbers swelled remarkably when the Central Pacific Railroad began importing them by the thousands to build its line across the Sierra Nevada, and California's farmers, beginning their long search for a cheap and invisible labor pool, added their own lures to the flood. As immigration increased, Americans' fear rose to meet it, and when the Burlingame Treaty of 1868 was signed, implicitly guaranteeing China the right of unlimited immigration to the United States, anger flared in a series of riots and semi-pogroms, the most deadly of which took place in Los Angeles in 1871, when twenty-two Chinese were killed and hundreds more driven from their homes. The situation degenerated still more in the generally depressed mid-1870s and came to a head in 1876, when twenty thousand Chinese immigrants poured into an already glutted labor market.

The Workingman's Party was formed, and its goals were bluntly stated by the fire-eating Denis Kearney: "By the heavens above and the stars that are in it; by the moon, that pale empress of the night; by that sun that shines by day; by the earth and all its inhabitants, and by the hell beneath us, the Chinese must go! . . . The workingmen in California are becoming overpressed. The capitalistic thief and land pirate of California . . . sent across to Asia, the oldest despotism on earth, and there contracting with a band of leprous Chinese pirates, brought them to California, and now use them as a knife to cut the throats of honest laboring men." (For more on the Workingman's Party, see chapter 10.)

Slowly the pressure began to be felt in Washington. In 1882, President Chester Arthur signed a bipartisan exclusion bill that put a ten-year moratorium on Chinese immigration. The bill was extended for another ten years in 1892, and in 1902, President Theodore Roosevelt signed an exclusion bill that prohibited any further Chinese immigration at all, ever.

Once again, as it had been doing for more than half a century, California made its needs felt on a national level. By 1902, however, the comparatively rational economic forces that had inspired the movement for Chinese exclusion had lost relevance, and the final, triumphant act of 1902 was very nearly an exercise in sheer xenophobia, as noted by the Chinese historian, Ping Chiu: "The Chinese in California increasingly left the fields in which they competed with white workers. By 1890 economic conflicts between the races were reduced to a minimum. However, whenever the American myth of unlimited opportunity for each and every individual needed reassurance, the mere presence of the Chinese in the state offered a ready explanation for the gap between ideal and actuality. It might not be an intelligent or well-founded explanation, but it satisfied deep emotional requirements even as it vouched for the adequacy of the American dream."

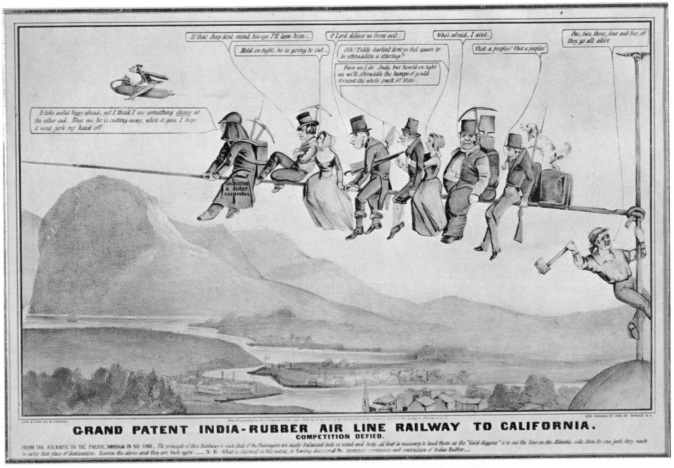

*A cartoonist's view of the California mania, 1849.*

# California Mirror:
# Getting There

*Lampooning the forty-niners, German style (F. A. Behrens, 1850).*

Before the completion of the transcontinental railroad in 1869, the most important consideration facing anyone who sought the promise of California was the matter of getting there. One could always walk (and an astonishing number did precisely that), but most of the perhaps one hundred thousand people who came over the various overland trails did so in wagon trains, creaking over dusty, well-rutted tracks laid down years before. Others, in more of a hurry, chose to endure the spartan pleasures of the Concord coaches and celerity wagons of the stagecoach lines. Still others selected one of several sea routes—via the Isthmus of Panama or across Nicaragua or through the treacherous waters around Cape Horn. However one got to California, one thing was made abundantly clear: there were no easy ways.

*"Crossing the Plains," an uncharacteristically impressionistic creation by Albert Bierstadt, ca. 1870.*

*"Snowstorm in the Sierra" by William Hahn, 1876. There may be no more evocative depiction of the travails of stagecoach travel in the West.*

If one were to believe the information in **Gregory's Guide for California Travels** (1850), the trip across the Isthmus of Panama was only a little more complicated than, say, making connections on the Baltimore & Ohio Railroad from New York to Washington, D.C.: "From New York to Chagres, the route may be considered plain sailing, and we will commence with the anchorage off Chagres, which is usually from one to two miles distant. The Steam Ship Company provides for the landing of passengers and their baggage. . . . Three or four taverns are kept at this landing by white men, one or two of whom are Americans.

"After seeing your baggage safely landed . . . your first object should be to secure a good canoe—one holding four or five persons is the most preferable. Then make your contract to convey yourself and baggage to Cruces, which will cost you from thirty to forty dollars the trip (six to eight dollars each person), usually occupying three days, during which time your pleasure will be greatly enhanced, if you have been provident in supplying yourself with a sufficient stock of provisions. . . . Take sufficient coffee, tea, loaf sugar &c., for five days consumption in crossing the Isthmus, and should there be anything left on arriving at Panama, **anything** you have is preferable to tropical fruit, **which should be avoided** by all means."

The author of the guidebook studiously avoided such matters as the lack of supplies at Chagres, the unreliability and extortionate instincts of the native canoe (or "bungo") paddlers, the mosquitoes, the moist jungle heat that sapped a man to his very marrow, typhus, malaria, yellow fever, dysentery (although his prejudice against tropical fruit may have been an oblique reference to it), or the most lethal of them all, cholera. The Panama crossing was too often a lottery played with death.

*Charles Nahl's "Incident on the Chagres," 1867, complete with Eden-like vegetation and Panamanian cows.*

*Overleaf: Perhaps the greatest barrier of them all, the desert,
where distance played tricks and heat shriveled the mind.*

And then there was the sea, always the sea, and most of those who came to California journeyed on its not always welcoming bosom. During the gold rush, they took passage on anything that would float—and some ships that did not, finally—enduring six months or more packed into an overcrowded vessel, grimly wolfing down what passed for ship's fare, rationing their water (by edict, more often than not), and risking shipwreck, fire, and all the standard diseases—with the added fillip of scurvy. In later years both the time and the traveling conditions were considerably improved, with regular service provided by ocean-going steamers and, for a few years, the magnificent clippers, probably the most beautiful vessels ever built.

Still, sea travel remained precarious—even after the California latitudes had been reached, a fact substantiated by Alfred Robinson, who once attempted to sail from Santa Barbara to San Francisco. His account appeared in **Life in California** (1846): "Twenty-one days afterwards, when in the latitude of Port Bodega [north of San Francisco Bay], whither we had been carried by adverse winds, we were obliged to heave to, and lay more than forty-eight hours drifting directly upon the land. Had the wind continued twenty-four hours longer, we should have been driven on the coast; but it hauled to the west, and Captain T——— ordered sail to be made, and the vessel was kept away for the Farallones. Five hours brought us to these islands; a short distance from them . . . the sea was covered with white foam, tumbling and breaking in every direction. It was fearful to look at. . . . In a moment the brig's bow became enveloped in foam; a heaver comber came inboard, rushing over spars and bulwarks, and furiously passed her sides. . . . Another and another sea came rolling behind us. . . . The orders of the captain . . . with the exception of the noise of the agitated bellows, were all the sounds that met my ear. . . . I jumped to the rigging, and there I remained firmly fixed."

*The Big Sur coast south of Monterey Bay —no haven for the shipworn and weary.*

# CHAPTER 8

# WHEELS, ROADS, AND RAILS

*With the energy of fanatics, Californians erect the most advanced*

*transportation network west of the Mississippi*

THAT AN ADEQUATE SYSTEM of transportation is the *sine qua non* of any developing region is a truism that hardly needs elaboration. What made California unique in this respect was that her transportation needs were massive—and *immediate.* The headlong boom of the gold rush could only be sustained if people, things, and money could be moved around and about in California with a speed and efficiency to match the emotional pitch of her inhabitants, who were first, last, and always in a devil of a hurry. With a pure American vigor, that need was met so completely that in less than ten years California had developed an internal transportation network whose complexity and sophistication compared well with that of any region of the country.

It helped no little bit, of course, that the state's centers of commerce, trade, and industry also happened to be within relatively easy access of her inland waterway system, which encompassed a remarkable spread of territory. San Francisco Bay and the Sacramento, San Joaquin, and Feather rivers comprised Northern California's first major interior highways, and for more than fifty years a clotted stream of passengers, produce, machinery, lumber, dry goods, food, tobacco, wine, carpet tacks, and gold dust went back and forth between Red Bluff, Marysville, Sacramento, Stockton, San Francisco, and a hundred brush-and-board riverbank stops along the way. These water highways were the first strands that tied together California's far-flung pinpoints of empire, from the gold camps of the Mother Lode to the wharves of San Francisco.

For the most part, it was steam that powered this intricate web of transportation. While quick little sloops, larger brigantines, and even an occasional square-rigger could be seen running through Carquinez Strait on the way to Sacramento, and while the charming and wonderfully efficient "square-toed packets," the scow schooners, continued to haul goods and produce well into the twentieth century, California's inland waterways were dominated from the beginning by the hissing stroke of the walking-beam engine and the waterfall sound of turning paddle wheels.

The first steamboat on San Francisco Bay arrived remarkably early. She was a ramshackle, narrow-beamed little Russian boat by the name of *Sitka,* which had been broken up in Alaska, put aboard the barque *Naslednich,* and hauled down to Yerba Buena in the summer of 1847. She was purchased by William A. Leidesdorff, who reconstructed her and began running her up to Sutterville, the embarcadero for New Helvetia. Powered with an arthritic little engine, the thirty-seven-foot *Sitka* was an unimpressive performer, but she continued in service until a roaring northeaster sank her in February 1848.

It was not long after the beginning of the gold rush that a substantial fleet of steamers was following in the wake of the *Sitka,* so to speak, and by the end of 1850 there were more than thirty churning the water between Marysville and San Francisco. Most of the early boats, such as the *California,* the *Sarah,* and the huge, 530-ton side-wheeler, *New World,* were eastern vessels that had made the perilous journey around the Horn to Cali-

*Donner Pass in winter; nearly buried in this scene are the ancient snowsheds of the Central Pacific (Southern Pacific) Railroad.*

*October 8, 1853: Passengers and crew of the "American Eagle" are propelled to meet their Maker.*

fornia, picking up passengers at ports along the way. Others were dismantled in the East and placed aboard larger ships for reassembly and service in California; some of the state's earliest industrial enterprises were shipyards devoted exclusively to the reconstruction of eastern paddle wheelers. Before long, however, many of those shipyards were building their own steamers, utilizing engines manufactured in eastern foundries and lumber shipped down from the redwood forests of the Mendocino Coast. The first California-built steamboat, the *Shasta,* slid off the ways in 1853, and while the records are too scattered and haphazard for us to know how many were constructed, it is certain that the state's yards contributed substantially to the total of 285 sternwheelers and side-wheelers that at one time or another graced California's landscape. Imported or California-built, they were magnificent vessels, whose construction displayed that combination of bulk, power, and delicacy that was the hallmark of Victorian technology at its best: they were wedding cakes on water.

They were also bloody dangerous, particularly during the early years, when a feral competition for the shipping and passenger trade thoroughly overwhelmed any considerations of safety. Most of the boats between 1850 and 1854 were independently owned and operated by rugged individualists who interpreted the term "free enterprise" with the latitude of an eastern robber baron, unregulated by anything more stringent than their flexible consciences. Forcing the competition's boat aground on a sandbar and even ramming it in midstream when the occasion presented itself were common tricks of the trade; and a certain careless inattention to

such things as boiler pressure while racing another boat to Sacramento, or Stockton, or wherever (often cheered on by the passengers) was the immediate cause of more than one explosion that ripped a steamer and most of her cheerleaders to shreds.

But when a group of riverboat entrepreneurs got together in San Francisco in March of 1854 to talk things over, it was not safety that troubled them: it was money. The same frenetic, cutthroat scramble that made it worth a man's life to book passage on one of the river queens had driven many of the individual captain-owners—and some of those few who had put together modest fleets—up against a financial wall, as each attempted to undercut the freight and passenger fares of his rivals. Prices had occasionally dropped to next to nothing, and in several instances to nothing itself, owners hoping to make up the considerable difference with liquor sales on the saloon deck. This, it was generally conceded, was no way to run a steamboat line, and the consequence of the March 1854 meeting was the formation of the California Steam Navigation Company, an organization which consolidated ownership of about 80 percent of the steamboats then operating in California—valued at some $1,250,000—standardized freight and passenger fares at prices with suitable profit margins, and gained effective control over most of California's inland waterway system for the next generation.

This was not the first consolidation in the Golden State. Even then racing toward the future at a speed few could calculate, California was rapidly shaking down the elements of her economic life, a life that would on several levels be dominated by the American genius for incorporation and control—or "monopoly," as it could be (and frequently was) called. In no other field of enterprise would this quality be more apparent or have more impact than in transportation, and it is fitting that the first major economic consolidation was engineered by yet another group of fledgling transportation magnates—only three months before the formation of the California Steam Navigation Company.

Where the paddle wheels left off, the wagon wheels began. As quickly as the inland waters became highways for steam, the Indian trails, deer tracks, and forty-niner footpaths of the Mother Lode country were carved and pounded into wagon roads—hundreds of miles of them lacing the foothills, gorges, and ravines from Poker Flat to Mariposa. Down in the flatlands similar roads thrust out to link major and minor settlements in a free-form spiderweb pattern. As early as 1849 these rocky, dusty arteries, primitive in their engineering and frequently lethal, were servicing an outpouring of ox- and mule-drawn wagons, long strings of mule trains, horsemen by the thousands, and an army of backpacking, footsore pedestrians in hot pursuit of the golden dream. The roads were, as Joseph Henry Jackson called them, "one of the major engineering accomplishments of early mining days in California."

The roads gave access, but it was the Concord coach that provided speed and reliability. These 2,500-pound, egg-shaped carriers were the land equivalent of the steamboats, in terms of both style and function. Superbly crafted by the firm of Abbott, Downing & Company in Concord, Massachusetts, and with a buoyancy provided by leather thoroughbraces, in which the body of the coach was slung like a sailor in a hammock, the Concord was the most efficient animal-drawn passenger vehicle the nineteenth century ever saw. Nor was it without its element of romance, for the image of the steely-gripped driver—the "Jehu" or "Whip"—guiding his six-in-hand and clattering stage at full gallop over some dusty, rutted western road is one of the most permanent memories we have of the West-that-was. Unlike a good many such memories, this one is substantially true to the facts.

The first Concord, stuffed in the bowels of a ship, appeared in California on June 24, 1850, and by the end of the year dozens more had arrived to be put to good use by the fistful of stage companies that had leaped into competition. Between 1850 and 1854, independent stage lines proliferated, lending the same air of confusion and feckless rivalry to the business of land travel that characterized inland water transportation. By the middle of 1853 it became obvious to one staging entrepreneur, James Birch, founder and co-owner of the Birch Lines, that something would have to be done. He got his money together, talked to a few people, and in January 1854 announced the birth of the California Stage Company, an amalgamation that incorporated 75 percent of the stage lines in the state, with Birch himself as president. Capitalized at a million dollars and ultimately to control more than fifteen hundred miles of staging routes in the state, the California Stage Com-

pany was the largest such organization in the world.

With extensive land and water routes established as early as the middle of 1850, California's express business—the business of getting packages, letters, bills of exchange, and money from one place to another with speed, safety, and regularity—flowered like a hothouse orchid and contributed substantially to the financial well-being of her transportation network. The state's first "expressmen" were hairy individualists who cheerfully exploited the miner's desperate need for letter-carrying. Gold diggers who were one continent and several months away from home would pay handsomely to receive and send messages, and men like Alexander Todd or A. T. Dowd were able to command as much as eight dollars a letter—no small enterprise, when one considers the number of letters a man could carry on his back or the back of a packmule. The United States Post Office, in the form of San Francisco postmaster William Van Voorhees, was suitably appalled by this gouging, but it had little choice in the matter. Underfinanced and understaffed throughout the Golden Era, the post office was forced to make do with the best carriers at hand—and the best at hand in 1849 and early 1850 were men like Alexander Todd, men who were willing and able to trudge the gullies and canyons of the Mother Lode for what they considered a reasonable price. As their reliability became established, these men also began carrying small shipments of gold dust, as well as bills and other papers, between merchants in San Francisco, Sacramento, Stockton, and the mining camps of the mountains. Todd himself so expanded operations along these lines that he was able to bill his enterprise as the Todd & Company Express.

But Todd and the rest of California's home-grown express companies were soon eclipsed by the arrival of eastern "professionals." The first was the Adams & Company Express, one of the oldest in the country, which began California operations in late 1849 and quickly absorbed many smaller companies. Powerfully geared to a program of expansion and domination, Adams & Company soon controlled most of the express business in the state, its nearest significant rival being the smaller, newer, and more cautious firm of Wells, Fargo & Company, a New York–based organization with close ties to the prestigious American Express Company. From the carrying and disposing of bills of exchange and the holding and shipping of gold dust, it was but a short step to the business of banking, and before long California's express companies were doubling as the state's most prominent banks (as noted in chapter 6).

Unfortunately for Adams & Company, the very instinct for expansion that had enabled it to gain the bulk of California's express and banking trade put it in a vulnerable position during the panic of 1855. Adams & Company folded, and while it was later reorganized into the Pacific Express Company, its days of preeminence were done. Wells, Fargo—always careful to maintain a strong cash position—not only survived the disaster of 1855, but went on to become the single most ubiquitous business institution on the entire Pacific Coast, as Samuel Bowles noted in 1865: "It is the omnipresent, universal business agent of all the region from the Rocky Mountains to the Pacific Ocean. Its offices are in every town, far and near; a billiard saloon, a restaurant, and a Wells & Fargo office are the first three elements of a Pacific or Coast mining-town. . . . It is the Ready Companion of civilization, the Universal Friend and Agent of the miner, his errand man, his banker, his post-office."

For a time the express companies were in direct competition with the post office, an institution regarded with something less than reverence by most Californians, as illustrated by an editorial in the *Alta California:* "The whole system, as now conducted, is utterly useless. It is so clearly and undeniably a nuisance, that we had hoped the press generally would have taken up the subject, for then it would in time be abolished. . . . He who depends on the mail for his newspaper, finds his neighbor who relies on the Express, will have it read through, and can lend it to him, while he is waiting for the post office to open." In an effort to stifle such competition, Congress passed a law in 1854 that required express companies to carry only mail bearing federal postage—but it made no real difference, for the express companies purchased stamps and stamped envelopes for their customers, who cheerfully paid the double postage involved for the privilege of seeing their letters arrive at their destinations with some reliability.

Indisputably trustworthy and remarkably efficient for its time and place, the express business in California nevertheless was not without its perils, principally robbery. Such colorful *banditti* as Tiburcio Vásquez, Rattlesnake Dick, and Black Bart, the "PO8" of cheerful memory, together with a host of their more or less anonymous brethren, continued to plague the stage lines of the state until the Concords were supplanted by railroad cars. The dimensions of the problem are suggested by the following table of charges for the year 1860 from the offices of Wells, Fargo, a company that went to extraordinary lengths to secure the arrest and conviction of highwaymen:

| | | |
|---|---|---:|
| Jan. 31. | Paid officers Gay and O'Neil for defending treasure in attempted robbery on Angeles Road | $1,330.00 |
| Apr. 30. | Louis McLane, traveling exp. | 2,141.69 |
| June 30. | Iowa Hill robbery | 11,811.25 |
| | Shasta robbery | 22,239.12 |
| July 31. | Judgment on O'Neal suit | 1,505.06 |
| | Robbery at Trinity Center | 1,839.30 |
| | Exp. paid officers—Shasta robbery | 649.00 |
| | Exp. paid officers—Iowa Hill robbery | 161.00 |
| Aug. 31. | Settlement with A. B. Brown, Agt, at Marysville—cash short | 1,716.00 |
| | Iowa Hill robbery—paid officers | 540.50 |
| | Trinity Center robbery—paid officers | 91.00 |
| Sept. 30. | Paid office exp., witness and cost | 239.00 |
| Oct. 31. | Paid officers reward for arrest and conviction of "Cassell" engaged in the Shasta robbery | 1,040.00 |
| | Officers' expenses, Iowa Hill robbery | 52.00 |
| Nov. 30. | Reward for recovery of portion of money stolen—Iowa Hill robbery | 778.00 |
| | Due to M. E. Mills—lawyer | 500.00 |
| | Sundry exp. officers and witnesses | 271.25 |
| | Reward officers—recovery of $1515 of the Shasta robbery | 475.00 |
| | Error Stable Acct. quarter ending Dec. 31 | 36.00 |
| Total Charges | | $48,415.17 |

Such figures are evidence that the many-times fictionalized cry of "Throw down the box!" had a base in hard reality—*expensive* hard reality.

W HILE THE STEAMERS, stagecoaches, and express companies were lacing together California's internal lines of communication, the old problem of isolation from the rest of the country remained, and throughout the 1850s numerous efforts were made to bridge the transportation gap—all of them colorful, some of them profitable.

Federal money fed such enterprises, as it had in the beginning. It had been fat mail contracts from the federal government in 1847 that had financed the launching of the United States Mail Steamship Company on the run from New York to Chagres, and mail contracts that supported the Pacific Mail Steamship Company on the run from Panama to California—and both companies continued to receive federal largesse through the 1850s, leading to complaints of a "steamship monopoly" in conglomerate-conscious California. Monopoly or no, the two lines provided the quickest and most reliable mail service to and from the Pacific Coast, a service greatly enhanced by the completion of the Panama Railroad in 1855, the Western Hemisphere's first "transcontinental" line.

The first attempt to carry mail overland was made by George Chorpenning, who set out in the spring of 1851 with a string of packmules to haul the mail from Sacramento to Salt Lake City. The travails and delays involved in the Sierra Nevada crossing, particularly in winter, were a constant drawback, however, and in 1857 the government authorized the so-called "Jackass Mail," the San Antonio & San Diego Mail Line from Texas to California. The "Jackass Mail" was short-lived, for in March of the same year Congress passed a bill that authorized the creation of the Butterfield Overland Mail, a semi-weekly, twenty-five day route that covered 2,800 miles from the railhead at Tipton, Missouri, through Arkansas, Texas, New Mexico, and Arizona to Los Angeles, then up the interior of California to San Francisco. John Butterfield, one of the founders of American Express, was no piker; armed with an annual federal grant of $600,000, he spent one million dollars and several months in preparation for

*California's first monopoly: The California Stage Company, organized and incorporated in 1854.*

the line—building and repairing roads, erecting stage stations twelve to fifteen miles apart, digging wells and building water tanks, buying 1,800 horses and mules and 250 coaches, and hiring 2,000 employees. His motto, it is reliably reported, was "Remember, boys, nothing on God's earth must stop the United States Mail!" The first stage left Tipton on September 16, 1858, and arrived in San Francisco on October 10, for a total time of twenty-three days and twenty-three-and-a-half hours (beating the steamship mail by some ten days), and for the next several years very little indeed would ever stop Butterfield's delivery of the United States Mail. By 1860 his Overland was carrying more mail than went by way of Panama.

By then, other mail was crossing the country via a financial disaster called the Pony Express. This venture was the brainchild of the St. Louis freighting firm of Russell, Majors, & Waddell, who also controlled the Central Overland California & Pikes Peak Express Company, a semimonthly service from St. Louis through Denver and Salt Lake City to Placerville, California, limping along on a measly annual mail subsidy of $162,000. It was their hope that if they could prove the practicality and speed of the Central Overland route, the government would cough up a major grant for daily mail service to and from California, one that might even eclipse that of the Butterfield Overland.

*The transcontinental railroad as dream and ideal: Currier & Ives' "Across the Continent," 1868.*

The Pony Express was their proof—and it *was* fast, covering the 1,966 miles from St. Joseph, Missouri, to Placerville (and later Folsom) in no more than ten days, and at least once in as little as seven and a half, with herds of tough, long-winded horses and a small army of leathery, nearly weightless young riders, many of them in their teens, like William F. ("Buffalo Bill") Cody. Service on the Pony Express began on April 3, 1860, and by March 1861 apparently had proved its point, for that month Congress passed a law that provided for daily mail service on the Central Overland route and a semiweekly Pony Express service; the combined subsidy amounted to one million dollars.

Unfortunately for the dreams of Russell, Majors, & Waddell, who had lost nearly five hundred thousand dollars on the Pony Express experiment (never designed to make money on its own), the Confederate States of America opened fire on Fort Sumter on April 12; the Postmaster General of the United States closed the southern mail route and ordered the Butterfield Overland to move its men, horses, and materials to the Central Overland route. An agreement worked out with Butterfield gave the Central Overland California & Pikes Peak Express control over the staging and Pony Express lines from the Missouri River to Salt Lake City, but the company was hopelessly in debt, a situation that hardly improved when a Pacific Telegraph line (also federally subsidized) was completed from Omaha, Nebraska, to Sacramento in October 1861, removing

whatever dubious need there had ever been for the Pony Express. The firm went bankrupt, and its men, animals, equipment, and share of the federal mail contract fell to its principal mortgage holder, Ben Holladay, who was busily knitting up all the strands of a western transportation empire that ultimately controlled more than five thousand miles of road.

At this juncture, Wells, Fargo & Company entered the picture—or at least, *openly* entered the picture. For some time, the company had had profound but generally obscure connections with both the Butterfield Overland Mail and the Pony Express (there are those who maintain, with some evidence, that Wells, Fargo in actuality controlled both organizations practically from the beginning). In any case, Wells, Fargo became a major force in the Central Overland route when it purchased John Butterfield's interest in the Salt Lake City to Placerville branch not long after his move north, and became the *only* force in 1866, when it bought out Ben Holladay's ownership of the eastern branch of the line. But 1866 was too late, for transcontinental staging was about to be sent into a long decline by the force of an idea whose time had come: the transcontinental railroad.

I T WAS NOT A NEW IDEA—for its time, in fact, it was quite an old idea. In the early 1830s, when the vision of a continental America was still as vague as smoke, eastern newspaper editors, filled with those gaseous certitudes characteristic of the breed, were wont to call upon Congress for the creation of a Pacific Railroad. Probably such proposals were no more seriously intended than they were received; it was an appealing way to fill up editorial space, being devoid of controversy and replete with assurances of America's present and potential greatness; moreover, newspaper editors have never been required by law to explain precisely *how* their prescriptions might be translated into reality.

But in 1845 a man stepped forward to explain how it might be made to work. His name was Asa Whitney, a New York merchant who had a strong interest in the China trade and a conviction that a Pacific Railroad would provide the ideal link to all those millions of Chinese. His scheme, put before Congress, was that a railroad run from Lake Michigan to the mouth of the

Columbia River, and that Congress should grant to its builder a strip of the public domain sixty miles wide along the whole line. He was only a little ahead of his time, but Congress nonetheless did not act on his proposal, and Whitney took to the stump, lecturing, writing, and petitioning for his idea over the next ten years.

Whether moved by Whitney's proselytizing or by the sheer inevitability of the whole business, Congress was soon giving the idea of a Pacific Railroad serious consideration—and recognizing, as well, that some sort of federal subsidy was going to be necessary, much as Whitney had suggested. Throughout the 1850s, however, the growing sectional rivalry between North and South utterly hamstrung Congress on the question of an appropriate route, and the only contribution made was the authorization in 1853 to have the army survey all practical routes between the Mississippi Valley and the Pacific. Yet the principal result of this study was the publication in 1855 of the ten-volume *Pacific Railroad Reports,* which outlined, not merely two, but *four* feasible routes, two in the north and two in the south—a conclusion which did little to relieve sectional bitterness; in fact, it amplified the opportunity for debate.

With the secession of the southern states and the outbreak of the Civil War in 1861, debate on the north-south routes ended, yet Congress might not have moved on the question of a Pacific Railroad for several more years, had it not been for the artful prodding of Theodore Dehone Judah, a brilliant young engineer who found the definition of his life in an obsession with a transcontinental railroad. After a precocious engineering career in the East, during which he helped to reconstruct parts of the Erie Canal and built bridges and railroads while still in his early twenties, Judah was called to California in 1854 by the officers of the Sacramento Valley Railroad, who wanted him to construct a line from Sacramento to Marysville. The little railroad—the first in California—never extended beyond Folsom, some twenty-five miles from Sacramento, but by then Judah was thoroughly entranced by his ambition. With his own money he financed survey trips to determine the best route across the Sierra Nevada and spent most of the rest of his time trying to drum up support for the idea in California. In 1859 the state legislature approved a Pacific Railroad Convention, which met in San Francisco and appointed Judah as

its official spokesman in Washington, D.C. While sectional problems blocked any significant progress that year, Judah took advantage of the experience to become one of the shrewdest of the mob of lobbyists who clustered like carpenter ants in the halls, offices, and closets of the Capitol building.

Back in California in 1860, the determined engineer made yet another survey, concluding that his Sierra Nevada route would wind up a long, gradual slope to Emigrant Gap and Donner Pass, and organized some of the financial support necessary to incorporate his dream—which he had already decided to call the Central Pacific Railroad. He turned to San Francisco for added money, but the city's financiers, profoundly involved in their own money-making schemes and taking a "wait and see" attitude toward congressional action, refused to support him.* In Sacramento he had better luck, for among those who came to hear him lecture one evening late in November 1860 was a local hardware dealer named Collis P. Huntington, a man with a sharply honed instinct for moneyed possibilities. Also in attendance were Huntington's partner Mark Hopkins and an associate by the name of Charles Crocker, a recently elected state assemblyman.

Huntington listened that night . . . and listened; he then invited Judah to come to his home and talk some more. Calculating to the point of cold-bloodedness, Huntington in his own way was still something of a romantic—if the term "romance" can be applied to the making of money. Judah's proposal excited his imagination, and he threw his considerable influence behind the project, ultimately convincing Hopkins, Crocker, and another associate, grocer Leland Stanford (an unsuccessful Republican candidate for governor in 1859), to join with him. This quartet would soon and forever after be known as the Big Four. The rest of the needed money (amounting to about $1,500 per man) was put together, and on June 28, 1861, the Central Pacific Railroad of California was officially incor-

---

*In his *California: Two Centuries of Man, Land, and Growth in the Golden State,* historian W. H. Hutchinson has another explanation: "This writer has gained the distinct impression that San Francisco's financiers were content to play the time-honored game of letting the Sacramento upstarts fail and then obtaining control of the railroad at a fraction of what an initial investment might have cost them. The game failed."

porated, with Stanford as president, Huntington as vice-president, Hopkins as treasurer, and Judah as chief engineer.

Reinforced by a workable route, an organization, and the opportunity provided by the Civil War, Judah once again assailed Congress in the summer of 1861. After months of haggling, feuding, wheeling and dealing—principally among various Mississippi Valley railroads vying for the privilege of building the eastern leg of the transcontinental line—a Pacific Railroad Bill was pried out of Congress on May 7, 1862, and signed by President Lincoln on July 3. Among other details, the bill divided the responsibility for construction between the Central Pacific Railroad and the still-unformed Union Pacific Railroad (the C.P. to start from Sacramento, the U.P. from a point near Omaha, Nebraska), but the provisions that undoubtedly most stirred the hearts and minds of the aspiring empire-builders were those regarding federal subsidies. Each railroad would receive free right-of-way along the entire line, permission to use stone and timber on the public domain free of charge, alternate sections of ten-mile strips of land on either side of the line, and government loans in the form of thirty-year, 6 percent bonds in amounts ranging from $16,000 to $48,000 per mile, depending upon the nature of the terrain over which the line was built.

Construction on the Central Pacific began on January 8, 1863, and on the Union Pacific on December 2 of the same year. On May 10, 1869, the two lines were joined at Promontory Point, Utah. It was one of the great climaxes of the nineteenth century, but Theodore Dehone Judah, whose obsessed energy had given birth to the transcontinental railroad, was not there to witness the occasion. In 1863, he had split from the Big Four and headed back to New York in an attempt to raise enough money to buy them out. In Panama he contracted a fever, and shortly after his arrival in New York, he died. In 1930, a monument to his vision was erected in Sacramento by the American Society of Civil Engineers.

MUCH HAS BEEN WRITTEN—and will continue to be written—concerning the federal government's massive subsidy to the builders of the transcontinental railroad, particularly the land grants, which amounted to some 45,000,000 acres. "While fighting to retain eleven refractory states," one critic of the day complained, "the nation permits itself to be cozened out of territory sufficient to form twelve new republics." Incredible power had been placed in the hands of a few men with the foresight, shrewdness, unenlightened self-interest, and raw determination to turn great dreams to their own ends, and frequently that power was badly used, distorting and sometimes crippling economic and political life, particularly in California.

Even so, the transcontinental railroad transformed the course of California's history; it ended her twenty-year isolation by cutting transportation to the East to a matter of days, vastly expanding her already astonishing potential for growth, and it linked the economic empires of the Pacific and Atlantic coasts, strengthening the power that these empires already exercised in the economic "colony" of the trans-Mississippi West. Moreover, it was not only Californians who danced in the streets when word came that the rails had joined at Promontory: Mormons gathered in the Great Tabernacle of Salt Lake City to lift paeans to a foresightful Providence, and New Yorkers, Philadelphians, and Chicagoans rejoiced; even Bostonians abandoned their composure, for the transcontinental railroad was a national dream, a national pride, and a national experience.

*Sixty-pound iron rails lie stacked in the Sacramento yards, 1864.*

# *California Mirror: The Muscle, the Gold, and the Iron*

*Crossing the Sierra required enormous fills, like this at Sailor's Spur. . .*

*. . . as well as great cuts and hardrock tunnels.*

"The skies smiled yesterday upon a ceremony of vast significance," the **Sacramento Union** reported on January 9, 1863. "With rites appropriate to the occasion . . . ground was formally broken at noon for the commencement of the Central Pacific Railroad—the California link of the continental chain that is to unite American communities now divided by thousands of miles of trackless wilderness. The muscle, the gold, and the iron were ready to make the railroad a reality."

Almost precisely one year later—December 2—the Union Pacific began building west from Omaha. On hand to document the building of the "Great Work of the Age" were two photographers: Alfred A. Hart for the Central Pacific, A. J. Russell for the Union Pacific.

*Windmill and water tank at Laramie Station, Wyoming —on the Union Pacific line.*

As the Central Pacific began to cut its way into the Sierra, the money situation seemed hopeless: "I would have been glad, when we had thirty miles of road built," Charles Crocker later recalled, "to have got a clean shirt and absolution from my debts." Another participant, attorney Alfred A. Cohen, remembered Huntington's frantic scramble for eastern money: "I have seen Mr. Huntington trudging about from office to office in New York trying to get people to lend him money. For months —almost for a year, if not more—he was traveling at night between Washington and Boston trying to raise money to send to California." With the completion of fifty miles of track at the end of 1864, however, federal loans of $48,000 a mile were forthcoming and the following year the Central Pacific pushed into the mountains in earnest.

One of the railroad's greatest assets was a force of Chinese laborers acquired in the spring of 1865. E. B. Crocker, a Central Pacific executive, described their advantages: "They prove nearly equal to white men in the amount of labor they perform, and are far more reliable. . . . We want a body of 2,500 trained laborers and keep them steadily at work until the road is built clear across the continent—or until we meet them coming from the other side." Ultimately, the Central Pacific employed nearly fifteen thousand Chinese.

For its part, the Union Pacific relied upon some ten thousand Caucasians, most of them veterans (on both sides) of the Civil War, many of them Irish. Like the Chinese gangs of the Central Pacific, they laid the rails down with an awesome, machine-like inexorability, a kind of "grand anvil chorus," as a newspaper reporter described it. "It is played in triple time, three strokes to the spike. There are 10 spikes to a rail, 400 rails to a mile, 1,800 miles to San Francisco—21,000,000 times are those sledges to come down with their sharp punctuation before the great work of modern America is complete."

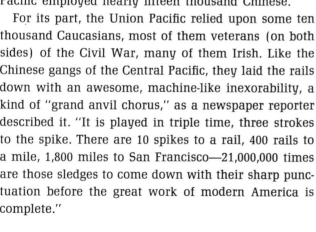

*The Union Pacific at Green River, Wyoming, Citadel Rock in the background.*

*Ten miles of track in one day: curving irons at Ten-Mile Canyon, Utah.*

Near the end of 1867, Collis P. Huntington urged his construction superintendent, Charles Crocker, to "work on as though Heaven were before you and Hell behind you," and Crocker announced his New Year's resolution: "A mile a day for every working day in 1868." By the spring of that year, the Sierra had been breached, and the rails were marching east across the deserts of Nevada. Steadily, Crocker's edict was exceeded again and again—three miles, four miles, five miles, six miles a day. "It would be impossible to describe how rapidly, orderly, and perfectly the work is done, without seeing the operation itself," a reporter for the **Alta California** wrote. Finally, on April 28, 1869—just two weeks and a few miles from the final joining at Promontory, Utah— the crew of the Central Pacific laid ten miles of rail in a single day, working from seven in the morning to seven at night—a construction record that has never been matched. Some compulsive statistician calculated that 25,800 ties, 3,250 rails, 55,000 spikes, and 14,080 bolts were used that day, and that each rail handler lifted 125 tons of iron.

*Ten miles of track in one day: the men who did it.*

*Left: Horny-handed sons of toil gather at the paymaster's car on the Union Pacific line.*

*Ten miles of track in one day: the memorial.*

*Done! The meeting of the rails at Promontory, May 10, 1869.*

And then it was done. Obeying a congressional order designed to keep the two lines from passing each other and heading off into the distance with federal loans, the Central Pacific and the Union Pacific joined their rails in the sagebrush desert of Utah, just a little north of Great Salt Lake, on May 10, 1869. The place was called Promontory. Of all the speeches given that day—and there were quite as many as one would expect—the shortest and best was given by Grenville M. Dodge, superintendent of construction for the Union Pacific: "Gentlemen, the great Benton proposed that some day a giant statue of Columbus be erected on the highest peak of the Rocky Mountains, pointing westward, denoting that as the great route across the continent. You have made that prophecy a fact. This is the way to India."

*Variations on a theme: Compare this German lithograph after the Great Event to the Currier & Ives print on page 154.*

*Overleaf: William Hahn's view of the Central Pacific's Sacramento station in the early 1870s.*

# SECTION THREE

# *The Wheel of Fortune*

The new era into which our State is about entering . . . is without doubt an era of steady, rapid and substantial growth; of great addition to population and immense increase in the totals of the Assessor's lists. Yet we cannot hope to escape the great law of compensation which exacts some loss for every gain. . . . The California of the new era will be greater, richer, more powerful than the California of the past; but will she be still the same California whom her adopted children, gathered from all climes, love better than their own mother lands; from which all who have lived within her bounds are proud to hail; to which all who have known her long to return? She will have more people; but among those people will there be so large a proportion of full, true men? She will have more wealth; but will it be so evenly distributed? She will have more luxury and refinement and culture; but will she have such general comfort, so little squalor and misery; so little of the grinding, hopeless poverty that chills and cramps the souls of men, and converts them into brutes?

Amid all our rejoicing and all our gratulations let us see clearly whither we are tending. . . . Let us not imagine ourselves in a fools' paradise, where the golden apples will drop into our mouths; let us not think that after the stormy seas and head gales of all the ages, *our* ship has at last struck the trade winds of time. The future of our State . . . looks fair and bright; perhaps the future looked so to the philosophers who once sat in the porches of Athens—to the unremembered men who raised the cities whose ruins lie south of us. Our modern civilization strikes broad and deep and looks high. So did the tower which men once built almost unto heaven.

—Henry George in the *Overland Monthly* (October, 1868)

*An abandoned tailing-wheel and (in the distance) the headframe*
*of the Kennedy Mine in Jackson.*

# CHAPTER 9

# THE CITADEL

*The Comstock Lode, William C. Ralston, and the uses*

*of economic power on the Pacific Coast*

THE CIVIL WAR left America haunted by nearly six hundred thousand dead, scores of shelled cities, ruined sweeps of land over which war had passed like a flame, thousands of bitter, sonless families—and the gray pall of Lincoln's assassination, which gave the country one more shroud in a time that stank of death. The four years of that ghastly conflict burned away much of whatever had been left of simplicity and innocence after the Mexican War. It was the single most traumatic episode in American history; from it the country emerged an industrial civilization whose strength and weaknesses had been fired, forged, and tempered by war, and America would never be the same again.

Out on the western edge of the continent, California lay almost untouched by the conflict that had transformed America. The state's pristine remove from war had to do with more than geographic distance, however. Her isolation was as much a matter of psychology as geography, the manifestation of a somewhat arrogant conviction among many of the state's inhabitants that California quite properly had removed herself from the sordid concerns of the American East, much as America itself had turned its back on the ancient travails of degenerate old Europe. In its most extreme form, this attitude—by no means unique to the Civil War years—inspired agitated discussions regarding the formation of an independent Pacific republic that would cast a pox on the houses of both North and South, as Governor John B. Weller vigorously noted early in 1860: "If the wild spirit of fanaticism which now

pervades the land should destroy this magnificent Confederacy . . . [California] will not go with the South or the North, but here upon the shores of the Pacific found a mighty republic which may in the end prove the greatest of all."

This is not to say that Californians as a whole exhibited a callous disregard for the forces that were ripping the nation apart; men do not escape their origins that easily, and the movement for a Pacific republic never advanced beyond the stage of political vapor and occasional newspaper editorials. A sizeable minority (perhaps as much as 25 percent in 1860 and early 1861) devoutly wished California to cast her lot with the Confederate States of America, and in common with most dedicated minorities, Southern sympathizers provided enough alarms and diversions to inject an element of color into the state's politics—for a time, at least. With the commencement of hostilities in the spring of 1861, whatever political clout the pro-South faction possessed dissolved in the face of a powerful surge of pro-Union sentiment. That fall Republican Leland Stanford, in his second try, won the gubernatorial election, carrying with him a healthy contingent of pro-Union advocates, and from that time forward there was never any question of California's loyalty to the North. In 1863 the Republicans coalesced with pro-Union Democrats to form the Union Party, a political monolith that held sway over California's public life until the end of the war.

Yet political fealty, then as at any other time, did not necessarily imply personal commitment; when it came

*The Montgomery Street carriage entrance to the Palace Hotel,*
*Ralston's folly and the grandest hostelry west of Chicago.*

*171*

*The mines of the Comstock, looking toward Mount Davidson, Virginia City.*

down to placing their bodies on the line, Californians displayed a certain reluctance. True, problems of transportation and logistics prevented the draft from being enforced in California, and for the same reasons the Union Army never actively recruited in the state; nevertheless, the 15,725 volunteers who joined the Union cause from California (most of whom served in various western garrisons and remained unacquainted with Confederate shots fired in anger or any other fashion), constituted less than 4 percent of the state's population of more than four hundred thousand in 1861—hardly a record worth writing home about, particularly in those years. But if Californians were less

than overwhelmingly generous in the donation of their flesh to the cause, they could not be accused of comparable frugality in the matter of money. When the Sanitary Commission of the East—the Civil War equivalent of the Red Cross—called upon California for donations, the residents of the state contributed $1,200,000 to the cause, not only the largest contribution of any state in the Union, but nearly one-fourth of all the money raised during the course of the war.

Money, in one form or another, remained California's major contribution to the war effort, for she was a new economic civilization, an imperial force whose tentacles already had reached out beyond her own borders—and she was precisely as useful to the Civil War North as any rich, friendly, independent nation would have been. In less than a generation, California had become a citadel of power.

For well over twenty years after the gold rush, the interior of the American West was distinguished by a phenomenon called, among other things, the "Old Californian"—as ubiquitous (if not quite so numerous) as bedbugs in a mining-camp flophouse. Such men, driven by failure in the California diggins, pursued the dream of easy wealth with a manic, obsessive determination, filtering sooner or later into nearly every inhospitable corner of the West in search of treasure. It was Old Californians who drifted north into southeastern Oregon in 1850 and 1851, there to discover only minor deposits of placer and lode gold; and it was Old Californians (23,000 of them) who scrambled for passage to the Fraser River of British Columbia in 1858, where even less gold was found; it was Old Californians who found placer gold above the Gila River in Arizona in 1858 and Old Californians who found it near the Rocky Mountains in that same year; Old Californians helped give birth to Florence, Idaho, in 1861 and to Helena, Montana (nee Last Chance Gulch), in 1864; California's grubby ambassadors-without-portfolio were spread across the whole spectrum of the mining frontier, from the Black Hills of South Dakota to the barren mountains of central Nevada, from the desert land of Cerrillos, New Mexico, to the icy sands of the beach at Nome, Alaska.

Numerically, the Old Californian was probably less important than people drawn from other sources, but he brought with him a body of knowledge that contributed significantly to the development of any given region—in a very real sense, re-creating the technology, law, and social structure of California's mining experience. Beyond this, the Old Californian was a symbol of California's first tentative thrusts toward empire, for behind him came California money. Profoundly committed to a hard-cash economy and entranced with the notion that money should generate more money, California was both able and willing to become the first—and for a time, the major—capital investor in the mining frontier of the Far West. With investment came

control, and California investment capital soon pulled the strings on some of the most successful mining ventures in the West—enterprises like the Homestake Mine of Lead, South Dakota, or the Anaconda Mine of Butte, Montana (both in operation today).

The monies received from such ownership increased the funds available for investment, and California interests in the West expanded with almost geometric progression into railroad speculations, land development, cattle and sheep ranching, farming, irrigation projects, banking, and the like, until by the end of the century, California money nourished and frequently dictated the economic life of communities scattered from the border of Mexico to that of Canada—and sometimes beyond both. In a kind of nineteenth century version of the mercantile system, these California-controlled "colonies" provided a ready market for the state's produce, lumber, mining, and farming machinery, and sundry hardware goods, thus providing even *more* capital for investment in the manic cycle of money feeding upon money to grow more money.

This neo-mercantilism was a central fact of California's nineteenth-century economic character, and nothing illustrated it more pointedly or with greater drama than the development and exploitation of the Comstock Lode of Nevada. Even the dimmest beginning of this spectacular silver bonanza had a California connection. In 1850 a party of California-bound Mormons —sent to the state to bolster the local extension of Brigham Young's theocratic empire—camped in the Carson Valley to wait for spring to make the Sierra Nevada passable. While there, they discovered traces of placer gold in an ambitious gulch soon to be called Gold Canyon. In the spring they abandoned their find and obediently crossed the mountains, but the news of their discovery spread behind them. The first to pick up the scent was a group of Mexican miners from Sonora, but these were soon followed by a ragtag and bobtail collection of Anglo hopefuls, and by 1851 Gold Canyon sported a typically primitive village called Johntown by those who bothered to mention it by name.

Gold Canyon was a ravine that cut far up toward the southern side of Sun Peak (later called Mount Davidson), and the persevering goldseekers patiently crept north, sometimes scraping as much as five dollars a day out of the reluctant hide of the canyon. Then in the

*The men and machines of the Comstock's "hole in the ground with gold and silver in it": interior of the Ophir hoisting works.*

early spring of 1859, four prospectors uncovered a comparatively rich outcropping of gold on a lumpy ridge near the canyon's head, and were soon washing out between eight and twenty-five dollars a day from their four fifty-foot placer claims. They were joined by one Henry T. P. Comstock, nicknamed "Old Pancake," presumably because of his talent with a wad of sourdough, but possibly because he spent most of his time, according to local legend, flat on his back. Comstock took

out his own claim, hired a couple of Indians to work it for him, and spent most of his time, as was his wont, wandering about the hills to see what he could see.

What Comstock saw about a mile to the north of the new diggings—quickly christened Gold Hill—were two Irish miners who had stumbled upon an outcropping fully as rich as the Gold Hill find. Comstock had a gift of gall and a persuasive manner; he convinced the two Irishmen that they were working on a "ranch" he was in the process of homesteading, but graciously allowed them to continue—providing he received an equal share in the enterprise. They agreed, named the working the Ophir Mine, and went back to their picks and shovels. It was on these two claims that Comstock later based his contention that he had "discovered" the great lode, and it was on this boast that the entire district was later named after him.

At both Gold Hill and Ophir, the quality of ore was richer than any the Nevada prospectors had ever experienced. Yet this gold had its problems, chief among them the blue-black sand with which it was mixed, a rather viscous material which clogged up the riffles of rockers and Long Toms—"damned blue stuff," as it came to be called. This nuisance, of course, was bloated with silver sulfurets, and far richer than the gold which was painstakingly separated from it. Blindly, the prospectors had stumbled upon the surface detritus of the south end of the Comstock Lode, a nest of out-croppings eroded by the wind and rain of epochs and covered by a thin blanket of gold-rich placer soil that had washed down from the peaks of the Washoe Range.* In June 1859 a rancher on the Truckee River Meadows by the name of B. A. Harrison and a local trader, J. F. Stone, became intrigued by the possibilities of the sand which the miners had been discarding; they sent two sacks of it across the mountains to California for analysis by experienced assayers, J. J. Ott in Nevada City and Melville Atwood in Grass Valley. The richness of the ore was unheard of. Atwood estimated that his sample was worth $3,000 per ton in silver and $867 in gold.

The ink had hardly dried on the assay reports before a contingent of insiders from Nevada City and Grass Valley were galloping across the mountains in a break-neck race for the mines, where they purchased mining claims from astonished miners for as little as two or three thousand dollars. (Sooner or later every one of the original claimholders on the Comstock Lode sold his interest to these and other California buyers—in-

cluding Henry T. P. Comstock, who characteristically boasted of having "taken" a naive Californian for $11,000.) Among these early arrivals was George Hearst, a mine speculator and developer from Nevada City, who purchased a one-sixth interest in the Ophir Mine for himself and several partners, constructed a pair of crude arrastras (stone ore-crushers), and before the first snows of winter, had crushed some thirty-eight tons of ore. By muleback the ore was hauled across the mountains to San Francisco for smelting, netting Hearst and his partners a clear profit of $91,000.

San Francisco, born in a frenzy for gold, found a new mania, as reported by J. Ross Browne in *A Peep at Washoe:* "But softly, good friends. What rumor is this? Whence come these silvery strains wafted to our ears from the passes of the Sierra Nevada? . . . As I live, it is a cry of Silver! Silver in Washoe! Not gold now. . . . But SILVER—solid, pure SILVER! Beds of it ten thousand feet deep! Acres of it, miles of it! Hundreds of millions of dollars poking their backs up out of the earth ready to be pocketed!" Browne's prose was only a little more excited than the city itself—although a certain skepticism remained from the brutally disappointing rush to the Fraser River mines the year before. Yet in the spring of 1860 at least ten thousand people, and possibly many more, streamed up the Placerville Road, trudged across Johnson Pass, down the Kingsbury Grade, up the valley of the Carson River, and finally clambered up the dry creek of Gold Canyon to the mines. By the end of the year, a burgeoning little town had been laid out and christened Virginia City.

They came with the typical allotment of picks, pans, shovels, and dreams, but the Comstock was no poor man's proposition. The ores of the district were indeed rich, but to get them out of the earth and reduce them to bullion would take money, labor, and machinery. The best of the early mines—Crown Point, Yellow Jacket, Ophir, Best & Belcher, Gould & Curry, and a handful of others—were taken up by those who could afford to develop them as they had to be developed: sink shafts hundreds of feet down and burrow drifts hundreds of feet in length; carve immense, cavern-like chambers into the friable ore bodies and timber them with massive wooden cubes; install steam hoists and huge Cornish pumps to keep the workings dry of the ever-present water; build mills to crush and refine the

---

*The presence of silver in significant quantities had been suspected as early as 1856 by Ethan and Hosea Grosch, who had abandoned the Mother Lode for more promising prospects in Gold Canyon. These brothers kept their suspicions to themselves, however, and both died before they could do more than exploratory work. Ironically, when the thin veins they had discovered were finally worked some years after their death, the silver content was too low to make them payable.

*William Sharon, general factotum for the Bank of California's manipulations in Virginia City.*

ore; and hire the hundreds of workers whose sweat would make it all possible.

In three years this kind of money planted a miniature industrial civilization in the sagebrush hills of Nevada, as described by J. Ross Browne in *Washoe Revisited:* "It is as if a wondrous battle raged, in which the combatants were men and earth. Myriads of swarthy, bearded, dust-covered men are piercing into the grim old mountains, ripping them open, thrusting murderous holes through their naked bodies; piling up engines to cut out their vital arteries; stamping and crushing up with infernal machines their disemboweled fragments, and holding fiendish revels amid the chaos of destruction." If they did indeed revel, there was reason enough: by the end of 1863, the Comstock mines had produced more than twenty-two million dollars in gold and silver bullion, a treasure that filtered back across the mountains to San Francisco and the coffers of men who struggled in the throes of the greatest game of all—the game of power.

Since she was the product of mass immigration, California distilled the best and the worst of men from distant places. Frontiers do not so much create types, as was once commonly supposed, as select them, and while California was in most respects light-years removed from the common frontier experience, she reflected a long heritage of selection: those who came and remained to prosper—and there were a remarkable number of these—did so because they carried within them the seeds of their survival. Unusually brilliant, sometimes ruthless, always obsessed with a passion for moving onward and upward, these men—for good or ill—were the architects of California's destiny; and on those occasions when what they built collapsed, as sometimes happened, it did so with a clatter and a crash whose reverberations defined the heights to which they had aspired.

William C. Ralston was such a man, but unlike many whose compulsion for power wore off the edges of subtlety and paradox in their character, Ralston remained until his death "a riddle wrapped in an enigma," to borrow Winston Churchill's description of Russia. A powerfully romantic—even visionary—streak colored his psyche, but he could be brutally hardheaded and realistic when he needed to be; indisputably a financial wizard, he was nonetheless capable of perfectly grotesque errors of judgment; he was able to make firm, quick, even dramatic decisions (often infuriating to those affected by them); his eccentricities endeared him to the people of San Francisco, who then as now were captivated by nothing so much as the presence of an antic soul among them;* he could (and frequently did) cheerfully ruin those who stood in his way, yet his loyalty to his friends was absolute, and his generosity open-handed to the point of lunacy; but his most striking, and in the end most durable, trait was his integrity, for he was one of those rare human beings who without rancor or whimpering actually accepted

---

*Among his eccentricities was the practice of boarding his four-in-hand carriage promptly at five o'clock and racing it against the evening commute train to his estate in Belmont—a distance of twenty-two miles; he usually won. Another was his habit of ripping up a piece of paper while someone was talking to him, methodically rending it into smaller and smaller bits, then reaching for another; the habit unnerved more than one petitioner, and would have intrigued a modern psychiatrist, whether of the Freudian or Jungian persuasion.

full responsibility for his actions, however outlandish —or expensive—they might have been. For that, if nothing else, he was ( and is) well remembered.

After a boyhood and young manhood spent in the riverboat trade of the Ohio and Mississippi, Ralston, like all those thousands of other young men, was drawn to California in 1849. At Panama City, however, he encountered two old friends engaged in the banking and shipping trade, and went to work for them, an enterprise which kept him on the isthmus for nearly two years. In 1851 he captained the 1,100-ton steamer *New Orleans* from Panama to San Francisco, and for the next three years made steady runs between the two ports. It was not until 1854 that he finally settled in San Francisco as agent for the Independent Opposition Line (later the Nicaragua Transit Company), a steamship venture organized by Commo. Cornelius Vanderbilt to undercut the virtual monopoly of the two Mail lines. Ralston then branched out into banking in 1855 with the firm of Garrison, Morgan, Fretz, and Ralston, later dissolved and reorganized as Ralston & Fretz, and even later dissolved and reorganized as Donohoe, Ralston & Co., Ralston's power and control rising with each dissolution and reorganization. When silver from the Comstock's first bonanza began streaming into San Francisco, Donohoe & Ralston got its share of deposits and by 1864 Ralston had become one of the city's principal nabobs, with a solid reputation and enough of a fortune to establish impressive digs in San Francisco and a palatial estate called Belmont south of the city.

It was not enough, for by then Ralston was stricken by a vision: California would become the most prosperous, self-sufficient region in the world, and San Francisco would be the richest, most beautiful, most cultured city in the world—and he, William Chapman Ralston, would do it all. But he needed a freer hand than he possessed with Donohoe & Ralston, and in June of 1864 he left the firm (taking most of the Comstock accounts with him) to organize the Bank of California, gathering about him as trustees some of the wealthiest, most respected men in the state, like banker Darius Ogden Mills (president of the new bank as well as a trustee) and Louis McLane of Wells, Fargo & Co. For himself Ralston took the position of cashier, or manager, which gave him the latitude necessary to pursue his dream. With a liberality unheard of even in free-

*James G. Fair, one of the "Bonanza Four" who would haunt the last days of William C. Ralston.*

wheeling California, Ralston began spreading the bank's money around, financing, sponsoring, or creating enterprises whose only qualification was their potential contribution to the prosperity, productivity and growth of the city and state: agricultural developments, township speculations, woolen mills, sugar refineries, foundries, San Francisco real estate, a railroad, a silkworm farm, a theater, a carriage factory, a tobacco plantation, a watch factory, a furniture factory . . . the list expanded with every twist of the man's remarkable imagination.

For the money to finance these ventures, Ralston looked to the Comstock, as other men were looking. But his sight went beyond that of others: he wanted nothing less than absolute control of this great money-making machine to assure a one-way flow of treasure into the vaults of the Bank of California (some idea of Ralston's attitude toward Nevada is suggested by his description of it as "a hole in the ground with silver and gold in it"). Shortly after the bank was organized,

*An 1867 view of Montgomery Street, San Francisco, looking west toward Telegraph Hill from California Street.*

Ralston sent William Sharon to Virginia City to act as manager of its Nevada branch, and over the next year Sharon loaned more than two million dollars of the bank's money to the mines and mills of the district at ridiculously low rates of interest for the time—sometimes as low as 1½ percent per month—giving the bank the status of the largest single mortgage-holder on the Comstock. When the mines hit borrasca (barren rock) in 1865 and 1866, the bank was able to foreclose those operations that could not meet their interest payments, thus acquiring effective control of most of the mines, mills, and machinery of the district. In March 1868 these were then reorganized under bank control as the Union Mill and Mining Company, an organization which ruled the Comstock like a sledge, freezing out the few independent mills by refusing credit to any mine that dared to send ore to any mill not under its management.

Borrasca or no, by this maneuver the Bank of California managed to lay hands on 95 percent of the sixteen million dollars' worth of ore processed during 1868 and 1869—and both Ralston and Sharon were convinced that there would be more, much more. Nor did the monopoly stop there. In 1869 the bank constructed the Virginia & Truckee Railroad from Virginia City to the mills in the Carson Valley, giving it control of ore and freight transportation; the following year it gained ownership of the major lumber companies that stripped whole forests from the slopes around Lake Tahoe and the Truckee River Valley and sent them to the Comstock as timbering and fuel; and soon after that it purchased a majority interest in the district's water company. As an added fillip, the bank also purchased the *Territorial Enterprise,* which had directed more than a little vituperation at William Sharon and the "Bank Ring." Ralston not only had economic control now, he had a good press—at least in Virginia City.

For five years the Bank of California ruled the Comstock as thoroughly as any Chinese emperor, a domination that extended from finances to politics; in an age in which city officials and state legislators could be purchased with considerable impunity, the bank's control of Nevada politics was nearly absolute—a state of affairs that eventually enabled William Sharon to buy his way into the United States Senate. In fact, during these five years only one item pricked at Ralston's bubble of monopoly—the efforts of a German Jew by the name of Adolph Sutro, who had his own kind of dream: he wanted to ram a four-mile tunnel through the mountains from the Ruby Valley to the lowest levels of the Comstock mines; this tunnel would provide ventilation to the miners, would drain the water from the lode, would establish a quick escape route in case of fire, and last—but by no means least—the tunnel would transport ore cheaply to mills established at its mouth.

It was a good idea, if somewhat startling, and when Sutro first approached him with it in 1864, Ralston was intrigued enough to give him letters of introduction to various sources of financing—and expressed the possibility of the Bank of California's participation. Later Ralston changed his mind; the tunnel's original appeal to him had been its usefulness in establishing the bank's monopoly—but that was soon accomplished by other means, and the tunnel could only be a threat. Ralston utilized his considerable influence to block Sutro's efforts to find someone willing to finance the project, and for five years Sutro floundered helplessly, turned down at every point.

But he was every bit as persevering in his dream as Ralston was in his, and in 1869 circumstances came to Sutro's aid. That year a fire broke out in the bank-controlled Yellow Jacket and Crown Point mines, killing 42 miners; by demonstrating that his tunnel would have saved them all, Sutro was able to raise a stock subscription from outraged Virginia City miners themselves. Construction began in 1869, but by the time of the tunnel's completion ten years later, the glory days of the Comstock were over, and the company that controlled the tunnel ultimately went bankrupt.*

THE FIRST WEDGE in the Bank of California's Comstock monopoly was driven, perhaps with a certain poetic justice, by two close associates of the ring itself: John P. Jones, superintendent of the bank's unsuccessful Crown Point Mine, and Alvinza Hayward, one of the trustees of the Union Mill and Mining Company. Late in 1870, while doing some exploratory work, Jones encountered streaks of rich quartz on the 1,200-foot level. Contemplating the fact that Crown Point stock was selling for two dollars a share, further contemplating the fact that the mine's owners did not yet know of his discovery, and even further contemplating the fact that he was tired of "supering" other men's mines, Jones took his information to Hayward, who had recently had a sharp disagreement with Ralston over one or another of the banker's projects. Quietly, Jones and Hayward began buying up blocks of Crown Point stock, until by May of 1871 they had acquired control—at precisely the point at which the Crown Point went into full bonanza, sending its stock to $180 a share. By 1872, the stock leaped to a screaming high of $1,825, and Jones and Hayward were very rich men indeed; they celebrated by organizing the Nevada Mill & Mining Company as a rival to the bank's conglomerate.

Ralston, reasonably enough, was nettled and more than a little worried. More than three million dollars of the bank's money was tied up in the Comstock—and at the first chance he had had to gain a substantial amount of it back, he had been done in by two of his own. Still, if there was rich ore in the Crown Point, logic indicated that there might be rich ore in the adjoining Belcher Mine. Gambling once more, Ralston sank more of the bank's money into a campaign to control the Belcher; he succeeded, and when an explor-

*It did so without Sutro, who sold out his interest in 1880 for something over one million dollars and retired to San Francisco, where he became a real estate and stock speculator, a renowned philanthropist, a champion of the people, and San Francisco's first and only millionaire populist mayor.

atory drift broke into the newest body of ore, it seemed that the long struggle was finally going to pay off.

But the biggest bonanza of them all was yet to come, and Ralston would get none of it. Since 1869, James C. Flood and William S. O'Brien, who owned a popular San Francisco saloon and a brokerage firm as a sideline, and John W. Mackay and James G. Fair, former mine superintendents, had been in partnership on the lode, patiently gathering up marginal and moderately successful properties. In 1872 they acquired a strip of presumably barren ground on the north end of the lode for less than $100,000 and proceeded to organize it into the California and Consolidated Virginia mines. After careful development, the partners struck a rich vein early in 1873; the vein widened, then widened again, and by the spring of 1874 it was obvious that they had encountered a "body of ore absolutely immense, and beyond all comparison superior in every respect to anything ever seen on the Comstock Lode," as San Francisco's *Mining and Scientific Press* later described it. The lode's production leaped to a total of more than forty-five million dollars in 1873 and 1874, most of it carved out of the workings controlled by the four men now called the "Bonanza Kings."* Following the example of Jones and Hayward, these newest Comstock millionaires proceeded to further weaken the bank's hold on the district by operating their own mills and by planning the founding of their own Bank of Nevada.

By the end of 1874 Ralston was desperate. His Comstock monopoly was steadily crumbling, diminishing his source of reserves. Moreover, four million dollars of the bank's money had been loaned to agricultural enterprises in the interior of the state to assure bringing in that year's wheat crop, and there had not yet

been any return. Another five million had gone to obtain control of the Spring Valley Water Company, San Francisco's principal water supply, in the hope of turning around and selling it to the city for ten million; that project aborted. More than a million dollars had already been spent on Ralston's most ambitious enterprise yet, the huge Palace Hotel, but it would not be complete until sometime in 1875, and could not expect to pay for itself for several years after its opening. Plummeting land prices were crippling his real estate interests, and most of his collection of industries—his furniture factory, his watch factory, his refineries, mills, and foundries—were on their way toward bankruptcy.

But the Comstock had never failed him before, and in an attempt to reproduce the Belcher bonanza of 1872, Ralston launched a heated campaign to gain control of the old Ophir Mine, situated not far from the glittering bonanza of the Consolidated Virginia. With William Sharon joining in the effort, Ralston spent nearly three million more dollars to buy controlling shares in the mine, most of them from E. J. Baldwin —called "Lucky" for good and sufficient reasons. There was only one thing wrong with the tactic: unlike the Belcher, the Ophir Mine did not and would never encounter any part of the Big Bonanza vein. Sharon learned this early on, and quietly began dumping his shares back on the market before anyone else discovered it, including his long-time colleague, Ralston. By the time Sharon recovered his investment, Ophir stock had tumbled from a high of $315 a share to only a little over $35. Ralston was left holding three million dollars' worth of stock in a nearly worthless mine which he could not resell for what it had cost him.

It was his last investment and his last mistake, for time and circumstance were about to catch up with William C. Ralston and the Bank of California; he would never live to see the creation of his Xanadu on the shores of the Pacific.

---

*Between 1873 and 1882, the year of its final decline, the Big Bonanza produced $105,168,859 in ore, more than one-third of the Comstock's total production.

*Stacking hay in the Diablo Valley, ca. 1890.*

# *California Mirror: The Resource Economy*

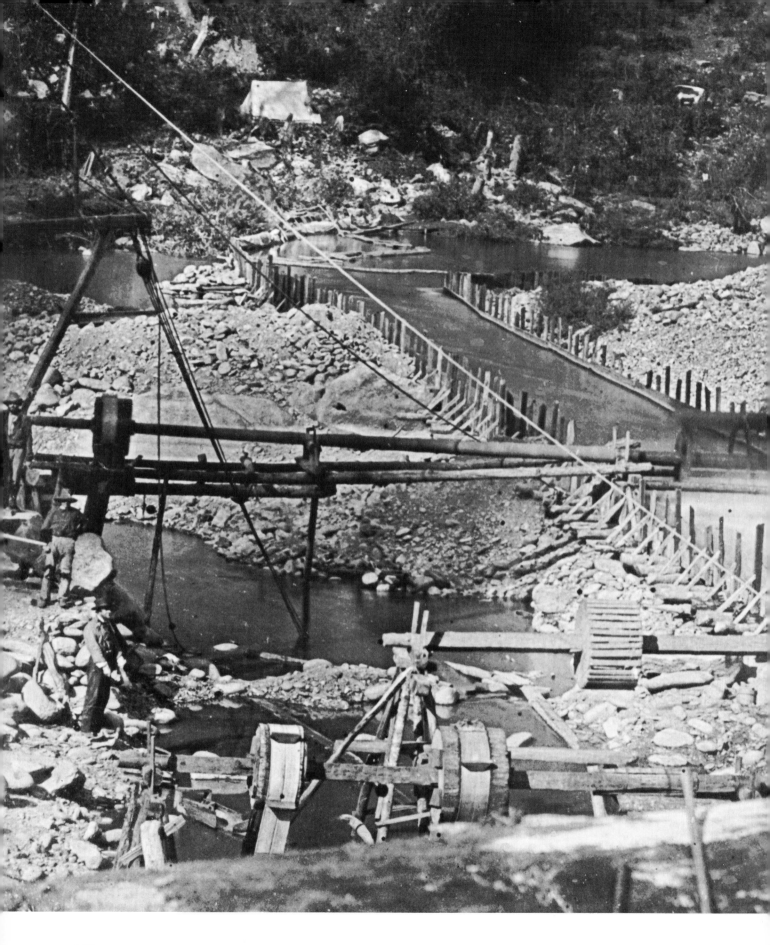

The one factor that put California several steps ahead on the road to an economic civilization was the ready availability of her immediate resources—chiefly gold, soil, and timber. Each helped support the others, but the main leg in this economic tripod was gold.

Not that it was particularly easy to get. As noted in "California Mirror: Pick, Pan, and Shovel," after 1848 and the first few months of 1849, the time was past when an individual could reasonably expect to find his fortune in simple placering by himself or with a few strong-backed friends. There was a great deal of gold left, but most of it lay in the bottoms of tumbling rivers, or was imbedded in the gravel of ancient streambeds buried under layers of sedimental deposits, or locked deep in the earth in the form of quartz. To get it, a man needed money, equipment, and a labor force of no small dimensions.

Quite early, men began banding together to form companies and associations for the purpose of river-mining, which involved nothing more or less than picking a river up and moving it out of its natural bed so that the deposits it covered could be worked. The scale of such operations is suggested by the unidentified 1852 scene at the left. The river has been dammed and channeled into a rough but serviceable flume that carries the water around the part of the bed being worked and then dumps it back into its normal course (where, if the operation was typical, it was once again diverted by another company, then another, and so on down the line for miles). The "current wheels" in the flume provided power to pump water out of the riverbed's potholes and depressed areas, and the derricks and slings (shown in the left part of the picture) were used to remove large boulders. In the decade of the 1850s, virtually every stream of respectable size in the Sierra was subjected to river-mining along at least part of its length—until the riverbeds, like the streambanks and gulches before them, were exhausted of their gold.

An even more ambitious form of large-scale placering was hydraulic mining, a process said to have been invented in 1853 by one Edward E. Mattison of American

*Technology: A California river dammed, moved, and put to work, ca. 1852.*

Hill in Nevada County. As the name suggests, "hydraulicking" utilized the power of falling water to "wash" gold-bearing earth and gravel on a scale never before attempted. Water from high mountain lakes and man-made reservoirs was carried for miles down the slopes of the mountains in flumes, then channeled into great iron nozzles (often called "monitors" after a popular make), and directed against the very hills themselves. The force of the water was astonishing; there are recorded instances of men and animals being killed by a direct shot of it from as far away as two hundred feet. What it did to the mountains can be imagined (or seen, for that matter, as at today's Malakoff Diggings State Park in Nevada County). The resulting mud was then directed into systems of sluices sometimes several miles in length to extract the gold, while the residue, or "slickens," was finally deposited in whatever river or stream might be handy.

At its height hydraulic mining was a gargantuan enterprise involving hundreds of individual companies, some eight thousand miles of flumes, ditches, and pipelines, and more than one hundred million dollars of invested capital. It produced approximately $270,000,000 in gold—and havoc for downstream farmers, much of whose land was buried under an avalanche of slickens every spring. Pressure from agricultural interests finally persuaded the U.S. District Court in 1884 to declare it illegal to discharge tailings into streams and rivers, a decision that all but destroyed hydraulicking. In 1893

*Washing away a sizable chunk of the landscape at the Haas Mine of Junction City, 1905*

*The crew of a mighty "monitor" studiously ignores several thousand pounds of pressure.*

*A gold dredge wallows in its own muck, building a windrow behind it.*

the state legislature revived the industry somewhat by allowing hydraulic mining only after the construction of holding basins for the slickens it produced. The cost of operating under such conditions proved too much for most companies, and by the turn of the century the method was only rarely practiced.

By then, however, gold dredging was becoming common as the most refined and ultimately practical of all placer operations. Wonderfully integrated into one functioning unit, ungainly dredges chewed their way across the landscape on their own little lakes, bringing sand, mud, and gravel into their innards by means of long bucket-chains, processing the muck with interior sluices, and spitting it out behind them in meandering windrows of tailings (the remains of which can be seen today in many parts of the state). Before the last California dredge closed operations in 1968, this form of mining had produced an estimated $400,000,000.

By far the major source of the nearly two billion dollars in gold produced in California by 1900 was quartz mining, beginning with the Gold Hill Mining Company of Grass Valley in 1851. By the 1880s quartz mining was the most thoroughly industrialized activity in the state, with shafts thousands of feet deep, immense pumps and steam hoists, pounding stamp mills to pulverize the ore in buildings that marched stair-step fashion down the sides of mountains, the stink of chemistry for refining, machine shops, blacksmith shops, workers' barracks, headframes towering against the sky, and thousands of employees. The names of the giant mines scattered from Jacksonville in the south to Alleghany in the north—the Eagle-Shawmut, the Argonaut, the Kennedy, the Keystone, and the rest—spoke of an age when the cry of "Boys! I believe I've struck it rich!" was drowned out by the inhuman thunder of a thousand falling stamps.

*No place for claustrophobics, with or without candles: working the face of a deep mountain mine, ca. 1885.*

*Gathering and stacking hay at Sherman, in the San Fernando Valley, ca. 1890.*

While river-miners and hydraulic nozzles were assaulting the landscape of the Sierra Nevada, the soil of California's coastal and interior valleys was being assaulted by the plow—not for what could be taken out of it, but what could be made to grow from it. The subsistence agriculture that had characterized the Spanish and Mexican eras—most of it centered around the missions —had been rudely brought up to date by enterprising Yankees by the middle of the 1850s, with the cultivation on a wide scale of truck crops, deciduous fruits, grapes, barley, and, most notably, wheat—the first "boom" crop in California history.

While the coastal valleys were more suitable for the growing of barley, since the humidity produced a variety of rust in wheat, the hot, dry Sacramento and San Joaquin valleys were eminently suited to the growing of a hard winter wheat (later called "California White Velvet") that could be harvested in the summer and shipped great distances with a minimum of deterioration. By 1856 the state was supplying all of her own

wants in wheat on 138,000 cultivated acres; by 1860 she was producing 6,000,000 bushels a year on 271,000 acres; by 1870, with worldwide commerce freed of the restraints of the Civil War, 16,000,000 bushels on 1,479,000 acres; by 1880, 29,000,000 bushels on 2,500,000 acres; and by 1890, 40,000,000 bushels on more than 2,750,000 acres. Thereafter, declining wheat prices and severe competition from Australia, Canada, and the Argentine cut into California production badly; but while it lasted, the boom of the 1870s and 1880s had made California one of the largest wheat-producing regions in the world.

Wheat-farming on the thousands of acres typical of California farms inspired the creation of machinery to match its demands. One such was the Stockton Gang Plow developed in the 1860s; a three-share device pulled by two or more spans of oxen (and later mules), it tripled the amount of ground that could be turned in a day. In 1867 a Martinez mechanic by the name of Philander H. Standish attempted to make the Stock-

*Grape-pickers harvesting a vineyard in the San Bernardino Valley, 1885.*

ton and all other plows obsolete with the invention of the Mayflower, an eight-ton steam plow with a series of rotary blades instead of shares. On one of its few successful test runs, the performance of this behemoth titillated a reporter from the **Mining and Scientific Press** as he watched it "throwing up and exposing the earth to aerating and fructifying influences of the atmosphere. . . . Surely the bosom of old mother earth was never before tickled in such a vigorous manner."

The Mayflower failed miserably, but it was only the beginning of the steam mechanization of California agriculture. By the 1890s gigantic rigs capable of harvesting, binding, and threshing wheat in one operation (combines)—many of them manufactured in San Leandro and Stockton—were lumbering and clanking outrageously across the fields of the Great Valley, belching clouds of oily smoke and tickling the bosom of old mother earth in a most vigorous manner indeed.

*Left: A hay-laden scow schooner, closely followed by a ferry, slips toward her dock in San Francisco.*

*A steam harvesting rig chews its way through a wheat ranch in the San Joaquin Valley.*

In any growing civilization probably the first resource to be utilized is timber; in order to build a civilization, one needs something to build with. As usual, California was uncommonly blessed with this resource. Billions of board-feet lay in the sugar pine and yellow pine forests of the Sierra Nevada, and billions more crowded the slopes of the Coast Range as redwood trees, from the Santa Lucias to the Trinity Alps. By 1860 there were more than three hundred sawmills in the state.

Although it supplied the mining industry (including that of the Comstock) with the wood for its flumes, dams, sluices, headframes, timbering, and towns, the timber of the Sierra Nevada did not begin to be fully exploited until the early 1860s, when the Central Pacific Railroad entered the mountains from Sacramento. The railroad enabled the lumber industry to expand beyond its local market into the Sacramento and San Joaquin valleys, whose needs it continued to meet almost exclusively for the rest of the century.

The most immediate major market for timber after the beginning of the gold rush was, of course, San Francisco—not only because the city grew with such speed, but because it kept burning down so often. The problem of transporting lumber, cut or raw, from the Sierra Nevada eliminated it as a practicable source of building materials for San Francisco, which looked instead to the redwoods of the Coast Range, particularly those on the coasts of Sonoma and Mendocino counties, where the mountains provided the timber, and the sea the transportation.

The great trees were felled and cut into logs ("take three logs and leave her" was the standard rule of thumb), which were linked together with chains and "snaked" out of the forest by teams of oxen or steam "donkey" engines. In regions near enough to the coast, seasonal floods carried the logs down the creeks to mills established at tidewater; in the more interior regions, they were dumped into whatever river was wide and deep enough to hold them and floated down to the

*An oxteam "snakes" a chain of redwood logs out of the Elk River Forest in Humboldt County, 1885.*

*Previous pages: Thompson & West's bucolic rendition of an Alameda County farm, 1876.*

*With a great white plume and a thunderous splash, a log is chuted into the Klamath River.*

mills. From the mills the finished planks, beams, and railroad ties were carried by tramways to loading points on the cliffs above the sea. Here the lumber was loaded onto the decks of one-topmast lumber schooners via chutes suspended one or two hundred yards out over the water. Standing on the deck of a ship that bobbed and rolled with every move of a nearly open sea, and handling heavy planks that shot off the end of a hundred-yard chute with alarming speed, was a job that required quick hands, strength, and a nearly total disregard for one's own survival.

By the 1880s this trade was at its height, with seventy-six loading points scattered from Humboldt Bay to Bodega Head. Writing in the **California Historical Quarterly** (March 1971), maritime historians Karl Kortum and Roger Olmsted said of this stretch of coast that it "might be loosely described as having a mill in every

gulch and a chute or two at every indentation that offered slight protection from the prevailing sea and deep water close inshore." The landing points were, at best, "outside" ports (that is, places where it was wiser to anchor in the open sea during storms), and, at worst, "doghole" ports ("big enough for a dog to crawl into, turn around, and crawl back out"). Such inadequate harbors, together with the justly notorious and unpredictable weather conditions of the north coast, made the coastal lumber trade probably the most dangerous occupation in the West; on the night of November 10, 1865, alone, ten schooners and their crews were driven onto the rocks. Nevertheless, more than three hundred lumber schooners at one time or another carried the materials of progress from the steaming mills of the north coast to the spreading metropolis on the shores of San Francisco Bay.

*With a fine load of redwood planks and a good wind behind her,*
*the lumber schooner "Big River" heads for home in San Francisco.*

# CHAPTER 10

# THE PARADOX OF PLENTY

*The demise of the Bank of California, the speculator's itch,*

*and the unstable mix of the depressed and unemployed*

THE BUSINESS WEEK of August 23 through August 27, 1875, was possibly the single most traumatic week in California's nineteenth-century economic history. "Sooner or later in life," Robert Louis Stevenson (no stranger to California) once wrote, "we all sit down to a banquet of consequences," and that week some of California's most glitteringly successful citizens ate more than they could have expected.

The catalyst for disaster was William C. Ralston and his Bank of California. During the first six months of 1875, he had spent more than twelve million dollars of the bank's money, eight million alone in his fruitless scheme to sell the Spring Valley Water Company to the city of San Francisco and in his acquisition of the Comstock's Ophir Mine. True, he had personally guaranteed to the bank's nervous trustees much of what he had spent, but the bank's treasure reserves nevertheless were badly depleted, a situation that was hardly improved when the Bank of Nevada—owned by the Bonanza Kings, Ralston's major competitors on the Comstock—was incorporated in May, "freezing" five million dollars of its own as a treasure reserve, an amount equal to nearly one-third of the available coin in San Francisco. Every depositor, however small, who came up to a teller's window in the Bank of California with a check or withdrawal slip in his hand was bleeding Ralston, and as the months passed, more and more of them came with those insidious slips—no run, but a constant, fearful drain. Public confidence in California's most influential bank began to slip, prodded along by innuendoes and attacks in some of the local news-

papers, particularly the San Francisco *Bulletin,* which was so incensed over his Spring Valley project that its editor became nearly incoherent: "Ralston's Ring is entrenched behind bank-counters and installed in comfortable chairs. His ring is powerful by reason of wealth. It is above the law. The influences which it yields are not of the bar-room, ward-gathering, or sailors' boarding-houses. Its methods resemble Washington rather than New York. Its head is depraved. It hatches the worst designs against its own body. Its dangers smack of the villa, bank and palace rather than the back-alley and slum. For all that, its bite is more vicious than that of New York's Tweed Ring."

Under mounting pressure, Ralston cast about in every direction for cash. He sold a 16,000-acre block of Kern County land for $90,000 and fed it into the bank's reserves. He borrowed on his Spring Valley stock but could get little. He sold his own one-half interest in the Palace Hotel to William Sharon for $1,750,000—only to have Sharon return the deed a few days later, saying he couldn't raise the cash. Sharon used the same excuse to refuse an outright loan; the Honorable William Sharon (he was now a United States senator) had amassed a huge personal fortune in his capacity as manager of the Virginia City branch of the Bank of California, but he was never one to let loyalty interfere with what he considered good business sense, and the odor of failure must have been strong about Ralston's person. Darius Ogden Mills, president of the bank, was less fastidious: he loaned Ralston $750,000. It was not enough—nothing was enough. By the last

*August 23, 1875: Chattering with panic and waving withdrawal slips, depositors assault the granite hulk of the Bank of California.*

*The end of a dreamer: some of the major legacies of William C. Ralston are sketched in this memorial tribute published shortly after his death.*

week of August, the bank's reserves were nearly gone. As a final attempt Ralston hauled $1,400,000 worth of bullion (most of it from other men's mines) from the bank-controlled Selby Smelting Works near Oakland, sent it to the United States Mint for coining, and by the morning of August 26, the money trays of the Bank of California glistened with piles of new money. (Though the ethics of this act may have been questionable, its legality was not. Under standard milling agreements, mills and refineries guaranteed to pay mines a percentage—rarely less than 60 percent or more than 80 percent—of the assessed value of the ore; the ore itself, and bullion derived from it, became the mill's property.

Not far from the California Street offices of the Bank of California, the San Francisco Mining Exchange was the scene of frenetic confusion and rumor that morning: William Sharon was "pounding" (selling) great blocks of bank-owned Consolidated Virginia and Ophir stock—whether acting at the instigation of Ralston in order to raise cash or on his own in an effort to cut Ralston's throat, no one knew. Whatever the reasons, Sharon's manipulations steadily gutted the market for mining stocks, depressing prices lower and lower; everyone was losing paper money, and a fever of uncertainty gripped Montgomery Street. By one o'clock that afternoon, a particularly significant rumor was in circulation: the Bank of California was in such bad shape that the Oriental Bank of London had refused it credit (not quite true; the Oriental Bank had simply not responded to Ralston's frantic cable).

The run that Ralston had feared for so many months began. Hundreds of depositors crowded through the great bronze doors of the bank, spilled down its steps, clamored at its windows, piled up in the street outside, waving checks and withdrawal slips, and chattering with panic. By 2:30 in the afternoon, the bank's reserves were down to a pittance of $40,000, and Ralston ordered its doors closed. In a little over four hours, more than $1,400,000 had been withdrawn and the Bank of California had failed. Frustrated, the milling crowd eddied over to the National Gold Bank and Trust Company across the street, stripping its coffers, then on to most of the banks in the city, who were judged guilty by association.

The next morning the trustees of the Bank of California, who had displayed a singular willingness to go along with Ralston's management so long as their salaries and dividend checks continued, demanded his resignation. He gave it to them, then signed a blanket deed conveying all his personal property to William Sharon, who was instructed to use all proceeds to reimburse the bank's depositors.* At three o'clock that afternoon, Ralston walked down Sansome Street to the bay for his customary swim. His body was recovered from the water some time later; the coroner's report attributed death to "congestion" of the brain and lungs, which suggests apoplexy or a stroke, but talk of suicide was not uncommon.

Five weeks later the Bank of California was reorganized, and its doors opened for business; in control now was a syndicate under the leadership of William Sharon and D. O. Mills, and while the first day's deposits by San Franciscans with short memories amounted to one million dollars, the bank never regained the prestige

---

*It is interesting to note what happened to that property, whose value was more than enough to cover Ralston's indebtedness of $4,500,000, with several million left over for his widow and children. Sharon, to put it bluntly, simply appropriated most of it for himself, including the Belmont estate, paying to the bank's depositors as little as sixty cents on the dollar and giving Ralston's family as little as possible. In most recorded instances, Sharon displayed all the generous instincts of a guttersnipe.

or power it had enjoyed under Ralston, whose memory was revered by most, but not all, of those who had been close to him.

Shortly after the recovery of Ralston's body, one story went, John W. Mackay, Ralston's enemy, asked William Sharon, Ralston's friend: "Did you do everything you could for him?"

"Yes," Sharon replied, "and, by God, for a while I was afraid he was coming to!"

---

THE RISE, DECLINE, and fall of the Bank of California was by no means an event sealed in a vacuum; it was both symbol and symptom of an age whose glitter obscured the darker corners of California's economic life and its profoundly unstable social conditions. Like dry rot, a fetid uncertainty ate away at California's underpinnings throughout the ten years between 1870 and 1880, giving the decade the gloomy sobriquet of "The Terrible Seventies."

The problems of the 1870s, like so much else in California's life, were the direct legacy of the gold rush and the Golden Era which followed it. For twenty years the peculiar psychology of the state had been dominated by the philosophy of boom, a condition demanding the constant repetition of spectacular success. "My opinion," a disgusted William Tecumseh Sherman had written in 1857 ( see chapter 6), "is the very nature of the country begets speculation, extravagance, failures, and rascality. Everything is chance, everything is gambling. . . ." Sherman had seen only the beginning, for the decade of the 1860s—coming on the heels of a depression from which little had apparently been learned—saw speculation and gambling bloated to such a degree that even the excesses of the Golden Era took on the aspect of marble-shooting games played by small boys on their hands and knees.

The Comstock Lode, whose silver and gold excited the imagination of the world, sent the majority of Californians to the edge of dementia. Not since the first careless rapture for gold propelled thousands into the gullies and gulches of the Sierra Nevada had California seen anything like the Comstock mania—yet there was a significant difference: whereas the gold rush had been the pursuit of the metal itself, the very *stuff* of treasure, the Comstock excitement was a chase after paper. The

*Speculation as fever: winners and losers alike mill around in the streets of the city during one of many Comstock excitements; most appear to be losers.*

lode's treasure, after all, was not something a man dug out of the ground with a spoon and exchanged for a drink at his favorite saloon; it was ore, and ore had to be processed through clanking machines and the spectral stink of chemistry before it could be rendered into bullion. If he couldn't dig it out and pocket it, however, a man *could* own a piece of the ground in which it sat. That piece of ground could then be translated into squares of paper, called shares, one square of paper for every foot of any given claim. Multiply that piece of ground by many more thousands of pieces of ground, and multiply its pieces of paper by many hundreds of thousands more, and some idea can be

gained of the absolute ocean of paper that was ultimately involved in the development of the Comstock.

During the twenty years of the Comstock's most productive life, nearly seventeen thousand claims were staked out, every one of which had its proportionate portfolio of shares issued by owners whose only dream was to sell their interests at an inflated price and return to California with a pocketful of dreams. The phenomenon was visible from the earliest beginnings of the lode, as limned by J. Ross Browne in *A Peep at Washoe*: "Nobody had any money, yet everybody was a millionaire in silver claims. Nobody had any credit, yet everybody bought thousands of feet of glittering ore. . . . All was silver underground and deeds and mortgages on top; silver, silver everywhere but scarce a dollar in coin."

Only a little over one hundred of those seventeen thousand claims ever developed into genuine working mines, and only a handful of those mines ever developed into genuine paying enterprises. Yet the clouds of paper securities which represented those mines, large or small, successful or not, became in a very real sense the principal paper currency of California for almost twenty years. The necessity for a clearinghouse to handle the sale and purchase of Comstock shares gave birth to the Hall of San Francisco Board of Brokers, later called the Mining Exchange, and still later the San Francisco Stock Exchange—even today the largest west of Chicago—and that building, or the transactions therein, inexorably governed the heartbeats of thousands of Californians, causing them to flutter in anticipation or stop dead in despair, depending on the fluctuations of the market at any given moment. For the beauty of Comstock speculation was the fact that anyone capable of coming up with the purchase price of a fistful of shares was allowed to play the game, risking everything he had on a stab at the long chance; and nearly everyone wanted to play the game, from washerwomen to housewives, shoe clerks to cable car conductors, miners to cigar-makers.

So while the power brokers of the Comstock—the mine and mill and bank owners—struggled in an earnest attempt to cut one another's throats, an army of small investors blindly threw their patrimony into the Comstock's wheel of fortune—and just as blindly lost it. They had forgotten, or ignored, or had never been told that the most important requirement of successful stock speculation is that one must be in a position to afford to lose. And for all but a few who were close enough to the situation to take their profits straight off the top of the Comstock's mountain of treasure, so to speak, it was first, last, and almost always a losing game. Less than half of the hundred or so working mines ever paid a dividend to their stockholders, and of the $125,335,925 that was dispensed, $73,929,355 was taken back in the form of assessments for mine development and improvement. In the lifetime of all but six mines, in fact, assessments actually exceeded dividends; for example, the Ophir—the Comstock's first major mine and William Ralston's Waterloo—paid out

$1,595,800 in twenty-four dividends between 1860 and 1880, and in that same twenty years charged its stockholders $2,689,400 in thirty-five individual assessments, for a net loss of $1,093,600.*

Unprofitable as it may have been for the overwhelming majority of participants, Comstock speculation nourished the continuing good health of what has been called the "boom psychology" that pervaded the state, a condition that was not particularly conducive to the making of a stable, steady, foresightful civilization—however rich. Consider, for a moment, one aspect of what might be called California's "cultural" life in this era. As noted earlier, the state's population was remarkably literate from the beginning. Its hunger for news inspired hundreds of newspapers, from San Francisco dailies like the *Alta California* to mining-town sheets like the *Downieville Old Oaken Bucket;* and its willingness to entertain sensationalism supported such efforts as the *San Francisco News Letter,* from which Ambrose Bierce assaulted propriety and progress with his "Town Crier" column, and the *Wasp,* whose front-page illustrations depicting sundry political and economic facets of life in California were frequently vigorous to the point of hilarity. As well, this population reflected more subtle literary interests, giving rise to one successful literary weekly, the *Golden Era* (founded in 1852), and one major quarterly, the *Overland Monthly* (founded in 1868), as well as the general-interest journal *Hutching's Illustrated California Magazine* (founded in 1856).

However literate—even literary—California's population may have been, it was singularly uninterested in learning as an institution. It was a full year after statehood in 1850 before the state legislature authorized local towns to establish public schools, 1852 before it got around to allocating state funds for the purpose, and not until 1856 were the state's first public high schools (two of them) founded. It might have been argued that since the state's population in these years was predominantly composed of wifeless, childless males, there was little need for schools—true enough, if one did not take into consideration the children of

*The six lucky mines were the Belcher, the California, the Consolidated Virginia, the Crown Point, the Gould & Curry, and the Kentuck.

Mexican Californians (which one did not in the 1850s and 1860s). By 1870, however, the argument no longer held water, since one-fourth of the state's population of 560,247 was by then native-born, but development of the public school system remained far behind the demonstrated need.

The fate of higher education was even more illustrative of California's apathy for learning. By 1880, when the population exceeded 850,000, only ten colleges existed in the state, and only two of these were state-supported, the rest being private or religious institutions. It was a full six years after the passage of the Morrill Act of 1862, which dispensed federal land-grant endowments to the states for agricultural colleges, before the state legislature authorized the founding of the first state-supported college, the University of California (founded privately in 1855 as the College of California and taken over by the state in 1868). By comparison, it is interesting to note developments in the state of Colorado during these years: by 1880—after only twenty years of development and with a population of only 194,327—Colorado was supporting, not one, but three state colleges. It seems reasonable to assume that for more than a generation most Californians simply did not consider the education of their children important enough to warrant the spending of their money.*

EDUCATION (or the lack of it) was the least of California's problems as it approached the 1870s, however aptly that problem illustrated the state's sluggardly approach toward building for the future. Others were more visible and possessed more immediate impact, and all of them were aggravated, if not caused, by the completion of the transcontinental railroad, whose long-term contribution to the state's growth cannot be argued, but whose short-term effect was almost crippling. Amid all the fervent predictions of unparalleled prosperity that anticipated the railroad's completion, the percipient, rational voice of Henry George (his

*The state's second major university was not founded until 1891, when Leland Stanford utilized his own money and his own land to establish the Leland Stanford Junior University some forty miles south of San Francisco.

*Progress and Poverty* will be discussed in chapter 11) cooly noted in the October 1868 issue of the *Overland Monthly* the pitfalls facing the future of the state: "And this in general is the tendency of the time, and of the new era opening before us: to the great development of wealth; to concentration; to the differentiation of classes; to less personal independence among the many and the greater power of the few. . . . Connected more closely with the rest of the nation, we will feel more quickly and keenly all that affects it. We will have to deal, in time, with all the social problems that are forcing themselves on older communities . . . with one of them, the labor question, rendered peculiarly complex by our proximity to Asia. . . . Let us not imagine ourselves in a fool's paradise, where the golden apples will drop into our mouths. . . ."

Few were listening. California land and lot speculators briskly laid out new developments in anticipation of the expected influx of immigrants and a corresponding rise in land values, while merchants laid in heavy inventories and manufacturers made plans for the expansion that ready access to eastern markets surely would demand. What happened, of course, was that a flood of goods from the East, particularly from Chicago, streamed into California almost immediately, glutting the market. California's business interests, hampered by the high cost of raw materials and high wages, simply could not compete, as Asbury Harpending, one of those affected, later recalled: "For months we had been living in a fool's paradise over the boom that the railroad would bring. That day came, but what a disappointment! . . . For the business people it spelled ruin. It brought an avalanche of goods from St. Louis, Chicago, and New York, at prices our local men could not meet. Many firms failed, some consolidated, some retired from business. Rents dropped like lead, real estate values shriveled to nothing. It was ten years before those values recovered to 1869 levels." (In San Francisco, real estate transactions had averaged $3,500,-000 a month through most of 1869; the following year, that average plunged to $1,300,000.)

In 1870 Samuel Bowles, a visitor from Massachusetts, commented in a letter home that "All of the great interests of the state are depressed. . . . Several thousand laborers are reported idle in San Francisco alone, and 50,000 to 100,000 in the state . . . ." Much of this army of

**CAN ANY WHITE LABORER AFFORD TO VOTE FOR AH-SING BOOTH GORHAM AND Cº AT THE COMING ELECTIONS NOT FOR JOSEPH**
**YOU KNOW HOW IT IS YOURSELF!**

*All the ills of "The Terrible Seventies"—unemployment, the unavailability of land, depression,*
*and starving widows—were ascribed to the twin evils of monopoly and Chinese labor.*

unemployed—which, even at the estimate of 50,000, amounted to perhaps 30 percent of California's total labor force in 1870—was made up of farm workers, as a drought in the winter of 1869–70 proved ruinous to many interior farms, reducing the demand for seasonal labor. Again, the influence of the transcontinental railroad aggravated an existing problem, for as the national depression of 1873 staggered the East, it sent thousands of unemployed men and their families to California, whose appeal as a land of gold and opportunity had not diminished. Between 1873 and 1875, 262,000 people arrived in California, most of them by rail, and at least

25 percent of them factory hands. What they found when they reached California, of course, were conditions that approached the worst the East could offer.

This unstable mix of the depressed and unemployed was stirred to the point of explosion by the presence of the Chinese. The completion of the transcontinental railroad released anywhere between fifteen and twenty thousand Chinese laborers, most of whom drifted back to California's urban enclaves and interior farms to compete for jobs. Added to this total was an influx of nearly eighty thousand Chinese immigrants between 1870 and 1875, each and every one of whom was willing to work for wages far below those of Caucasian levels. The temptation to employ them, in the face of the most virulent depression the state had yet seen, was nearly irresistible, and by the latter 1870s the Chinese were not only in competition with white workers, their labor population comprised 20 percent of the total working population in the state—a percentage twice that of the ratio of Chinese to the rest of California's population. Among other trades, the Chinese represented 52 percent of the boot- and shoemakers, 44 percent of the brickmakers, 84.4 percent of the cigar makers, and 32 percent of the woolen mill operators. The problem was undeniably real.

By the middle of the 1870s, then, the malaise that Henry George had predicted in 1868 was upon California. Great wealth had indeed been made and had indeed been concentrated in the hands of a few men and corporations; the relatively even distribution of wealth that had marked the Golden Era was thrown out of balance by the money and power that had been acquired by the exploiters of the Comstock, the builders of the state's railroads, and the largest of the landowners (for more on both of the last two, see chapter 11). Rigid class lines had indeed been drawn in a state that once prided itself on the looseness of its economic divisions; the average workingman in California could no longer consider himself a potential entrepreneur simply biding his time before striking it rich in one way or another. He *was* a workingman and his class was the working class. Deprived of the buffer of time and space, California now felt most keenly indeed the difficulties of the American East; the failure of the Bank of California in 1875 was its single most dramatic manifestation, and it would be more than a decade before the state's economy fully recovered. Finally, the labor question had indeed been rendered "peculiarly complex" by a continuing immigration from the coast of China.

It was a new society for California, and it bubbled with discontent. Unemployed workers from all over the state wandered into San Francisco, congregating on street corners and vacant lots to mutter darkly about their condition and cast baleful glances at the monuments to other men's wealth all around them. On the night of July 23, 1877, six or seven thousand gathered on a sandlot across from San Francisco's City Hall to express sympathy for workers in the great Pennsylvania Railroad strike of that year. Generally peaceful, the meeting took on an ugly tone when some lunatic fired a couple of shots into the crowd, wounding two workers; police apprehended him before he found himself at the wrong end of a rope, but the meeting was finally climaxed when a small contingent of workers split from the meeting and ran amok for a time, burning several Chinese laundries in the process.

The city's "better element," long apprehensive of a major riot among the local unemployed, gathered the next afternoon in the Chamber of Commerce and elected a Committee of Public Safety under the leadership of William T. Coleman. With some experience in extra-legal law enforcement, the old vigilante recruited a defense force of five thousand men, armed them with good hickory pickhandles, and sent them out to patrol the city streets. This "Pickhandle Brigade" came in handy two nights later, when a mob attempted to burn the docks of the Pacific Mail Steamship Company, said to be the largest single carrier of Chinese laborers. The docks were protected, but four men were killed, several wounded, and a nearby lumber yard went up in flames. No further rioting occurred, and a few days later the committee's army was disbanded, replaced by 150 special police financed by agitated property owners.

Over the next few months San Francisco's laborers gradually coalesced into a unified body called the Workingmen's Party of California, largely through the organizational efforts of Denis Kearney, a former sailor, the owner of a small drayage concern, and strangely enough, a recent soldier in Coleman's Pickhandle Brigade. With much arm-waving, pungent oratory, and the ever-present cry of "The Chinese must go!" Kearney addressed meeting after meeting on the sandlots of San Francisco throughout the summer and fall of 1877, was once arrested for inciting to riot (although no riot had occurred), and when the Workingmen's Party was officially organized, emerged as its president.

The following spring the Workingmen's Party got its first test of political strength. For two decades there had been a steady criticism of the state constitution of 1849 as being too brief and general for the needs of the more complicated times which followed its adoption. The problems of the 1870s sharpened such criticisms, and during the elections of September 1877 a referendum was passed authorizing a convention to lay out a

*Denis Kearney, whose cry of "The Chinese must go!" articulated frustration.*

new constitution. The election for delegates to this convention was held in June 1878, and at its conclusion the Workingmen had demonstrated remarkable strength: of the 152 delegates chosen, 51 were Workingmen, 78 nonpartisans (most a combination of Democrats and Republicans who had fused in an effort to undercut the convention's domination by Workingmen, but the nonpartisans included several small farmers representing the interests of the Grange, or Patrons of Husbandry), 11 Republicans, 10 Democrats, and 2 Independents.

The Workingmen's Party carried an impressive list of demands to the convention, which assembled on September 28, 1878: an eight-hour day, direct election of United States senators, a compulsory education law, the regulation of banks and railroads, a state board of equalization to enforce a more equitable system of taxation, and the prohibition of the use of Chinese labor by corporations or in public works. By combining with Granger representation to pass articles on which they could both agree—such as tax equalization, railroad regulation, and the regulation of corporations and banks—the Workingmen's Party effected most of its desired reforms, not including the eight-hour day or the direct election of senators; but necessary compromises so disaffected party membership that when the document was ratified in May 1879, the Workingmen's Party of San Francisco rejected it overwhelmingly. Statewide, the constitution was approved by a thin majority of eleven thousand votes.

What the convention of 1878–79 produced was one of the longest constitutions in the world, many times longer than that of the United States, and one of the most detailed and confusing ever contrived by any body of freemen anywhere, anytime. As a result California's

constitution has been amended more than three hundred times since its adoption. Virtually none of the reforms written into it ever proved effective; the methods used by corporations, banks, and railroads to evade or postpone conforming to regulations were the best that money could buy, and they generally gutted the power of regulatory agencies. Even the Chinese question lost much of its force with the passage of the exclusion bill of 1882 (see chapter 7).

The Workingmen's Party, the first political expression of California's laboring class, quickly disintegrated into various partisan fragments that were absorbed by larger entities. By 1882, it had disappeared—and with it disappeared the first and last major influence labor would have on the political destiny of the state during the nineteenth century.

A new society had evolved on the western edge of the continent in the decade of the 1870s, a society altogether too similar in too many respects to the tangled milieu of the industrial civilization that dominated the American East for the remainder of the century. The 1880s would see steady improvement in the general economic scene, but the problems bred in "The Terrible Seventies" would continue to shape both the character and quality of California's life well into the twentieth century.

"The California of the new era will be greater, richer, more powerful than the California of the past," Henry George had written in 1868, "but will she still be the same California whom her adopted children, gathered from all climes, love better than their own mother lands . . . ?" The prophet must face two unnerving possibilities when he imparts such wisdom: that he will be proved wrong—and that he will be proved right.

*A pair of romantics, old enough to know better, negotiate Lover's Leap in Southern California, 1898.*

# California Mirror:
# Having Fun

As noted elsewhere in this book, posterity owes a tremendous debt to the photographers of the nineteenth century, amateur and professional alike. Not only did they leave us a most useful record of the places and events of a time called history, helping us to understand the character of the forces that shaped the past, they have given us a broad and compelling portrait of the past's very essence: its people. Famous, infamous, and anonymous, the faces stare across the decades of time, projecting an uncanny sense of reality and immediacy, speaking of pride, humor, passion, fear, and foible.

What we are apt to forget when considering, as we must, such weighty matters as economics, politics, and social upheaval, is that, to most people of any given time or place, the concerns of daily living assume far more importance than the outcome of a gubernatorial election or the economic policies of any man or group of men. For every person who joined Denis Kearney in his rantings against the Chinese, there might have been a thousand who would have had difficulty recalling his name; for every individual who brooded over the evils of monopoly, another thousand might have brooded over unpaid bills, the slight received at a Friday-night soiree, or a sore tooth. The photographs remind us, when we allow them to speak to us, that we are dealing essentially not with parched statistics but with terribly human beings. And at no time are people more human than when they are having fun.

*Communing with nature (more or less) in Golden Gate Park, San Francisco, 1880.*

*Hikers in the San Fernando Valley, ca. 1890. Did the bucket carry chicken wings and beer, or just chicken feed?*

Nineteenth-century Californians—particularly those in Southern California—were wont to take their pleasures in the out-of-doors, even as today. On the previous two pages, the simplest form of recreation of all is demonstrated—walking, whose delights people began to lose when they attached themselves to four rubber-tired wheels and a gasoline engine. The oddly mixed group on page 210 has paused during a stroll through Golden Gate Park; what the young man's gesture signifies is anybody's guess. The charming quartet on page 211 has apparently interrupted a Sunday hike to feed the chickens. The top hat seems out of place for either occupation.

Probably the most popular social institution of the nineteenth century—at least in California, whose climate encouraged it—was the holiday picnic. Almost any occasion would do—the Fourth of July, a birthday, a wedding reception, or simply the occurrence of Sunday. The occasion that prompted the splendid document on the right was a subdivision sale at Lakeside, near San Diego, in 1887. The picture is a testament to fun: the skewed, perhaps bibulous expression on the face of the woman at the left end of the table; the portly bandleader with his magnificent uniform open to catch a breeze; the antic gaze of the man with the well-waxed moustache; the inevitable clown with the upturned bottle; the dear old gentleman with his comfortable paunch, his cigar, his straw boater; and most captivating of all, the beautiful imp peering over the shoulder of a most handsome young man—if the two were not together, they should have been. Whether or not any of these people bought or sold lots, won or lost money, it is obvious that they were having a fine time.

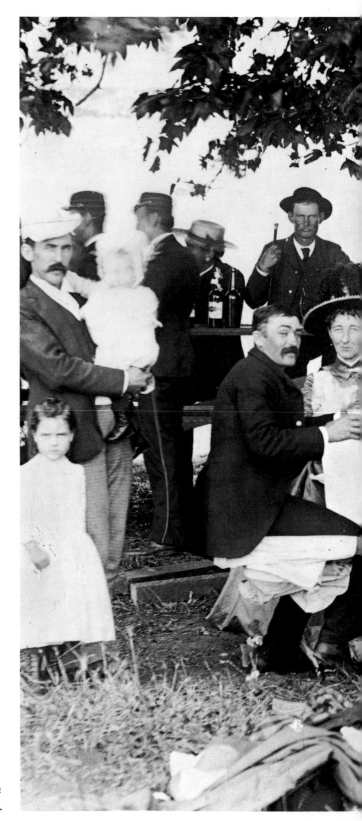

*Picnickers at Lakeside, 1887. Note the man with the bottle; there is one in every crowd.*

Water sports: When Californians were not walking or picnicking, they were liable to be off "bathing" somewhere. Three varieties of this pastime are presented here. Directly below, the term "old swimming hole" is given stunning definition by a scene on a San Diego ranch; the lad with the pinched expression seems unconvinced that the water is fine and appears destined for rotten-egg classification. On the top of the facing page is a beach scene at Santa Monica; while the somewhat bohemian gentleman in the center of the picture looks downright rakish in his swimming suit, the ladies look lumpish and uncomfortable in theirs (one wonders if they ever managed to get wet in such outfits).

In San Francisco, where swimming holes were in short supply and the beaches were usually cold and always dangerous, Adolph Sutro's splendiferous Tropical Baths (at the bottom of the opposite page) institutionalized swimming for the masses. Fed by the tidal surge of the ocean and warmed by the "greenhouse effect" of the huge glassed-in building, Sutro's immense pool remained in almost continuous service from 1896 to the mid-1950s (the building was destroyed by fire ten years later). The populace of the day was suitably impressed; one newspaper reporter was nearly overcome on opening day: "The baths rival in magnitude, utility, and beauty the famous abluvian resorts of Titus, Caracalla, Nero, or Diocletian. . . . These wonderful expressions of architectural skill—airy, graceful yet substantial. . . . Thus have the tides been harnessed and made subservient to the multitudes."

*Sea, sand, sun, and fun: beachcombers enjoying themselves at Santa Monica, ca. 1895.*

*The good old summertime defined: a swimming hole on the La Vida Ranch near San Diego, ca. 1900.*

*Sutro's Tropic Baths at the ocean's edge in San Francisco.*

One of the accepted modes of having fun was by subjecting oneself to potential mutilation or death on "rides" of one kind or another. One of the most spectacular of these was the Mount Lowe Railway of Thaddeus Sobreski Coulincourt Lowe, who might better have been remembered as a balloon-spy during the Civil War or as the scientist whose little mountaintop astronomical observatory ultimately became the famous Mount Wilson Observatory. Nevertheless, his railway was a major tourist attraction for more than twenty-five years. It was called "the trip of a lifetime," and judging from the view shown below, one would not care to argue with the description. Another popular ride was "The Chutes," examples of which could be found in both Los Angeles and San Francisco. One can almost feel the jolt as the little boat hits the water, feel the head snapping back, the muscles of the neck begin to tear . . .

*Rounding the bend on Thaddeus S.C. Lowe's Mount Lowe Railway on opening day, July 4, 1893.*

*Shooting "The Chutes" in Los Angeles, 1900.*

Ladies of the day were wont to engage in more genteel amusements than shooting "The Chutes." Proper ladies (that is, those with the leisure that affluence provided) pursued any number of gracefully vigorous activities, including croquet, horseback riding, bicycling, lawn tennis, and—as these photographs demonstrate—rowing and archery; rather odd, perhaps, but unarguably genteel. (That the two last-named exercises were extremely good for the development of the pectoral muscles was a fact probably not known among these ladies or, if known, not discussed.) Particularly impressive in the photograph of the San Diego Rowing Club is the starched and sparkling elegance of the uniforms. The archery scene is somewhat disturbing, however. Where has the arrow gone? Are the women in the center of the picture perhaps standing a bit too close to the archerette's line of fire?

*An afternoon of archery at San Diego's Hotel Del Coronado, 1900.*

218

*A morning at the oars for the ladies of
the San Diego Rowing Club, 1899.*

*Fun can also be good for you: the interior of Woodward's Museum, San Francisco.*

For more than a generation, Woodward's Gardens, opened in 1866, provided San Franciscans with a wide variety of sights and activities: camel rides, picnic areas, parades, concerts, animals (both stuffed and caged), an eight-foot Chinese who had to be supported by two six-foot Caucasians in order to walk, even a museum where the youngsters could be exposed (however reluctantly) to the refining influences of art.

*The entrance to San Francisco's world of oddities and excitements—including "California Lions!"*

*Negotiating the camel's hump in Woodward's Gardens.*

Southern California had no eight-foot Chinese, but it did have several ostrich farms, where the birds were at first raised for the sale of their tail feathers. When feather boas went out of style, some talk of attempting to market the birds' eggs went the rounds; nothing ever came of that idea, and the only profit the birds could contribute was as tourist attractions. Fifty cents or so enabled a customer to watch the creatures gobble down whole oranges and do other strange and exotic tricks. It was also possible to ride one—although not recommended, since a grown ostrich can kick a man to death.

Even more intriguing to the tourist was an alligator farm not far from Pasadena. One of the most popular attractions of this enterprise was the enclosure for infant alligators, as shown below. The scene prompts several questions: What is the point of the photograph? Where are the child's parents? Is it a good idea to have a toddler picking up things like that? Is that darling child about to eat the little beggar?

*A ride unconditionally guaranteed to be thrilling—and brief.*

*Trifling with baby alligators, Pasadena, 1900.*

THE CURSE OF CALIFORNIA.

# CHAPTER 11

# FEATURES PECULIAR AND DANGEROUS

*The tentacles of dread Monopoly stretch out for control*

*of California's nineteenth-century life*

ONE FACTOR REMAINED CONSTANT through all the vicissitudes of California's nineteenth-century development, through all the dips, spurts, and detonations of her economic and social evolution. That factor was land—or, more accurately, land monopoly. From the moment the first exhausted, hungry party of overlanders stumbled down the western slopes of the Sierra Nevada in 1841 and found that much of the land of milk and honey had been staked out in chunks of a size to rival most of the counties from which they had sprung, the concentration of California's land in the hands of a few was a fact of life that profoundly affected the entire fabric of her society.

It was a condition that violated the frontier experience, altering patterns that had been established when the first nauseous settler from England weaved ashore at Jamestown in 1607. As the cutting edge of the westward movement pushed across the Allegheny Mountains into the valley of the Ohio River, filling up the rich bottomlands of the Old Northwest, as it spilled through the Cumberland Gap into Kentucky and Tennessee and the rich valleys of the Mississippi and its tributaries, there was always one thing settlers could count on: good, bad, or indifferent, the land was there. For the first time since the dimmest beginnings of European civilization, there was land enough for all, and around this availability America built an entire culture, as outlined by Henry Clay in 1842: "Pioneers of a more adventurous character, advancing before the tide of emigration, penetrate into the uninhabited regions of the West. They apply the axe to the forest,

which falls before them, or the plough to the prairie, deeply sinking its share in the unbroken wild grasses in which it abounds. They build houses, plant orchards, enclose fields, cultivate the earth, and rear up families around them." Such land-breakers were the strength of America, it was believed, and to perpetuate their kind the federal government had passed a series of laws designed to increase the availability of land, climaxing with the Homestead Act of 1862.

In California that tradition, deeply rooted in the nation's image of itself, came to a nearly dead stop as the homestead culture of the Anglo met the ranchero culture of the *Californio* head-on. Accustomed to measuring his land in square leagues and using it for cattle graze, the *Californio* had little sympathy for the concept of the small, self-sufficient family farm; for his part, the Anglo settler could not bring himself to understand how any man could want or *need* all that land—it was greedy, selfish, and quite typical of a civilization hopelessly behind the progressivism of America. The resulting squatters' revolts and riots were as bitter as they were inevitable.

The massive estates of the *Californios*, of course, were eventually eaten away by years of litigation, taxation, and poor management, but it could have been little comfort to the settlers who had first challenged their concepts of land use. For the bulk of those lands fell into the clutches of speculators of one kind or another who viewed a piece of ground as a commodity—money to be used for the generation of more money. The land speculator was by no means unique to Cali-

*Never a publication that could be accused of subtlety, the* Wasp
*of San Francisco made its position on the railroad perfectly clear.*

223

fornia; he was, in fact, endemic to the American scene, from the time land jobbers lined up proxies for head-right warrants in seventeenth-century tidewater Virginia to the time land sharks hired armies of squatters to pre-empt government lands in the Midwest of the 1840s. But California did offer an uncommon opportunity to such men. On other frontiers speculators had been forced to manipulate ownership of pieces of the public domain; in California, to their delight, they found immense tracts of land in private ownership, held by men under constant harassment from squatters, government investigation of their titles, legal battles, and an uncertain and suddenly confusing financial atmosphere. Most of these owners were simply unequipped to deal with the situation, a state of affairs which proved fertile ground, so to speak, for those with the speculator's itch. For one example, in 1850 speculators laid out the township of Oakland on the San Antonio rancho of Don Luis Peralta, across the Bay from San Francisco; unfortunately, Don Luis, dead set against the urbanization of his land, neither sold them the land nor gave them permission to use it. Yet the speculators went ahead and sold their lots, confident that time and a growing town would eventually render the question of title irrelevant; they were proved precisely correct.

FOR ANOTHER, more dramatic example, consider what happened to the little empire owned by Don Abel Stearns in Southern California. A native of Massachusetts, Stearns had arrived in California in 1829 after a brief career in Mexico, during which he became a naturalized citizen. Like Thomas Larkin in Monterey, Stearns set up shop in Los Angeles as a merchant, trader, and "go-between" for the hide and tallow business. Over the next thirty years, through foreclosures and outright purchase, Stearns gathered up land until by 1862 he owned more than 200,000 acres in the Los Angeles–San Bernardino area. Like those from whom he had acquired his land, however, Stearns was badly overextended by that time, deeply in debt and owing thousands of dollars in delinquent taxes. The six years of periodic drought that followed the flood season of 1861–62 further crippled him, and in 1868 he was forced to sell 177,796 acres to the Los Angeles and San Bernardino Land Company (one of whose officers was

none other than Sam Brannan, still wheeling and dealing in grand fashion); the purchase price was $1.50 the acre, not a bad price for an area that would ultimately comprise a good portion of the twentieth century's definitive megalopolis.

Circumstances and an ever-willing phalanx of speculators, then, perpetuated the land-tenure system of the Mexican era, removing vast acreage from cheap access to small farmers. And with the force of a juggernaut, the system moved from Mexican grant lands into the public domain. By the use of "dummy" entries (a device so old in America that it was almost respectable), "land prospectors" took full advantage of the provisions of the Preemption Act of 1841 and the Homestead Act of 1862 to lay hands on millions of acres of federal land in the 1850s and 1860s. Millions more became accessible to them through the state itself, which had been granted two million acres of "swamp and overflow" lands in 1850, and another six million from the Morrill Land Grant College Act of 1862. The state administered these federal grants with what can only be called, politely, a certain laxity; the definition of what constituted a "swamp," for example, could be as loose as any speculator might have desired, and large sections of some of the richest land in the state were sold under conditions that approached outright fraud—not only were various enterpreneurs allowed to buy such land at the standard $1.25 an acre, the money was refunded if they "swore" they had spent an equal amount to reclaim the land, much of which was wet only during the rainy season.

The Desert Land Act of 1877 offered yet another opportunity, since it was designed to provide access to 640-acre parcels, rather than the 160-acre units applicable to the Homestead Act. Under its provisions a man could obtain tentative title to 640 acres of arid (i.e., less than 20 inches of annual rainfall) land for twenty-five cents an acre; after three years, if he could prove that he had irrigated a portion of the land, he would be allowed to gain final title for an additional dollar an acre. The act was, as historian Ray Allen Billington has written, "an open invitation to fraud," and Secretary of the Interior Carl Schurz launched an investigation of one such fraud almost immediately—significantly enough, at Visalia, in the southern end of California's San Joaquin Valley. With a certain one-

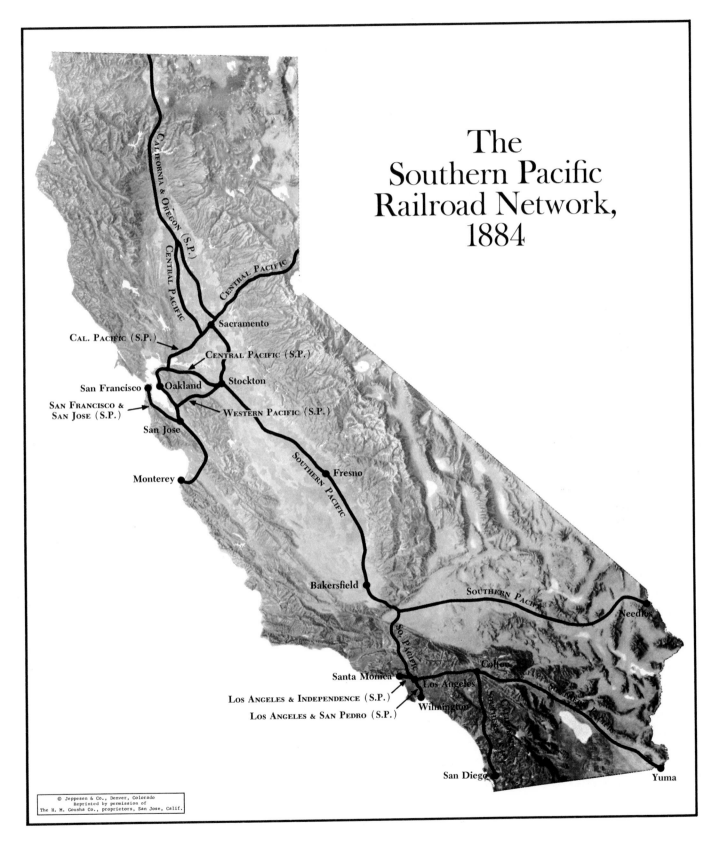

# The Southern Pacific Railroad Network, 1884

CALIFORNIA & OREGON (S.P.)

CENTRAL PACIFIC

CENTRAL PACIFIC

Sacramento

CAL. PACIFIC (S.P.)

CENTRAL PACIFIC (S.P.)

Stockton

San Francisco  Oakland

SAN FRANCISCO &
SAN JOSE (S.P.)

WESTERN PACIFIC (S.P.)

San Jose

Monterey

SOUTHERN PACIFIC

Fresno

Bakersfield

SOUTHERN PACIFIC

Needles

So. Pacific

Santa Monica

Colton

Los Angeles

LOS ANGELES & INDEPENDENCE (S.P.)

Wilmington

LOS ANGELES & SAN PEDRO (S.P.)

San Diego

Yuma

*Lloyd Tevis, a man who had more pies than fingers.*

*The oddly named James Ben Ali Haggin, partner of Lloyd Tevis.*

*Henry Miller, a German butcher turned California cattle king.*

sided relish, the *San Francisco Chronicle* summarized the investigation's findings, reporting that the investigator "discovered that the Desert Land Act of Congress was simply a Ring* job, and was made the medium for an organized colossal steal by the Ring, to the prejudice of thousands of thousands of honest, *bona fide* settlers, against whom it was so used as to prevent them enjoying the benefits of the letter and spirit of the Act. By arrangement and collusion, the thing was so managed as to furnish from Washington to the Ring here the instant information of the Executive approval of the Act, and in less time, by weeks, than it requires to officially communicate the necessary order to give proper operation to an Act of Congress on this coast, the Ring landgrabbers had been allowed by the officers of the Visalia Land Office to list and locate an immense area of the desert tracts."

---

*After more than ten years of "Ralston's Ring," the term "Ring" had become a commonplace description of any group of capitalists who, according to editorial opinion, had gathered together for the purpose of looting the people. The Ring mentioned here was dominated by Lloyd Tevis and James Ben Ali Haggin, predecessors of the Kern County Land Company and partners with George Hearst in many of his mining enterprises, including the Homestake and Anaconda mines. The newspaper gave the Ring altogether too much credit for the passage of the act, since cattlemen from the Great Plains, seeking cheap tracts of rangeland, had exerted far more influence.

Most of the men who engaged in such speculations—men like Sam Brannan, William C. Ralston, William S. Chapman (who ultimately controlled more than a million acres), Lloyd Tevis, and Ben Ali Haggin—were far more interested in the commodity value of their land than in its use as resource; to such as these, land meant lots, subdivisions, rental property, and salable farms with suitably marked-up price tags. To Henry Miller, a German-born butcher who had arrived in California in 1850 and had soon become the state's leading wholesale dealer in meat, land was nothing less than the making of an empire. Like John Sutter before him, Miller looked upon the interior of California's great Central Valley and saw in it an agricultural fiefdom; unlike Sutter, Miller made it work. Joining in partnership with Charles Lux and using every trick in the book, Miller accumulated vast holdings in the Sacramento and San Joaquin valleys with an obsessed determination. By 1880 the holdings of Miller & Lux amounted to an estimated 750,000 acres in California, most of it in a 100-mile strip on both sides of the San Joaquin River and a 50-mile strip along one side of the Kern River in the lower valley, with another 250,000 acres in Oregon, Nevada, and Arizona. On this land they ran as many as one million head of livestock at one time or another, and thousands of acres were given over to the growing of wheat and other grains; in sheer bulk it was one of the greatest agricultural enterprises in the world, and its "factories in the fields" helped shape the character of California's agriculture.

What the effect of such patterns of land ownership had on the character of the state itself was another matter. To some it was a disastrous condition that sapped California's economic lifeblood, created squalor and poverty, made wage slaves of men and millionaires of toads. That, at any rate, was the opinion of Henry George, a transplanted Philadelphian, printer, newspaper editor, and the only truly original economic thinker America ever produced.

That a man could buy, say, 10,000 acres of land at $1.25 per acre, then hold it unused until population growth increased its value—the "unearned increment"—was to George a perversion of proper land tenure; land was meant for people who would use it as a resource to support themselves and their families, and enrich the society around them. First in a small pamphlet called *Our Land and Land Policy* (1871), then in a major book called *Progress and Poverty* (1879), George analyzed the ills of society, linked them to improper land use, and proposed his solution: a massive "Single Tax" on unused privately owned land based on its rental value or unearned increment potential. This tax would not only be large enough to finance government by itself, its cost would have the effect of returning land

to the government and thence to the people. Given the number of land owners in this country, needless to say, the Single Tax was never remotely considered, but *Progress and Poverty* went on to become one of the most phenomenal best sellers of the nineteenth century, and while the Single Tax solution may have been simplistic, George's pointed observations on the country's social and economic agonies possessed both insight and permanent value to an understanding of his time.

Nor was George alone in looking askance at California's patterns of land use. In his brilliant *The American Commonwealth* (1889), James Bryce (British ambassador to the United States) summed up both those patterns and the problems inherent in them: "When California was ceded to the United States, land speculators bought up large tracts, under Spanish titles,* and others, foreseeing the coming prosperity, subsequently acquired great domains by purchase . . . either from the railways, which had received land grants, or directly from the government. Some of these speculators, by holding their lands for a rise, made it difficult for immigrants to acquire small freeholds, and in some cases checked the growth of farms. Others let their land on short leases to farmers, who thus came

---

*The titles, of course, were Mexican, not Spanish—a mistake as common then as it is today.

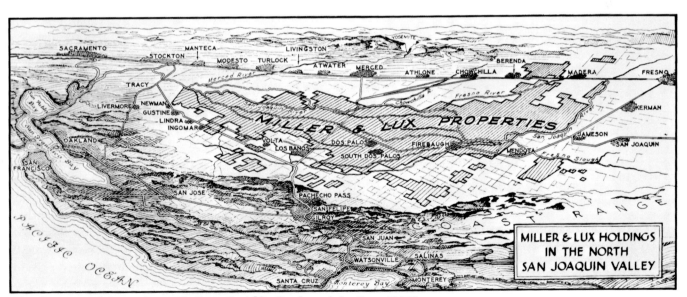

*Empire of land (map from Wallace Smith's* Garden of the Sun, *1939).*

*Henry George, whose* Progress and Poverty *influenced the economic thinking of a generation.*

into a comparatively precarious and often necessitous condition; others established enormous farms, in which the soil is cultivated by hired labourers, many of whom are discharged after the harvest—a phenomenon rare in the United States, which is elsewhere a country of moderately sized farms, owned by persons who do most of their labour by their own and their children's hands. Thus the land system of California presents features both peculiar and dangerous: a contrast between great properties, often appearing to conflict with the general weal, and the sometimes hard pressed small farmer, together with a mass of unsettled labour, thrown without work into the towns at certain times of the year."

As we shall see in later chapters, the "peculiar and dangerous" features of California's land system, shaped by nineteenth-century experience, have survived for more than a century; Bryce's words might have been written today.

IF LAND MONOPOLY and its consequences was one of the major thematic chords in California's life in the latter third of the nineteenth century, its counterpoint was the role of the railroad—specifically, the Southern Pacific Railroad.

The two were not disconnected, for the Southern Pacific was the largest single landowner in the state. The process by which this enviable position was attained stemmed from a moment of decision following the completion of the transcontinental railroad in 1869. At that time the owners of the Central Pacific—the "Big Four," Stanford, Huntington, Hopkins, and Crocker—were, by their own lights, feeling the pinch. The heavy construction costs they had expended in their race across the desert to Promontory had already forced them to sell most of their government and company bonds; not even the profits from the dummy corporation of the Contract & Finance Company were enough to cover those expenses, and except for fat salaries, which they had with some foresight been paying themselves, they had realized little of the profits that had seemed attainable when they met with Theodore Judah seven years before. It is not to be supposed that they were destitute; if they had, as Charles Crocker wished, simply put their Central Pacific stock on the market, historian David Lavender estimates (in *The Great Persuader*) that each would have realized about $780,000—less old debts, to be sure.

In any case, Huntington utterly opposed such a plan. With his eye on the immense profits hovering at the edge of the future, he persuaded his associates that the only recourse was not to retrench, but to expand. And so they did, energetically consolidating and refining an internal transportation network out of holdings acquired during the 1860s in an effort to stem potential competition. In the north they absorbed the California & Central and Yuba railroads and acquired a franchise for the California & Oregon, which effectively blocked any competition from that direction. Completion of the Western Pacific from Sacramento to Oakland gave them access to San Francisco Bay, and the absorption of the San Francisco & San Jose line gave them southern access to San Francisco. Most importantly, by obtaining the franchise of the Southern Pacific Railroad (still a "paper" road when they gained control) and beginning its construction in 1870, they had not only a line that connected north and south, but one whose franchise included congressional authorization to build the western link of a southern transcontinental railroad. With thoughts on federal land grants, the Big Four associates moved the planned route of the Southern Pacific from the coastal region, most of whose land was in private ownership, to the San Joaquin Valley, most of which was still in the public domain. As final links in this transportation chain, they purchased the California Steam Navigation Company, giving them control over the northern state's internal waterway system, and in 1874 started their own Pacific steamship line, the Occidental & Oriental, whose competition proved so ruinous to the Pacific Mail Steamship Company that it, too, was ultimately absorbed by the Big Four.

By 1872 the California & Oregon Railroad had been constructed to Redding, where its terminus remained for several years, and four years later the Southern Pacific had laid track down the San Joaquin Valley, across the Tehachapi Mountains, and through the San Fernando Valley to Los Angeles. In 1877 the line was extended to Yuma on the Colorado River, thus blocking the entrance of any competing line from the south (most especially the ill-fated Texas & Pacific, of which more in chapter 12). In 1882 the company completed its "Sunset Route" to New Orleans, giving it absolute domination of transcontinental railroad traffic to and from California—at least for a time. The entire network was organized in 1884 under the aegis of the Southern Pacific Company, a corporation formed in the state of Kentucky, whose corporation laws were among the most lenient in the nation.

No transportation enterprise in the world was so large or so devoid of competition as the Southern Pacific in its heyday. No transportation enterprise owned so much land, for in all its building up, down, and around the state, the Southern Pacific obtained 11,588,000 acres of federal grant lands. Much of this was in desert and mountain country; much of it was also in some of the most fertile areas of the state, such as the San Joaquin and the Sacramento valleys. That land provided (and still provides) the company with much of its annual revenues through land sales and short-term leases to tenant farmers. Huntington and his associates approached transactions along these lines with precisely the same hard-bitten regard for the value of their dollars that had enabled them to build their transportation empire in the first place—a fact illustrated by events in a corner of the southern San Joaquin Valley, a corner called Mussel Slough by some but "Starvation Valley" by others.

*Southern Pacific's roundhouse at Yuma, jumping-off point for the southern transcontinental route.*

When the Southern Pacific's line entered that section of the valley early in the 1870s, the company had issued brochures and pamphlets inviting settlement on its grant lands. Since it did not want to assume the tax costs of the land at the time, the railroad had delayed taking full title to the grants from the government; however, it did guarantee title to the settlers' claims, promised that they would be given the first opportunity to buy when the railroad decided to take ownership, suggested somewhat vaguely that the price per acre would be in the vicinity of "$2.50 upward," and finally guaranteed that, as noted in one of the pamphlets, "in ascertaining the value, any improvement that a settler or other person may have on the lands will not be taken into consideration: neither will the price be increased in consequence thereof. Settlers are thus assured that in addition to being accorded the first privilege of purchase, they will be protected in their investments."

The settlers came; land that cheap in California was not easy to come by, even if it was situated in a nearly waterless section of a seasonally arid country. Through the dry, one-hundred-degree summers and the crashing rains of winter, through drought, floods, frosts, and crop-destroying winds, the settlers fought the land. Banding together, they constructed irrigation ditches

THE OGRE OF MUSSEL SLOUGH.

*The tragedy at Mussel Slough provided an easy focus for anti-railroad sentiment.*

and brought seasonal overflow water to their crops from Mussel Slough, and by 1877 had generally won out against the vagaries of the land. In that year, the Southern Pacific took final claim to its grants and announced that the land was now for sale—to anyone who could meet prices that now ranged from $17 all the way up to $40, far above estimates the railroad had made several years earlier. Outraged, the settlers maintained that the higher prices were the direct result of their improvements on the land, a violation of the promise not to take such improvements into consideration. The railroad's reply simply noted that there was no specific contract involved, and that it was entitled, in Huntington's words, to "what the land is worth."

The farmers formed a Settlers' League and took their case to the U.S. District Court of San Jose in 1879; they lost, and the railroad began selling off the land to those willing to meet the price. The Settlers' League responded by degenerating into a kind of rural vigilante committee, complete with masks, drill practice, secret meetings, and actions as pointed as they were brutal. New settlers who had purchased at the railroad's price were persuaded of their folly, their possessions carefully removed from their homes, and their homes burned, a procedure that tended to dampen the enthusiasm of potential buyers. The railroad then hired two local toughs by the names of Mills D. Hartt and Walter J. Crow to function as "owners," obtained writs of ejectment against several original settlers, and gave the writs to the federal marshal with instructions to dispossess the specified farmers and turn over their lands to Hartt and Crow.

On the morning of May 11, 1880, Hartt, Crow, and the marshal were greeted by twenty grim, well-armed settlers when they tried to make the first eviction at the Henry Brewer ranch. The air was filled with imprecations and shouted arguments and much waving of arms and fists, and eventually shots rang out. Who fired them no one ever determined, but in seconds Hartt was killed, and five settlers lay dead or dying; Crow leaped from his buggy and escaped to a wheatfield, where he was eventually tracked down and killed.

While the Southern Pacific pulled every string at its command to be sure that its version of the affair was the first to gain common knowledge, the "Mussel Slough Tragedy" (as it came to be called) effectively distilled a widespread public resentment of the railroad. Ever since the Golden Era, when outcries had been raised against the conglomerate of the California Stage Company, Californians had been uncommonly monopoly-conscious, and there was no monopoly anywhere like the monopoly of the railroad. Nor, it must be noted, did the railroad itself go out of its way to seduce public favor (with such exceptions as that noted above); for the most part, its directors considered public opinion irrelevant to the larger question, which they saw as nothing less than survival, as David Lavender has written: "Self-defense and the survival of the fittest, their attitudes proclaimed, were the first law of economics as well as of nature. In fulfillment of that law they would do, with no sense of wrong, whatever was necessary to protect their great achievement against erosion by politicians . . . competitors, or raiding speculators, just as they would have protected their homes against robbers or wild animals. If this involved breaking unjust laws (and the associates could define injustice to suit themselves), then they would do it."

There was a multitude of men who held and exercised such opinions in the nineteenth century, of course, and in all fairness it must be pointed out that the very ruthlessness such attitudes represented had created a comprehensive transportation network whose long-term value to the economic development of the state cannot be questioned. It opened up vast new areas

THIS IS THE MONSTER CALIFORNIA MUST DESTROY NOW IF EVER.

*The* San Francisco Examiner's *variation on a theme by the* Wasp, *1896.*

of settlement, stimulated the continuing growth of the lumber industry (particularly in the Sierra Nevada), provided ready transportation of goods, both inside California and across the continent, made possible the growth of Los Angeles, and helped create an agriculture whose social value may have been questionable but

COLLAPSE OF COLLIS.

*Uncle Collis takes one on the chin from the* Examiner's *Ambrose Bierce when the railroad fights repayment.*

whose hard-cash results were obvious to anyone who could count.

Against this must be placed the railroad's use of power, and it is on this score that the Southern Pacific earned the criticisms that dogged it well into the twentieth century. It was called the "Octopus" (not coincidentally, the title of Frank Norris' novel based on the Mussel Slough affair), and with good reason, for the railroad's directors were not shy about exercising their power wherever and whenever they felt it would do them good. Their control of freight rates in the state was so nearly absolute that it was exercised with a kind of arrogance. Southern Pacific officials were not above demanding to see a shipper's books before quoting him a price, then determining the rate on precisely as much as they thought he could stand. When the market price of any given commodity took a sudden rise, the shipping rate for it increased correspondingly—and conversely, when a market price dropped, the rate price was cut only so much as to let the man who was trying to market his goods stay in business. "All that the traffic will bear" was a phrase that acquired profound meaning to anyone utilizing the rails of the Southern Pacific.

Attempts at regulation, most of them anemic to begin with in the nineteenth century, were hopeless; the railroad was superbly efficient at both bribery and litigation—if one didn't forestall attempts at regulation, the other one usually did. Similarly, the railroad successfully stalled the payment of its interest on the loans it had acquired from the government for the building of the transcontinental line—and when the principal on those loans fell due in the 1890s, continued stalling for nearly another decade.

Of all the criticisms leveled against the Southern Pacific, however, it was the company's vested interest in the political scene that aroused the most vehemence. Using its freewheeling rate system as either club or carrot, depending upon what it wanted done, the railroad was able to make friends and break enemies in municipal, state, and—on some levels—national politics.

It did not hesitate to do so when it was considered necessary, and it was considered necessary quite a lot of the time. Between 1874 and 1900, a full-time job was held down by a succession of three men whose duties were exclusively devoted to furthering the railroad's political interests: David Colton, whose addition made the railroad's directors the "Big Four-and-a-Half," according to some critics; W. W. Stow, who retired in 1893 to become commissioner of San Francisco's Golden Gate Park and have a lake named after him; and William F. Herrin, who organized the railroad's Political Bureau into a marvelously efficient machine. Under the direction of these men (most often with Huntington's guidance), the railroad's influence on California's politics was felt on a broad scale, affecting everything from the election of a San Francisco supervisor to that of a United States senator.

The Southern Pacific's political power was considerable (if not quite as considerable as critics of the day maintained), but its base was in the urban north, where control of local bosses was more easily obtained and where some assurance of a predictable response to the railroad's stimuli could be found. The "Cow Counties" of the south were virtually ignored, a mistake that came home to the railroad with great force when it lost the "free harbor" fight in 1890 (see chapter 12). The 1890s, in fact, were bad years for the railroad on several levels, in spite of Herrin's efficiency. For one, its traditional power base of San Francisco was badly crippled when Adolph Sutro, the "Tunnel King of the Comstock," faced the railroad's machine in the mayoralty election of 1894—and won. For another, the railroad was finally forced to deal with its debt to the federal government, and in 1899 signed an agreement whereby it would repay some $59,000,000, plus interest.

For thirty years, the railroad had been the single most powerful economic and political force in California. But now it, and the rest of the state, would have to face winds of reform that had been dormant for more than two generations.

*Mythic isle: an early Currier & Ives view of "The Coast of California."*

# California Mirror:
# The New American Eden

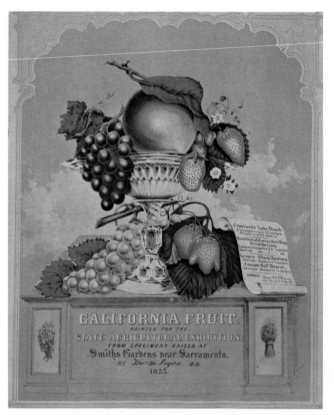

*This 1885 exhibition memorial was one of the earliest attempts at national advertising.*

California, the Spanish novelist Montalvo had written in 1510, lay "on the right hand of the Indies," and "very near to the terrestrial paradise." By the time of the gold rush, few people any longer took Spanish romances seriously, yet the region remained invested with a yeasty unreality quite as fanciful as anything that ever ran through the mind of any scribbling Spaniard. As a case in point, consider the Currier & Ives lithograph on the previous page, in which Mount Rainier appears to have been put down in the middle of a Panamanian jungle—the whole thing billed as a typical scene along the coast of California.

Californians were themselves guilty of perpetuating the image of a demi-paradise, motivated by simple greed as well as enthusiasm. From the beginning, the state advertised itself with a unique vigor no other state had ever matched, or ever would match. One of the earliest and most successful efforts in this regard came with the development of the canned and packaged food industries, and the dissemination of locally rolled cigars. A man not only heard and read about the glories of the Golden State, he ingested them—or in the case of cigars, puffed away at the very stuff of myth. In one way or another, the legend of California was consumed and remembered.

*In 1855 "California Fruits" were in a bowl; by 1876 they were packed in a can.*

*1871: Most of the early four-color labels were reserved for fairly expensive products, like cigars.*

Advertising worked—probably because so much of it was so close to the truth. There was an outlandishly Eden-like quality to the state's landscape. Who would have believed in the existence of trees thirty feet thick, three hundred feet high, and four thousand years old? California had them—and could prove it. Who would have believed that such wonders as the Yosemite Valley or the canyon of the Kings River were anything more than the fancies of some romantic's overheated imagination? California had them and a hundred more—and was never bashful about proving their existence.

*The prototype version of the raisin industry's "Sunshine Girl," 1890.*

*Nature as a marketable attraction: the Mammoth Tree Grove, 1855.*

*Like many others in the nineteenth century—among them, Albert Bierstadt,
Thomas Moran, Thomas A. Ayres, and Thomas Hill—the Scottish-born William
Keith found himself drawn to the spectacular wonders of the Sierra
Nevada and attempted to recreate them in almost photographic detail,
as in his panoramic view of the Kings River Canyon in 1878.*

237

The one image perpetuated more consistently than any other was that California was the Cornucopia of legend come to pulsing life—and this too was not so far from the truth that it could be easily dismissed. If such artists as Thomas Hill and William Keith presented Eden as wilderness, then the proud municipalities spreading across the land presented Eden as wilderness tamed and made fruitful, where man and his products could proliferate.

The bird's-eye view of Fresno in 1891 at the right was typical of the hundreds of such airscapes produced by virtually every hamlet, town, metropolis, or would-be metropolis in the state during the nineteenth century. Like a journeyman's card or a high school diploma, such documents marked a town's coming-of-age, announced its readiness to take on the world on its own terms, relinquishing to no other municipality or region the primacy of its place in the sun. Fresno's lovingly rendered banks, mercantile houses, churches, schools, gingerbread residences, bustling little locomotive with a trainful of rich produce, and spreading green fields— all documented a triumphant pilgrimage of thirty years from the days when the town could be described by William H. Brewer: "Fresno 'City' consists of one large house, very dilapidated, one small ditto, one barn, one small dilapidated and empty warehouse, and a corral. It is surrounded by swamps . . . the green of which was cheering to the eye after the desolation through which we had passed." Here, the drawing says, was a new kind of paradise; here was an American Eden.

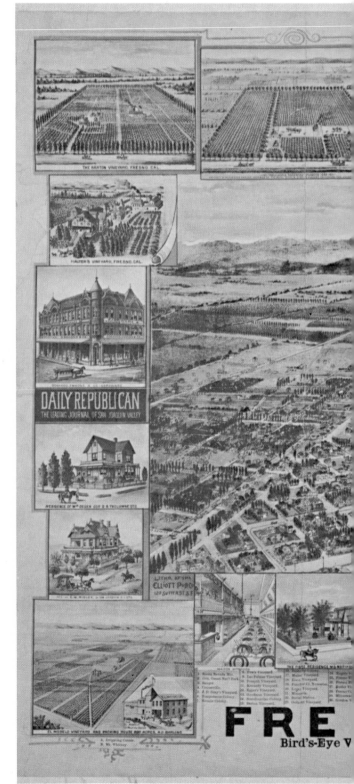

*A birds-eye view of Fresno in 1891,*
*the raisin-growing center of the universe.*

238

O, CAL. 1891.

sno, Fresno County, California—The center of the Raisin industries of the United States.

Issued by the "FRESNO DAILY REPUBLICAN" and "FRESNO WEEKLY REPUBLICAN." Jan. 1, 1891.

# CHAPTER 12

# ISLAND IN THE SUN

*Fifty years in Southern California—from the time of the rancheros*

*to the age of the real estate boomer*

For more than twenty years after American occupation, Southern California sunned itself like a lizard. Isolated both geographically and psychologically from the bustling mining and city-building counties of the north, the so-called "Cow Counties" of the south drifted in a backwash of time, changing little from the days when mission priests had called their Indian charges in from the fields with chiming bells, and *rancheros* with dark-eyed daughters and silver saddles dabbled in family politics and ruled over fiefdoms of grass.

It was a region that still found a definition of itself in the possession of land, and it felt its difference with both pride and pain. The pride was Hispanic and traditional; the pain was pure Anglo-Saxon and of recent origin; the mix produced a kind of mild paranoia that was not entirely without foundation. The more prosperous, progressive, and more nearly "Yankee" counties of the north did in fact look upon Southern California with something akin to condescension—even contempt—an attitude that combined ancient prejudices with a specific lust for the very land that was the source of the Southern Californian's pride. "Of what avail is it," Governor Bigler remarked in 1856, "that our soil is the most productive, and our climate admirably adapted to the culture of all the necessities and luxuries of life, if flowing vales sleep in native beauty and silence, and expansive plains are but the roaming grounds and rich pasture fields for the unchecked herd?"

Already harassed by the long processes by which they were forced to prove title to their land under federal regulations, the *rancheros* of the south regarded such sentiments with some resentment. An even more solid object of concern was the direct taxation of land, which Southern Californians saw as nothing less than an attempt to carve up their fiefdoms and hand them over to dirt farmers (this was, in fact, not far from the truth—although, as noted in chapter 11, the more immediate effect was to place the land in the hands of speculators of one ilk or another). Stephen C. Foster, son-in-law of San Bernardino County's Antonio Maria Lugo, articulated their sense of frustration in 1851: "The overwhelming influence of the north in the legislature is seen in every act which has been passed within two years. The northern counties are engaged almost entirely in mining and contain very little land liable to taxation [not precisely true]. As a consequence the burdens of taxation fall principally upon the south—burdens which our people are poorly able to bear."

Frustration gave way to expression quite early. In 1850 a collection of *Angelenos* petitioned Congress to declare the counties south of Monterey a separate territory under the name of Central California. Nothing came of the attempt, but the following year another group called upon the citizens of Southern California to form a convention to split the state: "It is the plain truth," this group maintained: "that whatever of good the experiment of a state government may have otherwise led to in California, for us, the southern counties, it has proved only a splendid failure." Again, nothing happened, and in 1859 yet another attempt was made—and this one came close to success. Andrés Pico, the

*Date palms in the Coachella Valley, just north of the Salton Sea.*

241

*Californio* hero of the Battle of San Pasqual, it will be remembered, introduced a joint resolution in the state assembly which called for the secession of the counties of San Luis Obispo, Santa Barbara, Los Angeles, San Bernardino, and San Diego to form a new political entity called the Territory of the Colorado. Southern members of the legislature supported the measure vigorously, and northern members were sublimely indifferent to Southern California's role in the future of the state; the measure passed both houses of the body, was ratified by the citizens of Southern California, then sent on to Washington for the reasoned deliberations of Congress. There it died, stifled by the sectional antagonisms that ultimately led to the Civil War.*

Trapped in its isolation and emotional separatism, Southern California was an island in the sun forced to work out its own destiny on its own terms, with results that lagged far behind the burgeoning growth of the north. When compared to the simple vigor of San Francisco and Sacramento, the towns of the south seemed preserved in aspic for nearly a generation, gelid in their development and more than a little primitive in their social character. San Diego and Santa Barbara had barely risen above village status as late as 1860, and even the region's leading metropolis, Los Angeles, could be described in that year as a "city of some 3,500 or 4,000 inhabitants, nearly a century old [the town, not the inhabitants], a regular old Spanish-Mexican town," where "fifty to sixty murders per year have been common."

Not even the great cattle boom that lasted roughly from 1849 to 1856 could make up the difference, however impressive it was on the surface. *Rancheros* found themselves courted by such wholesalers as Henry Miller, who were willing to pay the unheard-of price of $25 a head for their tough, black Mexican cattle for resale in San Francisco or Sacramento—for as much as $75 a head. Enormous drives that nearly matched those between Texas and Kansas in later years sent tens of

*Periodic enthusiasm for the division of the state would punctuate California's history for more than another century, however—in fact, right up to our own times. Ironically, in recent years, it has been the *northern* counties that have indulged in such dark mutterings, generally frustrated by the shift of economic and political power to the south and specifically annoyed by Southern California's appropriation of northern water.

thousands of cattle from Southern California north through the coastal valleys or the San Joaquin Valley, and millions of dollars changed hands, lending an air of furious prosperity to the southern scene, as reported by Maj. Horace Bell in his *Reminiscences:* "The streets were thronged throughout the entire day with splendidly mounted and richly dressed *caballeros,* most of whom wore suits of clothes that cost all the way from $500 to $1,000, with saddle and horse trappings that cost even more. . . . Of one of the Lugos, I remember, it was said his horse equipments cost over $2,000. Everybody in Los Angeles seemed rich, everybody *was* rich, and money was more plentiful at that time, than in any other place of like size, I venture to say, in the world."

The wealth was as permanent as steam, dissipated on the glittering refinements that appealed to a people whose experience had never before included such large amounts of money; what good was wealth if a man did not demonstrate his possession of it? As a result, almost none of the money from the cattle boom was translated into concrete wealth; for example, the assessed value of real and personal property in Los Angeles in 1859 was $2,370,529—less than 2 percent of the state's total valuation of $147,104,955. It was a shaky foundation on which to build; when more and more cattle began to be bred in the northern counties of the state, eventually dominating the local market, many *rancheros* found themselves rich in clothes and wines and silver trappings, but too poor to pay the taxes on their lands. The decline was accelerated in 1862, when floods drowned thousands of cattle, and given a further push over the next several years as a series of droughts almost annihilated the region's natural pasturage, climaxed by the drought of 1864, in which cattle died like fruit flies, as reported by the *Southern News:* "The cattle of Los Angeles County are dying so fast in many places, for the want of food, that the large rancheros keep their men busily employed in obtaining hides. Thousands of carcasses strew the plains in all directions . . . and the sight is harrowing in the extreme. We believe the stock interest of this county, as well as the adjoining counties, to be 'played out' entirely. Famine has done its work, and nothing can now save what few cattle remain on the desert California ranches."

The trade was not quite "played out," but it was crippled badly; in the ten years between 1860 and 1870,

*In the land of the specialty farm: Eagle Rock Valley near century's end.*

the cattle population of Los Angeles County dropped from an estimated 70,000 head to an estimated 20,000. The glory days of the *rancheros,* with their kingdoms of grass and indolent grace, were gone forever.

As the cattle industry began to disintegrate, carrying with it the life-style it had nurtured, it did not leave Southern California in a vacuum, however disruptive it might have been to those who had based their future on the "cattle on a thousand hills." For one thing, the sheep industry quickly rose to dominance. Begun with the mission fathers, sheep-raising enjoyed a healthy revival in the 1850s with a powerful demand for both meat and wool, and the number of sheep in the state rose from 17,554 in 1850 to more than one million in 1860; by 1870, given a push by the Civil War and the corresponding shortage of cotton fiber, the figure had risen to nearly three million, with a

season's "clip" of 11,400,000 pounds of wool—worth anywhere from two to three million dollars, depending upon quality and the fluctuations of the market. Southern California accounted for fully half these figures.

Less explosively, but with a steady inexorability, the region's agriculture began to blossom, enhanced no little bit by the existence of what might be called climatic "sub-regions" within the geographic complex of the southern counties. Although Southern California was (and is) a semiarid region, rainfall patterns varied widely—sometimes as much as six inches a year between places no more than a few miles apart. Temperature and soil conditions displayed a similar disparity, making it possible to grow corn with great success in one area, say, and over a range of hills, fruits whose soil and climatic requirements were vastly different. These peculiar qualities gave rise to the nurturing of exotic "specialty" crops, a characteristic of Southern California's agriculture for more than a century. Even on a

*Sell, sell, sell—by the middle of the 1880s, the real estate "style" was a fact of life.*

small patch of land, the sheer variety of crops that could be cultivated was startling, as noted by Charles Nordhoff in his *California for Health, Pleasure, and Residence* (1873): "As I drove out from Los Angeles into the country on a January morning with a friend, we met a farmer coming into town with a market-wagon of produce. . . . The farmer's little girl sat on the seat with him, a chubby, blue-eyed little tot, with her sun-bonnet half hiding her curls, and a shawl, which her careful mother had wrapped about her shoulders, carelessly flung aside. To me, fresh from the snowy Plains and Sierras, and with the chill breath of winter still on me, this was a pleasing and novel sight; but the contents of the man's wagon were still more startling to my Northern eyes. He was carrying to market oranges, pumpkins, a lamb, corn, green peas in the pod, lemons, and strawberries. What a mixture of Northern and Southern products! What an odd and wonderful January gathering in a farmer's wagon!"

Nordhoff was a railroad "boomer" and was therefore disposed toward hyperbole; he was not a liar, however, and his little vignette suggested much that was true about Southern California's agriculture in its earliest years. The garden-like appeal of such climate and soil conditions was nearly irresistible. As more and more ranchos succumbed to the pressures of drought, famine, taxes, and deteriorating cattle prices, more and more land fell into the hands of brokers like the Los Angeles

and San Bernardino Land Company (see chapter 11), who went to extraordinary lengths to broadcast both the real and the imagined advantages of the country for agriculture—inundating coastal steamers with brochures and pamphlets, collaring likely prospects on the streets of San Francisco, setting up land offices in Chicago, New York, and even London, and advertising whenever and wherever they could.

It was no dirt farmer's proposition. Prices for Southern California land in this period rarely fell below five dollars an acre and often went as high as twenty-five. Yet the resulting influx of settlers amounted to a genuine boom; they crowded steamers from San Francisco, came overland in wagon trains, and—after its completion in May 1869—over the rails of the transcontinental railroad. Those who could afford the land on their own came as individual families; those who could not banded together to create agricultural colonies, like those at Etiwanda, Ontario, Riverside, Compton, and Pasadena. Land sales in Los Angeles County rose from $40,000 a month early in 1868 to more than $200,000 a month early in 1869; by the end of the decade, the county's cultivated land had increased from a little over 5,000 acres to nearly 40,000. By 1872 Los Angeles had acquired a population of 17,000; two genuine banks (the Farmers & Merchants and the Temple & Workman); one railroad (the twenty-one-mile Los Angeles & San Pedro line to the sea at San Pedro Harbor); and thousands of acres of farmland that surrounded the city in a great checkerboard planted in wheat, barley, olives, tomatoes, corn, grapevines, lemons, limes, and oranges.*

By then Southern California also had its own somewhat miniaturized version of the Comstock Lode. In 1868 comparatively rich "galena" deposits of silver and lead had been discovered two miles above the sea on the crest of the Inyo Range, some two hundred miles north of Los Angeles, and by 1869 a mining town called Cerro Gordo had bloomed outrageously on those rocky timberline slopes. Pear-shaped furnaces melted the ore

---

*Of these crops the most steadily successful in the early years was grapes. By 1870 Los Angeles County was producing nearly one-third of California's total wine production of 1,814,656 gallons, and a similar percentage of its table grapes. Orange production, soon to be the principal "cash crop" of Southern California, had not yet began its first period of bloom, although by 1870 there were 34,000 trees in blossom.

*An excursion train of potential buyers regards a bleak subdivision called Coronado Beach, 1887.*

into eighty-five pound "pigs" of silver and lead, each worth from twenty to thirty-five dollars; these were then loaded into wagons and hauled the two hundred miles out of the mountains to the Los Angeles terminal of the Los Angeles & San Pedro Railroad. The citizens of Los Angeles soon became gratefully accustomed to the clatter and rumble of Cerro Gordo ore wagons in the dusty, rutted, unpaved streets of their town; there was reason enough to be grateful: in the ten years of its most productive life, Cerro Gordo produced nearly eight million dollars in silver and lead bullion—a trifle when compared to the production of the Comstock, perhaps, but a bonanza in Southern California terms.

Nearly all of the Cerro Gordo product was shipped by railroad to San Pedro, then up the coast by steamer for refining at the Bank of California's Selby Smelting Works near Oakland. Aside from viewing displays in bank windows and watching ore wagons on the way to the railroad station at the corner of Alameda and Commercial streets, Los Angeles had little connection with the silver itself. The trade that it stimulated was another matter, for Los Angeles became the major supplier of the Cerro Gordo mines. In exchange for the thousands of tons of silver-lead pigs unloaded at the railroad depot for shipment to San Pedro every year, the town's suppliers packed more than $700,000 worth of supplies into the empty wagons and sent them back to the mountains. Mule-train freighting firms, chief

among them Remi Nadeau's thirty-two-team enterprise, flourished to the point that freighting became, next to agriculture, the region's principal "industry." The more than five hundred mules engaged in freighting consumed nearly all the surplus barley in Los Angeles County, and Nadeau alone, in the words of the *Los Angeles News,* provided "employment to more men, and purchased more produce, and introduced more trade to Los Angeles than any other five men in this city."*

Slowly, then, with shrugs and an occasional twitch, the "sleeping giant" of Southern California was beginning to edge into the mainstream of California's nineteenth-century life by the early 1870s. Yet it was still a region forced to develop in isolation, an island on the land. Not since the Butterfield Overland Express had moved to the Central Route in 1861 had Southern Cali-

---

*The importance of the Inyo trade to Southern California is suggested by the fact that Los Angeles had to fight to keep it more than once. In 1871 it stalled an attempt by the little town of Ventura to steal the trade for its own port of Hueneme, but only by shipping ore on the Los Angeles & San Pedro Railroad at a solid loss. In 1872, Los Angeles did lose the trade for a few months when Bakersfield freighters in the southern San Joaquin Valley, anticipating the arrival of the Southern Pacific Railroad, outbid Remi Nadeau and the other Los Angeles freighters; bad roads and unexpected delays in railroad construction soon killed the enterprise, however, and by the summer of 1873, Cerro Gordo silver was once more rumbling through the streets of Los Angeles.

*The selling of Monrovia during the boom of the eighties; it was one of the few towns to survive.*

fornia enjoyed a direct link to the East, and connection with San Francisco was still by stage or steamer. Without more ambitious communications, the region would continue to feed upon itself; without such communications, the law of supply and demand would strangle its agriculture, and stunt its embryonic urban growth. Southern California needed a railroad; it needed, specifically, the Southern Pacific Railroad.

IN A VERY REAL SENSE, the emergence of Los Angeles as the leading metropolis of Southern California was in splendid defiance of all visible logic. Situated more than twenty miles from the sea on a semi-arid plain next to a nearly waterless river, there was no particular reason why Los Angeles should ever have been more than a modestly prosperous service center for the ranchos and farms that surrounded it—except that a handful of men had glimpsed a brighter vision.

"God made Southern California," Charles F. Lummis once wrote, "and made it on purpose." Similarly, man created Los Angeles—and did it on purpose. The men who made Los Angeles, if not out of whole cloth then out of fairly suspicious material, were not many, but they were vigorous partisans of the go-ahead persuasion, and their energy shaped the future of the city and the region: William Workman, who had led an overland party to Southern California in 1841, then acquired the El Puente rancho and later became partner in the Temple & Workman Bank; Benjamin D. Wilson, a member of the Workman Party of 1841, a rancher, an early railroad booster, and a state legislator; Francis P. F. Temple, who started as a rancher in the early 1840s and became a partner, in merchandising and banking respectively, with Isaiah W. Hellman and William Workman (Temple's father-in-law); John G. Downey, a former goldseeker of 1849 who drifted to Los Angeles in 1850, started a drugstore, acquired Rancho Santa Gertrudes, became governor of the state in 1859, and after the expiration of his term in 1862, invested his money, influence, time, and name in nearly every major enterprise in the Los Angeles region; Phineas Banning, who helped found the San Pedro Harbor town of Wilmington and built the Los Angeles & San Pedro Railroad; Isaiah W. Hellman, a Los Angeles merchant since 1859 and partner with Downey in the Farmers & Merchants Bank; and Robert M. Widney, Southern California agent for the Los Angeles & San Bernardino Land Company, among others, and editor and publisher of a prototype of the "boom" publications of future years, the *Los Angeles Real Estate Advertiser.* They were not alone, these men, but more than any single man or group of men, they were responsible for the early growth of Los Angeles; they were, as Remi Nadeau characterized them, the "city-makers."

To a man, they recognized the city's need for a major railroad connection, not only to San Francisco but to the markets of the East, and their hope lay in the Southern Pacific, whose charter included a stipulation for a branch through Southern California to Yuma, Arizona, and eventual connection with a southern transcontinental railroad. The charter did not stipulate, however, precisely which Southern California town would be chosen as the hub between the branch from the north and that to the Arizona border. The erstwhile architects of Los Angeles were determined that the city should be that hub. When Congress in 1871 began deliberation of the Texas Pacific Act, which would authorize federal land and money grants both to the Southern Pacific in its march down the San Joaquin Valley and across Southern California, and to the Texas & Pacific Railroad from New Orleans to San Diego, Benjamin D. Wilson traveled to Washington to represent the interests of Los Angeles. A persuasive en-

*The "First Special Fast Fruit Train" gets steam up for the delivery of oranges to the East, June 24, 1886.*

thusiast, he managed to have the phrase "by way of Los Angeles" stitched into the act, which was passed in March, 1871.

The city rejoiced at the good news but soon felt the heavy hand of the Southern Pacific and learned that getting itself a railroad was somewhat more complicated than had been supposed. Under the provisions of the state's "Five Per Cent" law, the cities of eight counties (unsurprisingly, those through which the Southern Pacific was building or planning to build) were authorized to issue bond donations to the railroad equal to 5 percent of their assessed valuation. The Southern Pacific, of course, tended to look upon these donations as part of its God-given patrimony; any city foolish enough to reject the issuance of such bonds would never see the railroad come within hailing distance of its limits—as Visalia in the San Joaquin Valley and San Bernardino east of Los Angeles would learn.* In the case of Los Angeles, the railroad let it be known that it didn't require just the standard donation—it wanted controlling stock in the Los Angeles & San Pedro Railroad, the city's pride and its only connection with the harbor at San Pedro.

---

*In these two instances, the Southern Pacific simply invented its *own* towns—Delano in the north and Colton near San Bernardino, the last named after the "half" of the "Big Four-and-a-half": David D. Colton.

The reaction to this gentlemanly extortion was vehement but useless; the city had no choice, for it feared the power of the Southern Pacific was quite capable of having the Texas Pacific Act altered so as to delete the stipulation regarding Los Angeles. The only alternative was a singularly unattractive one on several levels. Upstart San Diego, feeling the flush of its own railroad boom and backed by Thomas A. Scott, owner of the Texas & Pacific Railroad, offered to build a line to Los Angeles; all it required was the 5 percent subsidy, having no interest in the Los Angeles & San Pedro line. This was adding insult to extortion; moreover, if the proposal had been accepted, Los Angeles would have lost forever the chance to be the major railroad center of Southern California.

On the eve of the November 5, 1872, bond election, the *Los Angeles Star* stated the simple facts of life: "Without railroad communication, the future prospects of Los Angeles are not flattering. . . . It is in the hands of the people of today to decide what shall be the future of this valley—whether it shall overflow with life, animation and prosperity, or whether it shall sink back into a dreamy stupor." The bond issue, involving a total of $602,000 in bonds and railroad stock, was passed by a healthy majority. In exchange, the Southern Pacific agreed to complete twenty-five miles of road north to San Fernando Mission and another twenty-five miles east toward San Bernardino within fifteen

These Lots are the

# BEST OF INVESTMENTS,

and cannot fail to pay a handsome profit almost at once.   Also,

## BEAR IN MIND

that this property is ON THE HILLS, and on the line of the only Cable Railway System on the Pacific Coast outside of San Francisco.

No such opportunity has ever been offered the people of Southern California.

## PURCHASE NOW!    DON'T WAIT!

The most LIBERAL TERMS upon which this property is placed before the public, puts it

# Within the Reach of All!

A small amount of money in a safe investment has been the stepping-stone to fortune.

## TITLES PERFECT!

## LIBERAL CREDIT!

# CHOICE BUILDING SITES!

A Cable Road running Direct from the Center of the City.

## EVERY LOT MUST CHANGE OWNERS.

# Saturday, Jan'y 23d, 1886,

AT 11 O'CLOCK, A. M.

SEE MAP INSIDE.

*"Within the Reach of All!" The clarion cry of the real estate boomer was heard in the land.*

months and promised to complete the main line across the Tehachapis and through the San Fernando Hills by 1876.

The railroad, as agreed, began construction of the smaller branch lines early in 1873, and started pushing across the desert for Yuma. In its wake, the Los Angeles region enjoyed an exciting, if somewhat premature, boom; more farmers came, and new towns—Garden Grove, Downey, and Orange among them—popped up along the branch lines. The Los Angeles Chamber of Commerce was formed in April 1873 under the leadership of Robert M. Widney (by then a municipal judge) and John G. Downey, and began an intense advertising campaign, spreading the glories of Southern California wherever it could. From Nevada, John P. Jones, one of the Comstock "kings" and now a United States senator

(see chapter 9), entered the scene by beginning construction of a new harbor at Santa Monica and laying plans for the Los Angeles & Independence Railroad to compete with the Southern Pacific–controlled Los Angeles & San Pedro. Early in 1875 the Southern Pacific began its assault on the Tehachapi Mountains, and the fever of anticipation rose. "The operations of the Southern Pacific Railroad Company," the Chamber of Commerce noted in one of its flood of publications, "have revolutionized Los Angeles County, commercially and financially." And Los Angeles, the *Express* remarked fulsomely, "is going to be a city all the way down to Santa Monica."

But the city had not reckoned with the arrogance of the Southern Pacific, in spite of its experience with the subsidy of 1872. In January 1875, David D. Colton caused legislation to be introduced into Congress that would significantly revise the Texas Pacific Act along lines the Southern Pacific considered more equitable. One stipulation asked was that the railroad be allowed to construct a branch from the Tehachapi Mountains across Antelope Valley and through Cajon Pass to San Bernardino and connection with the line to Yuma; this would have the effect of reducing Los Angeles to branch-line status. Even worse, from the city's point of view, was a second request: that the Southern Pacific be allowed to postpone the completion of its Los Angeles connection through the San Fernando Hills until November 1, 1885—nearly ten years beyond the 1876 date it had promised the city. The railroad, it should be pointed out, was not just exercising an idle grudge against Los Angeles; it simply wanted to postpone the expense of tunneling through the San Fernando Hills for a few years, as well as obtain a shorter route to its transcontinental connection—all of this so reasonable and businesslike that the directors of the Southern Pacific could not understand why anyone would want to oppose the idea.

Los Angeles opposed it; under the leadership of the Chamber of Commerce and with the support of the Texas & Pacific's Thomas A. Scott, who viewed the progress of the Southern Pacific without enthusiasm, the city met the lobbyists of the Southern Pacific in a head-on conflict—and won. The Southern Pacific's bill was soundly defeated, one of the few legislative setbacks the railroad had endured since its founding, and the last obstacle to the city's emergence as a railroad center was removed. By August 1876 the Southern Pacific had "holed through" its 7,000-foot tunnel in the San Fernando Hills, and one month later Los Angeles enjoyed its own "golden spike" ceremony that tied it to the rest of the world.

Bᵁᵀ ᵀᴴᴱ ᵀᴵᴹᴱ ᵂᴬˢ "The Terrible Seventies," and railroad or no railroad, Southern California was as fully crippled by the depression of 1875 as any region in California. Towns and agricultural subdivisions built in the first flush of boom declined and died; the Temple & Workman and Farmers & Merchants banks of Los Angeles were forced to close, and although both reopened, the Temple & Workman quickly failed altogether; the Cerro Gordo trade dribbled away from the city to the railroad, and the Los Angeles Chamber of Commerce succumbed to desuetude; the vaunted Los Angeles & Independence Railroad became involved in a ruinous rate war with the Los Angeles & San Pedro, and it soon folded, John P. Jones selling out to the Southern Pacific and leaving Los Angeles in the "grip of monopoly," as newspaper editors were wont to put it; and finally, a drought hit the region in 1877, killing thousands of sheep and cattle, and withering most of its crops. By 1880 the population of Los Angeles had dropped from a high of 17,600 in 1876 to only a little over 11,000.

Ironically, it was the railroad, that "grip of monopoly," that began pulling Southern California out of the doldrums of the seventies. In 1877 the Southern Pacific completed its line to Yuma. When the Texas & Pacific went bankrupt later that year, getting no farther west than southern Texas, Southern Pacific continued pushing across Arizona and New Mexico on its own; in 1882, in exchange for the Texas & Pacific's western land grants, the Southern Pacific joined its rails with those of the eastern road at Galveston: the "Sunset Route" to Southern California was finally completed.

Fat with federal land grants, the railroad needed people—people to buy its land, people to settle and develop the country, people to buy and sell goods shipped over Southern Pacific tracks at Southern Pacific rates. In the railroad's view, what was good for the Southern Pacific was good for the country, and it began

*Waiting to dig into a mess of barbecued beef at a free-lunch auction near San Diego, 1887.*

to ballyhoo the joys of the Golden State in one of the most intensive advertising campaigns in American history. Handbills, posters, brochures, pamphlets, newspaper advertisements, magazine articles, and books sprouted like morning glories all over the world. Lecturers braved the "chicken a la king circuit"; land offices popped up in Chicago, New York, London, and Hamburg; and land agents bent the ears of farmers from Iowa to Ireland—Eden was for sale.

The campaign had the desired results. By the middle of the 1880s, several new towns had been laid out and occupied, farming had increased profoundly, and Los Angeles had acquired a population of more than twenty thousand, most of whom shared the convictions of the *Los Angeles Times:* "All the world is interested in California. As of old, when search was instituted for the fountain of eternal youth, and men dreamed of drinking its waters and living forever, so men today turn their steps in the direction of the Golden State, looking for the springs of health which are hidden in its atmosphere. Better than the Utopias of the ancients is this modern Utopia of the Pacific. Better than the Gardens of Hesperides, with their golden fruits, the gardens of this sunset land. . . ."

It was only the beginning. Late in 1885 the Atchison, Topeka & Santa Fe Railroad completed its own line

*Hollywood in the halcyon days — when it was more beautiful than the people who inhabited it.*

that year, another forty thousand boiled in San Diego, and thousands more fanned out into the warm countryside with money in their pockets and stars in their eyes. There weren't real estate agents enough to serve them all, but the problem was solved by the eager migration of veteran midwestern brokers, tract developers, auctioneers, and specialists in flimflam who detected the sweet odor of other people's money. Buying up chunks of railroad land and former Mexican ranchos, promoters built hotels and short-line railroads, laid out streets, sidewalks, and water lines, printed up magnificent brochures, maps, and bird's-eye views of their future metropolises, and brought the buyers out with free train rides, free barbecues, free band music, free lemonade, and something a little stronger here and there—everything free, "free as air."

A town is what you make it, and the promoters of the big boom were not shy about making them—anywhere they could. In the Mojave Desert, Widneyville-by-the-Desert featured a stand of Joshua trees on whose spiny blossoms oranges had been impaled, thus creating an orange grove within the reach of all. In the Sierra Madre Mountains near the border of Los Angeles County, Border City had been laid out on a rocky promontory so bleak that, according to the *Los Angeles Times,* even crows and eagles would "have to carry well-filled haversacks with them as they fly over that inhospitable waste." Swamps, mudflats, deserts, dry river bottoms—no place was considered unsuitable for the development of "choice villa and residence sites."

Not all the towns and subdivisions—more than sixty of them, finally—were quite so fraudulent, and many survived, places like Glendale, Alhambra, Monrovia, and Westlake Park. Yet dozens were as transient as smoke, and their names have a ghostly sound: Rosencrans, Walteria, Chicago Park, Dundee, Ivanhoe, Terracina, Morocco, La Ballona, Gladysta. . . . The towns were dream towns at best, and fabrications at worst, but with ten, twenty, or thirty dollars down and forever to pay, *everyone* was making money: buy today, trade up tomorrow, and the future has no end. "Millionaires of a day," in the classic words of Theodore C. Van Dyke, "went about sunning their teeth with checkbooks in their outside pockets." Real estate values all over Southern California bloated incredibly. City lots in Los Angeles and San Diego went for thousands of

from Kansas City to Los Angeles and San Diego. The two railroads promptly entered into a rate war on passenger fares in 1886 and 1887 that saw the one-way price from points in the Missouri Valley drop from $125 to $100, from $100 to $50, from $50 to $25—and finally, on March 6, 1887, fares opened at $12, fell to $4 within three hours, and at noon plummeted all the way down to a single dollar.

The combination of inducement and opportunity was irresistible. More than three hundred thousand people who had been hearing about Southern California for more than ten years decided to pack up and see for themselves. The boom—the *big* boom—was on.

As the trains came rattling in during the spring, summer, and fall of 1887, they spilled thirty and forty thousand people a month into Southern California. Eighty thousand wandered the streets of Los Angeles

dollars a front foot; former truck gardens and cattle browse were carved up and sold for $10,000 an acre; some days, nearly a million dollars in transactions took place, and by the end of 1887, it was estimated that more than $200,000,000 worth of promises had been traded. Southern California was "the land of opportunity and one-dollar bills," and one man's paper money was as good as another's.

And then it ended. No one seemed to know precisely why, but perhaps it was because people who had been making hundreds of thousands in paper money began running short of *real* money. In the lexicon of boom, any attempt to exchange the deed to, say, a "sure-fire" $50,000 lot for a thousand dollars or so of real, negotiable, cash money is coldly regarded as a violation of the rules of the game; when enough people try, however, the game is over.

So it was in Southern California by the spring of 1888. The boom, according to one of San Diego's 235 real estate agents, "went down like a chunk of sawed-off wood." Millions were lost as quickly and magically as they had been made. The populations of Los Angeles and San Diego dropped 50 percent in a matter of months. Some of the more sizable new towns were nearly depopulated, and dozens of towns that had had no inhabitants to begin with never got any. Worthless paper blew across the landscape like tumbleweeds.

The big boom ended, but the growth of Southern California did not. There were cities now where there had been towns, towns where there had been villages, and villages where there had been chaparral and creosote bush; farms were planted and irrigation companies formed; at least 130,000 of the boom's population remained to make the land their home; and in spite of paper profits and paper losses, the assessed *real* valuation of property in Los Angeles rose from $18,000,000 in 1886 to $46,000,000 in 1889. The more-or-less normal growth following the period of hysteria was as real as the anticipatory growth of the boom years had been hallucinatory, and the somewhat florid exclamations of one real estate firm in 1887 at least had the ring of prophecy: "Oh! generation of carkers and unbelievers. . . . This boom is based on the simple fact that hereabouts the good Lord has created conditions of climate and health and beauty such as can be found nowhere else, in this or any other land, and until every acre

*San Diego, for sale, for sale, for sale . . .*
*the punctuation for a boom that would be reborn.*

of this earthly paradise is occupied, the influx will continue."

And so it did. Largely responsible for that continuing influx was the startling rise in the citrus industry, particularly oranges, a rise made possible by the completion of the southern transcontinental railroad and ready access to eastern markets. The first special train loaded exclusively with oranges left Los Angeles for the east in February 1886, and from that time forward the orange became not only the principal cash crop of Southern California, but its living symbol; until halfway through the twentieth century, when Florida began to dominate the market, the California orange defined the essence of a land that saw itself and was seen by others to be colored with the magical. Requiring a minimum of both investment and maintenance, and blessed with an enormous profit margin, the orange was the aristocrat of agriculture, the ideal crop for gentlemen farmers as well as industrial farmers, and its appeal to both was phenomenal. In 1890 there were a little over one million orange trees in Southern California; after ten years of nationwide exposure to this new kind of gold, the number had risen to 5,648,714 trees, whose annual product exceeded one billion dollars.

This was the stuff of growth, and the "boosters" of Southern California took full advantage of it. The defunct Los Angeles Chamber of Commerce was revived under new leadership and began a proselytizing campaign that would not be matched by any organization on earth; the theme was grow, grow, grow! and Los Angeles grew with startling abandon, until its population leaped to more than 100,000 in 1900. Not only did it grow, it began to exercise muscle, and probably no other event so defined its new sense of power as its final conflict with the Southern Pacific Railroad.

At issue was the old harbor of San Pedro, which the citizens of Los Angeles wished to enlarge with several million dollars of federal money. At first, the Southern Pacific enthusiastically supported the idea, but when a new, independent railroad began operations between Los Angeles and San Pedro in 1891, the directors changed their minds. Viewing competition with their usual distaste, they maintained that it would be far better to spend the money on their own harbor of Santa Monica, acquired when they purchased the Los Angeles & Independence Railroad from Senator John P. Jones. Anticipating success in this regard, the Southern Pacific moved ahead and constructed a huge new wharf at Santa Monica, severely undercutting the trade of its own operation at San Pedro as well as the Santa Fe's new ocean terminal at Redondo Beach. In the meantime, Collis P. Huntington, an old dog who believed in old tricks, applied pressure to Southern Pacific men in Congress and attempted to browbeat the leaders of Los Angeles into dropping their plan for San Pedro.

He was only partially successful in either regard. In a secret vote held in 1894, the Los Angeles Chamber of Commerce voted in favor of San Pedro by more than two to one, and each of two investigative bodies sent west by Congress to determine the best location for a major port recommended San Pedro. Huntington did not give up easily, although he must have smarted from the almost continual attacks by the city's "Free Harbor League," an organization formed to press the campaign for San Pedro. In 1896, Huntington manipulated a River and Harbors Bill through the Senate's Commerce Committee that included an appropriation of three million dollars for the improvement of Santa Monica—and none for San Pedro. When the bill reached the floor, Senator Stephen M. White, a Los Angeles lawyer elected in 1893 and a vigorous champion of San Pedro, rose in a last-ditch effort to propose an amendment that called for another engineering study to determine whether Santa Monica or San Pedro should receive the federal grant. Pointing to the allies of the Southern Pacific, White cried, "They fear fairness!" in his finest courtroom manner, and for five days the winds continued to blow in the halls of Congress as the antagonists faced off in debate. The amendment carried, and with it the bill was passed and sent to the House, from which it emerged intact for President Grover Cleveland's signature. After the president signed the River and Harbors Bill into law, a third engineering report once again recommended San Pedro, and in the spring of 1899 construction of the Port of Los Angeles began, an event celebrated for two days in Los Angeles and Wilmington.

After fifty years of somnolence interrupted by sudden, disruptive spurts of growth, Southern California faced the twentieth century with a knowledge of its strength and a full-blown conviction that it held a firm grip on destiny, as articulated by a particularly excitable real estate speculator during the boom of the eighties. "We have seen the future," he had announced, "and it belongs to the Sunset Land."

*Schoolhouse and children, San Diego, ca. 1890.*

# *California Mirror:*
# *Portrait of the Sunset Land*

*Eagle Rock Valley, with Pasadena in the distant right, 1900.*

"Better than the Utopias of the ancients is this modern Utopia of the Pacific," flatly declared the **Los Angeles Times** in 1886. But was it? Some declared that Southern California had simply fallen in love with its own advertising. Unsurprisingly, much of such criticism came from San Francisco, one of whose newspaper editors took a genteel swipe at the city's little sister to the south: "Our brethren of the city and would-be state of the Angels know how to advertise. The average Eastern mind conceives of California as a small tract of country situated in and about Los Angeles. . . . The result shows the pecuniary value of cheek."

The response of Southern California to such jibes was usually mild; the regions, after all, were inhabited by

two different kinds of people, and there was little question as to which was the superior group, as one Los Angeleno wrote in the 1860s: "We are different in pursuits, in tastes, manner of thought and manner of life. . . . The restless, uneasy population of the north, ever drifting, without local attachments, has no counterpart in Southern California. . . . With this peaceable life . . . there has grown up in the people an intense love of their land. . . . We call ourselves, not Californians, but Southern Californians." He was writing in the years before the booms of the 1870s and 1880s, but the sense and tone of his feelings were mirrored even in those years.

Who was right? The portrait that follows may suggest an answer.

*Dairying in the Chino Valley south of San Diego, 1885.*

"Wherever you go, you need to take with you a cheerful and also inquiring spirit. The whole of Southern California is full of novelties and wonders to an intelligent person; but oftenmost he must discover them for himself. . . . You are expected to do what you please . . . and you carry with you, wherever you go, fine mountain scenery, bright sunshine—so constant that, when I remarked to a citizen of San Diego that it was a fine day, he looked at me in amazement, and said, after a pause, 'Of course it is a fine day; why not? Every day is fine here.' Moreover, at all these places you will meet pleasant, intelligent, and hospitable people. . . ."

—Charles Nordhoff, 1872

"It is held that Los Angeles, with its port of Wilmington, thirty miles away, should be, and will be, now upon the completion of the Southern Pacific Railroad, the entrepot and Pacific terminus respectively of a new commercial system. San Francisco has too long sat at the Golden Gate, as it is picturesquely put, 'levying toll on every pound of freight that passes through.' This selfish greed on the part of San Francisco is to be properly rebuked by the diversion of a part of its trade to the places named. . . . Los Angeles, it is held, is to be the Lyons, and San Diego, the Marseilles, of the State, this theory still leaving San Francisco the Paris of the Golden State. . . ."

—William Henry Bishop, 1883

*One of the earliest known photographs of San Diego, a daguerreotype of about 1860.*

*Overleaf: An 1885 view of a garden in Pasadena, where flowers bloomed even in the winter.*

*A stagecoach scene on the road to Naples, Los Angeles County, ca. 1880.*

"A low hand-car running on a track upon the long wharf conveys our baggage up into the town while we walk beside it. The town on being reached is found to be a place of loose texture. It has a disproportionately large hotel, the Horton House, which was built in anticipation of future greatness, and proved a loss to its proprietors. The blue shades are down and the plate-glass windows dusty also in much of the 'Horton Block' . . . which still wears an expectant look. After '73, it is said, half the shutters in San Diego were nailed up. They have now come down, however, no doubt to stay. . . . The chronic condition of shutters in San Diego 'Old Town' is to be nailed up. . . . Nothing is more desolate now."

—William Henry Bishop, 1883

"I am willing to take the country barefoot and wait for the shoes and stockings."

—David M. Berry, 1873

"I do not mean to say that everybody in Southern California is rich—but everybody expects to be rich tomorrow."

—Charles Dudley Warner, 1888

"Buy land in Los Angeles and wear diamonds."

—Real estate pamphlet, 1887

"FOUR EXCURSIONS—A REGULAR TOURIST ARMY ARRIVES"

—Headline in the **Los Angeles Times**, 1887

*Perhaps the definitive horsecar photograph: the Florence Heights Line, San Diego.*

*Rapid Transit personified forever: the electric line of San Diego, 1887.*

*Overleaf: Picking poppies at the end of the line in Altadena, 1886.*

"And the summer of 1886 came on. . . . By the middle of the summer Los Angeles was growing at the rate of about a thousand a month, and San Diego at the rate of about five hundred a month. The deposits in the banks were already several times the amount of the capital stock, and gold was more plentiful on the streets than silver in ordinary times. For property was selling every day in all directions, and selling generally for cash. . . .

"When the boom started the Californians laughed at it. The first stage was spontaneous and healthy. The crazy part of it was started by professional boomers flocking from Kansas City, Chicago, St. Paul, San Francisco, and other places, and showing the natives how to make money out of wind. Never were more apt scholars found, and they soon became dizzy with the rapid installation of wisdom. Farmers began to neglect their farms and go into town-lot speculation. Orchards and vineyards were given over to the malva and wild mustard, and too many bore only crops of town-lot stakes. It became far more dignified for the owner of town-lots that were advancing in value by the day to buy his eggs from Iowa, his chickens from Kansas City, his pork from Chicago, and his butter from the north, than to bother with raising them. All this was aggravated by the fact that it was now quite useless to talk to a newcomer about buying a farm. . . . Why buy a farm now when it was so much better to double one's money first on town-lots and then buy a farm? These were the sages who spread out their money as thin as possible . . . lost the whole of it, and then went back to tell Eastern editors that the whole of Southern California was cut up into twenty-five foot lots."

—Theodore S. Van Dyke, 1890

"This damned town is getting too crowded for me! I'm going to move out!"

—An anonymous Pasadenan, 1887

*Selling lots—2,500 of them—at San Diego's Ocean Beach, 1887.*

*Overleaf: The subdivider's dream—Westlake Park, Los Angeles, 1900.*

*Measuring the fruits of growth, San Diego, 1933.*

# PART TWO
# THE TWENTIETH CENTURY

# PROLOGUE
## Death With a Sound Like Thunder

APRIL 18, 1906, 5:12 A.M.: "The first shock came while still the mighty city lay deep in slumber," the *Los Angeles Times* reported. "Then came the rumble of deep thunder from the mighty bowels of the startled earth. The city shook like an aspen leaf, and her gray highways suddenly cracked and split as though the batteries of Satan and his upper hell had been opened. . . ." Paul Barrett, an editor for the *San Francisco Examiner,* recalled a scene of agony and chaos: "It seemed as though my head were split with the roar that crashed into my ears. . . . Great gray clouds of dust shot up with flying timbers, and storms of masonry rained into the street. Wild, high jangles of smashing glass cut a sharp note. Ahead of me a great cornice crushed a man as if he were a maggot."

*A section of the Embarcadero, one of the many San Francisco streets ripped and warped by the quake.*

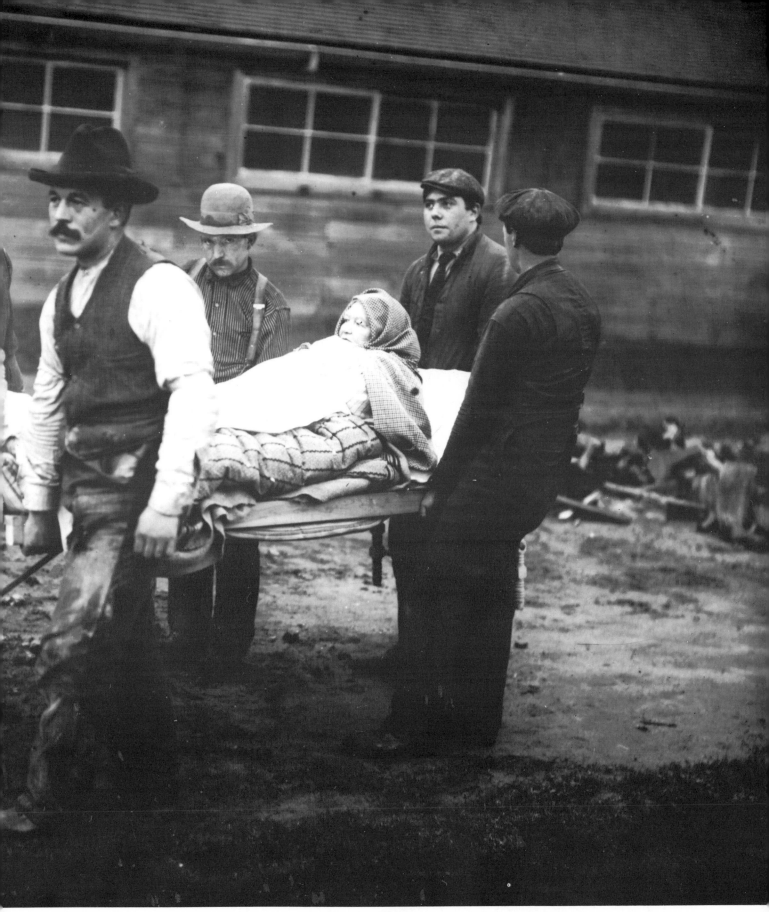

*One of the first rescue operations was the removal of hospital patients.*

*There was time for humor even in a crisis: outdoor cooking on California Street.*

*Singularly humorless were the special deputies on the lookout for looters.*

The San Andreas Fault, after eons of steadily building pressure, had suddenly slipped—a shift that took less than a second and amounted to no more than twenty feet, yet created an energy wave perhaps ten thousand times more powerful than an atomic bomb. Rupturing, twisting, tearing, and killing, the wave of destruction lashed the earth like the bitter hand of God—which many feared it was. The first and most intense shock lasted about forty seconds; the second, following the first by ten seconds, lasted only twenty-five seconds. In a little over a minute, much of San Francisco had been shaken into rubble.

And then the city began to burn. Disrupted stoves and fireplaces, and shredded, sparking electric wires touched off little fires all over the city—perhaps as many as seventy-five in the first few hours after the earthquake. Many of these were extinguished quickly. Many were not; they joined to become large fires, which joined to become great fires, and by the evening of April 18, swarms of flames were eating into the heart of the city with an awesome hunger. "All colors and shades were there," Henry Lafler wrote for *McClure's Magazine*. "Here, for a moment, showed a pale, clear yellow, then again a fiery red. There were perfect blues, there was violet, green, and rose yellow. Then would come dark, sinister, demoniac hues, hateful as hell."

Controlling the flames was an almost hopeless task. Water mains, ruptured by the earthquake, delivered little or no water. Dynamite, used to create firebreaks, was the only weapon left, and even its help was limited, as the *Call-Chronicle-Examiner*—an emergency issue printed in Oakland across the bay—pointed out on April 19: "During the day a blast could be heard in any section at intervals of only a few minutes, and buildings not destroyed by fire were blown to atoms. But through the gaps made, the flames jumped and although the failures of the heroic efforts of the police, firemen and soldiers were at times sickening, the work was continued with a desperation that will live as one of the features of the terrible disaster. Men worked like fiends to combat the laughing, roaring, onrushing fire demon."

*City on fire: a ruined city hall dome is framed in billows of smoke from the financial district.*

Not until the morning of April 21 were the flames finally halted. By then they had done their work well: 28,000 buildings in 490 blocks spread over 2,831 acres had been destroyed at a loss variously estimated at between 500 million and one billion dollars. The fire, with the earthquake, killed at least 450 people and left more than 200,000 homeless. Acre for acre, dollar for dollar, death for death, it was the worst municipal disaster in American history—and one whose agony touched the entire country. In days, more than eight million dollars was raised across the nation for the relief and rebuilding of San Francisco, and another million would come in over the rest of 1906. The money was a gift of the heart, as documented by William Marion Reedy, owner and editor of the St. Louis journal, *Reedy's Mirror:* "Vale et Ave Frisco the beautiful, the glad, the strong, the stricken, the invincible. Down with her went our hearts. Up with her go our souls. The country's hope and faith and love are more fired than the shuddering earth. . . ."

*Aftermath: a child finds refuge in a homemade swing that has incredibly survived the fire.*

*Aftermath: a group of rather elegant bachelors finds a home in the rubble of Mission Street.*

# SECTION ONE

# *To Grasp the Future*

This constant reaching forward to and grasping at the future does not so much express itself in words . . . as in the air of ceaseless haste and stress which pervades the West. They remind you of the crowd which Vathek found in the halls of Eblis, each darting hither and thither with swift steps and unquiet mien, driven to and fro by a fire in the heart. Time seems too short for what they have to do, and result always to come short of their desire.

\* \* \*

What will happen when California is filled by fifty millions of people, and its valuation is five times what it is now, and the wealth will be so great that you will find it difficult to know what to do with it? The day will, after all, have only twenty-four hours. Each man will have only one mouth, one pair of ears, and one pair of eyes. There will be more people—as many perhaps as the country can support—and the real question will be not about making more wealth or having more people, but whether the people will then be happier or better.

—Lord James Bryce (above, from *The American Commonwealth,* 1889; below, from a speech at Berkeley, 1909)

*With banners and bunting, the city of Oakland commemorates the completion of California's last transcontinental railroad, 1910.*

# CHAPTER 13

# THE MIDDLE-CLASS REVOLT

*In which the Good People of California rise up
and throw the rascals out of office*

As THE NINETEENTH CENTURY turned and the San Francisco that had captured the imagination of the world shuddered and flamed into memory, a movement of similar (if less destructive) force began to gather the momentum necessary to shake California loose from the political quagmire in which she had been caught for more than two generations. The men who engineered this movement, who gave it the strength of their determination, their hope, and their ambition, were inclined to view it as a genuine revolution of immense scope and glistening purity. That it was neither a revolution nor quite that pure should not be allowed to diminish the fact that this movement was the healthiest political manifestation exhibited to date in the state's history, and one that helped to set the tone for much of her twentieth-century life.

The forces against which the movement was directed were superbly illustrated by an event that took place less than six months after San Francisco's ruin. Early in September 1906 delegates of the Republican Party gathered in Santa Cruz to select a gubernatorial candidate. On hand were a number of reform delegates, most of them from the southern counties of the state, and most of whom were committed to the renomination of Governor George C. Pardee. Their influence was gutted by the efficient teamwork of a group of Southern Pacific lobbyists led by Walter A. Parker and dedicated to the nomination of Congressman James N. Gillett, who had proved himself a good and true friend of the railroad. The Pardee drive was further eroded by the efforts of Abraham Ruef, the little kingpin of San Francisco politics, who controlled the largest single body of delegates as surely as if they had been so many bits of paper carried around inside his black derby.

After a few days of the kind of wheeling and dealing its "Political Bureau" had raised to a refined art, the Southern Pacific faction managed to gain control over a substantial bloc of delegate votes. More were needed, and Ruef's contingent was available—eminently available. The matter of a $14,000 payment was discussed at meetings (presumably in smoke-filled rooms) between Ruef and Parker, and when the first ballot vote was taken on September 10, Gillett, the railroad's champion, was nominated by a vote of 591½ to 233½. Shortly afterward, the men who had negotiated the nomination gathered for a sumptuous victory banquet, and to document the bibulous occasion, a photographer snapped a most remarkable picture: seated in the center of the group, fittingly enough, was Ruef, flanked on either side by such plump dignitaries as Southern Pacific's Rudolph Herold, George S. Hatton, and Parker; and standing directly behind Ruef, with one hand gently resting in tender gratitude upon his shoulder, was the gubernatorial nominee himself.

That photograph, printed and reprinted over the next several years, became a kind of talisman for the reform movement in California, a visible expression of a blight that many people felt had reduced the state's politics to a nearly terminal condition. Around this picture, or what it represented, coalesced most of the fragments that had characterized the disorganized, fit-

*The strength to rebuild a city: the "Mechanics' Monument," Douglas Tilden's tribute to the workingmen of San Francisco, seen here in 1906.*

*James D. Phelan, San Francisco's liberal banker,
onetime mayor, and crusading philanthropist.*

and-start movement throughout the 1890s and the first years of the twentieth century. The movement in fact had been many movements, frequently as scattered geographically as they were varied in their allegiances, methods, and goals.

While statewide politics had remained pretty much the uncontested satrapy of the Southern Pacific Railroad throughout most of the 1880s and 1890s, an early, if somewhat abortive, sentiment of municipal reform was expressed in San Francisco in 1891. Democratic boss Christopher A. ("Blind Chris") Buckley, a myopic grafter who had manipulated city politics for more than a decade (profitably aiding and abetting the interests of the Southern Pacific whenever called upon), was inspired by a long overdue grand jury investigation to pack his bags and shake the city dust from his feet. He was replaced by Republican Daniel J. Burns, less nearsighted but no less willing to milk the city for whatever he could get, and fully as susceptible to the persuasions of the railroad. In 1894, Burns was actually brought to trial for graft, and although he won acquittal, the probability of coming to trial again caused him to leave San Francisco with all deliberate speed.

The city enjoyed a brief interlude of good government with the mayoralty election later in 1894 of Adolph Sutro, whose tunnel to the mines of the Comstock (see chapter 9) had given him the money to finance a career in San Francisco real estate and stock speculation. Sutro won the election under the banner of Populism, a radical faction of the Democratic Party whose eminently vocal national leader was William Jennings Bryan. Although the statewide influence of Populism was limited, garnering only a little over 20 percent of the vote in 1894, San Francisco's unionized labor supported it vigorously; this, coupled with Sutro's great popularity as one of the city's major benefactors, gave him a solid plurality.

By 1897, with the defeat of William Jennings Bryan in the presidential election of 1896, the Populist movement began to crumble, and Sutro was replaced by another, by no means like-minded, reformer: James D. Phelan, a banker. Remarkably liberal for his time and background, as evidenced by his conviction that the city's problems could be substantially solved by municipal ownership of all utilities, Phelan enjoyed a little over two years of a generally peaceful, progressive administration.

That period of grace came to an end in 1901, when union labor in the city began a series of strikes designed to make San Francisco the first closed-shop town in California. Soon nearly 60 percent of local businesses were closed by the strikes, and the streets rang with the traditional violence between union men and employer-hired strikebreakers and "special police." Phelan attempted to hold the middle ground, a stance that pleased no one. By refusing to call in state troops to put down the strike, he alienated the city's business element; by allowing city police to ride on drays next to strikebreaking teamsters, he became the enemy of organized labor. The strike was settled in October 1901 (to the advantage of the business interests), but by then Phelan's chances for renomination had disintegrated.

Enter Abraham Ruef and the Union Labor Party. Ruef was a native San Franciscan, a graduate of the University of California in 1883 at the age of eighteen, and was admitted to the California bar in 1886.

Supremely idealistic in his youth (his senior thesis in college was "Purity in Politics"), Ruef had acquired a fine veneer of cynicism after more than a decade of participation in the murkier levels of Republican Party manipulations under the tutelage of political thugs Martin Kelly and Phil Crimmins. The precocious Ruef was a quick study and between 1886 and 1888 had risen from lowly precinct captain to "boss" of the North Beach District. On that solid base he had developed a lucrative law practice, a profound respect for power, and a certain knowledge of how power could be made to work—for him.

In September 1901 he was given his chance. That month, San Francisco's disaffected labor unionists decided to make a bid for political strength by forming the Union Labor Party. On hand was Ruef with a carefully chosen claque, who quickly took over control of the new party's machinery. The next step was to choose a candidate for the coming mayoralty election, and Ruef went about it with a cool, perceptive calculation that would rival any of today's public relations firms. The man he chose was Eugene E. Schmitz, and the selection was little short of brilliant—in spite of the fact that Schmitz's only previous claim to public attention had been his orchestra-conducting at the fashionable Columbia Theatre. Nevertheless, Schmitz had two things going for him: he was the son of an Irish mother and a German father, giving him one foot in each of the city's major ethnic camps; and perhaps even more important, he was a most attractive man, tall, well built, with a powerful gaze, strong jaw, sweeping moustaches, and a shining black beard that positively shouted out his refulgent masculinity. Even in an age before woman suffrage—or television, for that matter—Ruef had shrewdly detected the value of charisma in the peculiar world of politics, as he later recalled: "The psychology of the mass of voters is like that of a crowd of small boys or primitive men. Other things being equal, of two candidates they will almost invariably follow the fine, strongly built man."

Schmitz's Republican and Democratic opponents were pale and lifeless by comparison, and with a strong showing in the city's working-class districts, he won the election handily. From that time forward, Ruef began weaving the strands of a little behind-the-scenes empire in San Francisco—and if union labor prospered

*The redoubtable Abraham Ruef in 1907. Is there a hint of mockery in that steady gaze?*

during the years of his dominance, succeeding in its goal of a closed-shop town, so did Abraham Ruef and those he let in for a piece of the action. Never had the wheels of municipal government been so well lubricated with the oil of graft, of payoffs and bribes and special favors, accompanied by the almost constant scrape of mutual back scratching. By 1905, when Ruef was able to pack the board of supervisors with Union Labor Party candidates, an extremely intricate web of greed and corruption had been spun through nearly every level of San Francisco's life.

The more it was spun, the more obvious that web became, particularly those filaments in the hands of Ruef's board of supervisors; these men, a gaggle of former saloonkeepers, draymen, and lower-echelon political functionaries, were so eager to better their condition in life that even Ruef said that they were prepared "to eat the paint off a house." That avarice was the system's downfall, for it fed the growing anger of the city's reform-minded element, led by Fremont

*Eugene E. Schmitz, an orchestra leader who danced to a tune composed by Abe Ruef.*

Older, editor of the San Francisco *Bulletin*.

Older was the very definition of the "crusading editor," and his *Bulletin* had begun casting barbs at the Ruef-Schmitz "machine" in 1903.* In 1905 he decided to engineer something more ambitious: a full-scale graft investigation. The earthquake and fire interrupted his preparations, but by June 1906 he had the necessary ingredients together. These included a guarantee of financing from former mayor Phelan and

---

*Historian James P. Walsh has recently argued (in the Spring 1972 issue of the California Historical Quarterly) that Ruef was not a boss in the traditional sense, nor was his machine a machine in that sense. The point is well taken, since the most apparent characteristics of a big-city boss and his machine are discipline and control. Ruef, a professional grafter surrounded by enthusiastic amateurs, was not able to control the greed of his cohorts—a situation that ultimately destroyed him.

Rudolph Spreckels, son of the sugar magnate, Claus Spreckels; a loan from the federal government of two machine-smashers, Francis J. Heney, a special prosecutor then spearheading some of the trust-busting activities of President Theodore Roosevelt, and William J. Burns, head of the Treasury Department's Secret Service and one of the most renowned detectives in the world; and an agreement to cooperate fully from San Francisco's district attorney, William H. Langdon, an honest man who had won election in 1905 as a Union Labor Party candidate. Understandably willing to see an end to municipal graft and not at all disheartened at the idea of crippling the influence of unionized labor, the city's business interests gave their enthusiastic support to the project—including, for a while, the Southern Pacific Railroad, which had found Ruef to be altogether too independent-minded for its tastes. (With Ruef's accommodating delivery of the San Francisco delegate votes at the gubernatorial convention in September, of course, the railroad curbed its support; there would soon be even better reasons.)

A grand jury was convened in November, evidence was presented, and indictments were issued against Ruef and Schmitz for accepting payoffs from various of the city's eating-places-cum-bordellos, the "French" restaurants. Before long, three of Ruef's hungry supervisors were caught with their hands in one cookie jar or another and, in return for a promise of immunity, confessed to their own crimes as well as those of the rest of the board; and again in a bargain for immunity, the remaining members fell over one another in their eagerness to testify. In May 1907, Ruef himself made a similar bargain, different only in one detail: he was promised immunity if he would not only testify to his own bribe-taking but give the names and numbers of the bribe-*givers,* which included some of the best people in town, such as William F. Herrin of the Southern Pacific and Patrick Calhoun, president of the United Railroads. With this ammunition in hand, Heney secured indictments spanning a broad spectrum of the city's business community.

Understandably, the business community's enthusiasm for the trials abruptly cooled after Heney's action, for that sort of thing simply was not done; it was tantamount to arresting a prostitute's customer along with the prostitute in a vice raid. The prosecution fell upon hard times. Ruef, having retracted his promise to testify, was himself put on trial and convicted to serve a term in San Quentin state prison, but his was the only successful conviction the graft prosecution earned. Although various trials dragged on until 1911, Heney was forced to leave the battle when a demented spectator shot him in the face during court proceedings, and his successor, Hiram Johnson, enjoyed better luck only in the fact that he was not shot. The conviction of Schmitz was overturned by a higher court; only two bribe-givers ever came to trial, and the closest they came to conviction was a hung jury.

Finally, a powerful coalition of antitrial people reformed the reformers by choosing a slate of "safe" candidates for the 1909 municipal election and won with ease. Frustrated by legal setbacks and deprived of public support, San Francisco's graft trials soon lost even their news value—for by 1910 a zenith was reached by a statewide movement for reform whose effects are with us yet.

T HOMAS ROBERT BARD was "a most reluctant candidate" for United States senator in the election of 1900. A pioneering oil developer (see chapter 16), rancher, farmer, and the leading light of Ventura County, Bard was a man whose granitic uprightness was unblemished by any trace of political ambition. But he was profoundly opposed to the continued influence of the Southern Pacific Railroad in California's public life and particularly incensed that the railroad's candidate was none other than Daniel J. Burns, the former Republican boss of San Francisco who had just barely escaped conviction for graft in 1894.

When Bard's name was placed in nomination before the state legislature in both the regular 1899 session and a special session in February 1900, he gave his supporters his qualified blessing. ("But we must remember," he had written one of them before the first nomination, "that I am not seeking for the honor.") The 1899 session ended in a stalemate, but during the 1900 session the office sought the man, and got him. Faced with yet another stalemate (which would deprive California of representation in Washington), the railroad finally abandoned its support of Burns, and Bard was elected unanimously by the Republican-dominated legislature.

*Fremont Older, an "editor's editor" who took on the forces of corruption in San Francisco.*

Like the successful "Free Harbor" fight of Los Angeles in 1896 (see chapter 12), the election of Senator Thomas R. Bard in 1900 helped to illuminate the cracks in the Southern Pacific's political armor—and it is significant that both events were the direct result of Southern California's growing power. For the major thrust of important reform in the state would come, not from urban San Francisco, with its long-held political and economic dominance, but from the "cow counties" of the south.

The first expressions of that thrust were as purely local as San Francisco's graft trials, if somewhat less spectacular. The "boom" of 1887 brought to Los Angeles a young Philadelphia doctor by the name of John R. Haynes, who had learned more than he cared to know about municipal corruption and machine politics in the City of Brotherly Love. Looking about him in

Los Angeles, he detected evidence of similar evils, particularly the dead hand of the Southern Pacific in the person of the portly, affable Walter Parker. He determined to do something about it and, gathering a few like-minded individuals about him, helped to form the Municipal League, whose avowed mission was to strip the local branch of the Southern Pacific of its power and return the city to its rightful owners, "the people."

To this end, Haynes and the league began to promulgate three of the most radical ideas then current in American reform politics: the initiative (legislation by popular vote), the referendum (popular veto of legislative action), and the recall (ousting of an elected official before the end of his term). An election was scheduled for December 1, 1902, and largely through the efforts of Haynes, all three measures were placed on the ballot as municipal charter amendments. Remarkably, three of the city's four newspapers vigorously supported the amendments, especially the Los Angeles *Express* of Edwin T. Earl, a liberal-minded agricultural entrepreneur who had invented the ventilated refrigerator car, thus making it possible to ship Southern California citrus products to eastern markets. Even more remarkably, Haynes had secured, for a short time, the support of the conservative Los Angeles *Times,* whose owner, "General" Harrison Gray Otis, sometimes found it difficult to admit that the industrial revolution had ever taken place. Shortly before the

*The good people, from left to right: Francis J. Heney, William J. Burns, Fremont Older, C. W. Coff.*

election Otis reversed himself, and never again would he and the city's reform element find much in common —save an everlasting dislike for the Southern Pacific Railroad and all its works.

The amendments carried handsomely, however, and in 1904 the citizens of Los Angeles carried out the first recall election in United States history. This noteworthy event took place when the city council voted to award the city's advertising contract to the *Times,* even though its bid for the job was much higher than that of the other three newspapers. The reformers set their sights on one councilman, J. P. Davenport, in order to set an example for the rest; after a bitter campaign, the offending Davenport found himself suddenly out of work, and the *Times* found itself out of a fat advertising contract. This in no wise increased Otis's regard for the Good Government movement, which he began characterizing as the "Goo-goos."

Even with the initiative, referendum, and recall, the city's government remained generally under the thumb of the Southern Pacific. With an eye to correcting this, four young men got together in early 1906; they were Edward Dickson, editor of the *Express;* Russ Avery and Marshall Stimson, lawyers; and Meyer Lissner,

*Abe Ruef lifts his eyebrows at some whispered advice during the San Francisco graft trials.*

a pawnbroker-turned-lawyer-turned-real-estate-speculator. They gathered enough support to organize what they called the Non-Partisan Committee of One Hundred, and went about selecting twenty-three candidates for the various city offices to be filled in December 1906. In spite of the vehement opposition of both Otis and the Southern Pacific, seventeen of the committee's candidates were elected—not including the mayor—an achievement that severely crippled the railroad's power and made San Francisco's attempts at reform look anemic by comparison.

It would not be until 1909 that the Good Government movement (which by then was calling itself the Good Government League) would take firm control over Los Angeles politics, but by then the four men who had engineered its first major victory were involved in an even broader, more ambitious assault on the power of the Southern Pacific. As noted earlier, the odoriferous Republican gubernatorial nominating convention of September 1906 provided most of the fuel for widespread anger at the arrogance of the railroad; the state legislature that convened in early 1907 did little to abate that anger, for the railroad, in full view of anyone who cared to watch, used its considerable weight to block reform legislation of any kind and promote legislation that served its own interests.

On hand to observe these proceedings were *Express* editor Edward Dickson and, next to him in the press row, Chester H. Rowell, editor of the Fresno *Morning Republican*. The two young men watched with growing repugnance while legislators sold themselves; and they talked, each feeding the other's conviction that the railroad must be stopped. At the end of the session, Dickson and Rowell returned to their respective cities and began a massive letter-writing campaign to promote yet another organization, this one aimed at rescuing the state government.

In May 1907 a meeting of the new group was held in Los Angeles, and the name Lincoln-Republicans was adopted. The reformers then issued an "emancipation proclamation," which declared their prime objective to be the "emancipation of the Republican Party in California from domination by the Political Bureau of the Southern Pacific Railroad Company and allied interests." It advocated adoption of the direct primary (in order to place the nomination of governors and

*Like an aging bantam cock, Hiram Johnson strikes a familiar pose near the end of his life.*

senators in the hands of the people); initiative, referendum, and recall; direct election of United States senators; stiff regulation of railroad and utility rates; prohibition of racetrack gambling; conservation of forests; a workmen's compensation act; a minimum wage law applicable to women; and women's suffrage. In August a statewide meeting was held in Oakland, where the organization's name was changed to the League of Lincoln-Roosevelt Republican Clubs—more commonly, and comfortably referred to as the Lincoln-Roosevelt League.

For the first time, the statewide reform movement had been given cohesion and purpose, and before long the league included in its membership most of the influential Republicans in California—a notable exception being Harrison Gray Otis, a man no more capable of endorsing such concepts as workmen's compensation or a minimum wage law than of flying. By 1908 the league had elected a sufficient number of legislators to secure passage of a direct primary law in the 1909 session, and the governorship itself was for the first time within their reach—if a candidate could be found.

On this point, the league's purity of purpose became somewhat tarnished, as a most unbecoming scramble for the candidacy developed between the extremist faction of the league, whose choice was Francis J. Heney, and the more conservative element, which held out for F. K. Mott, mayor of Oakland. Almost immediately C. H. Rowell began casting about for a potential compromise candidate and settled upon Hiram Johnson, Heney's successor in the San Francisco graft trials. As Rowell wrote to former Senator Thomas R. Bard, "If Johnson will consent to run, it will solve the whole situation brilliantly. I fear nothing else will solve it at all. . . . The radical vote is going to determine this election. Johnson can hold the conservative Republicans and get the whole radical vote, both Republican's and Democratic. To me it looks like certain victory with Johnson and like certain defeat with any other candidate."

Johnson, however, was almost as reluctant a candidate for governor as Thomas R. Bard had been for senator. He had built a good law practice in San Francisco, a practice enhanced by the publicity surrounding the graft trials, and he was understandably hesitant to abandon that for a stay in Sacramento. Moreover, his father, Grove L. Johnson, was an assemblyman from Sacramento who had long been subservient to the interests of the Southern Pacific, a relationship that had caused a painful rift between father and son. Hiram was not eager to open old wounds in that area by becoming a six-year resident of the governor's mansion. If anything, his wife was even more negative toward the idea, since she entertained the notion that her husband belonged in no office lower than that of a United States senator.

Yet, unlike Bard, Johnson's psyche contained more than a little political ambition wedded to a most sincere desire to see an end to the Southern Pacific's machine.

He weakened considerably as Rowell and other intermediaries repeated their conviction that not only could he win the nomination and the election but he was the only candidate who could. He finally capitulated when Heney was persuaded to swing his support to Johnson.

Accepting in February 1910, Johnson threw himself into the battle for the nomination with immediate and characteristic fury, although the primary election was not to take place until August. Armed with the support of a refined and enormously efficient league "machine," he drove up and down the state in his "red devil" Locomobile, hitting nearly every city, town, and hamlet along the way and, with the pugnacious tenacity of a bulldog, shaking the bloody shirt of Southern Pacific corruption at every audience he faced.

His was a simple theme: get the railroad out of California politics. Simple, and successful. In a four-way primary election, Johnson received an astonishing 46,276-vote edge over his nearest competitor. The league could expect no such margin at the November election, however, since the Democratic candidate, Theodore Bell, was fully as antirailroad as Johnson. Fortunately, William F. Herrin decided to support Bell on the assumption that he would be the lesser of two evils, and no amount of bleated protests from Bell could prevent Johnson from making political hay of his opponent's railroad endorsement. When the last vote was tabulated, Johnson had been elected governor of California by a margin of 177,000 votes to 155,000, and the league had won as well seven out of eight congressional seats and majorities in both houses of the state legislature.

After more than two decades, the "good people" of California, the middle-class progressives, had become the major voice in the state's government. How well they could make it work remained to be seen.

*San Francisco's city hall dome — after the earthquake, before the fire.*

# California Mirror:
# The Last Innocence

*Theodore Roosevelt's "Great White Fleet" sails into San Francisco Bay, 1908.*

It was still an age when men believed they could do anything they turned their hands to, with energy and determination enough. Rebuilding San Francisco on the "damndest finest ruins" left by the earthquake and fire of 1906 was a task beyond that undertaken by any other city anywhere, but there was little doubt that it could and would be done. "San Francisco will rise from its ruins and its ashes, grander, more beautiful, more influential than before," the **Los Angeles Times** had generously announced on April 19, 1906. "The men who have made the Pacific Coast what it is are not the men to be disheartened by the disaster. . . . They will con-

tinue to go forward in the magnificent work to which they have set their hands."

By the spring of 1908 the "magnificent work" was moving forward with startling speed. Most of the city's burned-over area had been rebuilt; surviving buildings had been restored, and seventy-seven new buildings, many of them "skyscrapers," were either complete or under construction. On May 6, 1908, Theodore Roosevelt's world-cruising "Great White Fleet" steamed magnificently through the Golden Gate in a gesture of tribute to the risen city, which her citizens accepted as no more than their just due.

*Panama-Pacific International Exposition: The eastern arch of the Court of the Universe.*

A salute from the United States Navy was all well and good, but San Franciscans felt the need to show the whole world what had been wrought on the tip of a thin peninsula at the western edge of the continent. They maintained that the rebuilding of the city was an achievement comparable to the digging of the Panama Canal, scheduled for completion on New Year's Day 1915. That being the case, why not commemorate both accomplishments with an international exposition—a Panama-Pacific International Exposition?

The canal exposition was an idea that had been promoted in fact as early as 1904, and with good reason. The canal in operation—cutting weeks from the long, costly, and dangerous sea route around Cape Horn—would be the most important contribution to California's transportation needs since the transcontinental railroad was finished in 1869. The earthquake and fire

had aborted the early exposition plans, but by the end of 1909 they had been reborn and were embraced enthusiastically. Some four million dollars for the project was pledged in one two-hour mass meeting, and another two million was pledged over a period of two months. A statewide bond issue garnered another five million dollars, and San Franciscans voted to raise their taxes to the tune of an additional five million.

Money was one thing; congressional approval of San Francisco as the official site of the exposition was another. A bid by San Diego was quickly done away with (although the southern city went ahead and put together its own, unofficial exposition, reminders of which can be seen in today's Balboa Park). New Orleans proved more stubborn as a competitor, and it was not until January 31, 1911, that Congress was persuaded of the innumerable virtues of San Francisco as the official site. "Thank you, Uncle Sam," a banner in the city proclaimed. "We'll do you proud."

And so they did. The spot chosen for the fairgrounds was a two-mile stretch of partially filled tidelands on the shore of the bay at the northern edge of the city, just inside the Golden Gate. After months of filling and grading, construction of the buildings began; most of them were composed of "staff," a plaster and burlap fiber mixture molded on wooden frames. Of little durability, the material did allow for a great variety of structural expression—which was exactly what the fair's architects wanted. What they built was an enormous fairyland, a wonderfully eclectic mix of Florentine, Venetian, Moorish, Spanish Byzantine, and Graeco-Roman styles. "If the plan of the Exposition were reduced in scale to the size of a golden **brooch and the** buildings made in Venetian cloisonné jewelry," Berkeley architect Bernard Maybeck exclaimed, "that brooch

would pass as jewelry without causing the suspicion that it represented a plan for a World's Fair."

The most splendid building of them all was Maybeck's own Palace of Fine Arts, which loomed in brooding magnificence over its curving lagoon, symbolizing, in the architect's words, "the mortality of grandeur and the vanity of human wishes." The grandeur of Maybeck's creation was less mortal than he probably intended; painstakingly restored in the 1960s, the Palace of Fine Arts stands alive and well today, the only remnant of that vast, innocent celebration (see page 296).

Equally impressive, on a different level, was the Tower of Jewels, the largest building of the exposition. Ornamented with 50,000 varicolored bits of glass hung from its edges and cornices, the tower glittered and twinkled enchantingly—particularly at night, when it and the rest of the buildings were washed in the light of thirty-six colored searchlights. The spectacle reportedly brought

*On the left, the Palace of Horticulture; on the right, the Tower of Jewels.*

tears to the eyes of poet Edwin Markham and definitely caused him to utter the following paean: "I have seen tonight the greatest revelation of beauty that was ever seen on this earth. I may say this meaning it literally and with full regard for all that is known of ancient art and architecture and all that the modern world has heretofore seen of glory and grandeur. I have seen beauty that will give the world new standards of art, and a joy in loveliness never before reached. That is what I have seen."

The exposition opened at ten o'clock on February 20, 1915, and from then until its closing less than ten months later on the night of December 4, an estimated two million people tasted its delights: the works of art in the great palace; the huge working model of the Panama Canal; the Fountain of Energy; the plants and flowers of the Palace of Horticulture; the mechanical gadgetry of the Palace of Machinery; the rides and restaurants of the Joy Zone. . . . The exposition was a last hopeful expression of a simpler age, and when its lights went out, that age ended with an ineffable sadness. Writing in the **San Francisco Chronicle,** Milla Logan remembered the final moments: "The night it went out, the Fair never looked lovelier. Every jewel in the Tower flashed for the last curtain call. Then a paralyzing dimness fell on the scene. The darkness drained the glow from the domes and palaces, bleeding them slowly to death. The walls turned cold and stiff. The last feeble lights gasped and then there was a dark void where a few minutes ago there had been a vision."

*The California State Building, Balboa Park—
a remnant of San Diego's 1915 canal exposition.*

# CHAPTER 14

# POLITICS, PEOPLE, AND POWER

*The short and happy reign of the California Progressives*
*ends with the ring of violence in the streets*

IRAM JOHNSON was a consummate, gut-fighting politician, but not even his most ardent supporters would have characterized him as an intellectual giant. It is reliably reported that shortly before his election in 1910 he turned to a companion and asked somewhat plaintively, "What in the world are we going to do after we do get in?"

Johnson may have been vague concerning the goals of the Progressive movement, whose figurehead he was, but the engineers of that movement were not; and the state legislative session of 1911 gave them the opportunity to exercise their convictions with a remarkably far-reaching effect. In eighty-five days both houses of the legislature passed more than eight hundred bills as well as twenty-three amendments to the state constitution. It was not only the most reform-minded session in the state's history but, in the sheer bulk of work accomplished, one of the most productive. Although a good many of the measures were passed over bitter opposition, some it from dissenting Progressives, it can be said of this session, perhaps more justifiably than of any other in the state's history, that it reflected with uncommon accuracy the will of most Californians of that time and place. In the special election of November 1911, all but one of the constitutional amendments were approved by the electorate.

The most important of these reforms included the initiative, referendum, and recall (the last including the recall of judiciary officials, which many Progressives considered radical excess); the direct election of United States senators (which some, like staunch old ex-Senator

Thomas R. Bard, believed was a crippling blow to traditional, selective representation); a reconstructed railroad commission whose new duties would include the supervision of *all* public utilities not municipally owned (an idea whose time had apparently come, for not even the Southern Pacific Railroad opposed it with much vigor); women's suffrage (in spite of conservative claims that it would "unsex" society); a workman's compensation law providing for the liability of employers in industrial accidents (at first voluntary, the law was later revised to become compulsory); an eight-hour-day law for women laborers (not including farm workers and employees of canning and packing factories); and a handful of measures designed to improve the quality of the state's moral character (the most prominent of which was a "local option" law that allowed cities and counties to pass and enforce anti-saloon ordinances).

The session of 1912 was considerably less productive, distracted by election-year maneuvering both inside and outside the state, but the session of 1913 challenged that of 1911 in the scope of its work. It introduced a bill for the creation of a conservative commission with the purpose of preserving and protecting the state's water resources (defeated the first time around, the bill was passed the following year); authorized a commissioner of corporations to examine and investigate all public issues of securities; created the Immigration and Housing Commission, as well as irrigation and rural credits commisisons; placed pipelines under the jurisdiction of the railroad commission; passed a licensing law for real estate dealers; established the Industrial Welfare Com-

*The Palace of Fine Arts, San Francisco, a serene monument that has*
*survived through the hard realities of the twentieth century.*

mission to regulate the wages, hours, and working conditions of women and children; enacted the cross-filing law, allowing a candidate to become the nominee of more than one party at a time for the same office; and finally, passed the Red Light Abatement Act, which sought to suppress prostitution.

With the legislative sessions of 1911 and 1913, the California Progressives accomplished most of the reforms they had sought. "From then on," as historian George E. Mowry has noted, "the current of the Progressive movement ran perceptibly slower." Republicans within the Progressive ranks made it clear that in their opinion reform had gone as far as God and the Angels had intended—perhaps farther—and that their future support, if forthcoming at all, would be sparingly measured. Even the more militant Progressives, whose success had blunted the cutting edge of enthusiasm honed in the days when any reform effort was a crusade, found their energies at a low ebb. In 1916, Hiram Johnson removed himself from the leadership post by finally achieving his wife's ambition to see him elected a United States senator.

Johnson's departure for the national capitol (where he would remain until his death in 1945) left the Progressive Party with a vacuum soon filled by factional squabbling for leadership and control. This acrimonious struggle for power, coupled with the beginning of World War I and a corresponding resurgence of conservative sentiment, so weakened the Progressives that by 1920 the voice of reform had deteriorated from a self-confident bellow to an uncertain whimper.

THE LIST OF GENUINE, working reforms produced by the California Progressives during their short reign of power was undeniably impressive. Their rallying cry had been a prototype version of "Power to the People!" and it is true that the changes they wrought provided the citizens of California with a more direct influence on the state's political and economic system than they had ever before enjoyed.

Yet, who were "the people"? In the eyes of most Progressives, the people were, in fact, themselves and others like them, who comprised the great middle segment of California's population. Most were well off, some were at least marginally wealthy, but only a few were rich, as the term is normally understood. Ever fewer were poor, as *that* term is understood. Most were well educated and of the professional stripe—lawyers, newspaper editors and publishers, real estate men, small businessmen, teachers, ministers, writers, librarians. With an innocent smugness that can be forgiven them, they quite self-consciously considered themselves the "good" people of California whose decent instincts reflected all that was best in the American dream.

They were an identifiable class, but they looked forward to an individualistic society *without* "caste or class," a society they liked to think existed in an earlier, simpler America. The movement they spearheaded was in a very real sense a response to what they considered an appalling division in society between the conglomerate rich and the swelling mass of industrialized workers. These two segments, in the Progressive view, spelled ruin for America. "My experience in public life," Thomas R. Bard had written in 1905, "has left upon me a lasting impression that never in our history as a Nation before have we been beset by so many serious dangers, threatening the National life, as now. The foundations, upon which our forefathers built, are rottening [sic]."

"A pox upon both your houses!" might have been the cry of the good Progressive, but when push came to shove, in California at least, he was inclined to fear the excesses of the workingman somewhat more than those of corporation capital. For all the evils of entrenched wealth he saw all around him, the average Progressive, possessed of enormous respect for private property and the inherent virtue of legitimately acquired money, found it considerably easier to identify with, say, a William F. Herrin of the Southern Pacific than with an unwashed foundry worker with a foreign-sounding name and a pronounced weakness for socialism—or even dread anarchy. Organized labor could be tolerated reluctantly as a short-term "war measure to provide relative justice to a few," but when it attempted to exercise muscle, particularly when it espoused the anti-individualistic idea of the closed shop, it became, in the words of Chester Rowell, "antisocial, dangerous, and intrinsically wrong."

As a result, the alliance between the Progressives and organized labor was an uneasy one in which each party took as much as it could from the other and gave back as little as possible. For its part, the Progressive Party supported such "reasonable" labor reforms as workman's compensation and minimum wage and hour laws for women and children, while opposing such items as bills designed to limit the injunction power of the judiciary during labor strikes and neglecting to include any major labor figure in the leadership ranks of the party.* Labor, on the other hand, embraced the Progressive movement simply because it was the only way it could achieve even its minimum goals. However reluctant, that support could at times be significant, as Michael P. Rogin and John L. Shover have pointed out in a recent study: in his second gubernatorial election in 1914, the working-class districts provided Hiram Johnson with 63 percent of his total San Francisco vote; in 1916 those same districts gave him 69 percent of the senatorial primary vote.

Nevertheless, however much the Progressive Party liked to think of itself as a "buffer" between the two great coagulating extremes of society, its real influence along these lines was at best transient. It gave to the middle-class Californian an avenue through which his grievances could be aired and, in large part, satisfied. It provided no such avenue for the working-class Californian, and that failure, if it did not cause, at least contributed to an era of violent confrontation.

F OR NEARLY FORTY YEARS, Harrison Gray Otis played John the Baptist for Southern California. A former Union officer in the Civil War (and later made a nominal general during the Spanish-American conflict), Otis had settled in Los Angeles in 1882, purchased a part ownership of the Los Angeles *Times*, later bought all of it, and from then until his death in 1917 proceeded to trumpet the glories of Southern California. Much of the character, and not a little of the growth, of the region in these years can be attributed to the efforts of this hard-headed visionary of material progress.

---

*Since the Progressive Party was—almost by definition—a non-monolithic organization, this lukewarm attitude toward the needs of labor was not universally held; Hiram Johnson, Francis Heney, Fremont Older, and William Kent, among other notable Good Government people, were in fact vigorous champions of the workingman on most occasions. Their influence, however, was only rarely enough to overcome the general lassitude and occasional antipathy that characterized the party.

*Harrison Gray Otis, the unofficial director of public relations for Southern California.*

His opinions were held with ironbound conviction, and among them was a muscular contempt for unionized labor. That contempt was translated into hatred in 1890, when the International Typographical Union objected to a citywide wage cut of 20 percent ordered by the Los Angeles newspapers. While the city's other newspapers responded to threats of a strike by entering into negotiations with the union, Otis refused even to discuss the matter. When the ITU consequently struck the *Times*, he promptly imported strikebreakers from Kansas City, and with the support of like-minded citizens set about satisfying a newly acquired ambition: he would make Los Angeles the most successful open-shop city in the United States.

It should be pointed out that Otis and his colleagues were acting out of more than simple antagonism. They believed, not without justification, that the only way Los Angeles could effectively compete with the older, more industrial, and largely unionized San Francisco would be to offer a substantially lower system of wages—and one way to assure this was to destroy unionism in the town, presenting potential investors and industrial-

*October 1, 1910: class warfare comes to Los Angeles, and the* Times *building succumbs to flames.*

ists with an enticingly cheap and timid labor pool.

Whatever the subtleties of motivation, the anti-labor forces went about the task of union-busting with enthusiasm and success. When local members of the American Railway Union struck, picketed, and demonstrated throughout the city in support of the Pullman strike of 1894, an uncommonly broad injunction against picketing was requested and obtained from the federal district court, resulting in hundreds of arrests. When the strike continued, federal troops were called in, more workers were arrested, union leaders were indicted, tried, and convicted, and in a matter of weeks the strike was broken locally. To carry on the good work, the Merchants and Manufacturers Association was established in 1896; with the vigorous support of Otis and the *Times,* the "M & M" became perhaps the strongest, most determined anti-union organization in the country. By the middle of the first decade of the twentieth century, wages in Los Angeles had dropped as much as 20, 30, and even 40 percent below those prevailing in San Francisco.

The surviving Los Angeles unions scrabbled desper-

ately for help outside the city, finally calling upon the American Federation of Labor in 1907. The AFL responded by pouring in a small army of organizers and agitators, and enough money to purchase the Los Angeles *News,* change its name to the *Citizen,* and begin countering the incendiary editorials of Otis's *Times* with vitriol of its own. More help came from the unions of San Francisco, although they acted out of something less than unadulterated charity; the merchants and industrialists of the "good, gray city" had been eyeing the lower wages of Los Angeles with both envy and fear for some time, and they finally delivered an ultimatum to their unions: either see to it that the Southland's wages are brought up to par or face wage cuts across the board. That was the kind of language any good union man could understand.

The battle lines drawn after 1907 were sharpened by the appearance and sudden rise of Los Angeles socialism, which waxed fat on the city's increasing ideological antagonisms. Socialist parades featuring as many as twenty thousand workers stalked through the streets of Los Angeles, terrifying not only the city's conservative element but its contingent of Good Government people as well. When it became obvious by the beginning of 1910 that the Socialist leader, Job Harriman, had his eye on nothing less than the mayoralty of Los Angeles, even the Progressive Meyer Lissner (a long-time foe of Otis), was driven to support the anti-labor fulminations of the Los Angeles *Times.*

In this more than slightly charged atmosphere, a series of strikes commenced in the spring of 1910, beginning with brewery workers and then spreading to the metals trades. In response, employers secured the standard injunctions against picketing. When these failed to quell the strikes, the Merchants and Manufacturers Association, with the willing assistance of most Progressive leaders, persuaded the Los Angeles city council to pass a broad anti-picketing ordinance, which swiftly resulted in the arrest of 470 workers. These arrests simply intensified the conflict; by the end of summer membership in the Socialist Party had doubled, picketing continued, and the streets echoed with the staccato ring of violence.

Then in the pre-dawn hours of October 1, a well-placed bomb ripped out one wall of the Los Angeles *Times* building, killing twenty employees and starting a fire that eventually gutted the interior of the masonry structure. "O you anarchic scum," cried Otis in a hastily printed edition of the *Times*, "you cowardly murderers, you leeches upon honest labor, you midnight assassins. . . ." His anger and his rhetoric were shared by most of the "good" people of the city, while labor countered with charges that the explosion and fire had been caused by a faulty gas line.

After a nationwide manhunt under the supervision of William J. Burns (who will be remembered for his part in the graft prosecutions of San Francisco), three alleged culprits were captured in Indianapolis and whisked off to Los Angeles without benefit of formal extradition: Ortie McManigal, a confessed professional dynamiter, and John J. and James B. McNamara, brothers with close ties to the International Association of Bridge and Structural Iron Workers, one of the youngest and most profoundly militant unions in the country, and one that had been linked to several explosions of an anticapitalist nature. While Ortie McManigal, giving state's evidence, fully implicated both the McNamara brothers in the crime, the labor movement gave out with cries of "kidnaping" and "frameup," and hired none other than Clarence Darrow to defend the two brothers.

The arrest and beginning prosecution of the McNamara brothers in the spring of 1911 did little to change the political situation in Los Angeles. In the primaries for mayoralty candidates that spring, the Socialist Party's Job Harriman garnered an impressive 58,000 votes, several thousand more than his nearest competitor. An uneasy alliance between the Merchants and Manufacturers Association and Good Government people immediately threw their weight behind his opponent, incumbent George Alexander; but as summer and then fall came on, it seemed more and more likely that Harriman would win in the election scheduled for December 5, 1911. The fondest nightmare of Harrison Gray Otis appeared to be coming true.

And so it might have—except that on December 1 the McNamara brothers changed their pleas from not guilty to guilty. Faced with a damning body of evidence and probable death sentences, Clarence Darrow had advised his clients to plead guilty in exchange for reduced sentences—John J. to receive life imprisonment, James B. to receive fifteen years. The brothers, now officially

*Surrounded by guards, the McNamara brothers are brought to trial in the summer of 1911.*

guilty by their own admission, saved their own lives but in so doing destroyed the Socialist Party in Los Angeles. Worker and non-worker supporters of the McNamara brothers felt betrayed in their faith, and because of his close identification with the case, Job Harriman was tarred with the brush of their resentment; on election day, discarded Harriman buttons and broadsides cluttered the streets of the city, and Alexander carried the vote by a massive plurality. That same bitterness fractured the labor movement in the city, robbing it of cohesion, support, and purpose, and the twenty-year crusade of Harrison Gray Otis ended with almost total victory. Until World War II, one of the attractions of Los Angeles most advertised by its chamber of commerce was an abundance of "cheap non-union labor."

THE TWO DECADES OF LABOR STRIFE in Los Angeles culminating with the Los Angeles *Times* bombing provided possibly the single most sharply defined conflict between capital and labor in the history of the state up to that time. In spite of the sloganizing and vague

*Hosing down a group of street-speaking Wobblies in San Diego, 1913;*
*firehoses were gentler weapons than pick handles or billy clubs.*

philosophizing that accompanied the struggle on both sides, the basic issue was clear from beginning to end: would Los Angeles be an open- or closed-shop city?

Other antagonisms of the state's early twentieth-century life could not be clarified so easily, for they involved one of the most visionary, ideologically confused, least-understood, and shortest-lived militant labor organizations in American history: the Industrial Workers of the World, the IWW—or "Wobblies," as Harrison Gray Otis is said to have called them. Born out of meetings in Chicago in 1905—largely through the efforts of Eugene Debs, founder and president of the American Railway Union, and William D. ("Big Bill") Haywood, secretary of the Western Federation of Miners —the IWW was a volatile mix of radical sentiments ranging from anarchy to Marxist socialism. Its organizers agreed, however, on one central point: that traditional labor unionism, in the form of the American Federation of Labor, had utterly failed the working class, for it had not recognized the revealed truth that industrial capitalism ("veneered cannibalism") would have to be totally eliminated before the American worker could receive the just returns of his labor. With that loudly proclaimed ambition as its primary goal (but with little that was specific in regard to ways and means), the IWW set out to organize what it saw as the great submerged mass of American workers — the un-

skilled factory hands, the migrant farm workers, the itinerant lumberjacks, the wandering miners.

Full of gusto, conviction, and the blind courage of zealots, IWW organizers spread the word across the western United States; and wherever they went, they were greeted by an outrage fully as paranoid as their own opinions and actions. At the height of its influence, the "One Big Union" probably never achieved a membership of more than seventy thousand (although a slipshod membership system left inadequate records), amounting to less than 3 percent of the country's total number of union workers; yet it challenged the very foundations of a new industrial civilization and was feared quite as passionately as if it had been an armed horde of millions.

The combination of IWW fanaticism and conservative reaction produced some of the most traumatic clashes in the labor history of the West, several of them in California. Oddly enough, two of those clashes featured a phenomenon that was revived in the 1960s as a political technique by eminently middle-class California students exercising protest against the "system": passive resistance.

The issue was "free speech," and after a trial season in Spokane in 1909, it erupted in Fresno, one of the major labor pools for San Joaquin Valley farmers. With soapbox clutched in one hand and a raft of literature in the other, IWW organizers drifted into Fresno in the fall of 1910, setting up business on street corners to spread the word—in spite of the fact that the local police chief had revoked the union's permit to hold street meetings and had declared it his intention to arrest on vagrancy charges any man who violated his prohibition. When he made good his word, the IWW responded by sending out a call for even more members. They came from all over the West—only to be dragged off their boxes, frequently beaten, and thrown into cells growing more crowded every day. By the end of January 1911, the Fresno authorities were desperate. The city's jails were stuffed with Wobblies, each of whom demanded a jury trial, insisted on directing his own defense, and when tried, contested as many jurors as he could—all of which had the approximate effect of a stillson wrench thrown into the gear box of the city's court system. On February 25, Fresno capitulated, releasing all IWW prisoners and guaranteeing the organization's right to use the city's street corners.

The outcome of a similar "free speech" fight in San Diego the following year was less felicitous for the union. San Diego, possessed of a small and generally contented labor force, had little to fear from the IWW, yet its citizens responded to the union's presence with astonishing ferocity. When the city banned all street meetings in the winter of 1911, the IWW sent out the traditional call: "Come on the cushions,/Ride up on top;/Stick to the brakebeams,/Let nothing stop./Come in great numbers,/This we beseech;/Help San Diego/To win *Free Speech!*" Members answering the call, however, were met at the city's railroad yards by vigilante mobs armed with pick handles and wagon spokes. After being forced to run pick-handle gauntlets and endure similar forms of civilized torture, those who survived in an ambulatory state were hauled to the city's jails, and when the population problem there became too great, it was solved by deportation sorties in which IWW members were escorted out of the county, forced to kneel and kiss the flag, and left to fend as best they could on foot.

The violence of San Diego's reaction was so great—even in an age when the IWW was generally acknowledged to have placed itself outside the bounds of decent treatment—that Governor Hiram Johnson was moved to send a personal investigator to San Diego. The investi-

*Preparedness Day, 1916: the human remains of a bomb explosion are covered over gingerly.*

gator compared the actions of the town's citizens to the atrocities typical of Czarist Russia, yet no one in the state government took any action beyond polite tongue-clucking; it was an election year. By October 1912 the streets of San Diego were silent.

Defeated in San Diego, the IWW nevertheless continued its almost formless assault on the Establishment of its time with unreduced vigor. When street speeches failed to obtain more than a handful of members from the ranks of California's migrant farm laborers, organizers took to the fields to work—and talk—side by side with prospective members. In the summer of 1913 several such organizers, including one Richard "Blackie" Ford and one Herman Suhr, gathered with 2,800 other men, women, and children on Ralph Durst's hop ranch, a huge "open-air factory" near Wheatland in the Sacramento Valley.

Following his usual practice, Durst had advertised all over the state for hop pickers, stating that he could provide ample work for everyone at relatively high wages. When the workers arrived, of course, they found there was *not* work enough for everyone, a state of affairs that allowed Durst to manipulate wages however he chose. Moreover, the only shelter he provided for the 2,800 were ragged tents that he rented to them for $2.75 a week, the only liquid he provided was sold from a "lemonade" wagon driven by one of his relatives, and

*Tom Mooney (center) grimly follows proceedings during his trial for murder.*

the only sanitation facilities were eight rancid toilets that overflowed daily.

When Durst refused to discuss worker complaints, Ford, Suhr, and the other IWW agitators (a description any self-respecting Wobbly would have welcomed) began to promote the idea of a general strike to force him to improve both wages and working and living conditions; a mass meeting to consider the proposal was scheduled for Sunday, August 3. Because such a strike would have crippled Durst's harvest, he called upon Yuba County authorities to break up the meeting and arrest the IWW men. In attempting to do so, one of the sheriff's deputies fired his shotgun into the air to "sober the mob," as he later put it, and a chaos of shots and confused fighting followed the sound like an explosion. At its end, four men were dead: a deputy, the county attorney, and two workers.

During the months that followed what the respectable press labeled an IWW atrocity, Ford and Suhr were rounded up, placed in jail, tried, convicted, and sentenced to life imprisonment for second-degree murder—although no evidence existed that either had had even an indirect hand in the deaths of the county officials.

The Wheatland "riot" of 1913 had two immediate effects: first, it inspired Governor Johnson to have his Immigration and Housing Commission investigate the working and living conditions of California's migrant labor force, which at least resulted in the implementation of minor reforms in the system (most of which were ignored, as we shall see in a later chapter); second, it pro-

vided the IWW with much-needed publicity among migrant workers, resulting in such a rash of sudden memberships that the union could feel that it was at last making significant headway.

The long-range effect of the Wheatland incident, however, was to help destroy the IWW. The image of the organization as a collection of anarchistic, sabotage-prone murderers—an image its own pronouncement did little to improve—solidified like obsidian after 1913. Even Simon J. Lubin, head of the Immigration and Housing Commission and an utterly sincere advocate of migrant labor reform, believed that "the existence within our midst of such a band . . . is a distinct menace to the public welfare." Similar attitudes (by no means exclusive to California) crossed nearly all political and economic lines, and in less than two years the IWW was nearly friendless.

When it became obvious that President Woodrow Wilson was not going to keep America out of the spreading European war as he had promised, antipathy toward the union was given a certain patriotic gloss: the IWW was loudly and consistently against the war —*ergo,* it was un-American. After the United States entered the war in 1917, federal agents instigated a series of raids from Chicago to Kansas City, Fresno to Spokane, in which IWW offices were broken into, records were seized or destroyed, and every leader the officers could lay hands on was arrested. Hundreds were tried and convicted on charges ranging from sabotage to treason. As labor historian Melvyn Dubofsky has written, "By April 1919 almost all the first- and second-line IWW leaders were in federal prison; those still at large were either free on bail, fugitives from justice, victims of the immigration authorities, or on the verge of being tried on criminal-syndicalism charges in various state courts." The dubious threat of the "One Big Union" had been eliminated with singular dispatch.

THE "THREAT" of radical unionism, in California as elsewhere, was more felt than real, as any impartial examination of the available evidence will suggest. In fact, if one looks at the record of the IWW, for example, it becomes obvious that, in spite of its belligerent rhetoric and pugnacious attitudes, the Wobbly organization was more often the victim of violence than the perpetrator of it. Yet it didn't really matter; people generally believe what they want to believe, and in the beginning years of the twentieth century, it took very little evidence to reinforce the preconceptions of most California citizens. Unfortunately, the "lunatic fringe" of the radical labor movement was almost masochistically inclined to provide such evidence (as witness the bombing of the Los Angeles *Times*). Nothing more thoroughly typified this phenomenon than the grisly disaster that occurred in San Francisco during its Preparedness Day Parade of July 22, 1916.

As noted earlier, the merchants and industrialists of San Francisco had for some years regarded the lower wage scale of Los Angeles with the lust of an alley mongrel watching a passing meat wagon. After the debacle of the McNamara confessions of 1911, when even the San Francisco labor movement lost much of its credibility, the city's employers, led by the chamber of commerce, began a concentrated campaign to destroy labor's power in the city. This resulted, of course, in a reaction on the part of labor, amplifying the voice of its radical element—particularly the voice of Thomas J. Mooney, local secretary of the International Workers' Defense League who had led an unsuccessful streetcar strike in the spring of 1916.

Just as San Francisco's labor pot began to stew, the United States began edging toward war, and "preparedness" parades became quite fashionable—exercises designed to emphasize patriotism and a willingness to support the upcoming war effort. Getting into the spirit of things, San Francisco decided to have its own parade —with an added fillip: the parade would demonstrate not only the city's patriotic fervor but the passion of its employers to bring back the good old days of the open shop. There was nothing secretive about this; employers of non-union help simply ordered their workers to march in the parade on pain of dismissal. The decision infuriated organized labor and inspired a series of anonymous threatening letters to various newspapers and city officials. They were ignored, and as the parade moved up Market Street on the afternoon of July 22, a bomb suitcase exploded, killing ten people and maiming more than fifty others.

In the days of ensuing hysteria, the authorities zeroed in on Tom Mooney, his wife Rena, a young associate Warren K. Billings, and two other minor radicals. They were arrested and placed on trial, and while Rena Mooney and the other two were ultimately released, Mooney and Billings were convicted on the strength of a tissue-like body of evidence that featured perjured testimony, manufactured documents, and conflicting sets of facts. Mooney was sentenced to death and Billings to life imprisonment, but the trial had been conducted so poorly that President Woodrow Wilson almost immediately forced the commutation of Mooney's sentence to life—and after a twenty-year crusade by sympathizers of the two men (which in time came to include some members of the prosecution), they were pardoned by Governor Culbert L. Olson in 1939.

The guilt or innocence of the two men may have been in question; the effect of the bombing and its aftermath was not. As in Los Angeles after 1912, the labor movement in San Francisco after the Preparedness Day Parade of 1916 was severely crippled, smothered by a rising conservatism that not only echoed but amplified reactionary sentiments then sweeping across the nation. In such an atmosphere, there was little room for tolerance, mercy, or forgiveness—and even abstract justice could be rendered irrelevant, as the editor of the Colfax *Record* succinctly pointed out: "The reason Mooney and Billings are in prison is because a majority of the people of the state of California want them there. . . . It is quite beside the point whether or not they are guilty of the particular crime of which they were charged and convicted. The question is: Are Mooney and Billings the sort of people we want to run at large? We have decided this in the negative and we have them locked up. We intend to keep them there."

The pendulum of social thought had swung from one extreme to the other in a single generation. The blossoming hope of the Progressives had been transmuted by twenty years of ideological contention and violence into the shriveled, bitter knot of what poet Langston Hughes once called the "dream deferred."

# CHAPTER 15

# REACHING OUT FOR WATER

*Water becomes a tool for growth, a point of contention, and its use*

*the province of earth-movers and dam-builders*

Wᴴᴇɴ "ᴅʀʏ ᴅɪɢɢɪɴꜱ" ᴍɪɴᴇʀꜱ of the gold rush years constructed primitive little flumes to divert the water from foothill streams and rivers to their hardscrabble placer operations, they established a tradition of water use whose ramifications are with us yet. For water was—and remains—the yeast for much of California's economic growth, a resource whose utilization has generated population increases, agricultural and industrial development, and a startling amount of confusion and contention between individuals, cities, counties, states, and—as will be shown in later chapters—even countries.

Those first minor diversions set the tone for the future, for they were in violation of the age-old English concept of "riparian rights" to water, a doctrine specifying that water diverted from a stream for nondomestic use (domestic use being urban and residential) must be returned to that stream undiminished. This was, to say the least, inconvenient, so California's miners came up with a new doctrine—"appropriation and beneficial use," which allowed the diversion of water for the benefit of enterprise without requiring return to its source. Hydraulic mining was the first major beneficiary of the new concept, and at its peak the industry's hundreds of miles of flumes and ditches delivered as much as 72,000,000 gallons of water a day to be used to flush out gold (see "California Mirror: The Resource Economy"). Yet it was farming that ultimately benefited most, for the doctrine of appropriation was the basis for passage of the Wright Act of 1887, a law that permitted regions to form and bond irrigation districts; this act was probably the single most important contribution to the growth of California agriculture.

Under the provisions of the law, farmers banded together, pooled their resources, and began bringing water from where it was to where it was needed. In California this was no small consideration. In the Great Central Valley, for example, one-third of the most arable land lay in the southern portions—while two-thirds of its water reposed in the northern region. It would be several generations before this "imbalance" was entirely corrected, but in the meantime agriculturalists tapped into what sources were available, diverting portions of the Merced, San Joaquin, and Kings rivers and their tributaries to their fields. Similarly in Southern California, private irrigation districts exploited the region's feeble water sources to the best of their ability, constructing not only intricate water-delivery networks but storage reservoirs as well.

By the turn of the century, then, water-moving of one kind or another had become an integral part of the state's development. But the century had already turned before the first hint came of the immense scale such projects could assume, given enough time and technology. That hint came in the Imperial Valley of the Colorado Desert, deep in the southernmost toe of California.

For eons, the Colorado River had been depositing at its mouth rich loads of silt in a delta extending from northwestern Mexico and southwestern Arizona to northern Baja and southern California. All that this

*Fully aware that they are taking part in history, engineers open the gates for the Los Angeles Aqueduct on November 5, 1913.*

*In a land of little rain, water becomes as salable as champagne; above, a rather
sordid-looking group gathers around Lyon's Well in the Colorado Desert.*

delta land needed to "blossom as the rose" was a reliable
source of water—and there was the Colorado, raised by
its own deposits some scores of feet above the level of
some of the richest sweeps of desert soil. The possibilities inherent in the combination of water, gravity, and
soil had been recognized as early as 1849, by one Oliver
Wozencraft, a forty-niner who had crossed the Colorado
Desert on his way to the gold fields. "It was then and
there," he later said, "that I first conceived the idea of
the reclamation of the desert." It took him ten years to
do much about his idea, but in 1859 he began a thirty-
year campaign to persuade Congress to give him six
thousand square miles of the Colorado Desert; he
would, he said, do the rest.

Wozencraft died before he could convince Congress
that he deserved that sizable chunk of the public domain, but in 1899 a group of more practical visionaries
took over his dream: Charles R. Rockwood and C. N.
Perry, construction engineers for the Southern Pacific
Railroad, and Anthony Heber and Samuel Fergusson,

real estate boomers who had learned the trade as agents
for the huge Kern County Land Company. Unlike
Wozencraft, they recognized the simple fact that ownership of Imperial Valley land was less crucial to successful exploitation than ownership of the water needed
to make it bloom—or, at least, ownership of the *delivery*
system for that water.

With this firmly in mind, they incorporated themselves as the California Development Company, staked
out a claim for twenty thousand acre-feet of Colorado
River water, filed for a canal right-of-way from the government, signed a canal contract with George Chaffey
(who had engineered and promoted the successful agricultural colonies of Etiwanda and Ontario in Southern
California), and began spreading the good word: that
they intended to bring Colorado River water to the
rich land of the Imperial Valley, land the government
was willing to give away in 160-acre parcels under the
Homestead Law or sell in 320-acre parcels for $1.25 an
acre under the provisions of the Desert Land Act—and

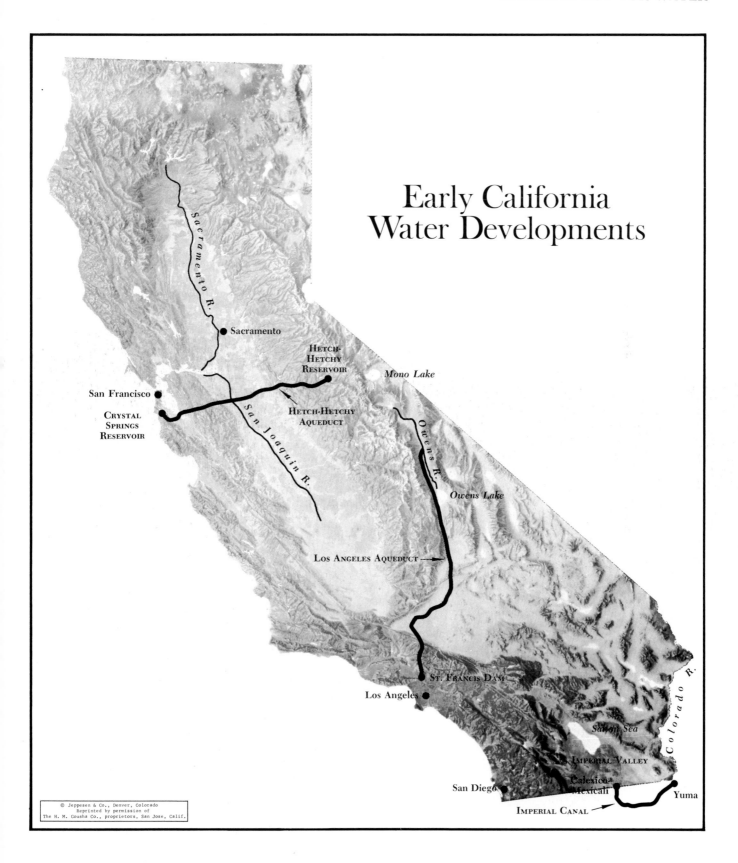

# Early California
# Water Developments

Sacramento R.

Sacramento

San Francisco

CRYSTAL
SPRINGS
RESERVOIR

HETCH-
HETCHY
RESERVOIR

HETCH-HETCHY
AQUEDUCT

San Joaquin R.

Mono Lake

Owens R.

Owens Lake

LOS ANGELES AQUEDUCT

ST. FRANCIS DAM

Los Angeles

San Diego

Colorado R.

Salton Sea

IMPERIAL VALLEY

Calexico
Mexicali

Yuma

IMPERIAL CANAL

water would cost settlers only fifty cents an acre-foot!

Settlers began trickling in almost immediately, but before Chaffey could even begin his canal, he found that the California Development Company was rich in promise but little else; it had no money for construction. He tore up his contract, raised his own money, and began his canal on Thanksgiving Day, 1900. When completed in the spring of the following year, the Imperial Canal, as it was called, was the most ambitious privately owned irrigation project in the West. Cutting into the Colorado River at Pilot Knob, just north of the Mexican border, it meandered nearly sixty miles, south into Mexico, west across fifty-two miles of purchased Mexican right-of-way, and north to terminate where the Alamo River enters the United States; here, the town of Calexico sprouted, a shack-and-shanty manifestation of Oliver Wozencraft's ancient dream.

Once done with the project, Chaffey sold it back to the California Development Company for $300,000 and went on to other things. What he left behind was more than a water-delivery system; it was a complex money-making machine, at least for those who could manipulate it. Water was conveyed from Pilot Knob into Mexico, where it was "sold" to a dummy Mexican corporation that delivered it to Calexico and the California Development Company; eight mutual water companies (organized and officered by executives of the CDC), then bought the water for fifty cents an acre-foot* for distribution to the individual farmers making up its membership; in return for furnishing the water at a minimal cost, the CDC was given all the "water stock" of the mutual companies; in turn, the Imperial Land Company, a CDC subsidiary that had been organized mainly to promote the sale of government lands (since it owned very little of its own), was allowed to purchase great blocks of this water stock at low prices for resale to individual farmers at $25 a share, each share representing one acre of watered land.

Water stock was the gimmick that made the whole machine work, for under the rules of the CDC only shareholders could receive water from the Imperial Canal; furthermore, each parcel of land had to be completely "covered" by stock before water was delivered (e.g., a 160-acre section had to be represented by 160 shares of stock). The Imperial Land Company, possessed of most of the stock, was quite willing, of course, to sell it on liberal terms of credit; should any farmer default on his payments, the company "foreclosed" on his share of water stocks. Without water the land was useless, and the farmer would have little recourse but to sell his parcel to the company at the company's price. The company was then quite free to turn around and sell the acquired land to anyone—including such outside investors as Harrison Gray Otis of the Los Angeles *Times,* who came to own more than a thousand acres of Imperial Valley land. As a kind of caboose on this gravy train, officers of the CDC and the Imperial Land Company also owned thousands of acres of Mexican land along the right-of-way of the canal, all of it watered with Colorado River water without the inconvenience of water stock.

By 1904 the Imperial Valley was booming. Seven thousand settlers had arrived to farm the land, producing that year more than one million dollars in dairy produce, barley, hay, cattle feed, honey, vegetables, fruits, and turkeys. And while the CDC struggled along on a very thin profit margin (as it was designed to do), the coffers of the Imperial Land Company swelled, as speculators and occasional farmers streamed in to buy the company's farming parcels, as well as town lots in Calexico, Brawley, Imperial, and Holtville. It was a prime year, and the last the valley would have for some time—for the Imperial Canal was beginning to silt up badly near its mouth, impeding the delivery of water. Taking their attention away from the selling of acreage, the executives of the CDC solved the problem by making a second cut into the river without bothering to provide adequate protection against the river's notorious flood season. Having made this last "improvement" on the canal, the company sold it to the Southern Pacific Railroad for $200,000 and went back to the making of money.

The railroad (under E. H. Harriman, successor to Collis P. Huntington) did little to improve the new cut. The flood season started, and the river broke through the canal; a brush dam was hastily thrown up, and quickly washed away. Again and again the river assaulted the breach. By the end of 1905, the gap had widened to more than six hundred feet, and billions

_____

*An acre-foot of water is enough water to cover one acre of land to a depth of one foot—or 323,000 gallons.

*A "street" scene in the desert hamlet of Imperial—before water enriched the land and town lots enriched speculators.*

of gallons of silt-laden water oozed down the "hump" of the Colorado delta to the Salton Sink, re-creating the Salton Sea, destroying farms, and washing out the tracks of the Southern Pacific five times. The railroad fought back, but it was not until February 10, 1907— after an expenditure of nearly two million dollars and the dumping of 2,057 carloads of rock, 321 of gravel, and 203 of clay—that the Colorado was returned to its proper channel.*

---

*Since they didn't yet know that the railroad had purchased the CDC and its works, the residents of the valley cheered it as the hero of the hour. The railroad was careful to continue keeping the sale a secret, thereby avoiding damage suits to which it was liable. Moreover, it made back its two-million-dollar expense and more by a $700,000 grant from the federal government for its flood-control work and, as noted above, its later sale of the whole distribution system to the Imperial Irrigation District.

The railroad had saved the valley, but there was no guarantee that there would not be a repetition. Seeking to control their own possible future, the residents of the valley banded together in 1911 to form the Imperial Irrigation District and with a bond issue of $10,500,000, purchased the entire water distribution system from the mutual water companies and the railroad (which received $3,000,000 for the canal). They then began a twenty-year effort to persuade the federal government to save them from the rampages of the river by the construction of a massive upriver dam for flood control. As we shall see in a later chapter, that campaign became a major force behind the creation of the Boulder Dam Project in the 1930s.

Being the very stuff of life, water and its use have consistently inspired an emotionalism that transcends all the intricacies of finance, of engineering reports, of acre-foot and gallons-consumed statistics. Nothing has illustrated this more thoroughly than the fury that attended the development of California's second major water project: the Los Angeles Aqueduct.

Between 1892 and 1904, Southern California was witness to two major phenomena, one natural, one man-made. The first was a series of droughts that severely crippled its agriculture. Possessed of only 6 percent of California's natural stream flow and an average of less than twenty inches of rainfall a year, the region had for years depended mainly upon thousands of artesian wells that sucked up groundwater. That resource had been used with little thought for the future—"wasted," as Carey McWilliams has written, "in a single generation"—and continued drought sank water-table levels to dangerous lows. Moreover, city water supplies were threatened.

The second phenomenon was growth on a startling scale, particularly in and around Los Angeles. It was a generated growth, deliberately wished for and calculatingly fashioned. Picking up the pieces after the collapse of the big boom of 1887, the Los Angeles Chamber of Commerce continued its advertising spree across the country, producing millions of copies of pamphlets and brochures, sending special trains loaded with California produce to midwestern and eastern cities, selling climate, land, health, and an easier, more serene life-style.

*Suburbia* was not yet a common American word, but in Los Angeles it was rapidly becoming a reality. Developers went on a subdivision spree, and one community after another popped into being throughout the Los Angeles Basin. Tying these scattered towns together into one metropolitan web was one of the largest rapid-transit systems in the world, the Pacific Electric Railroad of Henry E. Huntington (nephew of Collis P. Huntington), whose "Big Red Cars" whisked passengers over hundreds of miles of track throughout the basin, from one tidy residential enclave to another, each a comfortable little bungalow-with-lawn civilization. "To San Franciscans," historian David Lavender has noted, "it added up to overgrown Dullsville. For the newcomers themselves it was a Midwestern Eden stripped of farming's rigors but not of its Christian ethics, all within range of big-city conveniences, thanks to Henry Huntington's hurrying red cars. These, not

the automobile, were the true implementers of the Los Angeles sprawl that still baffles visitors from the East."

Sprawl, indeed. Between 1890 and 1900, the population of Los Angeles more than doubled, from 50,000 to 102,000; by the end of 1904, it was trembling at the brink of 200,000. And there it seemed suddenly fated to stay, for there simply was not water enough to support a population much larger, particularly in dry years. To the bulk of her citizens, to have blunted the city's thrusting growth would have been tantamount to denying Holy Writ, and among them was one man who believed he had a solution.

He was Fred Eaton, a former mayor of the city, and his solution lay 250 miles northeast of Los Angeles where the Owens River wound through a lush valley beneath the rising eastern scarp of the Sierra Nevada Range. This river, Eaton believed, could supply a city of two million, if need be, and he found agreement in William Mulholland, the Scottish-born superintendent of the Los Angeles Water Department. Early in 1905 the two men got to work laying the foundations for the most ambitious water project since the time of the Romans: a 250-mile gravity canal, or aqueduct, to bring Owens River water to Los Angeles.

While Eaton and several allies in the city government traveled to Washington in a successful effort to persuade the Bureau of Reclamation to abandon a major reservoir project then under consideration for the Owens Valley, Mulholland convinced the board of directors of the Los Angeles Water Department of the feasibility and desirability of the project and made a careful estimate of costs—$23,500,000, which would have to be raised by the largest bond issue ever undertaken by any municipality anywhere. When Eaton returned from Washington, he journeyed to the Owens Valley and, passing himself off as an ambitious rancher, began buying up land and water rights from willing valley farmers, who by dint of a generation's worth of money and work had converted a wilderness into a rich farming region. Still, Eaton was offering good prices, and money in the hand. . . . Soon, Eaton had secretly committed the city to more than one million dollars in purchase costs.

Eaton, Mulholland, and the Water Department found a powerful ally in a land syndicate headed up by Harrison Gray Otis and Henry E. Huntington. In

1903 this syndicate had laid out $50,000 for a three-year option to buy 16,500 acres of land in the San Fernando Valley—where Mulholland now planned to build a reservoir to hold Owens River water, calculating that water not immediately needed by Los Angeles could be sold to San Fernando farmers for irrigation purposes. With a certain understandable glee, the syndicate exercised its purchase option and threw its support behind the Owens Valley project.*

On July 29, 1905, the Los Angeles *Times* broke the good news to the general public for the first time: "Titanic Project to Give City a River!" In spite of murmurs in the Owens Valley from farmers who felt they had been cheated out of a higher price by Eaton's deception and cries of "Fraud!" and "Swindle!" from Otis's arch-enemy, Edwin T. Earl of the Los Angeles *Express,* the voters of Los Angeles turned out in the fall of 1905 and approved a $1,500,000 bond issue to back up Eaton's purchase commitments and to finance precise engineering studies. They turned out again in 1907 to approve (by a ten-to-one margin) the $23,000,000 needed to build the project, and the following year Mulholland supervised the turning of the first shovelful of earth on his enormous ditch.

Only the Panama Canal, Los Angeles declared, matched the size, scope, magnitude, and cost of its aqueduct—and the city was right. With more than five thousand men, Mulholland assaulted the deserts, canyons, and mountains between the Owens Valley and the San Fernando Valley, ramming 142 tunnels through ancient hills, erecting the largest inverted siphons ever built, and laying more concrete than anyone in the United States had ever laid before. After five years, the project was finished, on time and within the budget (not as rare for public projects then as it is today), and on November 5, 1913, more than fifteen thousand people gathered in the northeast corner of the San Fernando Valley to watch the first surge of water tumble

---

*The glee was understandable simply because the syndicate members expected that water would dramatically appreciate the value of their land. They were entirely correct; acreage that had cost them approximately five hundred thousand dollars leaped to nearly five million in value with the arrival of water. This, of course led to charges (periodically revived) that the Owens River project was no more or less than a "colossal swindle" conceived and perpetuated by Otis, Huntington, and their colleagues. Not so.

*William Mulholland, the architect of Southern California's empire of water.*

down an artificial cascade into the valley. It can be said that Mulholland had a proper sense of drama; as fifteen thousand people scrambled to see Owens River water dance down the slope of his cascade, he turned to the mayor of Los Angeles: "There it is," he said. "Take it."

Take it the city did. In 1915, Los Angeles reached out to annex most of the San Fernando Valley, and by 1920 its population had grown to 576,000—surpassing San Francisco for the first time in the state's history. It was also using nearly every drop of its original entitlement to the water of the Owens River, and in 1923 agents for the city once again journeyed to the Owens Valley to purchase more land, more water rights, while Mulholland began construction of a major dam and reser-

*A Model T Ford demonstrates the size of the pipes used in the construction of the aqueduct's immense siphons.*

voir in San Francisquito Canyon thirty miles north of Los Angeles to hold what the city would need.

This time, the city found few pushovers among the farmers of the Owens Valley, who now demanded what the city considered outrageous prices for their land and water. When the city refused to meet their demands, the farmers, led by Mark Q. and Wilfred W. Watterson (two bankers who were later convicted of embezzling the funds of their friends and neighbors), cried "Rape!" and proceeded to emphasize their protest by dynamiting portions of the aqueduct no less than nine times

between 1924 and 1927. It was not until the failure, arrest, and conviction of the Watterson brothers, which plunged many of the valley's residents close to financial ruin, that the situation was finally resolved—and it should not be said that Los Angeles took undue advantage of the valley in the final settlement: at prices prevailing during the "boom" year of 1923, the city spent more than twelve million dollars buying up most of the remaining land.

It spent even more in 1940 to thrust a tunnel through the mountains from the Owens River to Mono Lake

*A crew of "muckers" poses outside one of the 142 tunnels drilled and lined with pipe during the construction of the 250-mile aqueduct.*

for more water, and additional millions in 1941 for the construction of Long Valley Dam and Crowley Lake—today one of the favorite recreation areas for Angelenos seeking to escape the pressures of megalopolis. Thus, tourist dollars replaced the money that could have been made in agriculture—an irony given point by Remi Nadeau, the historian of Los Angeles: "Supported by this commerce, Owens Valley now numbers more permanent residents than it did before it came under the shadow of the monolith. But it is no longer the home of frontier farmers who breathed the exhilarating air

of self-reliance. It is a tributary province to the city it helped to build."*

---

*The story requires an additional footnote. Mulholland's San Francisquito Dam was poorly engineered. On March 12, 1928, shortly after its completion, it crumbled, sending millions of gallons of water down on the farms and villages of the Santa Clara Valley and drowning 420 people—next to the San Francisco disaster of 1906 the greatest catastrophe in California's history. To his credit, Mulholland assumed full blame: "If there is an error in human judgment, I was that human." It was an agony he carried with him for the rest of his life.

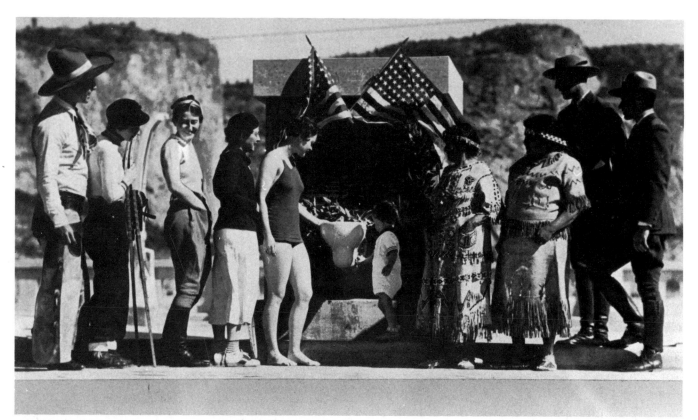

*After years of contention, World War I, the boom of the twenties,*
*and the Depression, San Francisco tasted its first Hetch Hetchy water in 1934.*

LOS ANGELES was not alone in the exercise of what has since become known, and not flatteringly, as "water imperialism." Almost simultaneously with the Owens River project, San Francisco did its own reaching out all the way to the Sierra Nevada—and if its grasp for water lacked the immediate drama of the very human conflicts that developed in the Owens Valley, it did engender, like a pebble in a pond, ripples of concern that have not been resolved to anyone's satisfaction yet.

As early as 1890, foresightful San Francisco city officials had wondered just how long the Spring Valley Water Company could satisfy the city's needs. The city, too, was growing, not as fast as Los Angeles perhaps and certainly never to match the southern city's ultimate bloat, but fast enough for some thought to be given to the demands of the future. An early engineering study had pointed out the advantages of a reservoir site in Hetch Hetchy gorge on the Tuolumne River, not far from Yosemite Valley, and by the turn of the century it was in this gorge that San Francisco saw the future of its water resources.

Unfortunately, the Hetch Hetchy gorge was contained within the bounds of Yosemite National Park, created in 1890, and was ostensibly protected for all time from exploitation. (The park did not yet include the Yosemite Valley, then administered as a separate park by the state of California; it would not be included in the larger park until 1905.) Citing San Francisco's potentially desperate need, Mayor James D. Phelan petitioned the Department of the Interior in 1901 for permission to utilize the gorge as a reservoir site. The department refused outright, but the city continued its petitions over the next several years.

The idea met with opposition on a number of fronts. First, the Spring Valley Water Company, like any other privately owned utility (the company, it will be remembered, had been purchased by William C. Ralston in the 1860s in his unsuccessful attempt to sell it back to the city), looked upon municipal ownership of vital services with absolute horror, and its stockholders vigorously maintained that the company could furnish the city's water indefinitely. Second, a corporation calling itself the Bay Cities Water Company (headed up, appropriately enough, by William S. Tevis, the son of land- and mine-speculator Lloyd Tevis) held a large parcel of land and water rights near Lake Tahoe and put pressure on the city government to buy its holdings for a mere $10,500,000 dollars; the pressure was applied during the reign of Abraham Ruef and his cohorts, and was sweetened with the offer of a one-million-dollar bribe—but the graft trials of 1907 soon removed the Bay Cities Water Company from competition. Third, private power companies, realizing that water streaming down a 156-mile aqueduct from Hetch Hetchy to San Francisco would inevitably generate municipally owned electricity, began a loudly voiced campaign of protest. Fourth, farmers in the northern San Joaquin Valley feared that a dam on the Tuolumne River would cripple the seasonal flows of water on which they depended.

Finally—and perhaps most importantly—the scheme inspired vigorous opposition on the part of a new and heretofore unimpressive faction of California society: militant conservationists. Led by John Muir, a poet of the wilderness and co-founder of the Sierra Club in 1892, these "preservationists" declared in no uncertain terms that to dam the Hetch Hetchy Valley was a veritable insult to Providence, a rape of Nature, a violation of the spirit in which Yosemite National Park had been created, and a spineless capitulation to the insensate demands of urban growth and "moneyed interests." This response was met with a mixture of disbelief and derision on the part of most San Franciscans, but however transient its immediate effect, it was the first significant articulation of the principle that man owed a debt not only to the needs of progress but to the natural world around him—and that this debt sometimes outweighed all other considerations. (For more details on John Muir, the Sierra Club, and the broader implications of the Hetch Hetchy controversy, see chapter 24.)

To all opposition, the proponents of a reservoir in the Hetch Hetchy gorge responded with the purest logic: it was the cheapest source available of all possible alternatives—and in spite of the claims of the Spring Valley Water Company, the city was going to need more water and need it soon. Possibly touched by San Francisco's rebuilding effort after the earthquake and fire of 1906, the Department of the Interior finally relented, granting the city's petition in 1908. Continuing opposition stalled the necessary congressional approval of the project until 1913, but in that year Congress gave San Francisco the water rights to approximately 420,000 acres of public domain in Hetch Hetchy Valley.

After a moratorium on public construction imposed by World War I, the city's engineers began work in earnest in 1919, erecting O'Shaughnessy Dam in the gorge and laying concrete for the Hetch Hetchy Aqueduct down the slopes of the mountains, across the San Joaquin Valley, and through the Mount Diablo Mountains. By 1934, the first water from the Tuolumne River was filling up Crystal Springs Reservoir south of San Francisco. The water had come late, but not too late, and once again a region reached beyond its own borders to appropriate a river. It would not be the last time.

As for man's debt to the natural world, today the Hetch Hetchy Valley—of which John Muir said, "No holier temple has ever been consecrated by the hearts of men"—lies buried under hundreds of thousands of acre-feet of water.

# CHAPTER 16

# CALIFORNIA CRUDE

*From tarry ooze to hillside gusher, "black gold" enters*

*the mainstream of California's economic life*

OR EONS the fuel that was to feed the twentieth century lay untouched and all but unnoticed just beneath the surface of the California landscape. Sometimes it crept out from beneath that surface, leaking into the sea in the Santa Barbara Channel and giving the water the radiant sheen of rainbow colors probably noticed by Cabrillo (Cabrilho) in 1542, or gathering in vast, viscous pools of tar, trapping outlandish creatures and preserving their bones for the future edification of their two-legged descendants on the tree of life. Sometimes, in places like the southern San Joaquin Valley, isolated pools of it bubbled and gasped with gases from the fractured innards of the earth, and sometimes it gathered at the heads of obscure canyons, oozing down with the deliberation of time itself, thick, black, and stinking of the ages.

It was petroleum in its crudest forms, as asphaltum, maltha, and liquid bitumen. When the Indians encountered this substance, they used it, according to its natural state, to secure arrowheads to their hafts, or waterproof intricately woven baskets, or seal the seams of plank canoes. Neither the Spanish nor the Mexicans had much use for the stuff, and not even enterprising Yankees were inclined to do much with it in the first years of American life. This indifference was quite logical, for there *was* no real use for California's viscous black treacle—yet. For generations, whale oil—in California as elsewhere—provided most of the illuminating fuel, and when supplies of whale oil began to decline, civilization turned to camphene, a distillate of turpentine, for home use and to coal gas for lighting the

streets of its cities. Coal oil and coal itself were, of course, the principal fuels of the nineteenth century. Throughout most of the 1850s, then, the only discernible use of California's natural petroleum was as asphalt, shipped to San Francisco to seal roofs and pave sidewalks.

Then in 1859, near a rivulet called Oil Creek in Pennsylvania, the first producing oil well in history came into being, issuing a superlative grade of crude petroleum that was refinable into both lubricants and an illuminating oil called kerosine. Within a matter of months, kerosine began to edge significantly into the market for household illuminants. And when the Civil War cut California off from any reliable supply of either the new kerosine or turpentine (most of which was at that time produced in South Carolina), it was natural enough for men to take another look at California's petroleum supply.

Former whale-oil entrepreneurs and amateur chemists struggled valiantly to contrive a way to refine California crude into something that did not, as W. H. Hutchinson once wrote, "char the lamp wicks and smoke the chimneys, nor stink like the back door to hell itself." Their attempts came to next to nothing, but they did not prevent the formation of the first identifiable oil corporation in the state in 1861: the Los Angeles Brea Company, whose announced intention was the manufacture and sale of something it called "coal oil" refined from asphaltum. In the same year, the state's first recorded oil well was also drilled, the Davis Well, an unproductive hole in the ground in

*With sterling indifference to the progress behind him, a young bull looks out from his pasture in the Los Angeles City Field, 1900.*

*Barreling asphalt in a Summerland refinery, ca. 1895.*

Petrolia, Humboldt County.

Other petroleum prospectors concentrated their efforts in and around the Ojai Valley, near the present-day town of Ventura, a country whose gullies, gulches, and canyons positively oozed with oil springs. Chief among the searchers was George S. Gilbert, a former whale-oil merchant who secured an oil lease on the Ojai Rancho and set up business near the San Buenaventura River in 1861, equipped with a massive iron retort and storage tanks. He was followed three years later by Edward Conway and James H. White, who under the aegis of Conway & Company purchased some 78,000 acres of oil rights around Ventura. It was here that California's first oil "boomlet" would take place—although it had to wait upon circumstances developing a far distance from the green and golden hills of the Ojai Valley.

THOMAS ALEXANDER SCOTT was a railroad man; he was, in fact, almost a definition of the breed. In 1850, at the age of twenty-six, he went to work for the Pennsylvania Railroad and by 1860 had become its first vice-president, with all the rights, duties, and privileges the position afforded—including the services of an assistant by the name of Andrew Carnegie. During the Civil War, Scott served as this country's first assistant secretary of war, with his function largely confined to running the railroads of the Union Army—a duty he performed so well that he was given the rank of colonel. After the war he continued to involve himself in railroad developments, not the least of which was the ill-fated Texas & Pacific, whose brief appearance in the California story has already been discussed.

The Texas & Pacific was not his only California connection, or even his first, for Scott was as much an incurable investor as he was a consummate railroad man. Constantly on the lookout for ways to fatten his stake in the world, he had thrown his considerable money in any number of likely directions—land and city-lot speculations, express companies, western mining prospects—and with a combination of shrewdness and plain luck had come out on top of several ventures. One of these (appropriately enough, given later developments) was the Columbia Oil Company, a very successful child of the Pennsylvania petroleum strike of 1859. Another was the Arizona Gold and Silver Mining Company, chartered in 1863 and destined to bring Scott his fair share of mineral deposits that had been discovered in western Arizona in 1862.

Late in 1863 Scott dispatched to San Francisco Benjamin Silliman, Jr., professor of chemistry at Yale College and an experienced and well-respected consultant to many industries (including the new Pennsylvania petroleum industry, which his studies had helped to found). From there, Silliman was to go to Arizona to examine and report upon Scott's mining properties, and thence to Nevada Territory to investigate new possibilities to appease the railroad man's insatiable hunger for investment.

Waiting in San Francisco for the world's leading (and practically only) oil expert were Edward Conway and James H. White, who greeted him upon his arrival with a proposition: would he, for a suitable fee, investigate their Southern California oil holdings? For a suitable fee he would and did, sailing down the coast and spending three days in the saddle being escorted around Conway & Company lands by James H. White and around several other prospects by George Gilbert.

Silliman was enthusiastic, to say the least. Of the Ojai Rancho he wrote, "As a ranch it is a splendid estate, but its value is its almost fabulous wealth in the best of oil." His comment on Conway & Company lands was hardly less sanguine: "The amount of oil you can supply is likely to be limited, within reason, only by the number of artesian wells you may bore."

These were words to be reckoned with, and when they got back to Thomas A. Scott, he quickly authorized his San Francisco agent, Levi Parsons, to buy and lease more than 450,000 acres in parcels scattered from Los Angeles County to Cape Mendocino. He then organized two corporations, the California Petroleum Company and the Philadelphia & California Petroleum Company, to develop his properties in and around the Ojai Valley. To supervise the drilling operations of the two companies, he hired two Civil War veterans, young Thomas Robert Bard (later a United States senator and the leading citizen of Ventura County) and Dr. Jonathan Letterman, the former medical director of the Army of the Potomac (whose name is left to us in San Francisco's Letterman Hospital).

Scott's enthusiasm for California oil set off a rash of speculations both in and outside the state. In California alone, more than seventy-five companies were incorporated for oil development, representing (theoretically) investment capital to the tune of fifty million dollars. It was all one more paper dream in the tradition of California's economic vicissitudes. No refining technique then known to man could adequately convert the state's tarlike crude to a product even approaching that of the Pennsylvania fields; and no matter how hard they tried, the scores of drillers scattered throughout the state (most in Southern California) could not find oil of appreciably better quality. And even though he had brought in the state's first recorded "gusher" (however minor, however brief) in 1867, Thomas R. Bard was soon urging Scott to sell at least portions of his immensely valuable land for farming parcels, a course to which Scott ultimately agreed.

Still, a new vision had been spawned in the fertile California psyche: black gold. Professor Silliman's words would not go away, and during the remainder of the 1860s and on into the 1870s and 1880s, the state's

*George S. Gilbert's pioneering refinery on the San Buenaventura River of Southern California, seen here in about 1885.*

*Another view of the little world of derricks and tanks in the Los Angeles City Field, where houses and oil rigs competed for ground.*

petroleum industry crept steadily upward. New sources were developed in such regions as the Newhall Basin and the deserts of western Kern County; new drilling techniques allowed deeper holes; new companies formed, dissolved, and reformed, including the Union Oil Company and the ancestor of Standard Oil of California; somehow, in spite of all visible logic, by 1890 more than three hundred thousand barrels of California crude were being produced and disposed of every year. It was still an infant, but the industry was at least up on its feet and taking its first hesitant steps. It would shortly be running, leaping, and brawling in the finest traditions of adolescence.

IN 1892 Edward L. Doheny wandered into Los Angeles, bent and weathered but not broken by twenty fruitless years chasing the Lorelei of gold and silver across the mountain West. His eyes never far from the ground and the treasures it might contain, he became intrigued by the tarry substance that seeped up here and there in the city, particularly in the area of Westlake Park. Proceeding in sublime ignorance, he got together with an old prospector friend, Charles A. Canfield, and the

two of them purchased a small lot near the corner of today's Second Street and Glendale Boulevard and began sinking a miner's shaft—the only kind of hole they knew how to dig. At 155 feet, they discontinued digging, contrived a primitive drill from a 60-foot length of eucalyptus tree, and probed even deeper. Shortly before Christmas 1892, gas hissed and oil spurted into the shaft, and soon their poorly engineered well was producing seven barrels of oil a day.

By California standards seven barrels a day was not a bad production statistic, and soon Doheny and Canfield's well was surrounded by three hundred additional wells and was the center of a genuine boom. Called the Los Angeles City Field, it produced in two years more than seven hundred thousand barrels of oil, more than half the production of the entire state in those years. By 1907 the field contained 3,000 wells (all within the city limits of Los Angeles), and California's petroleum industry had at last found its day.

The discovery and development of the Los Angeles City Field coincided almost precisely with probably the most important single innovation in the utilization of California crude. In 1894 the Union Oil Company persuaded the Santa Fe Railroad to test oil burners it had developed for use in fueling locomotives. Those tests, made on Southern Pacific tracks near Ventura, not only proved the feasibility of oil-burning locomotives but established a 25 percent saving in cost-per-mile over coal-burning locomotives. California's railroads needed little further persuasion to convert to oil.

Possessed of the first reliable market in its history (and soon to be given another in the form of a weird-looking contraption called an automobile), the petroleum industry blossomed—no, exploded. Extensive new strikes were developed in the Kern River, McKittrick, and Coalinga fields of Kern County at the southern foot of the San Joaquin Valley, raising the state's production to 77,000,000 barrels by 1910. After World War I, similar strikes occurred in the Los Angeles Basin—at Santa Fe Springs, at Huntington Beach, and most spectacular of all, at Signal Hill in Long Beach, a field that has produced more than one billion barrels of oil in its lifetime.

This was the stuff of empire, unmatched since the dear, dead days of forty-nine, and public reaction was just about the same. If San Francisco's streets had once been paved with gold, then the gutters of Los Angeles now ran with oil, and the city became a great charnel house of speculation. Literally thousands of oil "corporations" sprang into being, each of which belched forth a barrage of stock certificates and oily promises to the thousands of people streaming into the city from all over the country throughout the 1920s. A fever was in the air, as it had been in the air of San Francisco during the years of the Comstock mania, and otherwise practical businessmen—bankers, investment counselors, industrialists, newspaper publishers, even movie magnates—abandoned their composure. And the oil kept coming, with new strikes at Wilmington, Baldwin Hills, El Segundo, Venice, Torrance, Summerland. California soon led the nation in oil production.

In such an atmosphere, anything could happen—and something did: one of the largest stock swindles in American history. It began when Chauncey C. Julian, a former oil rigger who had saved his salary for bigger things, leased ten acres of oil property in the Santa Fe Springs Field in June 1922 and commenced an aggressive, folksy newspaper campaign for stock subscriptions. He was after the "little fish," and he got them with full-page advertisements that positively reeked of

*Part of Edward L. Doheny's holdings in the Coalinga Field of Kern County, 1910.*

down-home, just-us-folks hominy: "When we get this Corporation under way, we'll make that Standard Oil crowd turn flipflops. . . . I'm not kiddin', Folks, you're looking opportunity in the eye!"

By the end of the year, Julian had raised more than eleven million dollars from some forty-thousand subscribers. He leased more oil property, bought enough equipment to develop it, hired an office staff, bought or built thirty-five gasoline stations, and with the money left over began to raise inspired Cain in and around Los Angeles and Hollywood, throwing spectacular parties, commandeering nightclubs, getting into scrapes with the law and buying his way out of them, and generally thumbing his nose at the city's conventional society—including its bankers and stock brokers, whom he loudly, publicly, and repeatedly characterized as a bunch of "crooks, con men, and pawnbrokers."

These worthies retaliated by pushing his stock behind the counter, letting it linger unpromoted, and by shorting it at every given opportunity. By 1924 Julian was ready to capitulate, and sold out his entire interest in the Julian Petroleum Corporation for $800,000 to S. C. Lewis and Jack Bennett, a pair of experienced oil hustlers from Texas. They immediately launched

*The dream: peddling gasoline at the corner of Wilshire and La Brea in 1909,*
*Earl B. Gilmore's wagon was the first "service station" in history.*

a scheme to distribute great blocks of Julian paper in "stock pools," which they sold at prices substantially lower than those prevailing, to groups who promised not to put them on the market for a specified period of time. Unfortunately for the Texas hustlers, in the particularly savage little world of Los Angeles stock speculation, this device made about as much sense as trying to tickle a hungry shark under the chin. Threatening to dump their shares on the market at the end of the holding period, the stock pool owners forced Lewis and Bennett to award them enormous monthly bonuses, often as high as 19 percent. The Texans complied but then, to keep the money coming in, issued even more blocks of stock—to an ever-growing crowd of buyers eager to get its share of those monthly bonuses.

By the spring of 1927, Julian stock was the most active listing on the boards of the Los Angeles Stock Exchange. But then rumors began to insinuate themselves, whispers of concern that the Texans had issued far more shares than were authorized under the company's articles of incorporation—600,000 preferred, 600,000 common. Like a fire in the dry summer hills of the Coast Range, the rumors gathered force and spread,

driving the stock pool owners to the edge of panic. If the rumors were true, the value of their shares could be diluted to a fraction of their face value; slowly and then with an accelerated pace, the pools began dumping stock on the market one after another. Those who did so early got out with their skins intact; those who waited did not, for by the end of April the overissue was a known fact, and early in May, at Lewis's request, Julian stock was withdrawn from trading on the Exchange.

After investigators had sorted out the fishline tangle of financing, it was discovered that the stock had most certainly been overissued—to the tune of more than three million shares, a circumstance that simply wiped out whatever value the stock had possessed. Lewis and Bennett were indicted on a number of counts, including fraud, forgery, and embezzlement, and forty of the most respected men in Los Angeles, those who had participated in the stock pools, were indicted for usury. The two Texans were put on trial but acquitted by means of a carefully placed bribe to the district attorney (although they were later tried and convicted on similar charges stemming from yet another of their schemes). The forty stock-pool manipulators never came to trial.

*The reality: a fleet of "Red Crown" tanker-trucks leaves the Fresno refinery of Standard Oil of California, 1920.*

As is often the case in such outsized examples of genteel thievery, the ones who lost the most were those who could afford it the least—the "folks" to whom C. C. Julian had promised the sweet nectar of easy money but whose savings were now gone along with the bubble of their hopes. Diminished and bitter, they might have taken some comfort in the fact that if one had to go broke, there was no better climate in the world in which to do so.

The Julian fiasco was certainly the most colorful indicator of California's wildcat years of oil production, but it was by no means the only one. Another such was the Elk Hills scandal of 1923. After the war, the federal government had established the Elk Hills Naval Oil Reserve in the San Joaquin Valley as a resource to be tapped in the event of a war in the Pacific. That it was off limits to private development rankled in the minds of many of California's oil men, including Edward L. Doheny. In 1923 Doheny persuaded Albert B. Fall, secretary of the interior and an old companion of Doheny's New Mexico mining days, that the proper way to preserve Elk Hills oil would be to pump it out and store it in tanks, here and at Pearl Harbor, where it could be gotten at in a hurry if needed. Doheny, of course, would be quite willing to develop the field and build the tanks for a share of the oil. Fall went along with the idea.

As it turned out, part of Doheny's arsenal of persuasion was a satchelful of money—$100,000 as a matter of fact—delivered to Fall by Doheny's son. This fact was brought out during the investigations of Wyoming's Teapot Dome affair, and Fall was convicted of bribery and sent to federal prison (the first and only time a cabinet officer was ever so convicted). Doheny, paradoxically, was acquitted of *giving* the bribe on the grounds that he thought of it as nothing more than a convenient loan to an old friend who needed money. This turn of events inspired one observer to remark that it was "a waste of time to try any man in America for a crime who was worth one hundred million dollars."

Yet another indicator of wildcat promotion appeared in 1931, when the Richfield Oil Company went into receivership. An examination of the company's books peeled the lid off a veritable can of worms, revealing an operating loss of $54,000,000, most of it the direct result of a stunning degree of corporate irresponsibility. Among other peccadillos, the company's officials had maintained a suite of hotel rooms in Los Angeles for $50,000 a year and had consumed another $600,000 a year for what was vaguely labeled "entertainment." Several of the officials had been allowed to borrow sums from five thousand to five hundred thousand dollars, and others had charged to the company's books such items as private parties, alimony payments, speedboat repairs, and yacht purchases.

One salutary effect of the Depression, which crippled the oil industry as fully as any other in the state, was to force a shakedown of its scores of companies, systematically eliminating those whose financial strength was based mainly on a foundation of paper. One by one such companies failed or were absorbed by their larger corporate brothers, and by the middle of the 1930s the bulk of California's oil production lay in the hands of a relatively small group of entities, many of which are still with us today: Shell, Standard Oil of California, Standard Oil of New York (now the Mobil Oil Corporation), Richfield (reorganized), Union, Tidewater, Associated, and Doheny's own Pan-American Petroleum Company.

By 1935 yearly oil production, while never matching the 1930 figure of 227,000,000 barrels, had levelled off at two hundred million barrels, more or less; and with a total production of $265,385,925 in 1935, the refining industry stood at the top of eighteen manufacturing industries. The production and consumption of natural gas in the state led the nation, exceeding three hundred billion cubic feet every year, and the stimulus of oil in the Los Angeles Basin had transformed the little harbor at San Pedro into the richest port in the western United States. The demands of World War II caused oil production to leap to new highs, and by 1950 it had risen to more than three hundred million barrels.

Even before then, however, the industry realized that California's oil reserves were less than infinite. Looking about for new sources, it hit upon the idea of drilling offshore along the southern coast, particularly in parts of the Santa Barbara Channel. The state, presuming ownership of tidewater property extending three miles to sea, leased the offshore areas to oil companies during the war for a healthy slice of royalties per barrel.

At the end of the war, the federal government contemplated this new enterprise with its generous royalties and informed the state of California that her territorial waters were, in fact, federal property and please to vacate the premises. California resisted even when the United States Supreme Court ruled in 1947 that the rights of the federal government to tidewater strips were preeminent. Joining with Texas and Louisiana (whose concerns were similar), California lobbyists persuaded Congress to pass a bill that forced the government to return tidewater rights to the states; and while President Harry S. Truman vetoed the bill in 1952, it was revived the following year and signed into law by Truman's successor, Dwight D. Eisenhower.

Even with tidewater oil the supply was not enough. For the first time since the 1890s, California began importing oil, oil products, and natural gas to help meet her demands. Even today, with an annual production that reaches nearly four hundred million barrels a year, importation continues (as it does throughout the country, where the annual demand for gasoline, kerosine, and fuel oil exceeds production by more than six hundred million barrels). Seeking to tap into the estimated reserve of twenty billion barrels that was "lost" by poor production methods during the 1920s, engineers are pumping water into wellholes to force the oil to rise to the surface and using the "whipstock" method of drilling, which allows several holes to be sunk in different directions from the same drilling platform, but there seems little hope that this oil will ever be fully recovered.

The answer for California, as elsewhere—short of drastically revising our patterns of consumption (and our way of life)—probably lies in new discoveries outside the state, and it is not surprising to find California's oil companies playing a major part in the development of the fields off the bitter northern coast of Alaska. In a little over a century, Benjamin Silliman's remark, "It is plain to the least instructed people that the amount of oil capable of being produced here is almost without limit," has come up against the hard realities of a world neither he nor any contemporary could have foreseen.

*Something besides real estate to sell: the automobile comes to Southern California.*

# California Mirror:
# The Romance of Wheels and Wings

*A troupe of auto-excursionists on the road near Grossmont, 1909.*

In 1930, President Herbert Hoover's Research Committee on Social Trends issued its official recognition of the automobile's impact on American life: "It is probable that no invention of such far-reaching influence was ever diffused with such rapidity, or so quickly exerted influences that ramified throughout the national culture." If the statement was true of the rest of America, then it was—as usual—more so for California, which succumbed early to a lasting infatuation with the fascinating gadgets that, in the words of one owner, "shook and trembled and clattered, spat oil, fire, smoke and smell." Trembling or not, the contraptions moved, and there was nothing that Californians loved to do more.

The state's first encounter with an automobile, according to most accounts, occurred in 1898, when one W. L. Elliott drove his sputtering, handmade car down the streets of Oakland, terrifying horses and mystifying pedestrians. For the first few years after that, the automobile was little more than a rich man's plaything; in the opinion of Woodrow Wilson (then president of Princeton University), it was a major cause of social unrest: "Nothing has spread socialistic feeling in this country more than the use of the automobile," he said. "To the countryman, they are a picture of the arrogance of wealth, with all its independence and carelessness." That image was rectified somewhat after the San Francisco earthquake and fire, as noted in the **Overland Monthly**: "While beloved San Francisco was being devastated last April the automobile was making the greatest record in history. Without its aid, the damage done the city . . . and the sufferings of the inhabitants would have been immeasurably increased." Then in 1908 came Henry Ford's Model T—and from that time forward, California was on the move.

*The proud young man in the driver's seat of this glittering Davies-Overland is about to bridge the generation gap with wheels.*

*This 1900 Locomobile may have been the first motor car to enter Yosemite Valley.*

By 1910 there were 460,000 automobiles in the United States, and 36,000 of them were in California. Although they never matched the severity of a 1902 Vermont law that required every automobile to be preceded by a responsible adult waving a red flag, or a Tennessee law that demanded a week's notice before the beginning of a trip, early California laws were reasonably strict. At street intersections, for example, the speed limit was four miles an hour, in business districts six miles an hour, and in residential areas a nearly reckless eight miles an hour.

Still, little daunted the California driver. He had discovered a way of life. As the **Los Angeles Times** put it, "Our forefathers in their immortal independence creed set forth 'the pursuit of happiness' as an inalienable right of mankind. And how can one pursue happiness by any swifter and surer means . . . than by the use of the automobile?" One of the places in which the early automobilist was determined to pursue happiness was, improbably, Yosemite National Park. Under pressure from such organizations as the Motor Car Dealers Association, a reluctant Secretary of the Interior Walter L. Fisher put the question of admitting automobiles before the National Park Conference of 1912. Sentiment in favor of automobiles in the park was surprisingly broad, including even William E. Colby, the otherwise militant secretary of the Sierra Club: "We hope they will be able to come in when the time comes, because we think the automobile adds a great zest to travel and we are primarily interested in the increase of travel to these parks."

Others were not so sure, among them the British ambassador to the United States, James Bryce: "If Adam had known what harm the serpent was going to work, he would have tried to prevent him from finding lodgment in Eden; and if you were to realize what the result of the automobile will be in that wonderful, that incomparable valley, you will keep it out."

Secretary Fisher agreed with Bryce, but his successor, Franklin K. Lane, did not, and on April 30, 1913, he announced, "I have decided to allow automobiles to enter the Yosemite Valley." The prescient wisdom of James Bryce has since been demonstrated in the crowded, smog-ridden valley.

*A drive through the Wawona Tree of the Mariposa Grove of Big Trees was the most dramatic exploit of any automobile trip to Yosemite National Park.*

*"You know," Interior Secretary Walter Fisher said in 1912, "there are automobilists who apparently would . . . run their automobiles into St. Peter's."*

SAN FRANCISCO, CAL., SUNDAY, SEPTEMBER 17, 1916

### Studebaker Car Driven to Very Edge of Famous Overhanging Rock
### Automobile Figures in Unequaled Feat in History of the Yosemite

**Arthur Pillsbury Thrills Visitors in Valley by Daring Act to Obtain Unique Pho'o**

MAKING history in Yosemite National Park, Arthur C. Pillsbury, a photographer well known throughout California, Tuesday drove a Studebaker six to the extreme edge of the noted Overhanging Rock at Glacier Point, a rock varying in width from six to eight feet, jutting over a precipice 3240 feet deep. The sturdy six responded like a human to each purr of the engine and twist of the steering gear.

Pillsbury and his Studebaker six are the wonder of Yosemite. It has heretofore been considered a perilous task to walk out on Overhanging Rock, and to drive a car weighing 3700 pounds on this narrow shaft of granite was thought an impossibility. While the merry driver was worming his way out over the valley, the guests of the Sentinel Hotel and El Capitan Camp, who had been apprised of the feat to be performed, trained scores of glasses on the driver. Gathered at the summit of Glacier Point were a hundred or more hotel guests, who snapshotted every move of the Studebaker six.

**ADDED ATTRACTION**

Pillsbury had been engaged by D. J. Desmond, president of the Desmond Park Service Company, to take a series of motion pictures of the Desmond camps and concessions in Yosemite. To illustrate the Glacier Point trip, Pillsbury added the passage of Overhanging Rock as an attraction not in the original scenario.

When Pillsbury first stated he intended driving his Studebaker six to a point adjoining eternity, his claim was received with incredulity. Early Tuesday morning he wired D. J. Desmond in San Francisco:

"I am going to drive my auto across Overhanging Rock today. I will win this test as easily as I made the fastest run from San Francisco to Yosemite."

Pillsbury left Yosemite early in the morning and made the twenty-six-mile trip to Glacier Point in leisurely fashion. A survey of the approach to the Overhanging Rock showed the necessity of a runway necessary to surmount several granite boulders which barred the way.

*Overleaf: Automobiling as pure adventure—braving the perils of the coast road north of Santa Monica in 1912.*

Wherever one went by automobile in the early years, the difficulties of getting there were manifold. Local roads were little better than wagon tracks, rutted and pockmarked with holes, and the farther one traveled, the worse conditions became. Some idea of the pitfalls inherent in any ambitious excursion can be gained from a 1911 motoring magazine's suggested "minimum" list of basic tools and supplies: 34 tools, including "1 Small vise to clamp to running board," "1 Small short-handled axe," and "1 Towing cable"; 51 spare parts, including "1 Package assorted cement patches," "1 Small package raw rubber for vulcanizing," and "1 Assortment cotter pins, nuts, lock washers, wood screws, and nails"; and emergency food supplies for four people, including "2 Two-gallon canvas water bags," "4 Pound-packages hardtack," and "4 Half-pound cans meat or fish." Not since the days of the forty-niners had Americans set out to conquer a wilderness who were loaded down with so much equipment, most of it designed to avoid the need to "get out, get out and get under."

*For years, negotiating the Old Plank Road across the sand dunes of the Colorado Desert into Arizona was the epitome of exciting motoring.*

*That the six-hundred-mile trip across the desert was not to be taken lightly is suggested by the signs of the California Highway Commission, left.*

*For all its travail, the cross-country desert trip was a surefire publicity gimmick—a fact discovered early by circulation-hungry newspapers.*

As the automobile entered the mainstream of California life—becoming a means not only of travel, but of entertainment and even of advertising—the demand for more and better roads reached epidemic proportions. On the national level, the demand was reflected in the Lincoln Highway, a cross-country route from New York to San Francisco that was opened in time for a five-car cavalcade to rattle across the country to the Panama-Pacific International Exposition in 1915. Open, but not complete: a transcontinental speed record later that year took 19 days, 18 hours, and 15 minutes—and required no less than 505 miles of detours.

*As early as 1920, automobile manufacturers were testing the merchandise at public "meets".*

*The automobile as a permanent, portable advertising sign.*

*Left: There will always be an advertising man—in some peculiar way this 1920 photograph was meant to demonstrate the virtues of the Overland.*

*A study in contrasts: highway-building with horse-drawn Fresno scrapers.*

Long before the opening of the Lincoln Highway, Californians began to assume the task of building a statewide system of roads. Largely through the influence of the California State Automobile Association (San Francisco) and the Automobile Club of Southern California (Los Angeles), each founded in 1900, the state legislature authorized a road-building bond issue of $18 million in 1909, and the voters approved the issue the following year. In 1911 a State Highway Commission (now the Division of Highways) was created, and construction began. In 1916 another bond issue provided an additional $15 million, and in 1919 a third gave the commission another $40 million for construction purposes. After 1919 the adoption of the state gasoline tax made further bond issues unnecessary—a development aided considerably in 1921 when Congress passed the Federal Highway Act, providing the states with dollar-matching federal grants for an interstate highway system.

*Dedication day on the Mountain Springs Highway, 1912.*

*Right: The highway through Cahuenga Pass in 1928, its concrete, asphalt, and busy lanes providing a hint of the impending future.*

Many of California's early highways—like most in the rest of the country—were inadequately engineered. But these were quickly and unceremoniously replaced, for California soon achieved an expertise in highway technology that only the state of New York could match. By 1930 an expansive and sophisticated network of paved roads linked one end of the state to the other. It was just as well that it did, for by then there were more than two million automobiles in the state. The greatest single concentration was in Los Angeles, where there was one automobile for every three people. California had become what she would remain: a civilization on wheels.

*Off for a Sunday drive—a glimmering definition of the automobile's role in California life.*

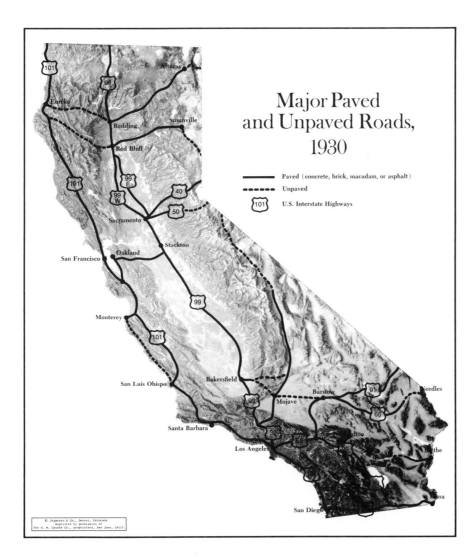

Major Paved and Unpaved Roads, 1930

— Paved (concrete, brick, macadam, or asphalt)
---- Unpaved
(101) U.S. Interstate Highways

© Jeppesen & Co., Denver, Colorado
Reprinted by permission of
The H. M. Gousha Co., proprietors, San Jose, Calif.

*For an interesting comparison, see the freeway map on page 459.*

*Left: There are very few photographs that truly make words superfluous; this is one of them.*

The romance of wheels was no match for the romance of wings, for the dream of flight is perhaps the oldest of man's atavistic yearnings. California's experience in flight had a discernible history even before the turn of the century. From the 1850s on into the 1890s, hot-air and gas-filled balloon flights were featured at nearly every public fair of more than passing consequence, and balloonists like Thomas Scott Baldwin achieved daredevil reputations throughout the state and the country.

More suggestive of the future was the remarkable "Aviter" of Frederick Marriott. A Native of England, Marriott had associated himself in the 1840s with a British group called the "Aerial Transit Company," which advocated the crossing of the Atlantic Ocean by air. Nothing came of the venture, and sometime around 1850 Marriott came to San Francisco, where he founded the **San Francisco News Letter.** He had not abandoned his

dreams of aerial transport, however, and after several years of research into the dynamics of flight—much of it stemming from the observation of Chinese kites flown from the roof of the city's Montgomery Block—he devised the notion of a blimp-type vehicle capable of crossing the continent in a matter of days. The degree of California's desperation for quick communication with the East was evidenced in Marriott's convincing a number of San Francisco financiers (including William C. Ralston) to invest time and money enough for the incorporation of the Aerial Steam Navigation Company in 1866; plans were immediately laid for the construction of a working model of his airship.

The model was finished by the end of June 1869. It was 37 feet long and 14 feet wide, and sported two startling innovations: the first, a small brass alcohol steam engine, designed by George K. Gluyas, president of the

*Romance, distilled and incandescent: above, on the beach at Coronado . . .*
*. . . and on the right, a "sunset flight" above the sands of Santa Monica.*

342

*French aviator Louis Paulhan and his Farman biplane, with William Randolph Hearst astraddle.*

*Paulhan makes aviation history at 4,149 feet —Dominguez Field, Los Angeles, 1910.*

California Steam Navigation Company; the second, a pair of muslin wings, or "inclined planes," which flanked the gas bag on either side and had attached at the end of each a propeller driven by the little steam engine. The airship was christened the "Avitor Hermes, Jr.," and a flight test was scheduled for the morning of July 2, 1869. The flight was a rather startling success, as reported by a correspondent for **Scientific American**: "With the first turn of the propellers she rose slowly into the air, gradually increasing her speed until the rate of five miles per hour was attained. The position of the rudder caused her to describe a great circle, around which she passed twice, occupying about five minutes each time. . . . Cheer upon cheer rose from the little group of anxious spectators." They had reason to cheer: the Avitor's maiden voyage was the first powered flight of a lighter-than-air craft in America.

*Lincoln Beachey scampers the catwalk of a Knabenshue dirigible, Dominguez Field, 1910.*

Unfortunately, that flight was the project's only moment of glory, for the completion of the earthbound transcontinental railroad that same year dissipated public interest. The Aerial Steam Navigation Company went bankrupt, and after several months of demonstrations at San Francisco's Mechanics' Pavilion, the little Avitor caught fire and was destroyed.

The Avitor died, but the dream of flight did not. In 1883, John Joseph Montgomery, a professor at the University of Santa Clara, made a successful manned glider flight off Otay Mesa near San Diego—twenty years before the Wright brothers accomplished manned flight at Kitty Hawk. And some rather vaguely documented accounts maintain that one Lyman Gilmore of Calaveras

County made a steam-powered heavier-than-air flight near Lake Almanor in 1902—months before the Wright brothers went aloft in their gasoline-powered craft. Another candidate for this particular "first" in California was Glenn Curtiss, a motorcycle builder who is said to have constructed and flown an airplane in San Diego as early as 1906. What is definitely known is that he founded the first flying school in the state and designed his own monoplane and seaplane before moving on to Long Island.

The first fully documented instance of powered flight in California took place in January 1910 at a place called Dominguez Hill, between Compton and Long Beach in Southern California. The occasion was the first air meet in United States history, sponsored by William Randolph Hearst's **Los Angeles Examiner,** and the powered

flight was made by the French airman Louis Paulhan in a Farman biplane. During the ten-day meet, Paulhan also set a world's altitude record of 4,149 feet, fully verified by an **Examiner** balloon. Other notable events of the meet included Lincoln Beachey straddling the catwalk of a powered dirigible, Glenn Curtiss doing tricks in his own biplane, and Paulhan's safe delivery of a passenger on a twenty-mile flight to Redondo Beach. The excitements continued. Later that same year San Francisco held its own air meet at the Tanforan Race Track, and in 1911, Eugene Ely accomplished the first aircraft-carrier landing in history by bringing his Curtiss "pusher" biplane down safely on the deck of the U.S.S. **Pennsylvania** in San Francisco Bay.

Such stunts and exhibitions were good for more than entertainment; they demonstrated the practicality and

*The state of the passenger arts in 1931: Century Pacific Lines, Los Angeles.*

*1932: A Ryan high-wing monoplane soars above Long Beach and the derricks of Signal Hill.*

increasing efficiency of airplanes, as well as the singular attractions of the California atmosphere for the pursuit of aviation—or, as the **Los Angeles Examiner** expressed it, "A new use has been discovered for the overflow of climate." Slowly, what had been an oddity of technology took on the outlines of an infant industry. In 1909, Glenn L. Martin began manufacturing airplanes in an abandoned church in Santa Ana. He later moved his plant to Los Angeles, and then east to Cleveland—but one of the products of his short stay in the state was his chief aeronautical engineer, Donald W. Douglas, who returned to Los Angeles in 1920 to set up his own "factory" in the back room of a barber shop on Pico Boulevard.

After fulfilling a navy contract for three torpedo planes, Douglas moved to Santa Monica, where he was soon turning out one airplane a week. In 1924 he designed and constructed four "World Cruisers" for the Army Air Service, three of which accomplished the first round-the-world flight in history that year. Douglas's most notable achievement before World War II, however, was the development of the DC-3 transport in 1936, probably the most reliable and well-used aircraft of its time.

In 1916, Alan and Malcolm Loughead began the manufacture of airplanes in the back of a garage in Santa Barbara. After some success in the 1920s—during which Loughead became Lockheed and the operation was moved to Burbank—the company went into bankruptcy in 1931 and was purchased for $40,000 by a group of eastern investors headed up by Robert E. Gross. In 1934 the company's health was assured with the development of the twin-engined Electra, a craft that proved eminently adaptable to military purposes and challenged the workhorse qualities of the DC-3 for civilian purposes.

A third Southern California pioneer in the manufacture of airplanes was T. Claude Ryan, an army pilot during World War I. In 1922, Ryan established the country's first regularly scheduled airline passenger service with daily flights between San Diego and Los Angeles, and in the next year he founded the Ryan Aeronautical Company in San Diego, where he began to turn out a particularly sturdy version of a topwing monoplane. An adaptation of this design became the **Spirit of St. Louis,** which Ryan constructed for Charles A. Lindbergh's solo transatlantic flight of 1927. The performance of the rugged single-engine craft gave Ryan Aeronautical a national reputation and made the Ryan monoplane one of the most popular passenger airplanes on the West Coast for a number of years.

By the middle of the 1930s, when Ryan, Lockheed, and Douglas—the early giants of the industry—were joined by a handful of other companies, among them North American Aviation, Northrup, and Consolidated Vultee (later Convair), Southern California had the largest collection of aircraft manufacturing plants of any region in the country. Yet the relative importance of the young industry's role to the economic life of the state is illustrated by the fact that its 1935 production output of $20 million amounted to less than 3 percent of California's annual agricultural product. Not until the dogs of war were slipped did the situation change.

*The U.S. Army's bomber squadron—all of it—*
*wobbles through the Golden Gate, 1932.*

# CHAPTER 17

# THE ANATOMY OF LOTUS LAND

*The quicksilver shift of power to the land south of the Tehachapis,*

*where oranges and fortunes blossomed and died, and blossomed again*

FOR SEVENTY YEARS San Francisco was California's Rome, the center of her arts, commerce, industry, and population. Not even the disaster of 1906 could fully diminish her role, one which the city's residents accepted with the aplomb of a chosen people whose preeminence stemmed from divine ordination.

Yet even as San Francisco quietly celebrated her dominant place in California's life, the city was being challenged by Los Angeles—by all of Southern California. In fits and starts, in times of boom and times of a kind of languid inevitability, Southern California was filling up with people. They were drawn by the climate and the glittering promise of escape; as Louis Adamic once wrote, "Toil-broken and bleached out, they flock to Los Angeles, fugitives from the simple, inexorable justice of life, from hard labor and drudgery, from cold winters and blistering summers of the prairies." They were drawn, too, by opportunity; mid-western wheat farmers came west to grow oranges, lemons, grapes, grapefruit, and sundry other specialized crops; bankers and brokers and merchants fled hundreds of small towns where growth had sputtered out, and workingmen streamed in to find a substitute for the grinding, antlike existence they knew in the industrialized East. In 1910 the population of Los Angeles was 319,000; by 1920 it had grown to 576,000—and those San Franciscans who bothered to notice would have learned that for the first time in the history of the state, the population of Los Angeles was greater than that of "the cool, gray city of love." It was only the beginning of a quicksilver shift of power to the land south of the Tehachapis.

Between 1920 and 1930, 2,251,000 people were added to the state of California, an increase that surpassed even that of New York in the same period. Of this number, 1,900,000 were out-of-state migrants, and of these 1,368,000 settled in Southern California. It was the largest internal migration in the history of the United States, surpassing by far the population boom of the gold rush years. Freed of the constraints of World War I, the migrants came for all the old reasons, reasons now given a bloated significance by the heavy smell of oil and booming prosperity and the iridescent sheen of Hollywood glamour. California had become something more than the land of promise it had always been; it had become a magic land, a lotus land, a confusion of myth and all the yeasty hopes that had ever driven the footling soul of man to defy logic and reach for the nearest available star.

The migration was the first national expression of the transformation the automobile was beginning to work on American life. Across the rutted dirt roads, the graveled wagon tracks, the partly paved highways of the trans-Mississippi West, they clattered and rumbled in twentieth-century equivalents of the Conestoga wagons and handcarts that had labored over all the rocks and hard places nearly three-quarters of a century before. "Like a swarm of invading locusts, migrants crept in over all the roads," an observer wrote. "For wings, they had rattletrap automobiles, their fenders tied with string, and curtains flapping in the breeze; loaded with babies, bedding, bundles, a tin tub tied on behind, a bicycle or baby carriage balanced precariously

*Sylphlike and cheery, a Matron of the Grapefruit cradles an armful of the sun's golden harvest in Southern California.*

*351*

*Main Street, Los Angeles, in 1906, when horses could be seen among the autos and streetcars.*

on the top. Often they came with no funds and no prospects, apparently trusting that heaven would provide for them. . . . They camped on the outskirts of town, and their camps became new suburbs."

It was a migration partly spontaneous and partly induced in traditional fashion. In 1921, Harry Chandler, publisher of the Los Angeles *Times* and—appropriately enough—son-in-law of the late Harrison Gray Otis, gathered a few colleagues around him and formed the All-Year Club of Southern California. Financed by both private and municipal funding, the All-Year Club soon transcended the Los Angeles Chamber of Commerce as the leading publicity organization in Southern California. Chandler had been deeply moved by complaints from the region's hotelkeepers and apartment owners that, while business boomed during the winter months, it fell off miserably during the summer, and the All-Year Club dedicated itself to selling Southern California as a year-round mecca for victims of eastern weather, a land whose delights of winter were second only to the glories of summer. "Sleep under a blanket every night all summer in Southern California," it boasted in one of its scores of advertising pamphlets. In another it extended itself beyond reason, as it attempted to persuade readers that the California sun was almost a marketable commodity: "The sunshine of Southern California is so beneficial, due to the violet rays therein, that scientists are endeavoring to reproduce it artificially."

The propaganda of the All-Year Club was supported by the continuing efforts of the Chamber of Commerce, real estate associations, the Automobile Club of Southern California (the first and largest of its kind), and even the Southern Pacific Railroad (it was still an age when railroads *wanted* passenger traffic). Through magazine articles and advertisements, planted newspaper features and advertisements, a blinding array of publications, and "California booths" set up in every county fair and state exhibition into which they could insinuate themselves, the California boosters put together the longest, most successful "saturation campaign" in the nation's history—long before the term or technique became common in the advertising world.

And so they came, by the tens and the hundreds of thousands. Waiting to meet them were real estate agents, 43,000 of them in Los Angeles alone. "One has hardly registered at a hotel," a new arrival marveled, "before the telephone and a little later the mail bring offers of real estate opportunities." Agents hired gray-haired matrons and willowy young blondes to prowl the streets of downtown Los Angeles, collaring pedestrians with fistfuls of boom pamphlets, tract maps, and artists' conceptions of the future appearance of one new subdivision or another. Free excursion buses were parked at strategic points, ready and more than willing to whisk prospects off to sites of some future Eden; most of them threw in a free lunch, too, in a manner reminiscent of the boom days of 1887. "Sightseers," wrote one reporter, "can get along with two meals and no automobile indefinitely in Los Angeles."

The theme was sell, sell, sell—and buy, buy, buy. The litany was repetitive, persuasive, and suffused with an optimism that simply glowed, as illustrated by a typical agent's spiel (quoted in Remi Nadeau's *Los Angeles: From Mission to Modern City*): "Follow my advice and buy one, or ten, of these lots, regardless of the sacrifice it might mean. Ten thousand banks might close, stocks may smash, bonds may shrink to little or nothing, but this tract and Los Angeles real estate stand like the Rock of Gibraltar for safety, certainty and profit. Don't be satisfied with six per cent on your money. Don't be satisfied with twelve per cent. Buy property like this and keep it, and as sure as the world moves it will pay you one hundred per cent to one thousand per cent and more per annum. Be among those who earn from one hundred per cent to one thousand per cent. We offer you the opportunity. . . ."

In some areas such breathless prognostications came true in startling fashion. Out on Western Avenue, for example, a group of businessmen decided in 1922 to erect a business center in the middle of what was then a quiet residential neighborhood. The resulting scramble for a piece of the action caused property values to skitter upward from $50 a front foot to as much as $2,000. Homes were torn down or carted off, replaced by block after block of two- and three-story business buildings. Those lucky enough to have purchased homes before the mercantile rush were offered prices that surpassed belief; one such homeowner, it is reliably reported, bought his house and lot for $4,500, and less

than two years later was able to sell it to a trembling speculator for $60,000—an interest rate considerably *over* that 1,000 percent mentioned by the real estate agent above. Similar developments grew like hypertrophic mushrooms along Vine Street, Melrose Avenue, and Beverly Boulevard, as downtown merchants, bankers, and brokers fell over one another in their efforts to erect branch locations.

The key to the success of such developments was the automobile, for it removed the necessity of developing only those areas where there were, or might be, streetcar lines. If the "Big Red Cars" of Henry E. Huntington's Pacific Electric Railway had provided an outline for the metropolitan sprawl characteristic of the Los Angeles Basin, it remained for the automobile to carry that outline to its logical extreme. "Now," as Remi Nadeau has written, "wherever the Model T could go, the surveyor could go." And he went.

*Opening day at the Montrose tract in 1913, complete with a free barbecue.*
*The presence of automobiles marks the only difference from a sale during the boom of 1887.*

*Growth, growth, growth: Culver City was not the only town
in Southern California to make such boasts, but it did so with style.*

In the middle of a sheep pasture and along a beaten dirt road called Wilshire Boulevard, four miles removed from anything close to civilization, realtor A. W. Ross bought eighteen acres of property for $54,000 and began selling lots for business property. In less than ten years, Wilshire Boulevard had become a six-lane paved thoroughfare, and its towering walls of business buildings had become known the country over as the "Miracle Mile." Cattle pasture in the San Fernando Valley, farmland in the Eagle Rock Valley, semidesert on the plain extending east to San Bernardino—much of it fell to the frantic onslaught of piecemeal development.

By 1924 the Los Angeles Planning Department (one of the first such in the nation) was approving as many as forty new subdivisions every week. One estimate had it that at least three hundred thousand lots had been sold in the county since the end of the war. Subdivisions became towns, then cities; several new cities with populations in the thousands were added to the county, including South Gate, Bell, Lynwood, Torrance, Hawthorne, Maywood, and Tujunga, and dozens of cities that had been born during previous booms swelled and expanded. In 1919 the total value of real estate permits in Los Angeles had been $28,000,000; in 1922 the value jumped to $121,000,000, and by the end of 1923 to more than $200,000,000. In five years 1,400 housing tracts were laid out.

Statistics to make the collective heart of any chamber of commerce pulse with delight—but by 1924 the boom had reached its apex. Refusing to believe there could ever be an end to anything, developers had reached beyond the future to subdivide everything in sight. William May Garland, who had learned the real estate trade in the 1880s and 1890s (and who was the creator of Westlake Park, one of the most exclusive and attractive of the region's many subdivisions), vainly sounded

*Boost, boost, boost: the scene is Southern California gone rampant, with palm fronds, Moorish-Spanish architecture, and a patriotic hot dog stand.*

an alarm in 1922: "We have enough subdivisions and lots for sale and in process of development to accommodate the cities of New York, Philadelphia, and Detroit."

Few listened in 1922, but by the end of 1924 even the most sanguine dealer in quarter-acre lots was forced to admit that the industry had overextended itself: there were simply more lots than there were people. Money that had been loose suddenly became tight, as banks and lending institutions curtailed their real estate loans; scores of ambitious tracts stood empty, not to be filled until the war boom of the 1940s; a rash of bankruptcies cluttered court dockets, as brokers and building contractors went under; employment in the building and service trades fell, and even the ever-optimistic All-Year Club was forced to temper its continuing promotion by warning immigrants not to expect to find work readily in Southern California—none of this im-

proved by the national recession of 1924, which had its effect in California as it had throughout the rest of the country (a brief harbinger of worse to come).

Yet like the decline of the 1887 boom (see chapter 12), the failure of the bubble of the 1920s was more in the nature of a gradual, fairly even deflation after the initial burst rather than a total collapse. The migration slowed but it did not stop. The seekers of California's promise kept coming, spilling across her borders in a steady stream that was less than the flood it had been in the first half of the decade but considerably more than the trickle it might have been to other regions. That stream provided a kind of cushion that kept the economy of Southern California from feeling the clammy touch of rock bottom—for a time, at least. And while it served this welcome function, that stream contributed many of the pieces to a cultural puzzle called Southern California.

For more than fifty years, one of the most per-

*Easter sunrise services at the Hollywood Bowl—
one of the region's oldest cultural traditions.*

sistent questions posed by sociologists, psychologists, writers and other students of human behavior has been: just what *is* a Los Angeles (or a Southern California, for the terms are used synonymously)? The society that evolved south of the Tehachapi Mountains was perceptibly unlike that which had evolved anywhere else on this continent, or any other, for that matter.

Vaguely structured and littered with a thousand conflicting dreams, demands, backgrounds, and attitudes, it was a society that somehow became more than the sum of its parts. As such, it captured (indeed, invited) the fascinated regard of much of the western world. It still does today, but it is well to remember that many of the definitions by which modern Southern California is measured have their roots in the observations and attitudes of the California-watchers of the 1920s. Their conclusions were often less than precise then and are certainly no more accurate today, for Southern Cali-

fornia was, and is, in a state of becoming, disinclined to remain in one condition long enough for a solid determination to be made concerning exactly what it is that is being watched.

Still, even as the automobile expanded upon patterns of physical growth that were shaped in the 1880s and refined after the turn of the century by electric railway lines, the societal web of modern Southern California is an enlarged (and sometimes distorted) reflection of cultural patterns spun, however falteringly, during the 1920s. That being the case, it would be well to take a closer look at both the origin and character of the population that established such patterns.

Writing in *Harper's* in 1925, Louis Adamic laid down at least one man's interpretation of the social structure of Los Angeles: "The people on the top in Los Angeles, the Big Men, are the business men, the Babbitts. They are the promoters, who are blowing down the city's windpipe with all their might, hoping to inflate the place to a size that will be reckoned the largest city in the country—in the world. . . . These men are the high priests of the Chamber of Commerce whose religion is Climate and Profits. They are—some of them —grim, inhuman individuals with a great terrifying singleness of purpose. . . . And trailing after the big boys is a mob of lesser fellows . . . thousands of minor realtors, boomers, promoters, contractors, agents, salesmen, bunko-men, officer-holders, lawyers, and preachers—all driven by the same motives of wealth, power, and personal glory. . . . They exploit the 'come-ons' and one another, envy the big boys, their wives gather in women's clubs, listen to swamis and yogis and English lecturers, join 'love cults' and Coué clubs in Hollywood and Pasadena, and their children jazz and drink and rush around in roadsters. Then there are the Folks . . . the retired farmers, grocers, Ford agents, hardware merchants, and shoe merchants from the Middle West and other parts of the United States, thousands and tens of thousands of them . . . here in California—sunny California—to rest and regain their vigor, enjoy climate, look at pretty scenery, live in little bungalows with a palm-tree or banana plant in front, and eat in cafeterias."

Adamic, bitten at an early age by H. L. Mencken, was obviously writing with an eye bloodshot with cynicism, and his view of life in Los Angeles rivals that of Nathanael West in his later novel, *The Day of the*

*Locust.* Nevertheless, his outline quite accurately divided Los Angeles society (and, by implication, Southern California society) into its three basic elements.

At the top were, indeed, the "Big Men," the promoters. They were men like Harry Chandler of the *Times,* real estate giants like A. W. Ross and William May Garland, or the oddly named Motley H. Flint, vice-president of the Pacific Southwest Trust and Savings Bank. Most were transplants to Southern California, but most had sunk their roots into the region long before the boom of the 1920s. For them, the sunset land was something more than a resource to be exploited; is was a new homeland to be developed. Believing in the inherent virtues of Growth, Progress, and Enterprise with the sincerity of nuns contemplating the doctrine of Virgin Birth, they were utterly convinced, right or wrong, that their own success was inseparable from the success of the region as a whole. They were the faith-keepers, the visionaries whose lambent optimism was reminiscent of that of San Francisco's William C. Ralston fifty years before.

"I am a foresighted man," Henry E. Huntington had written before the turn of the century, "and I believe that Los Angeles is destined to become the most important city in this country, if not in the world. It can extend in any direction as far as you like. Its front door opens on the Pacific, the ocean of the future. Europe can supply her own wants; we shall supply the wants of Asia. There is nothing that cannot be made and few things that will not grow in Southern California."

That optimism, linked with the power of the money behind it, almost literally "conjured" Los Angeles into existence, as Carey McWilliams once put it. Conservative in their social view to the point of becoming mossbacks, these shapers of Los Angeles were progressive, sometimes even radical, in their economic attitudes. When they failed, as they sometimes did, they did so with a crash and a clatter that shook the world around them. They were the architects of Southern California's future, and if they were sometimes grim in both their acts and attitudes, they were always human.

The "mob of lesser fellows" was less clearly defined.

*Seeking sun and surcease from the rigors of midwestern life, the Folks gobble up the free lunch at a land sale near Point Loma in 1928.*

*Sister Aimee's Angelus Temple in 1926—spiked with radio towers like the horns of righteousness.*

Most, but not all, were as new to Southern California as the boom they experienced and helped to promote. They, too, had faith in the virtues of Growth, Progress, and Enterprise but a little less faith in themselves. They had pulled up roots, some of them quite deep and secure, in other places and moved west, seeking the means by which mere security could be exchanged for greatness of one kind or another. They were "on the make" in the finest American tradition, driven, as Francis Parkman once put it, "by an insane desire to better their condition in life." Many had wagered all they had and their insecurity manifested itself in an eagerness to acquire the trappings of success even when success itself evaded them: memberships in country clubs and beach clubs, glittering new automobiles (in this era, Pierce-Arrows as often as not), stuccoed Spanish-style homes in the best districts, carefree frolics in local supper clubs and even occasional forays onto the fringes of Hollywood night life.

At their best, they were community leaders, councilmen, primary lights of the Rotarians, the Lions, and the Elks, pushing with whole-souled enthusiasm to make their lives and the lives of their towns something better.

At their worst, they were shallow, cheap-jack confidence men, morally threadbare, ready and willing to make the quickest of quick deals, skim a profit off the top, and move on to repeat the performance. Well or corruptly motivated, most were inclined to spread themselves dangerously thin, trusting in the religion of Climate and Profits to pull them through.

Their wives, bored and glittering with the freedom of a new age, did in fact pursue enlightenment into some fairly strange byways, including the lairs of swamis and yogis, and embraced a number of fashionable doctrines, particularly the murky theories of Emile Coué. Like their eastern counterparts, they played bridge and Mah-jongg, dabbled with ouija boards, and established the cocktail party as a social institution. They also contributed time, enthusiasm, and often money to the region's fluttering, embryonic cultural life, supporting and sustaining such efforts as the Los Angeles Philharmonic Orchestra, the Hollywood Bowl concerts (originated in the 1920s and still a tradition), the Belasco Theatre, and the Pasadena Community Playhouse. There was not much in the way of what the Germans call *kultur* in Southern California, but what there was was largely effected by such women.

What, then, of "the Folks," the bottom third of Southern California's social pyramid? They were fully as numerous as Adamic suggested, although not quite so voiceless as he implied. For years they had been the moral barometer of Southern California, the single standard by which the ethical character of the region was measured. "These good folks brought with them a complete stock of rural beliefs, pieties, superstitions, and habits," Willard Huntington Wright had written in 1913, "the Middle West bed hours, the Middle West love of corned beef, the church bells, *Munsey's Magazine,* union suits and missionary societies." Their quiet fervor for propriety had made temperance a political force, and anti-saloon ordinances a fact of life for many a thirsty drummer; that same fervor had given strength to the Good Government movement and the Progressive era that followed it, and had invested the towns and cities of the region with a homogeneous, village-like character not too distant in quality from the towns and cities left behind.

They were still coming in the 1920s, these good Folks, carrying with them most of the same rural certainties.

By 1930 the population of Los Angeles included 72,933 former Illinoisans, 49,590 Missourians, 42,212 Ohioans, and 41,352 Iowans, not to mention 49,337 former New Yorkers, most of them from the rural upstate region, whose character was not noticeably different from that of the Midwest. But now they had "pursued a yearning for self-fulfillment into strangeness," as David Lavender described it. Under the assaults of the developer and the automobile, the homogeneity that once might have given them assurance was dissolving, and the vague outlines of the megalopolis to come could be seen. It was an accelerating society that they now encountered, one that not only reflected the swift changes overcoming America but exaggerated, distorted, and elaborated upon them. Old institutions, old religions, old mores seemed to have lost relevance somehow, and the folks desperately turned to new answers, new definitions of themselves and the society in which they floundered.

Many joined lonely-hearts clubs in an attempt to assuage a terrible, rootless loneliness. Many thousands more took an active part in "state societies," organizations designed to bring former residents of individual states together in a kind of continuing reunion. The largest of these was the Iowa Society, whose annual picnics drew scores of thousands for fried chicken and nostalgia (much diminished today, these picnics continue in many regions of the southland). Still others abandoned the fundamentalism that had sufficed in the simpler world they had known and turned to a confusion of new ideologies, giving the region the reputation of welcoming cranks, cults, and the generally weird—a reputation it has not fully escaped today. They gathered once a year in the Ojai Valley to worship at the feet of Krishnamurti, the "New Messiah" of something called the "sixth sub-race," or made pilgrimages to Krotona, a fifteen acre "place of promise" in the middle of Hollywood.

They embraced the dogmas of New Thought and theosophy and a hundred strange offshoots of the fundamentalism they had known, including, most especially, the "Four Square Gospel" of Sister Aimee Semple Mc-Pherson, who arrived in Los Angeles in 1922 with one hundred dollars and eight years later had emerged as the most prominent religious figure in California. Her followers numbered more than fifty thousand, who worshipped in "lighthouses" scattered from San Diego to San Bernardino; and her Angelus Temple in Los Angeles, built at a cost of $1,500,000, boasted an auditorium with 5,000 seats, a $75,000 radio station, and classrooms that graduated as many as five hundred young evangelists every year.

Beset by a multitude of illnesses (most of which may have been as psychological in nature as they were physical), the Folks supported a phalanx of unconventional medical practitioners, including hydrotherapists, naturopaths, osteopaths, and chiropractors. Culturally confused, deprived of former certitudes (by their own volition, but deprived nonetheless), the Folks of Southern California painfully reached out for stability in all the ways they could. When they failed, they were inclined to kill themselves; throughout the 1920s, San Diego had the highest suicide rate of any city in the nation, and Los Angeles was not far behind.

These three—the Big Men, the Go-Getters, the Folks—comprised the matrix of Southern California's social life in the 1920s. (For the simple reason that they were culturally invisible, without voice, power, or even recognition, the two principal minority groups of Southern California—the Mexicans and the Japanese—have been left out of this discussion; their time would come.) Loose, fluid to the point of formlessness at times, dedicated to extremes of behavior, and too often economically shallow, it was a civilization ill equipped to withstand the debacle of the Depression to come. Yet, some of its forms and many of its attitudes would survive not only the Depression but the traumatic boom of the war years and the explosive growth of the 1950s. Some of both have survived to our own time, not the least of which is an unconquerable infatuation with the promise of Tomorrow, as expressed by one boomer of the 1920s: "Anything seems possible. The future is yours, and the past?—there isn't any."

# SECTION TWO

# *Interregnum*

Is California civilized? Yes, California is civilized. That is what is the matter with it. . . . It will be forty-three years in August of this year since I first saw California, after a long ride through the desert. . . . For more than four decades I have been privileged to live in one of the fairest and kindliest of all the regions of the earth. California is, indeed, a marvelous land, beyond anything the passing tourist can ever know, and many of its people are among the choicest fruits of human evolution. All of this only accentuates the bewilderment and bitter disappointment which must be felt by any thinking man at the social barbarism of California . . . of our ignorance, our intolerance, and above all, our complacent social inertia.

—Robert Whitaker in *The Nation* (April, 1931)

*The hope of tomorrow: this sleek, sturdy young member of the Civilian Conservation Corps (CCC) was doubtless meant to symbolize strength in adversity.*

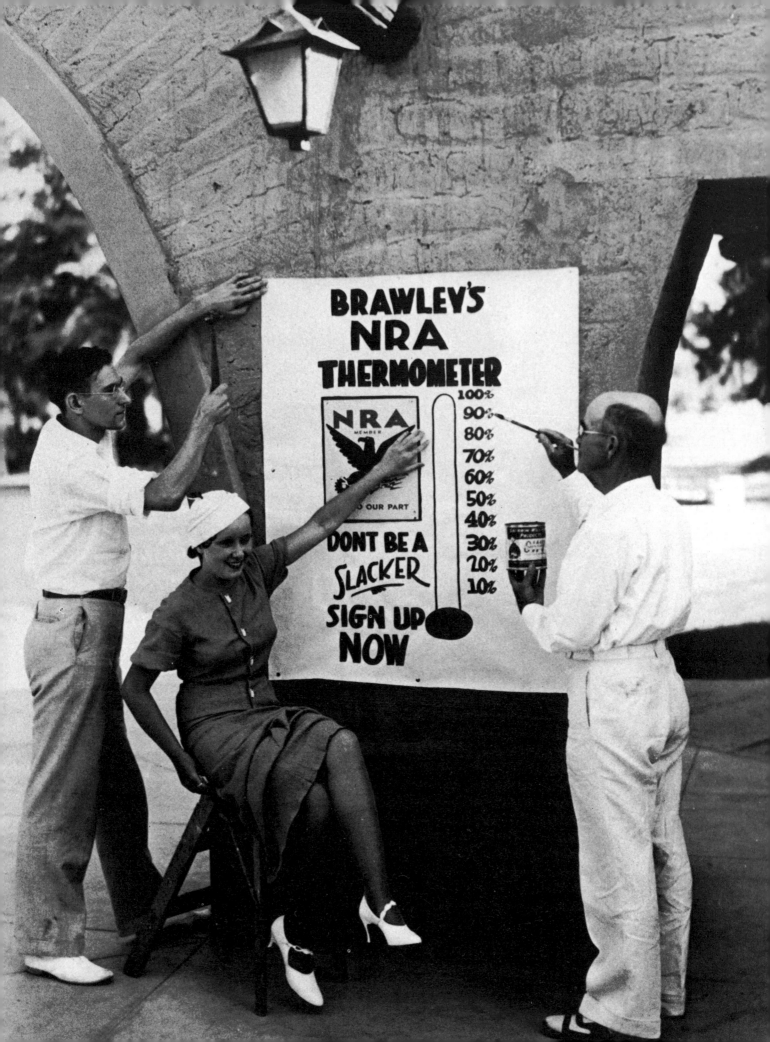

# CHAPTER 18

# PERILS AND PANACEAS

*The depression sweeps through the California economy like a scythe,*

*creating a welter of problems and a dearth of solutions*

THE WAVE OF PROSPERITY, on whose dizzy crest Californians had enjoyed an exciting ten-year ride after World War I, hit the beach in October 1929 with a fearful rumble, scattering financial wreckage along a suddenly lost and silent shore. For the first time in history, California would feel the full and undiluted effects of a national depression. No longer protected by the buffers of time and space, with economic tendrils spread throughout the continent and much of the world, California was now as vulnerable as any other state in the republic to the manic dips and spurts of the national economy. And, even as her response to prosperity had been to invest it with an intensity all her own, the state's response to the sink of the Depression possessed a unique flavor.

The disaster cut through the underpinnings of California's economy like a scythe. It was bad enough for the state's "real" industries, those turning out actual products; agricultural revenue, for example, dropped from $750,000,000 in 1929 to $327,000,000 in 1932, and the oil industry found itself producing more than 200,000 barrels a day above and beyond what a suddenly shrunken market demanded. For businesses like real estate promotion, the Depression was nothing short of Armageddon—and Southern California, the Shangri-La of real estate men, was devastated. Development firms, banks, savings and loan associations, and construction firms crumbled into receivership, accompanied by investigations into fraud, embezzlement, and other esoteric forms of financial jobbery. In 1930 alone Southern California led the rest of the nation not only in the total number of its bankruptcies but in the amount of losses incurred in said bankruptcies. In two years fraud investigations suggested that as many as seventy-five thousand people had been done out of as much as two hundred million dollars. No less than five hundred thousand people had been pauperized in the region, reduced to selling pencils and apples, cleaning off windshields at intersections in hope of a tip from the driver, and living off the pittances provided them by state and municipal relief checks. Between 1930 and 1933 seventy-nine people threw themselves from the lovely bridge spanning Arroyo Seco near Pasadena, causing the area's residents to declare that property values were being irrepairably damaged.

Throughout the state the bread lines grew, and while migration to California dropped to only 40 percent of what it had been during the 1920s, the state's pull was not completely diminished. Operating on the superficially logical assumption that conditions could not possibly be worse in California than where they were, and might even be better, thousands of hollow-eyed, wasted refugees guided their broken automobiles into the state, seeking jobs, seeking sunshine, seeking hope. By 1934 there were 1,250,000 people on the relief rolls of California—nearly 20 percent of the total population. Most of them clustered in the benign climate of Southern California, drawn like moths to a flame by a generation's worth of propaganda. In three years the costs of public welfare in Los Angeles County alone increased more than ten times, and by 1935 officials were desperate enough to launch a scheme whose out-

*The desert hamlet of Brawley does its bit to meet the requirements of the National Recovery Act.*

landish directness was utterly typical of the region: beginning on February 4, 1936, 136 Los Angeles city policemen (the county sheriff's office refusing to have anything to do with the operation) set up guard posts at all the rail and highway entrances to the state from Arizona, Oregon, and Nevada. Their orders were to refuse entrance to hitchhikers, boxcar riders, and "all other persons who have no definite purpose for coming into the state." This action, it should be emphasized, was strictly the doing of the city of Los Angeles, not of the state government, a fact that seemed to bother the city not at all and the state very little—although the legislature eventually passed a law that closed California's borders to "undesirables."

In spite of protests from civil libertarians that the whole business was transparently unconstitutional, the city of Los Angeles continued its blockade until almost the end of the decade. In 1941 a somewhat belated decision of the United States Supreme Court declared the practice to be, not unconstitutional, but "in restraint of interstate commerce"; but by then the decision was largely irrelevant. One estimate had it that the County of Los Angeles, through the "courageous" action of its principal municipality, had saved as much as $300,000 in welfare costs. Similarly, the city attacked its problem of resident Mexican aliens by periodically loading them into trucks and hauling them, free of charge, back to Mexico (from which, after a short vacation to visit friends and relatives, the aliens blithely slipped back across the border).

As if the invasion of destitute outsiders were not problem enough, the California labor movement, nearly dormant for more than a decade, became restive. Some of the earliest and most brutal confrontations between capital and labor during the 1930s took place on California's farms (see chapter 20), but the single most dramatic manifestation of the resurgence of old antagonisms took place on the waterfront streets of San Francisco.

In 1919 waterfront employers had systematically broken a strike by the International Longshoremen's Association, replaced the organization with a company

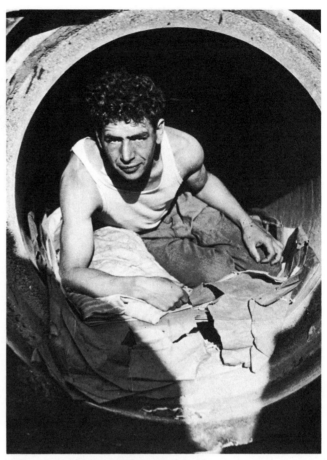

*A local resident of "Pipe City" in the San Joaquin Valley. This shot is not posed.*

*An apple-seller on San Francisco's Market Street in 1932. Is the shot posed?*

union, and joining with most of the rest of San Francisco's employers, dedicated themselves to the task of making the oldest union town in California an open-shop city. By the end of the 1920s that goal had been accomplished, giving California one of the tightest lids on the labor movement of any state in the nation. But in 1933 Congress passed the National Industrial Recovery Act, which contained one insidious clause (7a) declaring it to be one of the natural rights of workers to "organize and bargain collectively through representatives of their own choosing."

Taking heart from this official recognition of a right they had believed was theirs all along, laboring men slowly began to reorganize. One of the first groups to do so was a collection of longshoremen under the leadership of Harry Bridges, a former Australian seaman

*The dispossessed, the rootless, the exhausted: the refugees of the
Dust Bowl made home how and where they could.*

*The disenchanted and the angry: made eloquent by frustration, a street speaker harangues a crowd on Market Street, San Francisco.*

who had been working on the San Francisco docks since 1921. Leather-tough, devoid of humor, and possessed of a singleness of purpose that approached obsession, Bridges revived the San Francisco local of the defunct International Longshoremen's Association and managed to gain, by the democratic elections specified in the NRA, a membership that included most of those in the company union established in 1919. He then presented the Waterfront Employer's Union with a set of sweeping demands: that the hourly wage be raised to a minimum of one dollar, that a thirty-hour week be established, that a coastwide labor agreement be signed, and, most importantly, that the union be given control over hiring halls, then run by the employers on the "shapeup" system, whereby workers gathered daily to be told by a hiring boss where, when, and if each would be working that day. (Aside from giving the

employer almost absolute control over work assignments, the shapeup system was an open invitation to bribery, favoritism, and blacklisting.)

The Employer's Union responded by charging Bridges with communism and refusing to negotiate.*

---

*The charge of communism was by 1933 a fairly ancient liturgy. Ever since United States Attorney-General Mitchell A. Palmer had declared it his intention in 1919 to rid the country of Bolsheviks, California had enthusiastically embraced anti-communism. Hundreds of people had been arrested, tried, and convicted under the state's Criminal Syndicalism laws in the 1920s (laws broad enough to include Communists, often their main target), and "Red Squads" modeled after those of federal agents had abounded in the state. California's employers made no secret of the fact that such charges were reserved almost exclusively for unions, since in their eyes unions were, by definition, communistic. As one police captain allegedly told his men before they went out to break up a picket line, "If it moves, paint it red and beat it with a stick."

*National Guard troops invade Berkeley during the general strike*
*of 1934; it would not be the last time.*

On May 9, 1934, all the longshoremen in the major Pacific Coast ports went on strike, soon followed by seamen's unions and the Ships Clerks' and Licensed Officers' Labor Union. In a few days shipping had literally ceased from Seattle to San Diego (not including military, hospital, and relief supplies, which the unions allowed to be handled), and the Waterfront Employer's Union called upon the San Francisco Chamber of Commerce and the Industrial Association for support. It came in the form of funds for the importation of strikebreakers, who began to be hauled into the city by the end of June.

On July 5, 1934, the Employer's Union requested and received 1,000 city policemen to escort strikebreakers to jobs on the Embarcadero beneath the hump of earth called Rincon Hill. The policemen and strikebreakers were met by an estimated 5,000 union pickets. Rocks and bottles flew, fistfights and mutual clubbings broke out, and ultimately gunshots were exchanged by both sides. Sixty-four people were injured, and two strikers were killed on this "Bloody Thursday" (to this day, July 5 is observed by longshoremen as a solemn holiday; Harry Bridges does not forget). When National Guard troops were sent in to quell further outbreaks of violence, the unions of the Bay Area, in a rare show of unanimity, joined with the ILA in a general strike on July 16. One hundred and fifty thousand workers left their jobs in the first (and so far, only) general strike in California's history.

As a tactic, the strike could be characterized as either a qualified failure or a qualified success, depending upon where one sat. In four days it alienated much of the public sympathy the labor movement had attained after Bloody Thursday, and union leaders fell to bitter internal squabbling. (It is interesting to note that while employers of this era tended to look upon the labor movement as a monolithic entity staffed and directed mainly by world-devouring Communists, the ironic fact was that individual unions were fully as competitive and enterprise-minded as their capitalistic counterparts, a state of affairs that frequently did them more harm than good.) On July 19 the strike was called off amid a general air of dissatisfaction and frustration.

On the other hand, the great shutdown did inspire President Franklin D. Roosevelt to send federal arbiters to San Francisco in an effort to settle the waterfront strike that had precipitated the whole shutdown. Brought together with Bridges and representatives of the Waterfront Employer's Union, largely through the mediation of John Francis Neyland, personal counsel to William Randolph Hearst, the federal agents managed to hammer out an agreement in October that both sides could sign. From the point of view of the union, the most important clause in this contract was one that stipulated union control of hiring halls. Harry Bridges had won his major point, a victory that carried

him into the leadership of the Pacific Coast division of the ILA; today, the union is called the International Longshoremen's and Warehousemen's Union, and Harry Bridges is its president.

The agreement of October 12, 1934, was a watershed date in the story of California's labor unions. Encouraged by the success of the ILA (and in many cases advised, directed, or led by Bridges himself), organized labor all over the state enjoyed new life (always excepting agricultural labor). Unions grew in membership and power; concessions from employers were demanded and won more and more frequently; and by the end of the decade the labor movement had established a solid foundation on which it could build during the boom years of World War II. That it did so build can be ascertained by contemplating the unchallenged power that organized labor exerts in the state today (including, inevitably, Harry Bridges and the ILWU—as recent Pacific Coast dock strikes illustrate).

Faced with the most devastating economic and social crisis in California's history, the state's political leadership, from the governor's office down through the state legislature, displayed an attitude that at best can be called laissez-faire, and at worst criminal negligence. Part of the problem was the massive imbalance of political affiliation among that leadership, for Republicans controlled virtually every important office in the state, a condition that had existed ever since the first triumphs of the Progressive Era (although the party had long since abandoned its progressive instincts). Fractured, weak, and almost continuously at cross-purposes, the Democratic Party had been either unable or unwilling to pick up the Progressive gauntlet abandoned by the Republicans, and while the state voted overwhelmingly Democratic in the presidential elections of 1932 and 1936, it was not until the gubernatorial election of 1938 that the Democrats gained enough strength to make a dent in the Republican wall. Deprived of an effective loyal opposition, which might have forced it to deal realistically with at least some of the problems of the Depression, the state's Republican leadership vacillated, sometimes appearing to believe that the whole mess would go away if it were left alone.

The first governor of the Depression years was James

("Sunny Jim") Rolph, Jr., elected in 1930. For nineteen years Rolph had played mayor of San Francisco, and during the 1920s had more than once been compared (to his delight) to New York City's ebullient young mayor, Jimmy Walker. Dapper, quixotic, and a great crowd-pleaser, "Sunny Jim" possessed enormous personal charm, a jolly good nature, and the political, administrative, and social instincts of a doorknob. His administration was noteworthy mainly for two incidents. The first occurred in 1933, when the state legislature passed both a general sales tax (including a tax on food) and an income tax in an effort to raise money for the state's crippled educational system. Heeding the words of his personal banker and closest adviser, Rolph promptly signed the sales tax bill into law and vetoed the income tax measure—thus making his stand on taxes perfectly clear, at least to those who opposed him: he was in favor of taxing the poor and against taxing the rich. The second incident occurred in November 1933, when a San Jose mob, driven by God only knows what bloodlust and inchoate frustration, broke into the county jail, beat the sheriff senseless, and carried off two men who had confessed to the kidnapping and murder of the son of a rich San Jose merchant; the mob hanged the two men from a tree, by the light of a bonfire. "This is the best lesson California has ever given the country," Rolph announced, praising "those fine, patriotic San Jose citizens who know how to handle such a situation." They had "pioneer blood in their veins," he said.

Rolph, dying in June 1934, never learned whether his sales tax or his praise of barbarism might have cost him the gubernatorial election of that year. He was succeeded by his lieutenant-governor, Frank Merriam, a transplanted Iowan, a Long Beach realtor and newspaperman, and a former state assemblyman. One of Merriam's first moves as acting governor was to send in National Guard troops during the San Francisco water-

*"Sunny Jim" Rolph shows off*
*a new pair of boots in 1932.*

*A lynch mob batters down the*
*door of a jail in San Jose.*

front crisis of July (even though the city's mayor, Angelo Rossi, had not requested them), an act that made him a hero in the eyes of many Californians. Equally conservative but infinitely more tactful and shrewd than Rolph, Merriam won the gubernatorial election of November 1934—but not before he and most other conservative citizens received the political scare of their lives.

It has always been in the nature of California to abhor a vacuum, and in their apparent indifference to the plight of those citizens most injured by the Depression, the Republicans left a yawning chasm that had to be filled—by something, somehow. The result was a rash of political, economic, and social schemes, which varied mainly in the degree of their radicalism and their popularity. One of the first to be expressed during the Depression was Technocracy, a crypto-scientific view of the cosmos first promulgated in 1932. It was the opinion of the Technocrats, as illuminated mainly in the pages of the *Los Angeles Daily News,* that there would be "Plenty for All" if only the enormous productive energy of the nation could be restructured, reorganized, and rechanneled so that each American received his rightful share. As usual, with such cure-all schemes, the Technocrats were a little vague as to how this might be accomplished, but for at least three months the philosophy inspired agitated discussion in California, particularly south of the Tehachapis.

Like the popular song "Happy Days Are Here Again," the slogan of "Plenty for All" was well-nigh irresistible, speaking to an essential optimism as old as the country itself. After all, this was the biggest, richest country in the world, was it not? That being the case, there was no reason its problems could not be eliminated, provided everyone somehow got together, adopted the right philosophy, and made some changes in the way the system worked, or didn't work.

That wellspring of hope was next tapped by an organization called the Utopian Society, founded in 1933 in Los Angeles by three out-of-work promoters. Using the chain-letter technique to recruit members and

*"Bad Boys Thwarted Again," reads the caption on this uncommonly gentle political cartoon during Upton Sinclair's campaign of 1934.*

*Upton Sinclair, who saw too many jobless, too many starving children, too much graft.*

setting up elaborate secret rituals (thus satisfying the traditional American fascination for secret fraternities of any kind), the Utopian Society soon found people practically begging to join, handing over their pennies, nickels, dimes, and dollars with primitive abandon—all this without the organization's having offered any more specific program than the general idea that if people got together they could control at least some portion of their lives. By 1934 the society had an estimated half-million members, most of them in Los Angeles (where the army of unemployed had risen to 300,000); as many as 250 individual Utopian Society meetings were held every night—and at least once, 1,063 meetings. Lacking any specific solutions to the problems of the period, the organization ultimately fell of its own weight early in 1935, but by its very size and meteoric rise and fall, the

*CCC members at work in the Sierra Nevada, 1938—the year of the Munich Pact and the year before the Nazi invasion of Poland.*

Utopian Society suggested the degree of desperation many Californians felt.

Another such indication was the success of the Townsend Plan, or OARP (Old Age Revolving Pensions), Ltd. Of all the victims of the Depression, the aged were hit the hardest, and in 1934 an out-of-practice doctor, Francis Townsend, happened upon an idea warmed over from one originally proposed by the Technocrats: the issuance of a sizable monthly stipend to the elderly, which they would be required to spend completely before the next installment. Theoretically, this device would not only keep old people well fixed, it would

open up a vast new "captive" market, thus spurring the economy on to bigger and better things.

With the financial backing of a Long Beach realtor, Townsend opened an office and began a newspaper called the *Townsend Weekly* (which, logically enough, had a healthy revenue not only from subscription fees but from the advertisement of trusses, patent medicines, and sundry gland-renovating concoctions). He penned a catchy chant for his organization: "Two hundred dollars a month, / Youth for work, age for leisure, / Two hundred for the oldsters, / To be spent in ceaseless pleasure." By 1936, OARP had a membership of hundreds of thousands of elderly sybarites scattered through California and most of the other western and midwestern states, 150,000 of whom subscribed to the *Townsend Weekly,* and Townsend and his backer were splitting a weekly revenue of more than two thousand dollars. That was the organization's peak year, however, for the reelection of President Roosevelt and the passage of the social security program took much of the steam out of Townsend's pension scheme.

The Utopian Society and OARP were only two of the scores of outlandish programs that sprouted from the debris of the Depression; others, somewhat less visible, included Tradex, Syncrotax, the Americanist Plan, the New Exchange Tax System, Dated Money, the Universal Research Foundation, New America, and Plentocracy (this last possessing an understandable name, at least). Nearly all were more short-lived than the other, more dramatic two, and few could be said to have enjoyed even a modicum of their influence. One which did, however, was the EPIC (End Poverty in California) plan of Upton Sinclair, a utopian Socialist who very nearly became governor of the state of California in 1934.

When not running for governor, Sinclair's principal occupation had been as one of the most prolific muckraking novelists in the history of this or any other country. With the publication of forty-seven books to his credit, including *Oil!, The Jungle, King Coal, The Brass Check,* and *The Profits of Religion,* he had already produced his own five-foot shelf of books, and would add another shelf before his death in 1968. By the end of 1933, however, he had decided that it was time to put more than words into his crusade to change the world. "I saw old people dying of slow starvation," he later recalled, "and children by the tens of thousands growing up stunted by the diseases of malnutrition—the very schoolteachers dipping into their slender purses to provide milk for pupils who came to school without breakfast. I saw hundreds of thousands of persons driven from their homes; the sweep of an economic process which had turned most of California over to moneylenders and banks. I saw one colossal swindle after another perpetrated upon the public; and for every official who was sent to jail I knew that a thousand were hiding with their loot." Men have thrown themselves into politics for worse reasons.

Changing his registration from Socialist to Democrat early in 1934, Sinclair launched his campaign for the Democratic gubernatorial nomination by writing yet another book: *I, Governor of California and How I Ended Poverty: A True Story of the Future.* Old-line politicians laughed at his audacity, but the Folks did not, for his plan was simple, direct, and immensely appealing. He would institute a strong graduated income tax and an even stronger corporation tax, while eliminating the general sales tax; he would place a penalty of 10 percent per year on the valuation of unused land (thus echoing the "Single-Tax" theories of Henry George); he would buy up land and establish farm colonies for the unemployed, and would appropriate all the idle industries, factories, and other establishments and operate them for the public welfare; and he would give people over sixty a monthly pension of fifty dollars.

Buying hundreds of thousands of copies of *I, Governor . . . ,* contributing both money and time to his campaign, the Folks of California gave Sinclair the Democratic nomination in the August 1934 primaries. Not only did his total vote exceed that of his Democratic opponents, it exceeded that received by Frank Merriam in the almost uncontested Republican primary—a fact pointed enough to put the fear of God into any proper politician. Not since the Los Angeles campaign of Job Harriman in 1911 had the conservatives of California been faced with the horrendous possibility that a Socialist—a *Socialist* (and never mind what Sinclair's registration was)—would achieve a major political office in the state. Although it must have made his gorge rise, Merriam promptly endorsed the Townsend Plan in an effort to siphon off some of Sinclair's support and hired the young advertising firm of Campaigns, Incorporated,* to direct his campaign.

It was the most exciting, and bitter, gubernatorial campaign Californians had witnessed since the days of the Progressives. Using billboards, radio "spots" and features, magazine advertisements, and even movie "shorts" (with the full cooperation of Louis B. Mayer

---

*Founded by Clem Whitaker and Leone Baxter (who were later married) in 1933, the firm is today known as Whitaker & Baxter. It still espouses politically conservative candidates and causes (e.g., the 1966 campaign of Ronald Reagan) and remains a potent political force in the state.

of MGM) in the first mass-media campaign in the state's history, Campaigns, Inc., hammered at Sinclair's socialism, his probable Communist connections, his "fuzzy-headed liberalism"; they found a treasure trove of quotes (many taken out of context, many not) from his squadron of books to prove that Sinclair was against everything dear to the heart of America except Mom and apple pie. It was a thorough, even relentless performance, but it might not have been enough if it had not been for the candidacy of Raymond Haight, a Progressive, who severely undercut Sinclair's anti-Merriam vote. The final result in November was 1,138,000 votes for Merriam, 879,000 for Sinclair, and 302,000 for Haight.

Merriam breathed a sigh of relief, read the handwriting on the wall, and promptly advocated the passage of a graduated income tax and several minor corporation taxes. And Sinclair? He did what might have been expected of him; he wrote another book, this one entitled *I, Candidate for Governor: And How I Got Licked.*

WHERE THERE WAS HOPE, there was also hatred; both could be exploited, as the frenzied "Ham and Eggs" movement of the late 1930s illustrated. Founded in 1937 by Robert Noble, a radio performer specializing in directed vitriol, this movement predicated itself on a demand for "$25 every Monday" for the old folks. It was soon taken over by a pair of promoters who owned an organization called the Cinema Advertising Agency. Changing the slogan to "$30 every Thursday," they contrived a plan that called for the establishment of a state bank and the issuance of paper script to finance pension payments. Encouraging the bitterness, anger, and hatred (and the anti-Semitism) of its membership, the promoters instituted the cry of "Ham and Eggs" as a kind of mesmerizing chant, which at least one observer compared to the "Sieg Heil!" of Nazi Germany. By the beginning of 1938, the organization's membership had swollen to more than seven hundred thousand, and the Cinema Advertising Agency found itself with a potent political force. In the middle of 1938, the secretary of state received a petition from the organization that called for an initiative measure to be placed on the ballot in November, an initiative calling for the establishment of the state bank dreamed up by the promoters. The initiative was barely defeated, losing by only 255,000 votes out of a total vote of more than 2,400,000. And shortly after he took office in 1939, Democratic Governor Culbert L. Olson was presented with yet another petition from the movement, this one with 1,103,000 signatures calling for a special election. Again the proposal was narrowly defeated, but by the end of 1939 California was beginning to feel the first flush of wartime prosperity, and the movement declined, eventually degenerating into a bitter little club for practicing anti-Semites.

The Ham and Eggs movement was the last expression of any political attempt to solve the Depression problems of California. In the end, none of these movements, whether orthodox or fantastic, had anything close to the effect the war would have, and not even the booming prosperity of the war years would be completely effective in solving the social agonies laid bare by the Depression. A revitalized economy went far toward eliminating some of the problems and significantly alleviated others, but many lay unresolved for the uneasy perusal of another generation.

*The definitive mission: San Carlos Borromeo de Carmelo.*

# *California Mirror:*
# *The Sense of the Past, I*

*Mission San Francisco de Asis (Dolores).*

*Mission San Antonio de Padua.*

*Statue of Serra at Mission San Juan Capistrano.*

Given the virulence of California's twentieth-century growth, we should probably be astonished that every known vestige of the past—relatively recent as well as genuinely aged—has not long since been obliterated. Californians have always been caught up in a kind of cultural schizophrenia, reaching with one hand toward the future while fumbling behind their backs with the other, patching up bits and pieces of worlds they have conquered and passed beyond—perhaps creating signposts in an attempt to convince themselves that they do, too, know where they are going. In any case, the ambivalence has resulted in the existence of little islands of time encapsulated, some of which are shown on these pages as well as pages 441-446, places where Californians can obtain a tactile and visual sense of their historical legacy.

*Mission La Purisima Concepción, rebuilt from the ground up.*

*Interior of chapel, Mission Santa Inés.*

By the 1880s most of California's original twenty-one missions could have been described as J. Ross Browne described Mission Nuestra Señora de la Soledad in 1849: "A more desolate place cannot well be imagined. The old church is partially in ruins, and the adobe huts built for the Indians are roofless, and the walls tumbled about in shapeless piles." As the turn of the century neared, however, these crumbling wrecks became major tourist attractions as well as subjects for painters (particularly Edwin Deakin), photographers (particularly Adam Clark Vroman), and writers (particularly poets, who dedicated more than one trembling verse to the defenceless missions). A movement for restoration consequently developed, much of it inspired by Charles F. Lummis, editor of **Land of Sunshine,** who organized the California History and Landmarks Club in 1897. The club's pioneering efforts were later aided by state projects and private foundation work, and today each of the original missions has been partially or fully restored.

379

*In the years since 1814, the Monterey Custom House has seen three flags: Spain's until 1822, Mexico's until 1846, and America's since 1846.*

*Interior of the Custom House, featuring the press used to imprint California's first state seal.*

Throughout most of the Spanish and Mexican years of rule in California, Monterey was the real as well as the titular capital of the province—the center of her commerce, industry, and culture (what there was of it). It is fitting, then, that today Monterey retains more flavor of the pre-American past than any other city in the state.

The Monterey Custom House (above) has been registered by the Department of the Interior as a National Historic Landmark. It was here that American and British traders were forced to pay sometimes onerous duties (as well as occasional bribes) for the import and export of goods. It was here that the luckless Commodore Thomas ap Catesby Jones ceremoniously raised the American flag on October 19, 1842, claiming California for the United States by right of war—only to take it down two days later when he discovered there was no war—yet. The American flag was raised here permanently on July 7, 1846.

*Erected in 1847 by Walter Colton, Monterey's first American alcalde, Colton Hall served as constitutional hall, schoolhouse, courthouse, and church.*

Built in the traditional Mexican-Californian style, the Larkin House (right) was erected in 1834 by Thomas Oliver Larkin, California's first and only American consul. Nestled next to it is an adobe that was once part of Larkin's house.

A building that documents the transition from Mexican to American rule is Colton Hall (above), whose sharp-edged architecture is reminiscent far more of New England than of anything uniquely Californian. It was constructed by Walter Colton, first American alcalde of Monterey, in 1847 and later served as the meeting place for the first California state constitutional convention in 1849.

Aside from these, Monterey possesses many other adobe buildings of considerable antiquity, most of which have been marked by the Monterey History and Art Association and most of which can be seen by following the "path of history" on the city's streets.

*The Larkin House, built in 1834. Next to it is the headquarters adobe of Gen. William T. Sherman.*

381

*Sutter's reconstructed mill and millrace.*

The event that captured the imagination of the world and transformed California from a thinly settled frontier outpost into a citadel of power on the West Coast has been memorialized in Marshall Gold Discovery State Historic Park near the town of Coloma. Among the park's attractions (including a stone monument over the grave of James Marshall) is a full-scale replica of Sutter's Mill and millrace (left) constructed in 1965-66.

Covering two city blocks in the middle of Sacramento is Sutter's Fort State Historical Monument (below). The discovery of gold, which he had unwittingly initiated, surrounded Sutter with the fruits of civilization in the 1850s but eventually drove him from his fort. He moved to Lititz, Pennsylvania, and died in a Washington, D.C., hotel room in 1880. The fort itself was little more than a picturesque ruin by 1890; only the large central building remained in a condition approaching the original. In

*Russian Orthodox Church, Fort Ross. Burned in 1970, it is scheduled for reconstruction.*

1891 the state of California undertook the task of reconstruction, refurbishing the central building and re-creating the walls, shops, storerooms, and blockhouses that marked the fort in its prime.

Another victim of time and circumstance was Fort Ross on the bluffs of northern California overlooking the ocean near the Russian River. Founded by Russian fur traders in 1812, the fort was sold to Sutter in 1841. It was acquired by the state in 1906 and partially restored as Fort Ross State Historical Landmark. Unfortunately, the fort's lovely Russian Orthodox chapel (above) was destroyed by fire in 1970.

*Sutter's walled fortress of empire. Once surrounded by a sea of grass, it sits today in the middle of metropolitan Sacramento.*

# CHAPTER 19

# THE NEW RAINMAKERS

*Water is moved, and moved again—and its use remains tangled*

*in a confusion of social, political, and economic needs*

IN A REGION that seemed to sprout flimflam men like mushrooms in a spring meadow, Charles Mallory Hatfield stood like a giant among pygmies. For twenty-five years, this gentle dissembler made an extremely good living in the practice of what he called "pluviculture"—the making of rain. His career began in Los Angeles (appropriately enough) in 1903, when he signed a contract with a local farmer to produce rain. Setting up several evaporating tanks clouded with "certain chemicals the character of which must necessarily remain secret," Hatfield proceeded to make it rain, producing a full inch in five days. The delighted farmer paid him a fee of fifty dollars and began spreading the word of Hatfield's astonishing gift.

From then on "Hatfield the Rainmaker" was rarely without clients. Nearly every city and town in Southern California hired him—at fees that sometimes went as high as $10,000—to make rain at one time or another, and for several years in a row, farmers in the San Joaquin Valley did likewise. He rarely failed them. One year he gave the Lake Hemet Land & Water Company eleven inches of rain; in another year he produced eighteen inches in four months for Los Angeles. In the Mojave Desert, legend has it, he once made the heavens open to the tune of forty inches in three hours, and in San Diego in 1916, he not only filled the municipal reservoir, as requested, but overfilled it, causing a major flood (it was one of the few times any client refused to pay him his fee—on the flimsy grounds that he had produced too *much* water).

Hatfield's secret was simple enough, and had nothing to do with his mysterious chemicals. He studied weather charts avidly, carefully calculating the movements and inclinations of the climate. Offering his services always near the end of a long dry period (which of course was when prospective clients would be desperate enough to put up the required money), he would promise to deliver rain within a suitably extensive period of time: twenty, thirty, or sixty days, depending upon what his charts told him. So carefully evaluated were his prognostications, however, that he frequently managed to produce rain well ahead of deadline, a feat that added to his reputation immeasurably. By the early 1920s, that reputation had led him to projects in places as far removed as Alaska and Honduras, but by the end of the decade his career was over, done in by a new breed of rainmakers whose expertise had little to do with evaporating tanks and a great deal to do with slide rules, blueprints, concrete, and money. The terminal date of Hatfield's heyday, in fact, can be pinpointed: December 21, 1928, the day President Calvin Coolidge signed into law the Swing-Johnson Bill (to become known as the Boulder Canyon Act), designed, among other things, to bring Southern California all the water it would need for at least forty years.

THE BOULDER CANYON ACT had its genesis in the sweltering Imperial Valley, a land of factory-like farms wholly dependent upon the turgid waters of the lower Colorado River for survival (as discussed in chapter 15). The river was an unreliable ally; when it was not

*Water for land, water for growth: an aerial view of the long, wide, and very rich San Joaquin Valley.*

*During the drought of 1934, Imperial Valley residents were given water by the Southern Pacific.*

flooding, which it did with depressing regularity, it was being reduced to an effluent trickle by drought; furthermore, the Imperial Canal, which carried the river's water into the valley, was constantly filling with silt in amounts that its twenty-four-hour dredges could barely keep pace with; finally, the residents of the valley were forced to watch helplessly while hundreds of thousands of acre-feet of "their" water were siphoned off for use on land below the border simply because much of the Imperial Canal ran through Mexican territory.

What the valley needed, as expressed by the Imperial Irrigation District, was a large flood-control dam somewhere on the river, a second dam for water storage (including spreading basins so the water could be desilted before delivery), and a new—"All-American"—canal. The valley could afford to build none of this itself, of course, so in 1917 the Imperial Irrigation District sent its lawyer, Phil D. Swing, to Washington for intensive talks with Arthur Powell Davis, head of the Bureau of Reclamation. Swing (who became the dis-

trict's congressman in 1921) was a persuasive man, and the Bureau of Reclamation was in the business of building dams and canals; Davis agreed to investigate the proposal and after four years of study the bureau issued a recommendation that supported the desires of the Imperial Valley. The site chosen for the flood-control dam (which by now had grown to include functions of water storage and power production) was Boulder Canyon, some two hundred miles above Yuma.

However, in spite of the fact that many of the state's southern citizens would have wished it so, the Colorado River did not belong to California. Its watershed also included parts of New Mexico, Colorado, Utah, Wyoming, Nevada, Arizona, and Mexico, each one of which possessed, and intended to exercise, rights to the river's water. To iron out exactly what belonged to whom, seven state commissioners met under the supervision of Herbert Hoover, secretary of commerce, in Santa Fe in November 1922. After fifteen days of frequently contentious bargaining, the group hammered out the Colorado River Compact to divide the river's annual average flow: 7,500,000 acre-feet would be allocated to the states of the river's Upper Basin (Colorado, Utah, New Mexico, and Wyoming) and a like amount to the Lower Basin states (California, Nevada, and Arizona); if needed, an additional 1,000,000 acre-feet could be appropriated by the Lower Basin states yearly; and finally, if an international treaty allocated water to Mexico, it would first come from the excess over the already apportioned 16,000,000 acre-feet. The compact was signed by Hoover and the seven commissioners and sent to the individual states for ratification.

Arizona refused, fearing that the impending Boulder Canyon project would forever block her *own* designs on the Colorado, particularly a massive dam it wanted constructed on the upper reaches of the river so that a gravity canal could carry water to her southern midsection. "I'll be damned," said Arizona's governor, George W. P. Hunt, "if California ever will have any water from the Colorado River as long as I am governor of Arizona."

The remaining states rewrote the agreement and passed it through again as a *six*-state compact, and in 1923 Congressman Phil Swing from the Imperial Valley introduced legislation that would authorize funds for the construction of the Boulder Canyon project. The

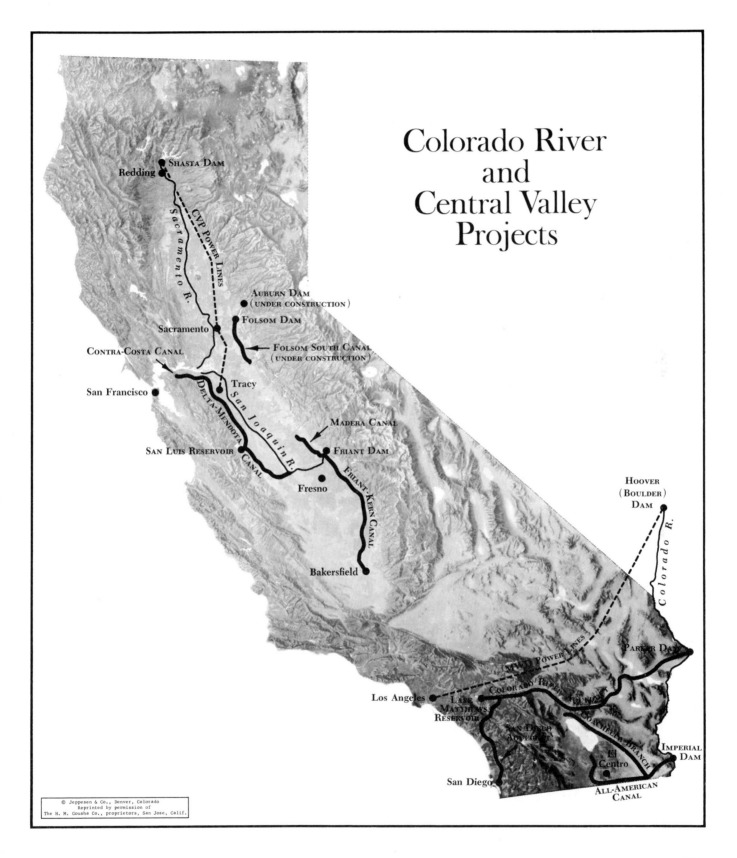

# Colorado River and Central Valley Projects

Redding
Shasta Dam
Sacramento R.
CVP Power Lines
Auburn Dam
(Under Construction)
Folsom Dam
Sacramento
Folsom South Canal
(Under Construction)
Contra-Costa Canal
Tracy
San Francisco
Delta-Mendota Canal
San Joaquin R.
Madera Canal
San Luis Reservoir
Friant Dam
Fresno
Friant-Kern Canal
Bakersfield
Hoover (Boulder) Dam
Colorado R.
Parker Dam
Los Angeles
Lake Matthews Reservoir
Colorado River
MWD Power Lines
San Diego Aqueduct
Southern Branch
Imperial Dam
El Centro
San Diego
All-American Canal

*Hoover (Boulder) Dam: "It is the human answer to a human need, / Power in absolute control. . . ."*

bill, meeting opposition not only from Arizona and the friends of Arizona but from private power companies with a morbid terror of public power projects, died in committee. It, and a similar bill later introduced into the Senate by Hiram Johnson, would continue to languish in committee for the next several sessions of Congress. A powerful ally was on its way, however, in the form of the Metropolitan Water District of Southern California, one more product from the mind of William Mulholland, chief engineer of the city of Los Angeles and head of its Water and Power District.

Shortly after World War I, Mulholland, keeping a close eye on the spiraling population figures of Los Angeles, made some calculations, and came to the conclusion that within a few years the city would need more water than the Owens River could possibly supply. In 1923 he and his subordinate engineers looked to the next logical source, the Colorado, and determined that an aqueduct should be built from the river at a point near the town of Parker to a reservoir near the city of Riverside, just east of Los Angeles. On behalf of the

city of Los Angeles, Mulholland put in a bid for 1,100,000 acre-feet of Colorado River water, made further calculations, and estimated that the proposed 242-mile aqueduct would cost $223,000,000.

This was more than even the go-ahead thinking of Los Angeles—boom period or no boom period—could regard comfortably, but many of the cities in or around the Los Angeles Basin were equally desperate for water. Perhaps some way of sharing both costs and water could be worked out . . . and so it was: Los Angeles and ten other cities joined to produce their own compact, which they called the Metropolitan Water District of Southern California. Sent to the state legislature for approval, the agreement was sanctioned in 1927, and the district immediately sent lobbyists to Washington to help win congressional approval of the Boulder Canyon project. The district's reasons were threefold: first, it wanted the government to add a storage dam for district water (Parker Dam); second, it needed the flood-control and regulatory functions a large upriver dam would provide; and third, in order to lift its water over mountains and deserts to Riverside County, it would require a healthy share of the power the dam would produce.

Throughout most of the congressional sessions of 1927 and 1928, the Swing (House) and Johnson (Senate) bills stirred up flurries of debate, acrimony, and pressure politics, including two separate filibusters by Arizona's senators. But in May 1928 the bill passed the House, and in mid-December it passed the Senate (a victory aided in no little part by the election of Herbert Hoover, a Californian, as president of the United States in November; Hoover was known to be in favor of the project and few senators, particularly of the same party, cared to alienate a new president right off the bat). A week later President Coolidge signed the Swing-Johnson Bill. It provided for the construction of Boulder Dam,* Imperial Dam on the lower reaches of the river, and the All-American Canal (Parker Dam

---

*An explanation would be useful here. Before its construction, the big dam was named for its proposed site at Boulder Canyon; that site was later shifted to Black Canyon, but the name remained until Secretary of the Interior Ray Lyman Wilbur, a Hoover appointee, changed it to Hoover Dam. In 1934 his successor, the "terrible-tempered" Harold Ickes (a Roosevelt appointee) to whom the name Hoover was anathema, changed it back to Boulder. Then the Republican Congress of 1947 changed it back to Hoover, as it is supposed to be known today. Is the reader taking notes?

would be added later). It limited California's share of Colorado water to 4,400,000 acre-feet a year, plus a share in any surplus in any given year, and up to half the "extra" one million acre-feet provided to the Lower Basin by the Colorado River Compact. It also gave Arizona and Nevada a royalty on the electric power produced at the dam and, undercutting the objections of private power companies by providing that the government would not build the dam's generating stations itself, proposed to sell nothing more than the power of falling water to outside companies. In later contracts, the Bureau of Reclamation "sold" the dam's power-producing potential, allocating 36 percent to the Metropolitan Water District, 19 percent to the Los Angeles Water and Power District, and 9 percent to the Southern California Edison Company; Arizona and Nevada were each apportioned 18 percent, but since neither could yet find enough customers for the power, no contracts were signed, and the two states were simply given the right to exercise their claims within fifty years.

After further surveys and estimates, the Bureau of Reclamation invited bids for the construction of Boulder Dam, with a deadline of March 4, 1931. Only three bids were submitted, for this would be one of the largest single construction projects in history and there were few engineering firms willing to accept the responsibility. The winning bid of $48,890,000 (just $26,000 under the estimate of the bureau itself) was submitted by a firm that had been assembled specifically for the project, the Six Companies, Inc., a conglomerate comprised of the Utah Construction Company, the Morrison-Knudsen Company of Idaho, the J. F. Shea Company of Los Angeles, MacDonald & Kahn, Inc., of San Francisco, and a separate triumvirate (itself organized for the project) that included Henry J. Kaiser, W. A. ("Dad") Bechtel, and John Dearborn. With Kaiser as chairman of the group, the Six Companies turned the first spade of earth in Black Canyon on the Colorado River on May 12, 1931. Chief engineer for the project was Frank Crowe, a former Bureau of Reclamation employee who was, in his own words, "wild to build this dam. I had spent my life in the river bottoms, and Boulder meant a wonderful climax—the biggest dam ever built by anyone anywhere."

While construction began on "the biggest dam ever built by anyone anywhere," the citizens of the Metro-politan Water District prepared to vote on the largest bond issue ever considered by any group of cities anywhere: $223,000,000 for the construction of the Colorado River Aqueduct. After a six-week saturation campaign that took advantage of every means of communication then known to the mind of man (including messages on milk bottles and a full-length sound movie entitled, with a stroke of genius, *Thirst*), the voters went to the polls on September 29, 1931, and passed the issue—not only an indication of the region's compelling urge for water but a tribute to its unflagging optimism in the midst of the most horrendous economic crisis it had ever known.

BOULDER DAM—the name has an aura of romance to it even today, when we have grown weary, suspicious, and even critical of engineering marvels. But the romance that is left is nothing compared to the romance it evoked while it was abuilding, for the 1930s may be characterized as perhaps the last great age of American engineering, when people could look upon such projects and not only find them good but find in them the very essence of what America was all about. That sense of wonder and celebration was captured by poet May Sarton in 1942:

> *Not built on terror like the empty pyramid,*
> *Not built to conquer but illuminate a world:*
> *It is the human answer to a human need,*
> *Power in absolute control, freed as a gift,*
> *A pure creative act, God when the world was born,*
> *It proves that we have built for life and built for love,*
> *And when we are all dead, this dam will stand and give.*

It was an object worthy of marvel, this dam. When complete, it stood 726.4 feet high, 1,244 feet across at its crest; it was 660 feet thick at the bottom, and 65 feet thick at the top. Its building consumed 3,250,000 cubic yards of cement, more than 3,000,000 board-feet of lumber, 662 miles of copper tubing to keep the cement at an even temperature while drying, and the lives of 110 of the more than three thousand men whose sweat had gone into its making. And when President Franklin D. Roosevelt dedicated the dam on September 30, 1935, the Six Companies, Inc., divided a profit of $10,400,000.

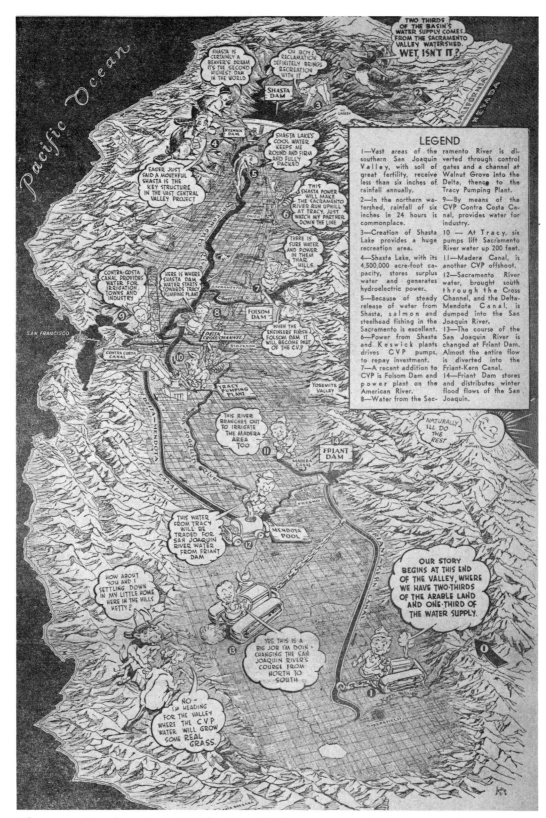

*The new rainmakers at work in the Great Valley—a cartoonist's interpretation of the Central Valley Project, from the* San Francisco Call-Bulletin, *1947.*

The rest of what had become known as the Colorado River Project lacked the brute drama of the great dam in Black Canyon, but taken all together it comprised a separately impressive marvel. Construction on Parker Dam (again by the Six Companies) began in November 1934 and was completed in 1938; if Boulder Dam was the world's tallest dam of the time, then Parker Dam was the "deepest," for engineers had to dig down 233 feet before reaching bedrock for the dam's foundation. Construction on the Colorado River Aqueduct began in early 1933 and was finished in late 1939; its 242-mile length included 42 tunnels, 144 siphons, and five electric pumps capable of lifting 1,605 cubic feet of water a second, the largest in the world. Because Congress was dilatory about allocating funds, work on Imperial Dam and the All-American Canal did not begin until November 1933. The dam, with its six huge desilting basins, was completed in 1938. The canal, whose construction machinery featured a 650-ton dragline crane that "walked" across the desert on two flat mechanical feet, was finished in 1940.

The total cost of the Colorado River Project was more than four hundred million dollars, and it provided jobs to eleven thousand men—most of them previously unemployed Californians. It was something for Southern California to crow about, for not only had the region assured itself of a water supply to last for at least two generations (or so it thought), it had demonstrated astonishing muscle in the halls of Congress. And even as President Roosevelt gave his dedication address at Boulder Dam in his nasal, insistent voice, the state (if not Southern California) was getting ready to exercise additional muscle in the matter of water-moving.

As noted in a previous chapter (chapter 15), the Central Valley of California suffered from a water "imbalance"; the northern section, watered by the Sacramento River and its tributaries, received two-thirds of the valley's water, but contained only one-third of its arable land, while the southern section, watered by the San Joaquin and a few anemic tributaries, contained two-thirds of the arable land but only one-third of its water. To juggle water flow for a more reasonable balance was the purpose of the Central Valley Project, one of the largest irrigation enterprises in history.

*Prefabricated concrete pipe to carry water pumped from Tracy to the Delta-Mendota Canal, C. V. P.*

The project, which was largely a matter of bringing water from the Sacramento River watershed down to the San Joaquin River for distribution to irrigation districts in the southern end of the valley, was first articulated in the "Marshall Plan" of 1920, a rather simple, two-canal system promoted by a visionary retired army engineer named Robert Bradford Marshall. In 1921 the Water and Power Bill, introduced into the state legislature to give the plan official approval, was defeated, largely through the lobbying efforts of the Pacific Gas & Electric Company (P.G. & E.), a private utility company that thoroughly dominated central and northern California and possessed, in common with most such enterprises, a healthy fear of anything that smacked of potential public power. As an initiative measure the proposal was placed before the voters of the state in 1922, 1924, and 1925, was opposed by P.G. & E., and was defeated each time.

Yet it was an idea whose time had to come, in spite of the efforts of P.G. & E. In 1930 the first California Water Plan was issued by the state. It was the first general inventory of California's water resources, devoting itself

*Like a great, watery snake, the Delta-Mendota Canal slithers down the Great Valley. Note the relative size of the farm at the bottom.*

to all phases of the problem, including flood control, saline intrusion from the sea, groundwater sources, power, and irrigation. Among its many considerations was a plan for the development of the Central Valley, which became the structural basis for the Central Valley Project Act, introduced and passed by the state legislature in 1933. The act called for the construction of Shasta Dam on the far northern reaches of the Sacramento River, the Delta-Mendota Canal to carry water from the "pool" of the Sacramento–San Joaquin Delta to the west side of the San Joaquin Valley, the Contra Costa Canal to carry water to farms in the valleys of the Contra Costa range, Friant Dam on the San Joaquin River, the Madera and Friant-Kern canals to carry water to the east side of the San Joaquin Valley, and a power transmission system to carry electricity generated

at Shasta and Friant dams. In passing the act, the legislature also called for the issuance of $130,000,000 in revenue bonds to finance the project.

The P.G. & E. went into action immediately, sponsoring, through one of its attorneys, Fred G. Athearn, the circulation of a petition to force a referendum on the issue. The necessary signature secured, the petition was presented to state officials and an election was held in December 1933. By the thin majority of 33,000 votes, the citizens of the state gave their approval to the project. (It should be noted that Los Angeles County voted against the project by a margin of two to one; after all, Los Angeles *had* its water—or would soon be getting it.) California had committed herself to the most ambitious reclamation project in any state's history.

Or had she? The revenue bonds she issued went beg-

*Construction on the route of the All-American Canal. The walking-bridge dredge shown above was first used on the Panama Canal.*

ging, 1933 not being the best year for speculating in bonds or much of anything else. Having conceived, planned, and authorized the project, the state then invited the Bureau of Reclamation to participate in its completion—in fact, it simply asked the bureau to take over, since it was obvious that the state could not afford to swing it alone. Some observers have maintained that the state legislature never intended for California to finance the project, assuming that its approval would guarantee the extension of federal funds for completion. However devious the legislature's reasoning may have been, the result was the same: the bureau accepted the state's invitation, and in 1935 President Roosevelt authorized the expenditure of $12,000,000 to begin the project.

The valley's large landowners viewed this turn of

events with loud alarm. They were willing enough to use the project's irrigation water, but they feared the "catch" that went along with any water delivered through facilities constructed by the Bureau of Reclamation: the 160-acre limitation law. This law, passed as part of the Newlands Act of 1902 (which created the Bureau of Reclamation), was designed to break up precisely the kind of land monopoly that was exhibited so dramatically in the San Joaquin Valley. It provided that landowners contracting to buy cheap irrigation water from federal reclamation projects agree to sell their holdings in excess of 160 acres (320 acres under California's community-property statutes) within ten years after the signing of water contracts. Taking little comfort from the fact that in the more than thirty years since its passage the acreage limitation law had not been enforced with any enthusiasm or consistency, the Kern County Land Company, Standard Oil, the Southern Pacific Railroad, and others of the valley's corporate owners set about attacking the whole water plan, concentrating on a campaign in California to persuade the state to "take back" ownership of the project and a constant lobbying effort in Washington to get the limitation provisions stricken from reclamation law. Neither effort succeeded—but neither was the law enforced, leaving the whole issue in limbo.

In the meantime, the Bureau of Reclamation, being a go-ahead organization, went ahead. Construction on the various elements of the project began in 1937 and continued over the next decade and more before completion. Even while the work was going on, the P.G. & E. refused to give up its fight to maintain dominance in the field of Northern California power. For year after year, congressional session after session, its lobbyists managed to block every appropriation for the government's proposed transmission lines. In 1944, when Shasta Dam was completed and ready to produce power, the Department of the Interior temporarily conceded to the strength of the power company, allowing it to buy all the electricity generated at the dam; it then used a threat to refuse to continue selling the power to force the P.G. & E. into a compromise agreement with which neither party was particularly happy. The company agreed to let the government use its lines from Shasta for delivery of some of its power and promised to refrain from blocking appropriations.

The Central Valley Project remains a growing child. By 1969 the bureau had completed the original elements of the project contained in the authorization act of 1933, and had added Keswick Dam, Folsom Dam and power plant, Nimbus Dam and power plant, Red Bluff Diversion Dam, San Luis Dam, the Corning Canal, and scores of miles of additional canal works. Future elements of the project (which by now is delivering more than seven million acre-feet of water to the San Joaquin Valley) include Auburn Dam and reservoir on the North Fork of the American River and the Folsom South Canal (both under construction), as well as a number of smaller projects.

The question of reclamation law remains as unsettled today as it was in 1935—although a rare case of implementation took place in 1964, when the Di Giorgio Corporation, which had signed its contract for water in 1952, finally broke up its $7,000,000 farm, offering its "excess" acreage (i.e., land not entitled to project water) for sale at pre-project water prices, as the law stipulates. In auctions held in 1964 and 1965, only three buyers made bids for the land. Opponents of the limitation law pointed to this example as evidence that the limitation provisions were simply unworkable in modern California, since only on vast spreads of land could a man expect to reap his fair share of profit. Proponents of the law replied that many people were in fact "making it" quite nicely on parcels of 160 acres or less (on the east side of the San Joaquin Valley, for example, or in the Coachella Valley of Southern California). They also claimed that local appraisers had inflated the preproject water price of the land, and argued further that since most of the land went to a San Francisco shipping magnate and his wife, neither of whom were residents of the valley (as required by the law), the legality of the sale itself was placed in question. In any case, the Di Giorgio sale gave no clear resolution of the problem.

"In the past it was gold that came from the fabulous Sierra streams to bring men wealth," Robert de Roos wrote in his 1948 study of the Central Valley Project, *The Thirsty Land.* "Now from those same hills, from those same streams, comes the one inexhaustible resource, the one sure wealth of the state. The rancher knows and the city dweller is coming to realize that the snow on the Sierra and the rain of California's gray winters are the future. How the water is used will determine what California is to be."

Today, after the expenditure of billions of dollars on massive water projects, the question of water's fair and proper *use* is no closer to an answer than it was in 1948.

*Hollywoodland, where dreams were made, some of which came true.*

# *California Mirror:*
# *The Dream Machine*

*Dreams amid clutter: the back lot of the William Fox Studio, 1927.*

Hollywood was founded as a temperance subdivision during the boom of 1887 and specialized in the production of watermelons, tomatoes, green peppers, and sundry fruits. It was a center of virtue, probity, and sobriety. Twenty-five years later, Hollywood had become the center of a major industry whose relationship to virtue, probity, and sobriety remains questionable even today —the movies.

California's first connection with the motion-picture industry occurred near the hamlet of Niles, just south of Oakland, where between 1908 and 1912 the Essanay Company ground out no less than 375 one-reel "Broncho Billy" westerns. Hollywood did not enter the picture, so to speak, until 1911, when a group of film-makers rented the Blondeau Tavern for a primitive studio; but over the next several years the town was invaded by a small army of moviemakers who were attracted by its favor-

able climate and its proximity to the Mexican border for purposes of escaping summonses in patent disputes.

After its first blockbuster success—D. W. Griffiths' **The Birth of a Nation** in 1915—the industry boomed like the oil fields of Signal Hill, until by the end of the 1920s "Hollywood" and "movies" were synonymous from Montreal to Marrakech. The town had become a great dream-making machine, a rigidly structured business ruled by a handful of fiefdoms called studios— principally Paramount, 20th Century–Fox, MGM, Warner Brothers, RKO, and Universal. The core machinery of what came to be known as the studio system was the "lot," a thirty- or forty-acre walled dominion that Carey McWilliams described in 1946 as "neither a factory nor a business establishment nor yet a company town. Rather it is in the nature of a community, a beehive, or, as Otis Fergusson said, 'fairy-land on a production line.'"

*Acres of worlds that never were by land or sea: the "Street of Cities" on the Universal Studio's lot, 1930.*

*Grauman's Chinese Theater shortly after its opening in 1927.*

If the studios might be called baronies, then their most impressive palaces were the motion-picture theaters, hundreds of which across the country were studio owned until the government put an end to the practice as a violation of antitrust laws. The chief owners of such theaters were Paramount, RKO, Fox, and Loew's, Inc. (which owned MGM), and the palaces they erected stood as monuments to kitsch gotten out of hand. Perhaps the greatest such monument, however, was the independent Grauman's Chinese in Hollywood, opened in 1927 and still operating today.

*Left: The interior of Grauman's was the epitome of movie-palace rococo.*

*Right: One of the most splendiferous premieres of the era was that for* Hell's Angels *in 1933.*

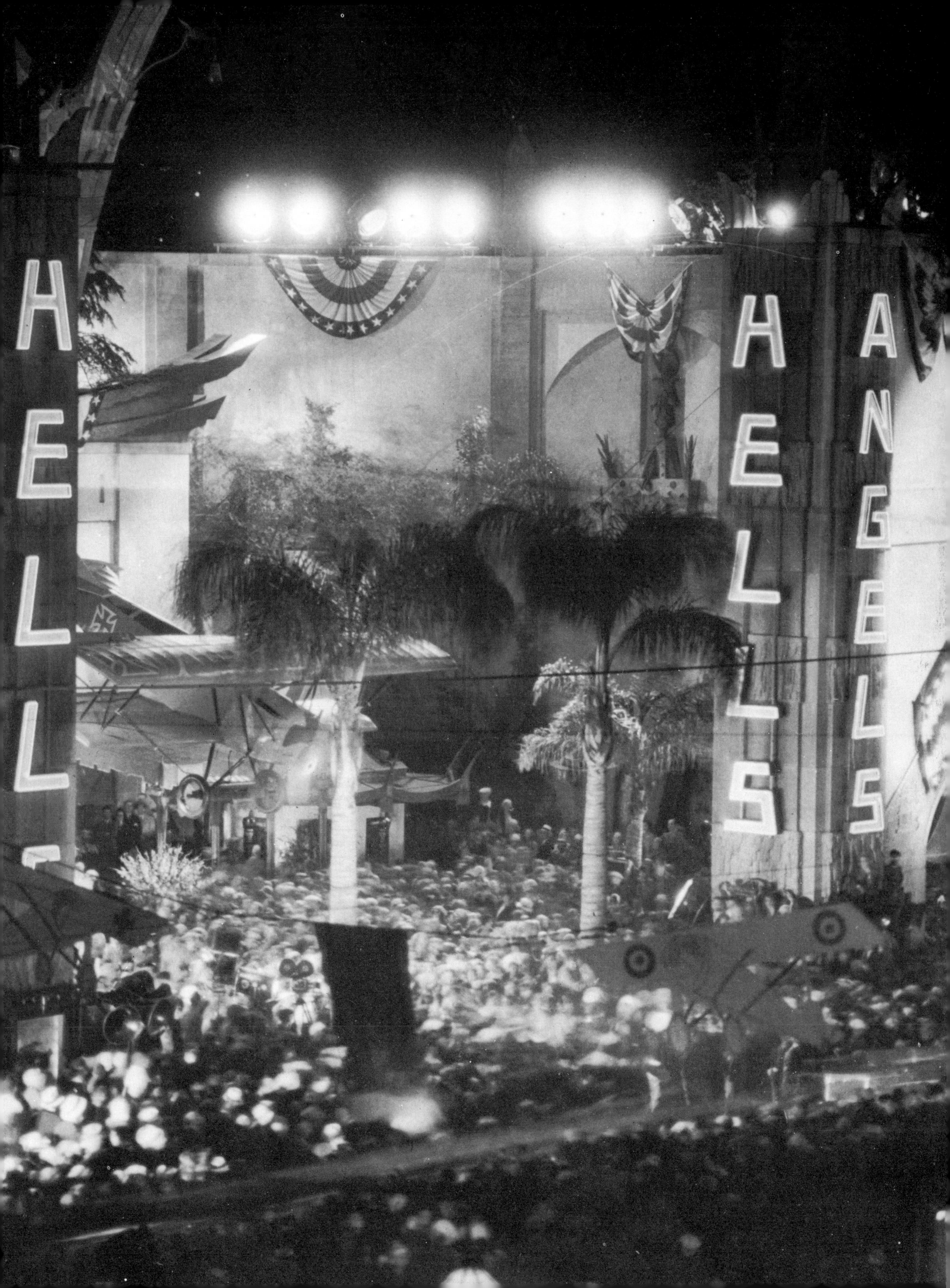
HELL
HELLS
ANGELS

*Observing the rites of wet cement: Harpo Marx, Mary Pickford, Douglas Fairbanks.*

For the talented and/or beautiful, the studio system trough fed very well indeed. Yet even the biggest stars were little more than platinum cogs in a machine whose ability to use up talent and people was described by screenwriter Gene Fowler: "The chief drawback of the enjoyment of Hollywood fame is that it comes all at once and departs at the same rate of speed. After the celluloid dream is done, the ex-star awakens in a world of toothless tigers . . . and groggy gypsies of Hasbeen Land. . . . Hollywood is a celluloid gut that must be nourished endlessly, an all-devouring gut that greedily takes in and speedily rids itself of talents fed to it from enchanted salvers. A victim of this gluttony enjoys a drugged moment of wealth, huzzas, and statuettes . . . but once the jaws of the man-eater close upon him, his lot becomes that of any other morsel."

No studio more typified the golden era of Hollywood—

*Of these two starlets, only Laraine Day (left) made it big enough to marry into baseball.*

*Louis B. Mayer surrounded by most of the inventory, 1943.*

with all its excesses, wretched or otherwise—than Metro-Goldwyn-Mayer, and no studio head quite so characterized the breed as Louis B. Mayer, a former junk dealer who ran MGM like a personal satrapy from its founding in 1924 to his departure in 1951. For twenty-seven years, the roar of the MGM lion was the sound of Mayer clearing his throat.

Stubborn, frequently dense, and pugnaciously defensive of banality ("I think my mother may have been a whore," actor John Gilbert once told him in idle conversation; Mayer promptly hit him in the mouth for besmirching the name of Motherhood), Mayer nevertheless possessed a canny perception that enabled him to erect the most stupendous movie-making machine in motion-picture history. He was gifted with a self-admitted (and often proclaimed) identification with the tastes of the American public, and he molded MGM into

the **Saturday Evening Post** of the movies with a reliance upon films that delineated, frequently with charm if rarely with art, the solid, middle-class virtues of mainstream America.

One day in 1943, Mayer called to his side three score of the more shimmering stars on whom he had built his kingdom, summoned the press, and threw a luncheon bash to celebrate (a year early) MGM's twentieth anniversary. It was an impressive gathering, a mighty distillation of the Mayer years, as the photograph above, taken by **Life** photographer Walter Sanders, illustrates (count the stars). Mayer gloated with forgivable pride. "This is the only business in the world," he said, "where the inventory goes home at night."

It was just as well that he gloated while he could, for by the time the company's twenty-fifth anniversary rolled around in 1949, both he and MGM were in trouble

*Ribbons, silks, and satins: costumes at the MGM auction, 1970.*

—as was the entire movie industry. Hollywood's version of the gold rush, like the original article, was coming to an end, done in by a little home-owned electronic box called television and by its own inability to satisfy the demands of an audience that had been tempered, and perhaps sophisticated, by war; the great studios fumbled through the 1950s like dinosaurs out of their time, their machinery arthritic and unresponsive, a flivver in the age of the atom. Independent productions filmed outside studio control and released through equally independent distribution agencies proliferated; in 1940, 90 percent of all the films produced in the United States had been made in Hollywood studios; by 1969 that figure had

*Left: Flanked by statuary is the gown worn by Greer Garson in* The Magnificent Ambersons.

dropped to less than 20 percent. One by one the studios either folded or turned themselves over to the mercies of the television industry.

The cruelest blow of all came when MGM itself was purchased by an eastern industrial syndicate headed by Kirk Kerkorian, who made a former president of CBS-TV, James T. Aubrey, Jr., head of the studio. Aubrey promptly announced that all but 30 of the 183 acres of lots the studio owned in Culver City would be sold off to developers, and turned over the firm's forty-five-year collection of props, equipment, and costumes to an auction company for $1.4 million. At a ten-day public auction in May 1970, these internal organs of MGM's physical plant were yanked out and sold to the highest bidder—a genuine wake in the land of celluloid dreams.

In late 1972 a movement took form to restore the huge "HOLLYWOODLAND" sign that had loomed over the town since 1923 and have it preserved as a cultural and historical landmark—sure evidence that one more of California's civilizations was gone.

*The sternwheeler "Cotton Blossom," used in* Showboat.

*Western freight wagons for sale in a fraudulent ghost town.*

# CHAPTER 20

# THE GIANT WITH FOUR LEGS

*The rise of California agriculture—an epic of*
*water, land, industrialization, and labor*

THE SIMPLE TERM "agriculture" does not begin to suggest the sheer immensity of what had been achieved in California by the end of the 1930s. *All* states had an "agriculture"; none approached in scope and complexity the industry that existed in the sweeping fields of California. It was not even just an industry; it was *the* industry, an overwhelming giant, an empire whose contribution to the web of California's economy outstripped that of any other single resource —including gold, which had given birth to the state nearly a century before.

Consider this: by 1940 California's annual crop production of more than $700,000,000 was the greatest in the nation, and the value of her livestock production exceeded $130,000,000, almost precisely one-tenth of the nation's total production of $1,289,537,600. California produced almost half the country's fresh fruit, one-third of its truck crops, and nearly one-third of its canned fruits and vegetables. She enjoyed first place in the production of many of the most important fruit and field crops (such as oranges and lettuce), and in some, including lemons, dates, figs, and olives, she held a monopoly on commercial production. Her nearly five hundred thousand acres of vines produced 58 percent of the wine consumed in the United States and 93 percent of the table grapes. The annual wool cut of nearly thirty million pounds ranked her third in the nation, and her more than three million head of cattle gave her more meat (or milk) on the hoof than any other state west of Kansas. Only five states raised more chickens, and only one surpassed her egg production.

Even as Rome, California's agricultural empire encompassed a huge spread of territory, from cattle ranches in the far northern reaches of the Sacramento Valley to rows upon rows of "money crops" in the sere boot of Southern California's Imperial Valley. In between lay fertile pockets and subpockets of a bewildering abundance and variety. Apples, pears, and almonds grew in Sacramento Valley orchards beneath the easy-rolling slopes of the Sierra Nevada foothills; the golden heads of wheat and barley whispered and clicked with the wind in the upper San Joaquin Valley. In the diked and leveed peat-bog islands of the Sacramento–San Joaquin Delta, asparagus ripened in black soil and rice wallowed in man-made pools; over the round green hillocks of the Napa and Sonoma valleys, terraced vine-yards perpetuated the strains of Zinfandel, Pinot, Cabernet, Reisling, and Traminer first introduced to the region in the 1850s by the "father" of California's wine industry, Agoston Haraszthy. In the hills and pocket valleys of Marin County, cows produced milk and milk products and armies of chickens cackled by night; along the worn and fog-drenched tableland of western San Mateo County, artichokes swelled within sight and sound of the sea. Truck gardens checkerboarded the flatlands east of San Francisco Bay, producing carrots, beans, celery, and squash for the markets of the urban Bay Area; and orchards south of San Jose turned the Santa Clara Valley into a sea of blossoms every spring.

The "long valley" of the Salinas was the "lettuce bowl" of the country, accounting for more than half the state's annual crop of $25,000,000; and across the

*Orange groves in the Santa Clara Valley*
*of Southern California, 1943.*

*California's exportable sunshine: fat crates of oranges being stacked for shipment, ca. 1920.*

navel orange took precedence (giving the state a year-round production of oranges), extending in an almost unbroken line east through Arcadia, Monrovia, Azusa, Glendora, Claremont, Upland, Pomona, Ontario, Colton, San Bernardino, and Redlands, and then spreading south to beyond Riverside—more than seventy miles of orange trees. In the coastal plain, Valencias, grapefruit, and lemons flourished, creating an independent belt from Fullerton south through Anaheim, Orange, Santa Ana, Tustin, and San Juan Capistrano—another fifty miles of citrus trees. Interspersed here and there were sub-belts: walnuts in Orange County, olives in Riverside County, lima beans and great fields of sugar beets along the coast.

Then to the desert region: just south of Palm Springs, huddled beneath the granitic hulk of Mount San Gorgonio, lay Indio near the head of the Coachella Valley; virtually all of the dates produced in the United States, four thousand short tons a year, were grown in the immediate area and packed and shipped from this desert hamlet. The Coachella Valley itself, extending south from San Gorgonio Pass to the northern shores of the Salton Sea, produced grapefruit, cotton, and vegetables. Finally, the Imperial Valley, a cornucopia of winter lettuce, sugarcane, grapes, white head lettuce, alfalfa, cantaloupes, tomatoes, cotton. . . .

No other state's agriculture could boast of producing so much of so many different things over so large a spread of territory as did that of California. It was a giant, and it stood on four legs: water, land, industrialization, and labor.

THE IMPORTANCE OF WATER to the state's agriculture has been discussed, but it should be emphasized once again that California's agricultural economy was an *irrigated* economy, profoundly dependent upon the act of moving water from where it was to where it was needed. That need had already inspired a number of major irrigation projects and would inspire more, but even in 1940 two-thirds of the state's cultivated land was under irrigation.

The pattern of land ownership made another important contribution to both the character and growth of California agriculture. As noted in earlier chapters, a combination of circumstances had produced one more

hills of the Coast Range, a part of the San Joaquin Valley was the "peach bowl" of the country, producing 36 percent of the state's whole crop. Fresno was the raisin capital of the country, Castroville the artichoke capital. In the lower San Joaquin Valley, immense fields of waving, dark-green alfalfa could be seen shoulder to shoulder with large fields of the bushlike, high-quality, and very rare Acala cotton (quite typically, while the state accounted for only 2 percent of the nation's cotton production, it *led* in the production of Acala; moreover, its yield per acre was more than twice the national average). Artichoke fields spread once again around San Luis Obispo, flower-seed and cut-flower farms around Santa Maria, pea fields around Lompoc and Buellton.

With lemons and summer-ripening Valencia oranges (which thrived in the coastal zone), Southern California's great citrus belt began at Santa Barbara, spreading southeast to fill the Ojai and Santa Clara valleys, then skipping the San Fernando Mountains to pick up again in Pasadena. Here, the winter-ripening Mission

of the state's peculiar social and economic phenomena: a degree of land monopoly unprecedented in the frontier experience. As a result, the small, self-sufficient family farm common to the American scene in other parts of the country was of marginal importance in California from the beginning. Bigness, in agriculture as in so much else, was a California tradition, and bigness breeds bigness. Steadily, more and more land fell into fewer and fewer hands until, by 1940, 2 percent of California's farms controlled 25 percent of her cultivated land and produced more than 30 percent of her crop value. "Of all farms in the United States whose product is valued at $30,000 or above," economist Paul S. Taylor wrote near the end of the decade, "nearly 37 percent are found in our own state. California has within its borders 30 percent of the large-scale cotton farms of the country, 41 percent of the large-scale dairy farms, 44 percent of the large-scale general farms, 53 percent of the large-scale poultry farms, 60 percent of the large-scale fruit farms of the United States."

A tradition of bigness, in turn, bred a tradition of industrialization and all that went with it—capitaliza-

*Wonderful, wonderful, wonderful—the packing shed of the Rosecrest Fruit Exchange, Porterville, in the 1920s.*

*Before Rachel Carson—cyanide fumigation was a messy, complicated, and dangerous business.*

tion, sophisticated organization, efficiency, mechanization, double-entry bookkeeping, and other aspects of the balance sheet. Under such a system farming became intensive, which is to say that as much of a single crop as possible was planted in fields that often ran to the thousands of acres, to be stripped at harvest time and replanted as soon as possible. It also became specialized to a fine degree, what with California's nearly three hundred individual agricultural commodities. Single farms would "manufacture" peas or carrots or artichokes much as factories would have turned out widgets or flanges or boiler casings.*

Organization, either corporate or cooperative, streamlined the production of the state's agribusiness. In the hands of a corporation, it quite often amounted to total supervision and control from field to grocery shelf. A

*Acknowledgement must be given here to the work of Luther Burbank, the horticultural scientist who took up residence in the Sonoma County town of Santa Rosa in 1875. In his fifty years of experimentation, Burbank developed sixty new varieties of plums and prunes, ten varieties of berries, and many important varieties of peaches, apples, nectarines, quinces, pears, cherries, asparagus, tomatoes, squash, and corn, as well as the Burbank potato and several varieties of flowers, including the Shasta daisy.

single company would own not only the acreage on which crops were grown but the factories in which they were canned, packaged, or packed, the distribution system (including fleets of trucks) that carried them to market, and, sometimes, the grocery stores themselves. In such a way, the brand names of the California Packing Corporation, or CalPac (Del Monte brand), and the Di Giorgio Corporation (S & W Foods) were spread throughout the state and the country. In addition to cultivating their own land, such corporations frequently contracted with individual farmers to produce selected crops according to company specifications, usually under the supervision of company fieldmen and sometimes with financing furnished by the company. Thousands of previously self-sufficient family farms were thus converted into satellites of corporate agriculture.

While cooperative organization had had its roots in the formation of irrigation districts in the nineteenth century, by 1940 it had come to include a wide variety of forms and functions. For small farmers the California State Grange provided a center around which community social life could revolve and a voice to express the farmer's needs on a political level. The corporate grower had the Associated Farmers, Inc., whose function was far less social than political, concentrating especially on vigilant efforts to protect California's migrant labor force from the evils of creeping unionism (as we shall see). Similarly general organizations included the Farm Bureau Federation, which dispensed information on the more technical aspects of fertilizing, soil nutrition, irrigation, and stockbreeding, and the Farmers Educational and Cooperative Union, whose function was similar to that of the Grange, though its influence was not as widespread.

The most numerous such organizations, however, were marketing cooperatives formed to control the price, shipping, and marketing of particular products —although many also operated processing plants, provided purchasing and advertising services, and performed technological research to improve production quality and efficiency. There were 450 such cooperatives with a total membership of more than eighty thousand, but whether the California Date Growers Association, the Walnut Growers Association, or the Prune and Apricot Growers Association, they all found their model and their inspiration in the biggest and

*Imported black field hands at work as strikebreakers during the Salinas lettuce strike of 1936.*

oldest cooperative in the state—the California Fruit Growers Exchange.

Founded in 1905, the Fruit Growers Exchange had grown to a membership of 13,500 by 1940 and comprised 210 local packing associations in twenty-six districts. Under the Sunkist label, it handled more than 75 percent of California's citrus crop, shipping and selling 75,000 to 100,000 railroad cars of oranges, lemons, and grapefruit every year for a gross income of $100,000,000 to $125,000,000. It was an all-purpose organization, as fully integrated as any corporation, from timber properties and a lumber mill in northern California for building packing crates to subsidiary plants for converting culls into citric acid, sodium citrate, lemon oil, pectin, orange oil, and orange pulp. Its advertising budget of $1,000,000 a year spread the name of Sunkist across the land, together with its slogan: "California for Health—Oranges for Wealth!"

The Sunkist monolith both capitalized upon and made possible a phenomenon peculiar to Southern California—a subculture of well-to-do "farmers" whose only direct connection with the land was through ownership and whose most strenuous agricultural activity was in stepping out the back door and picking

a few oranges for breakfast. The exchange did everything else: it planted, irrigated, pruned, sprayed the necessary pesticides, operated smudge pots on bitter winter mornings to prevent frost,* harvested, culled, packed, shipped, and sold the product for the farmer, who would then walk down to his mailbox one day and find a fat check, less a suitable fee for services rendered. There were worse ways in which to make a living.

Slick, efficient, and wonderfully complex, California's agriculture was a huge machine for making money, and its basic units were not so much farms as factories. But it was a system that not only fed but fed *upon* people, and behind all the rich, streamlined productivity of those factories lay the squalid, shadowed reality of what James Bryce had called California's own "peculiar institution": her migrant labor force.

---

*To anyone living in Southern California citrus-raising communities in this period, "smudge" (a combination of "smoke" and "sludge") was one of the more unpleasant facts of life. Produced by thousands of crude-oil-burning pots scattered throughout the groves, smudge hung in the air like a greasy, gritty black fog, hiding the sun for hours, smearing car windshields, eating at house paint, settling on windowsills, clothes, and hair, and penetrating with maddening persistence eyes, ears, noses, and throats. Housewives hung out no laundry on smudge days.

*With heavy mesh windshield screens and a police escort, trucks get the lettuce out of Salinas, 1936.*

IT HAD ALWAYS BEEN THERE, that army of seasonal farm laborers, California's largest and cheapest human resource—and, like the state's other resources, too often badly used. In the beginning it had been made up of waste products of the gold rush, refugees from urban failure in San Francisco and Sacramento, and luckless prospectors whose pans had never shown that heart-stopping flash of color, together with a number of Indians and a few Chinese. With the completion of the transcontinental railroad in 1869, the proportion of Chinese began to grow, and by 1884 they comprised more than half the migrant worker population, driving down wages that were already below subsistence levels

for Caucasian workers. After Chinese exclusion began to take effect, Caucasians once again came to dominate the migrant labor pool; but employers had enjoyed their first taste of a cheap, undemanding, and unorganized working force that could be counted upon to observe the first law of California's agricultural labor relations: Be there when you are needed; disappear when you are not. The hiring of cheap, transitory labor was an experience not easily forgotten, and growers began a continuing effort to re-create it.

The wave of Japanese immigration that began near the turn of the century seemed at first to be the ideal source for the large grower. Unfortunately, the Japanese not only tended to be less docile than the Chinese, they also were inclined to view themselves as farmers, not farm workers, buying or leasing their own land (by 1940, for example, Japanese were farming 26,045 acres in Los Angeles County alone, controlling 90 percent of its truck crops). After the "Gentleman's Agreement" of 1908 (see chapter 21), growers turned next to Hindus for a major labor source, and then increasingly to Mexicans, particularly after the Wheatland Riot of 1913, which made it clear that American workers simply could not be relied upon.

By 1920 there were 88,771 people in California who had been born in Mexico, and most of them followed the crops. By 1930 the figure had climbed to 368,013, so many that agitation began for a bill to prohibit any further Mexican immigration, just as the Chinese and Japanese had been excluded. No legislation came of the effort, but foresightful growers imported some 30,000 Filipinos just in case.

Just as the full weight of the Depression settled on the state, California found herself with a massive oversupply of migrant labor at a time when she needed it least. Most of it was Mexican, and most of these people settled down in the *barrio* of East Los Angeles, which acquired a Mexican population second only to that in Mexico City itself. As noted in chapter 18, Los Angeles County made valiant efforts to repatriate Mexican aliens so as to relieve its welfare costs, but this was no more than a stopgap measure; the Mexicans had come to Southern California to stay.

Relatively few, however, returned to play a dominant role as migrant laborers for the rest of the Depression, for by the time the agricultural industry began its rapid recovery, yet another body of imported workers had arrived on the scene: American refugees from the ghastly wasteland called the Dust Bowl. Between 1935 and 1938, an estimated 350,000 "Okies" and "Arkies" fled their homelands for the Eden of promise, and until the beginning of World War II, they comprised the majority of California's migrant labor pool.

Like their predecessors for seventy years, the new American migrants endured an existence that can only be described as submarginal and brutally insecure. Barely mobile in their wracked and beaten flivvers, they followed the harvest route from crop to crop, valley to valley: chopping cotton in the Imperial Valley, picking oranges in the San Bernardino Valley, lemons in the Ojai Valley, peaches in the San Joaquin Valley, lettuce in the Salinas Valley, cherries in the Santa Clara Valley (north), apples and almonds in the Sacramento Valley. . . . Wandering and utterly homeless, they lived where they could, sometimes in growers' camps that were grotesquely inadequate, most being no more than a collection of riddled shacks with overpriced rents, overcrowded and equipped with the most minimal of water and sanitation facilities. During the peak month of September, as many as 190,000 jobs were available (they fell to about 40,000 in December), but there were still many more thousands of migrants than there were jobs, and wages were abysmally low, even for a Depression. At ten, fifteen, but rarely more than twenty cents an hour, it was all a family could do to keep itself in food, much less put together enough to buy gasoline to reach the next harvest—even if every member old enough to walk and not suffering from rickets worked the standard ten-hour day. In 1935 the annual wage of the average migrant family (family, remember, not individual) was $289. With whatever thin shavings they had been able to carve off that annual intake, the migrants sat out the winters by clustering on the fringes of whatever towns they happened to be nearest when they had finished the season's last harvest, painfully contriving villages of rags and tar paper, sleeping in their automobiles, offending decent citizens everywhere by their starved and exhausted presence.

Migrants, of whatever time or origin, had been unable to do much themselves to improve conditions that had congealed into tradition over the years. As we have seen (chapter 14), the first major attempt to unionize farm laborers ended in bloody defeat at Wheatland in 1913, and those attempts that followed were no more successful—and hardly less bloody. In a purely grassroots attempt, Mexican cantaloupe-pickers in the Imperial Valley had tried manfully to strike for higher wages in 1928 and 1929; they were crushed by the full weight of police, judicial, and corporate authority. Similarly free-lance efforts throughout the state between 1930 and 1932 (forty-four brief strikes in all) were smashed with equal dispatch. Leaderless, rootless, disorganized, and abandoned by the traditional labor movement, migrant workers floundered helplessly. In 1933 many of them turned to the Cannery and Agricul-

*Destitution was no respecter of sex or age, and many migrant families traveled by freight.*

tural Workers' Union, organized by the Communist Party in an unsuccessful bid to gain a foothold in the California labor movement. Although the new union organized and led twenty-four strikes, chief among them a cotton-pickers' strike in the San Joaquin Valley, its most telling effect was to inspire the large growers to form the Associated Farmers, Inc., one of the most efficient strikebreaking organizations ever put together.

With the backing (both moral and financial) of such groups as the California State Chamber of Commerce, the Southern Pacific Railroad, the Industrial Association of San Francisco, Pacific Gas & Electric, and the California Packing Corporation, the Associated Farmers erected a smooth-functioning machine whose influence soon dominated every agricultural community in the state. By maintaining a statewide blacklist of known Communists, union agitators, and present or former union members; by drafting "citizens' armies" from the ranks of its managerial employees and arming them with brand-new pickhandles and occasionally shotguns;

by pressing the state attorney-general's office to enforce California's criminal-syndicalism laws vigilantly; and by "cooperating with" (i.e., directing) local law-enforcement officials—the Associated Farmers, Inc., managed to put the lid on every attempted strike throughout the rest of the 1930s, including the Salinas lettuce strike of 1936, the longest and most violent agricultural strike in the state's history up to that time. The organization not only destroyed the Communist union but so hamstrung the efforts of its less radical successor, the CIO's United Cannery, Agricultural, Packing, and Allied Workers of America, that it very nearly ceased to function in California by the end of the decade.

Deprived of any viable union leadership to assuage their ills, migrant workers could expect even less help from the state itself. Throughout the 1920s and most of the 1930s, the Commission on Immigration and Housing, which might have materially aided the living conditions of the migrants, sat in a kind of bureaucratic catatonia under a succession of disinterested Republican governors and legislatures. Even Simon J. Lubin, its founder and first director, had abandoned the organization in disgusted frustration in 1922. Federal aid was more substantial—but not until 1935, when the Farm Security Administration began a program to construct federally financed labor camps to replace those provided by the growers.

However, since there were approximately 5,600 camps scattered through the state, and since the initial appropriation allotted a mere $200,000, the government was never able to achieve more than a small part of its goal.

Yet public concern for the plight of the migrant worker slowly began to be felt both inside and outside the state, possibly inspired in part by the fact that the most recent migrants were not Chinese or Japanese or Hindu or Filipino or Mexican; they were *real people* —white, Anglo-Saxon, Protestant Americans. Two of the prominent figures who helped to generate this concern were John Steinbeck, a young novelist whose *In Dubious Battle* (1936) and *Of Mice and Men* (1937) had centered on the field hand's life, and Carey McWilliams, a lawyer, former newspaperman, and frequent contributor of social criticism to such magazines as *The American Mercury* and *The Nation.** In 1936,

---

*McWilliams later became editor of *The Nation*.

*Waiting for work, waiting for food, waiting . . . a group of idled men
talk it over in a tent village in the San Joaquin Valley, 1937.*

McWilliams and several staff people from the Farm Security Administration formed the Simon J. Lubin Society (Lubin had died that year), which was designed, in McWilliams' words, "to demonstrate the real nature of the controls which operated in the field of industrialized agriculture." One of the means to this end was *The Rural Observer,* a weekly newsletter under the editorship of Helen Hosmer, which set its sights on the Associated Farmers, Inc., and all its works and served as the closest thing to a farm labor newspaper that existed in the state. More directly, McWilliams assumed the chairmanship of the Steinbeck Committee to Aid Agricultural Workers in 1938, campaigned vigorously that year for the election of Culbert Olson for governor, and in Washington attempted to persuade the La Follette Committee (a subcommittee of the Senate Committee on Education and Labor) to undertake an intensive investigation of farm labor in California.

Aside from lending his name to the Committee to Aid Agricultural Workers, Steinbeck's contribution to the effort resided in his writings, particularly the two novels mentioned, a 1936 article for *The Nation,* and a seven-part series he produced for the *San Francisco News* called "The Harvest Gypsies"; later reprinted by *The Rural Observer* in pamphlet form under the title of *Their Blood Is Strong,* the series sold out its printing of 100,000 copies and is today a collector's item.

By the end of 1938, the names of McWilliams and Steinbeck were already anathema to the Associated Farmers and its allies; after the spring of 1939, neither name would smell as sweet. To begin with, in January 1939 Governor Culbert Olson appointed McWilliams director of the Division of Immigration and Housing (which replaced the former commission), and he began the first careful investigation of the living conditions in the state's labor camps since the administration of Simon J. Lubin, including unannounced personal inspections. Secondly, in the spring Steinbeck's evocative and deeply moving novel of the Joad family appeared, *The Grapes of Wrath*—and shortly afterwards, Mc-

Williams' own exhaustive, documented study of California farm labor was published, *Factories in the Field.*

The hue and cry that greeted the publication of these two books was remarkably virulent, even for California. To many, McWilliams' new position and the nearly simultaneous publication of the books amounted to nothing less than a Communist conspiracy. REDS BLAMED FOR BOOKS ON MIGRANT LABOR, ran a headline in William Randolph Hearst's *San Francisco Examiner,* and Elsie Robinson, Hearst's female version of Westbrook Pegler, issued a call to arms: "Get busy. Decide once and for all whether we're mice or men. Stop being played as suckers. Refuse to be taken for a ride. Throw every Red out of office." *The Grapes of Wrath* was branded as not only obscene but subversive, and was systematically removed from hundreds of library shelves. *Factories in the Field,* being a sexless historical and sociological study, could not be dispensed with so easily, but the Associated Farmers got in its licks during its annual meeting in December 1939, classifying McWilliams as "California's Agricultural Pest Number One, outranking pear blight and the boll weevil." It also persuaded the ever-obliging state legislature to pass a bill eliminating the position of director of the Division of Immigration and Housing, which bill was quickly pocket-vetoed by Governor Olson. "All of this frenzied activity," McWilliams recalled with visible pleasure in the May 1970 issue of *The American West,* "greatly stimulated the sale of both books."*

The books (or perhaps just their enormously successful reception by the public) also convinced Congress that it should send the La Follette Committee to California, where, during twenty-eight days of public hearings in December 1939 and January 1940, it considered the testimony of more than four hundred witnesses. Studying and evaluating the material from these hearings over the next two years, the La Follette Committee finally presented it to Congress in October 1942, together with recommendations for sweeping reforms.

It was too late, for by then World War II had "solved" California's migrant labor problem, as it had solved so many other problems of the Depression, by smothering it in a welter of more immediate concerns—like gearing up for a wartime economy. By the scores of thousands, the "Okies" and "Arkies" fled the factories in the fields for the aircraft, shipbuilding, textile, and armament factories in the cities. In their places came once again the Mexicans, who inherited, with some marginal improvements, the legacy of *The Grapes of Wrath* (see chapter 23). Once more, California's agri-industrialists were provided with the cheap and undemanding labor force they had come to view as their natural right.

As for the American migrants, they had found, transmuted, at least a part of the dream that had urged them west. But they had tasted bitterness along the way. "I like to think how nice it's gonna be, maybe, in California," Ma Joad had mused early in *The Grapes of Wrath.* "Never cold. An' fruit ever'place, an' people just bein' in the nicest places, little white houses in among the orange trees. I wonder—that is, if we all got jobs an' all work—maybe we can get one of them little white houses. An' the little fellas go out an' pick oranges right off the tree." After the family's arrival, she amended that hope: "We got a bitter road. . . . We got a long bitter road ahead."

Like hundreds of thousands before her, Ma Joad had learned that the promise of California was a two-headed coin.

---

*In that same article ("A Man, A Place, and A Time") McWilliams dispensed with the charges of a Communist plot: ". . . there is, I regret to report, one thing wrong with the conspiracy theory; namely, I never met John Steinbeck."

*Like spiderwebs of progress, suspension cables swoop across the Golden Gate.*

# California Mirror:
# The Celebration of Steel

*Nearing completion, the Golden Gate Bridge looked for all the world as if it had been slashed with a gigantic axe.*

Like many people possessed of an outsized dementia, Emperor Norton of San Francisco frequently displayed a flash of antic wit so close to gentle mockery that it made one wonder whether the old boy had not been pulling the collective leg of the city for years. One such occasion was his ambitious edict of 1873, which forecast the future in a startling fashion: "Now, therefore, we, Norton I, Emperor of the United States and protector of Mexico, do order and direct . . . that a suspension bridge be constructed from . . . Oakland Point to Yerba Buena, from thence to the mountain range of Sausalito, and from thence to the Farallones. . . ."

It took the citizens of the Bay Area nearly sixty years to obey the emperor's orders, and even then they didn't get it quite right; of the three sections he outlined, the span to the Farallones was never built (the emperor would not have been amused). The first section, called the San Francisco–Oakland Bay Bridge, was begun in 1931 and finished in November 1936 at a total cost of $77,000,000. Utilizing Yerba Buena Island as a stepping-stone between Oakland and San Francisco, the bridge was one of the biggest construction operations of its time in sheer size and engineering achievement. The massive concrete central anchorage for the suspension portion of the link from Yerba Buena to San Francisco (constructed by the Six Companies, Inc.) was equal to the height of a forty-story building and used nearly as much concrete as had gone into the construction of Boulder Dam. The tunnel rammed through Yerba Buena Island was big enough to accommodate the two decks

of the bridge, and was the largest-bore tunnel in the world at the time—and at twelve miles (including approaches) the bridge itself was the longest in the world.

But it was the Golden Gate Bridge, long since the working symbol of San Francisco, that captured the public imagination. The bridge had been the dream since 1917 of a "five-foot giant" named Joseph Strauss, but it took the engineer thirteen years to convince the citizens of the six-county region to commit themselves to the $27,000,000 bond issue that would be necessary. Many of those opposed to the idea maintained that it was impossible to bridge the Golden Gate; the immense daily flow of tidal waters—fourteen times as much as the average flow of the Mississippi River—they said, would prohibit the construction of solid anchorages. Others objected on purely aesthetic grounds—"The Golden Gate," one newspaper advertisement read, "is one of nature's perfect pictures—let's not disfigure it."

But Strauss was more than an engineer; he was a poet and a visionary, and his enthusiasm was contagious. The bond issue passed, and construction began in January 1933, largely under the supervision of Clifford Paine, a Chicago engineer who simplified and refined Strauss's original design for the bridge, giving it the shape it bears today. The distinctive facing decorations and the choice of international orange as the color it should be painted were the contributions of Irving F.

*Like creatures out of H. G. Wells'* The War of the Worlds, *the two ends of the Bay Bridge's cantilever section prepare to meet.*

Morrow, a young San Francisco architect. The bridge was completed on May 27, 1937—but not until ten workmen had plunged to their deaths—and thousands of pedestrians jubilantly crossed the Golden Gate for the first time in history.

The response of Strauss was to compose a poem:

> At last the mighty task is done;
> Resplendent in the western sun,
> The bridge looms mountain high;
> Its titan piers grip ocean floor,
> Its great steel arms link shore with shore,
> Its towers pierce the sky....
>
> High overhead its lights shall gleam;
> Far, far below, life's restless stream
> Unceasingly shall flow;
> For this was spun its lithe fine form,
> To fear not war, nor time, nor storm,
> For fate had meant it so.

*Opening day on the San Francisco–Oakland Bay Bridge, November 15, 1936.*

*In the spring of 1937, Golden Gate Bridge pedestrians rushed to meet the future.*

The response of San Francisco—since it was San Francisco—was to throw a party and invite the world. With some twenty million tons of sand and mud dredged from the bottom of the bay, a man-made island was built off the northern edge of Yerba Buena Island— dubbed Treasure Island (now a permanent navy base). On this island was erected the Golden Gate International Exposition, which opened in 1939. Like the Panama-Pacific International Exposition of nearly twenty-five years before, however, the Golden Gate exposition opened not only to the sounds of celebration but to the chilling thunder of war in a distant land, a sound that no amount of carnival noise could obscure.

Another world was coming to an end.

*Opening day on the Golden Gate Bridge, May 27, 1937.*

*The stern-wheeler "Delta Queen" salutes the opening of a bridge—and the end of her way of life.*

*The San Francisco–Oakland Bay Bridge today, looking toward San Francisco. On the following two pages is a view of the Golden Gate Bridge.*

# SECTION THREE

# *The New West*

California has always been part fantasy and proud of it. Where else is the range so broad between fairyland and nightmare? Since the early days, the state has amply justified her fairyland motto: "The Golden State." It began first with the hope of gold, then with the fact of it. . . . When that played out, other golden vistas remained: a horizon of orange groves which led, in time, to the nation's richest and most varied agricultural production; the lure of black gold . . . the golden wings of a sky's the limit aerospace industry; and possibly the most irresistible gold of them all, that sun-gold which makes the flowers bloom very big, and which makes the middle-aged seem a little less so.

In contrast, there are the nightmares: the heat of Death Valley; the tastelessness of Los Angeles; the stink of the microclimate which encompasses California's freeways. The bad is everywhere with the good; even the great redwood monuments to nature's majestic durability yield to increasing exploitation. Fertile valleys have been destroyed forever in the uncivilized conviction that every man is entitled to his own drab little box. In too many of the choicest coastal areas, California has become a vast unkempt and unlovely bedroom.

Thus, a profound tension is created, a tension between land and people, between reality and hope, with the present drawn taut to the very breaking point between. Here is the challenge of the limits to which human ecology can become complex. Man and his environment interact in an explosive and perplexing contest. It is an incomparable challenge for human wisdom, judgment, and restraint. . . .

—Robert C. Cook in *Population Bulletin* (June, 1966)

*Cauldron of light: the Los Angeles basin at dusk from the hills above Griffith Park Observatory.*

# CHAPTER 21

# A STATE OF WAR

*California learns, like the rest of the nation, that the quickest solution to the depression is the agony of international war*

IN 1898 the United States completed its first territorial expansion since the Alaska Purchase of 1867, and its first by war since the Mexican Cession (including California) of 1848: by solemn treaty with Spain, ending the "splendid little" Spanish-American War, America acquired possession of Puerto Rico in the Caribbean Sea and the Philippine Islands in the Pacific Ocean. In that same year it also annexed the Republic of Hawaii. These acquisitions gave rise to much throat-clearing oratory in the halls of Congress concerning whether the United States was going to remain a continental republic or become an imperial power, attempting to re-create the British Empire in her own image. The question was not resolved to anyone's satisfaction (and has not been to this day), but one thing remained certain: America had acquired a stake in the Pacific Ocean, and much of her future history would be written there.

And America's window on the Pacific was California. For California as for America then, the year 1898 was a kind of watershed marking a major change in the state's image of herself. For fifty years California had seen herself and been seen as the logical terminus of the westering urge that had crossed, then filled, a continent. But now her citizens could sense that California was not an ending after all but a kind of beginning, the literal and symbolic threshold to the vast Pacific; like poet Robinson Jeffers, they could feel behind them "Mountain and plain, the immense breadth of the continent, / before me the mass and doubled stretch of water." Somewhere over that "doubled stretch of water" lay more of the promise that had driven them west. "Less often did they look back toward the East," historian John Carl Parish wrote in 1932. "They glanced over their shoulders and saw Hawaii. They turned about and there was an awakened Japan, a China with its eternal problems, a Russia on the sea at the end of a transcontinental march like their own. The Pacific was no longer an empty room, a vacant space setting them apart from the Old East. It introduced them to a strange world. They had settled and tamed a land. Now they found themselves in the open doorway to a new life."

California echoed and sought to fulfill the ancient dream that had inspired Columbus, Cavendish, Frobisher, Hudson, Major Robert Rogers, Jonathan Carver, Alexander Mackenzie, and a score of other explorers to seek out the magical, mythical Northwest Passage through the mass of the North American continent, the passage that would lead to all the riches of Cathay. California was the ultimate expression of what Senator Thomas Hart Benton had meant the day in 1842 when he stood up in the chamber, pointed his fine Missouri arm west, and said: "There. There lies the road to India." Whether he knew it or not, Henry E. Huntington was paraphrasing the words of Benton when he said of Los Angeles in 1901, "Its front door opens on the Pacific, the ocean of the future. Europe can supply her own wants; we shall supply the wants of Asia." Hawaii, Samoa, New Zealand, Australia, New Guinea, Malaysia, the Philippines, Indochina, China, Korea, Japan.... Who knew how many customers there

*The California arsenal: view of a liberty ship under construction in the San Pedro yards of Kaiser Industries, 1943.*

*"Herd 'em up. . . . Let 'em be pinched, hurt, hungry, and dead up against it" (Shugimoto painting, 1943).*

were out there? Five hundred million? A *billion*? Who knew what resources, what pockets of wealth could be exploited and fed into the consuming maw of the California economy?

So a new obsession, a new dream: it would be two generations yet before that dream could become fully grown, but it was there through all the years California was developing her black gold and her green gold, enduring the delights and agonies of boom-and-bust and the horrors of Depression. Its presence helps to explain the furious intensity of her reaction to an event that took place in December 1941.

WHEN THEY ALLOWED THEMSELVES to admit it, most Californians, like most of the rest of the country, knew perfectly well that America's entry into the spreading world conflict was inevitable—indeed necessary. Since the Nazi *blitzkrieg* of Poland in September 1939 and the consequent declarations of war from England and France, war and the news of war were never long out of the public consciousness. With a kind of controlled anxiety, American people scanned the front-page war bulletins of their daily newspapers and gathered around their radios in the evening to listen to crackling, static-ridden reports from across the Atlantic, particularly the gravel voice of Edward R. Murrow: "This . . . is London."

One by one, European nations fell to the inexorable colossus of Nazi Germany: Norway and Denmark in April 1940; the Netherlands, Belgium, and Luxembourg in May; France in June. And across the Pacific, the Japanese invaded Indochina and swept down the Malay Peninsula, capturing Singapore on February 15, 1942. President Franklin D. Roosevelt initiated the Lend-Lease Program to aid a desperate England and issued a call for the manufacture of 50,000 warplanes a year. "All that could be heard as the Depression ended," social historian Robert Goldston has written, "was the summons of the steady drummer; a continuous rolling of the drums now, ever louder, ever nearer."

Then, on December 7, 1941, the tension broke with the Japanese attack on Pearl Harbor. Shortly before 8:00 A.M., Hawaiian time, more than one hundred carrier-based Japanese planes and a number of submarines launched a surprise assault on the U.S. Pacific Fleet anchored within the harbor. At its end the attack had destroyed or irreparably damaged ten American ships and severely damaged eight more. The Americans lost 177 warplanes, most of which never got off the

*"During the months of confinement, our minds lived in the future—not the past" (Ishigo painting, 1945)*

ground, 4,303 men killed or missing in action, and 1,272 wounded. On December 8, 1941, the United States declared war on Japan and three days later extended the declaration to include Germany and Italy.

California's response to the Japanese action and its aftermath could hardly have been more emotional had the planes strafed and bombed Catalina Island. Having celebrated their presence on the edge of the Pacific, the state's residents suddenly felt desperately exposed by their position, vulnerable to whatever move the Japanese cared to make next, including, the burning rumors had it, a massive invasion. They grew no more secure as Hitler's European triumphs began to be duplicated by Japan in the Pacific; between January and May, 1942, Thailand, Burma, much of Malaysia and Indonesia, and—most terrifying of all—the Philippines fell to the sweep of the Japanese.

While the string of conquests mounted, stories began to circulate that the attack on Pearl Harbor had been made possible only by the collusion—direct and implied —of Hawaii's 160,000 Japanese, who, it was said and widely believed in California, gave their hearts' allegiance to the land of the Rising Sun. Californians soon regarded their own Japanese with increasing suspicion —all their more than ninety thousand Japanese *Issei* (persons born in Japan), *Nisei* (American-born), or *Kibei* (American-born persons who had been partly educated in Japan). In this atmosphere hearsay gained the weight of documented fact: Japanese farmers were plowing and planting their fields in the shape of arrows pointing to military and industrial targets; Japanese fishermen were in reality enlisted men and officers in the Imperial Navy; Japanese field hands were militiamen; Japanese gardeners, household workers, laundrymen, butchers, bakers, and candlestick-makers were actually intelligence agents in a vast espionage network that blanketed the state, financed by Tokyo through Japanese banks and other businesses; all were simply waiting for the day of invasion to rip off their masks and attack the land that had given them welcome.*

It was not long after Pearl Harbor before the first

---

*Anyone not present in California and other parts of the West Coast in these months may find it hard to credit that people actually believed such things; they did, with an absolute, even fierce conviction.

"*Life in the camps was not easy. It was inadequate and morale-killing*" (Estelle Ishigo, 1945).

voices began to be raised in favor of removing people of Japanese descent from the entire West Coast (which was then considered nothing less than a war zone). One of the first to speak out publicly was John Hughes, a popular radio commentator. His views were quickly supported by a wide spectrum of public opinion, at least as expressed by such organizations as the Los Angeles Chamber of Commerce, the State Chamber of Commerce, the Native Sons of the Golden West, the California State Grange, the Associated Farmers, Inc., the State Federation of Labor, and the California Department of the American Legion, as well as most of the public press, particularly the Hearst newspapers, whose San Francisco columnist Harry McLemore was driven to eloquence by his passion for Japanese removal: "Herd 'em up, pack 'em off and give them the inside room of the badlands. Let 'em be pinched, hurt, hungry and dead up against it." That great a bulk of public opinion was simply too much for the average politician to bear comfortably, no matter what his personal feelings, and most of the state's elected officials— including Mayor Fletcher Bowron of Los Angeles, State Attorney-General Earl Warren, and Governor Culbert Olson—added their voices to the demand for removal.

For a while in January 1942, the federal government, in the person of Lt. Gen. John L. DeWitt, head of the Western Defense Command, resisted the idea. As DeWitt put it, "An American citizen, after all, is an

*Hollywood does its part, 1942. Immediately identifiable in the throng are Loretta Young, Bette Davis, Edward Arnold, Pat O'Brien, Claudette Colbert, and Charles Boyer.*

American citizen." By the end of January, after continuing pressure, he had changed his mind—influenced in no little part by the fact that Lt. Gen. Walter C. Short and Adm. Husband E. Kimmel had been removed from command for "dereliction of duty" in failing to provide proper protection of Pearl Harbor.

"I am not going to be a second General Short," DeWitt reportedly announced; he then proceeded to issue a formal recommendation for removal to the secretary of war, a report that contained one of the most astonishing non sequiturs in the annals of military jargon: "In the war in which we are now engaged racial affinities are not severed by migration. The Japanese race is an enemy race and while many second and third generation Japanese born on United States soil, possessed of United States citizenship, have become 'Americanized,' the racial strains are undiluted. . . . It therefore follows that along the vital Pacific Coast over 112,000 potential enemies of Japanese extraction are at large today. There are indications that these are organized and ready for concerted action at a favorable opportunity. *The very fact that no sabotage has taken place to date is a disturbing and confirming indication that such action will be taken.*" (Emphasis supplied).

*Interior of one of the shops of the Ryan Aeronautical Company of San Diego, 1935.*

The flaws in this "fantastic line of reasoning," as historian Walton Bean characterized it, apparently escaped the attention of DeWitt's superiors in Washington. On February 19, 1942, President Franklin D. Roosevelt signed Executive Order 9066, which authorized and directed "the Secretary of War, and the Military Commanders whom he may from time to time designate, whenever he or any designated Commander deems such action necessary or desirable, to prescribe military areas in such places and of such extent as he or the appropriate Military Commander may determine, from which any or all persons may be excluded,

and with respect to which the right of any person to enter, remain in, or leave shall be subject to whatever restrictions the Secretary of War or the appropriate Military Commander may impose in his discretion."

And so it was done; under the direction of the WRA (War Relocation Authority)—one of the many initialed organisms in the alphabet soup of the several Roosevelt administrations—110,000 people of Japanese descent, citizens and aliens alike, were ordered into "assembly centers" (former racetracks, fairgrounds, livestock exhibition halls) with no more personal belongings than they could carry on their backs, stuff under their arms,

*The aircraft industry boomed with the order for 50,000 warplanes in 1940 — but not without problems.*

or hold in their hands, and after weeks of waiting were transferred to "relocation centers" in ten singularly unstrategic locations, from Tule Lake in northern California and Manzanar in the Owens Valley, to Minidoka, Idaho, and Jerome, Arkansas. Housed in crowded, jerry-built barracks surrounded by barbed wire, guard towers (complete with searchlights), and posted sentries, the evacuees may not have been hungry or hurt, but they were certainly "pinched" and "dead up against it," much as Harry McLemore and the Hearst newspapers wished them to be.

Most of them remained in the relocation centers until well after the Battle of Leyte Gulf in October 1944 (which destroyed the Japanese Navy), and the last evacuees did not leave until 1946. Those who were allowed to leave before the end of 1944 and early 1945 included more than 17,000 army recruits, many of whom served in the famous 442d Regimental Combat Team, an all-Japanese force that was the most-decorated regiment in the history of the United States Army. There is

visible irony in that fact, and in the words of President Franklin D. Roosevelt when he authorized the formation of the combat team in February 1943: "No loyal citizen of the United States should be denied the democratic right to exercise the responsibilities of his citizenship, regardless of ancestry."*

DREAMS DEFERRED, AGAIN. . . . There are several things that can be said of the relocation of the West Coast's Japanese. One of the first is simply that by no stretch of the military imagination was it necessary. The Japanese never contemplated an invasion of the West Coast of America, and no American military commander—including General DeWitt—ever maintained that they did. As for sabotage, it is interesting to note that among the 160,000 Japanese in Hawaii, who were *not* removed from what was incontestably a military zone, not a single documented case of sabotage was recorded.

Secondly, as has been shown, the relocation was not imposed upon Californians from above; it was an act they both conceived and demanded—and it could not be attributed wholly to wartime hysteria. In a very real sense, it was the culmination (one hopes) of nearly a century's build-up of anti-Oriental feeling in California. Shortly before the turn of the century, the sentiments once directed against the Chinese (see chapters 7 and 10) shifted to the Japanese and grew in intensity as immigration from Japan increased between 1900 and 1910. As with anti-Chinese feeling, it was first expressed by a fearful labor movement, but the industry, thrift, and pride of the Japanese soon inspired a like feeling among the higher levels of California society. As Gover-

---

*It has been estimated that the economic loss to the Japanese community through the forced sale of homes, businesses, and land, the loss of salaried income and interest, and sundry forms of fraud, thievery, and vandalism to abandoned property was in the neighborhood of four hundred million dollars. Between 1950 and 1965, the United States settled 26,561 claims against itself for a total of $38,474,140—probably less than 10 percent of the total loss. Another financial note: in the appendix to his *Uprooted Americans* (1971), former WRA Director Dillon S. Myer notes that of the $190,170,000 appropriated to the WRA, the agency saved $24,432,970. One is allowed to wonder—just wonder, mind you— why it was considered necessary or even desirable to "save" money appropriated for the care, feeding, and housing of these 110,000 casualties of war.

nor Hiram Johnson put it in 1916, "Their superiority, their aesthetic efficiency, and their maturer mentality make them effective in competition with us, and unpopular and a menace."

In order to deal with this "menace," in 1906 the San Francisco Board of Education had ordered the city's Japanese children out of the general public schools and into an "Oriental School" originally established for Chinese children. This act outraged the assertive Japanese government, and a major diplomatic crisis was averted only when President Theodore Roosevelt persuaded the Board of Education to amend its order

drastically and broaden it to include *all* alien-born children. In exchange, the president in 1908 negotiated the so-called "Gentleman's Agreement" with Japan, by which the Japanese government agreed to limit the issuance of emigration passports to those who "seek to resume a formerly acquired domicile, to join a parent, wife or children residing there, or to assume active control of an already possessed interest in a farming enterprise."

That agreement was not quite what the anti-Japanese movement in California wanted—wholesale exclusion—but it was at least a step in the right direction. In

*The Douglas Aircraft factory at Santa Monica in 1938. In the foreground, a new DC-4; in the rear, the workhorse DC-3.*

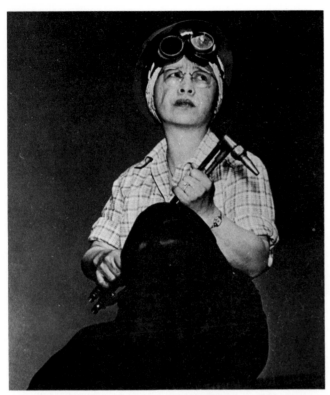

*The Chinese-American version of Rosie the Riveter
—although her name was Edna (1943).*

the meantime the California state legislature went ahead and passed the Alien Land Law of 1913, which prohibited aliens ineligible for citizenship (i.e., Japanese and Chinese) from buying farmland in the state or leasing it for more than three years. Strengthened and amended in 1920 and approved by a general election, the Alien Land Law was nevertheless no more than a stopgap measure; the offspring of these aliens, after all, *were* citizens and could own and lease all the land they could lay hands on. The only real solution was absolute exclusion, and organizations like the California Joint Immigration Committee (formed by Valentine S. McClatchy, publisher of the *Sacramento Bee,* in 1921) continued to push for the cessation of further Japanese immigration. That wish was satisfied in 1924, when Congress finally passed the Oriental Exclusion Act.

Once again the citizens of California had pressured the federal government into excluding a sizable segment of the world. The fears and prejudices that had given birth to exclusion did not die with its passage,

however, and the fact that those elements were alive and well in 1942 is illustrated by the candid admission of Austin Anson, managing secretary of the Grower-Shipper Vegetable Association of central California: "We're charged with wanting to get rid of the Japs for selfish reasons. We might as well be honest. We do. It's a question of whether the white man lives on the Pacific Coast or the brown men. They came into this valley to work, and they stayed to take over." Like some kind of waxy, unreal hothouse flower, then, Japanese relocation blossomed in a compost of both wartime jitters and aging prejudices.

However traditional its motivations may have been, Japanese relocation was a wrenchingly dramatic event, one utterly typical of California's wartime years.

It was a maddened and maddening time, that era of war, one for which not even California could have been prepared. It has been said that the Depression stood like a semicolon between the boom of the 1920s and that of the 1940s; it might be more accurate to say that the Depression was like that millisecond of time between the flash of a dynamite cap and the ripping explosion of the dynamite itself. All the patterns of growth that had been exhibited in the 1920s were bloated almost beyond control by the pressures of war —most particularly the pressures applied by the injection of no less than $35,000,000,000 of federal money between 1940 and 1946. Even without war, that amount of money would have done violence to the social and economic fabric of the state, for at an average of seven billion dollars a year, it was nearly twice the average annual value of California's economic output for the years just before the war. Like an overdose of bottled oxygen, federal money sent the state skittering into an unnatural frenzy of industrial activity that did not begin to taper off until the end of 1943. Yet, frenzied or not, that activity established a base from which, for the first time in her history, California could become one of the major manufacturing states in the nation.

One of the first industries to be affected was that of aircraft production. As pointed out earlier (see "California Mirror: The Romance of Wheels and Wings"), the aircraft industry had already established a beachhead, so to speak, in Southern California by the middle of the 1930s, with the founding of the Douglas Company, the Lockheed (Loughead) Company, Consolidated Vultee, and Ryan Aeronautical. Even before America's entry into World War II, several of these companies had obtained contracts from foreign countries for the construction of warplanes, most notably the Hudson bomber, more than three thousand of which were constructed for the British Royal Air Force by Lockheed. Even so, as late as 1939 the American aircraft industry, including California's firms, could produce not quite six thousand airplanes a year.

That changed, and changed most dramatically, in the spring of 1940 when President Franklin D. Roose-

velt, making his first major preparation for war, issued a call for the construction of 50,000 warplanes a year—and obtained the federal funding necessary to do it. After Pearl Harbor even more planes were called for and more money was made available, and Southern California's aircraft industry blossomed, specializing in the construction of airframes and the assembly of completed planes from motors, propellers, and other parts manufactured in other sections of the country (most in the converted automobile plants of Detroit). From less than 20,000 workers in 1939, the industry was employ-

*Victory-minded shipyard workers in San Pedro—a good many women among them—raise a few jubilant hats in the spring of 1945.*

ing more than 243,000 in California by 1943, and federal aircraft construction contracts in Los Angeles and San Diego counties alone accounted for more than twelve billion dollars of California's "share" of wartime construction money, transforming the pioneering firms of Douglas, Lockheed, Consolidated Vultee (or ConVair, as it was known by then), and Ryan from struggling "backyard" enterprises into enormous complexes whose operations covered thousands of acres in Los Angeles, Long Beach, Santa Monica, San Diego, and El Segundo, all of them painted over or covered with the patterned, olive-drab netting of what passed for camouflage. In these and plants like them (including such new firms as North American, Northrup, and Hughes), production was phenomenal; Lockheed alone manufactured more than twenty thousand aircraft during the war, accounting for nearly 6 percent of the total United States production.

Shipbuilding underwent a similar transformation in the harbor cities of Eureka on Humboldt Bay; San Francisco, Sausalito, Vallejo (and Mare Island), Rich-

mond, Oakland, and Alameda on San Francisco Bay; San Pedro in the Los Angeles Harbor; and San Diego. The federal government's wartime investment in California shipbuilding was comparable to that for aircraft —but in this case most of it (three billion dollars) went to the San Francisco Bay Area, rather than Southern California, and most of the Bay Area's share went to the Richmond shipyards of the Permanente Metals Corporation, a subsidiary of the imposing conglomerate then being erected by Henry J. Kaiser, whose propensities for dam-building we have already seen.*

Shipyard production rivaled that of the aircraft in-

_____

*In chapter 19. After the Six Companies had finished Boulder and Parker dams on the Colorado River, it went on to aid in the construction of the San Francisco–Oakland Bay Bridge. Kaiser then left the chairmanship of the company to form Kaiser Industries, playing a major role in the construction of the Bonneville and Grand Coulee dams, and to found among other enterprises the Oregon Shipbuilding Corporation at Portland, the California Shipbuilding Corporation at San Pedro, the Permanente Cement Company at Redwood City, and the Permanente Metals Corporation at Richmond. He was only beginning.

*The launching of a new "liberty" in Richmond was always the occasion for a gathering of friends and relatives of the engineers and workers ...*

dustry. Seagoing tugs, tankers, amphibious landing craft, P-T boats, C-2 and C-4 freighters, and Victory ships slid off the ways in astonishing numbers; but no statistics could match those of the Liberty cargo-carriers, those ugly and utterly reliable "rustbuckets" that provided the war effort with its most efficient line of supply. Of the 2,158 Liberty ships finished between the summer of 1941 and the summer of 1944, 53 percent were built in the yards of the Pacific Coast, and 23 percent were built in Kaiser's Richmond yards, which employed more than one hundred thousand workers. Kaiser, with a mountain of experience in handling men, machinery, and materials in outsized projects, operated his shipyards with a streamlined efficiency that ultimately broke all construction records. The first Liberty ship required 244 days for completion and delivery; by the summer of 1943 that time had been reduced to an average of 50 days per ship—and one ship, the *Robert E. Perry,* was completed in 8 days, a record that stands to this day.

In order to fulfill such production schedules, Kaiser needed steel—California steel—and being Henry J.

Kaiser, he decided to make it himself, even though both Bethlehem and United States Steel (together with more than six hundred smaller plants) were then producing a little over a million tons of steel every year. With subsidiary funding from the Reconstruction Finance Corporation, a federal entity, Kaiser planned and built the state's first completely integrated steel plant near Fontana, a small hog-raising community on the windswept plain between San Bernardino and Los Angeles. The iron ore for its operation came from the Eagle Mountains of the Mojave Desert (California's only significant source) and the coke for its furnaces from the ovens of Utah. At the plant's dedication in September 1942, Kaiser expressed forgivable pride: "For the first time on this side of the Rockies, we begin the manufacture of iron—the most fundamental element in modern industry—from ores mined in our own mountains. For the first time metallurgical coke is to be made in this western area by the modern by-product coke oven method. For the first time on this Pacific slope, we have under one complete control the manufacture of steel

*. . . as well as some rather notable dignitaries and their own families.
Above, Governor Earl Warren, his wife, six children, and daughter-in-law.*

*In San Francisco, some of California's permanent floating wartime population sleeps where it can in a crowded hotel lobby.*

from the selection of the ores and other raw materials, all the way through to the final finished products. For the first time in our own West, steel can be made to fit a pattern in a completely integrated plant."

Heavy industry, on a monumental scale, had taken its place in the California scene, but the federal money that made it possible seeped into nearly every other nook and cranny of the state's industrial life, from oil production, which rose from $226,000,000 in 1939 to $378,000,000 in 1946, through textiles, machinery, metals products, chemicals, electronics gear, and agriculture, whose product leaped from $625,000,000 in 1939 to $1,700,000,000 in 1944. Even the movies, the state's first all-weather industry, came in for its share of the federal bonanza, with training films, propaganda films, and a ready, captive audience in the form of millions of enlisted men who trooped down to hundreds of mess halls in camps all over the United States to watch the Saturday night special, furnished by the government at government expense. (The general public, it should be pointed out, was equally captive in the war years. Worried, preoccupied and hungry for the solace of entertainment, people were in no mood to be hypercritical; if it moved, they watched it.)

Twenty or more years of industrial growth were packed into the space of five, but it was by no means an unmixed windfall. Industrial growth of that scope meant people—a great many people, more people in a more volatile mix than even burgeoning, crowded California had ever experienced. As the shipbuilding, aircraft, and other industries expanded, they soaked up the state's available labor supply swiftly; from an unemployment level of 380,000 in 1940, the figure had dropped to just 25,000 by the end of 1943—the closest thing to full employment the state had ever known, or has known at any time since then. When that "pool"

*Housing was the bane of the wartime years. Here, a young family looks at likely prospects in a "used-house lot" in Los Angeles, 1942.*

was exhausted, the industries went out and found workers where they could, advertising all over the country, particularly in the South, where hundreds of thousands of Negroes read such advertisements as "Help Wanted!!! Male or Female, Young or Old, Experienced or Inexperienced," packed their belongings, and headed for the Golden State—often transported by the employee-hungry companies. Settling in the Watts (Mudtown) and Central Avenue districts of Los Angeles, the Fillmore and Hunters Point districts of San Francisco, and major portions of Vallejo and Richmond, these black workers gave California her first sizable Negro population—and established a pattern of black migration to the state that would continue for another quarter of a century.

The inducements of California's wartime industries were considerable, for prosperity greatly stimulated the labor union movement, giving rise to much-improved wages and working conditions; between 1939 and 1944, the average weekly earnings of manufacturing workers increased from $27.80 to $55.21. As well, employers went out of their way to make their jobs as attractive as possible; Kaiser Industries, for example, not only paid good wages, but offered on-the-job training and the most progressive group medical insurance plan in the country. Add to this the fact that those working in essential wartime industries were exempt from the draft, and one begins to understand the remarkable increase of manufacturing workers from 461,000 in 1940 to 1,186,000 in 1943. The total California labor force in all segments rose from 2,703,000 to 3,854,000.

This predominantly out-of-state working population was augmented by hundreds of thousands of servicemen from all parts of the country stationed at training camps like Camp Pendleton and Camp Roberts; at navy facilities on Treasure Island, Long Beach, and San Diego;

at airfields like the Alameda Naval Air Station, Hamilton Field, or March Air Force Base; and at embarkation and debarkation assembly centers, like the Oakland Army Base or the San Francisco Presidio. Homesick, apprehensive over their future, painfully young and filled with all the juices of youth, these soldiers, sailors, and marines were a kind of floating urban population, wandering the streets of the cities on one-, two-, or three-day passes—particularly the streets of San Francisco (when they could get there), considered then as now the greatest "liberty town" in the continental United States. A great sea of faces, ever changing but never diminishing.

"During the war Californians were aware vaguely of a phenomenal increase in population," Carey McWilliams wrote in 1949. "From time to time officials made speeches heralding the dawn of a *New West* and occasional headlines hinted at a great post-war expansion. But everyone was too preoccupied with the war itself to give much thought to what was happening in the state. In fact the full 'shock of recognition' did not come . . . until the Bureau of the Census released a report on population shifts for the period from April 1, 1940, to July 1, 1947. If the nation was amazed to learn that, in this period, California had gained 3,000,000 new residents, it would be fair to characterize the reaction in California as a curiously ambivalent mixture of pride, consternation, and dismay."

Pride, certainly—was not growth like this a part of the California tradition? But consternation and dismay simply because the state was not mechanically equipped to handle such an influx. Too much was needed too fast —homes, household goods, and food, not to mention such amenities as telephones, gas and electricity, schools, and sewers. Inevitably, the efforts made to deal with the situation were hasty and inadequate. Thousands of families lived in thin-walled, ramshackle housing projects, crowded into boxlike little rooms with rebellious plumbing and arctic-like heating systems; and in the summer, the inhabitants baked like muffins. Sewers backed up; septic tanks ruptured; water lines broke; electricity failed. Not until well after the war were these and a hundred other growing pains remedied.

The social impact of this swelling population was hardly less traumatic, particularly when it is remembered that hundreds of thousands of white people from prejudice-ridden parts of the South and Midwest were confronted with hundreds of thousands of black people—some of them in direct competition. In parts of the East—particularly Detroit in 1943—this situation created such tension that vicious rioting erupted. Yet in California, the closest approximation to such racial explosions took place not between whites and Blacks, but between whites and Mexican-Americans. In Los Angeles in the spring of 1943, three thousand white "vigilantes," soldiers and civilians alike, banded together to sweep so-called Mexican "zoot-suiters" from the streets of the city. They succeeded. Armed with clubs and followed by patrol cars, bands of white men beat every Mexican youth foolish enough or slow enough to be caught; the police then arrested the youths on charges of rioting and assault. After two days of this singularly methodical "rioting," the job was done; just to make sure it stayed done, the city then instituted a curfew that lasted for months.

Altogether, California was justified in viewing its swelling population and industrial boom with mixed feelings. There were many who welcomed V-J Day in 1945 not only because it meant the end of war but because it also meant the end of the constant influx of new people—or at least a marked slowdown in the rate of that influx. It meant that industry would inevitably face sharp cutbacks, perhaps even a depression of sorts, that would force it to shake down to a level of steady, less spectacular development. There would be time for the state to relax, settle down, and begin solving some of the problems brought on by the war.

What they could not know was that the fantastic growth of the wartime years was not a climax; it was merely a prelude.

*Headframe and hoisting shed of the Kennedy Mine, Jackson.*

# *California Mirror:*
# *The Sense of the Past, II*

*Express office and stagecoach, Columbia.*

*Vintage houses in Nevada City.*

*Camino, Cable & Northern Railroad near Placerville.*

More islands of time remembered: By its very nature gold-mining was a transient, extractive business and left much ugliness to mark its passing. It could be an impressive ugliness, however, as in the headframes shown on page 441 and the massive Pelton waterwheel shown at the left; thirty feet in diameter, the wheel was used to produce compressed air at the North Star Mine of Grass Valley near the turn of the century. More of a grace note is the Camino, Cable & Northern Railroad engine at the right, the last remnant of one of the many narrow-gauge "sugar pine" railroads that once hauled timber up, down, and around the mountains. Of the gold towns themselves, many have been partially restored, such as Columbia (above), a state park, or Nevada City (upper right), a town holding strongly to the past.

*Left: The world's largest Pelton waterwheel at the North Star Mine, Grass Valley.*

*Two Cape Horners: the "Balclutha" of San Francisco*

*...and the "Star of India," San Diego.*

*The "Skunk" line of the California Western Railroad, Fort Bragg.*

*Sail and steam: the scow schooner "Alma," steam schooner "Wapama," codfisher "C. A. Thayer,"
and the ferry boat "Eureka."*

The problems of getting from one place to another within California and from California to someplace else were considerations that occupied much of the nineteenth century's attention. Elements of that heritage have been preserved, sometimes with great style, as shown on these pages. At the top of the facing page are two well-restored relics of the last days of ocean-going sail. The older of the two is the "Star of India," launched under British registry as the "Euterpe" in 1863. The "Balclutha" was launched in 1886, one of the last of the fleet of grain ships that made San Francisco home port. Above, San Francisco's Maritime State Historic Park beautifully illustrates the city's maritime traditions.

The California Western Railroad (left) is one of the few working narrow-gauge roads remaining in the country; the "Skunk," its passenger line from Willits to Fort Bragg, is a favorite of tourists.

Outsiders do not think of Los Angeles in terms of the past —nor do most of the city's inhabitants. As one of them put it in the 1920s, "The future is yours, and the past?—there isn't any." Some of the past does remain, however; not quite so much as in San Francisco perhaps, or even Monterey, but it is there for those willing to search it out. A good place to begin would be the Bradbury Building at Third and Hill streets (left). Designed in 1893 by George H. Wyman, the building's exterior is unimposing, but to step inside is to find oneself in a sudden, light-washed world of carved woods and ornamental iron, an airy world whose panels and balconies and staircases seem to glow with muted fires. Few

*Grace and light: interior of the Bradbury Building, Los Angeles.*

*Time arrested: Mendocino City spreads along a bluff on the north coast.*

buildings of any kind have ever used light so well.

All the way up at the other end of the state is the Carson Mansion of Eureka (right), whose exterior seems to be its whole reason for being. Built in the 1880s by redwood tycoon William Carson, this eighteen-room crenelated wonder is the most photographed Victorian home in the state.

In different ways the Carson Mansion and the Bradbury Building speak for the architecture of another age; one hundred miles to the south of Eureka lies an entire town that does the same—Mendocino City (below), a former lumber port whose string-along charm has survived the worst the twentieth century could offer.

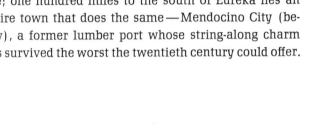

*Carpenter's Gothic defined: The Carson Mansion of Eureka.*

# CHAPTER 22

# THE DANCE OF GROWTH

*In which California explodes like an expanding star, speeding*

*toward the future at a pace unmatched in history*

IN *The Inland Whale,* a collection of California Indian tales, Theodora Kroeber tells the story of the "dance madness" of the Wintu, a tribelet that once inhabited the middle valleys of the Cascade Range. One spring a very long time ago, the tale goes, the people gathered to feast and sing in celebration of the coming-of-age of one of the tribe's most beautiful daughters, Nomtaimet. "Holding hands and singing," she writes, "they formed a moving circle around Nomtaimet, dancing the old circle dance which had been the coming of age dance for girls since the beginning of time.

"Hearing the singing and the familiar rhythm of the shuffling side step of the dance, the old men and women came from their fires and their houses, and the children who were big enough to dance came with them, all of them joining the moving circle which grew bigger and bigger. . . . For ten days and ten nights they ate and sang and danced. At last the feasting was over. The tenth night of singing and dancing came and went. But the pale dawn of the eleventh day found all those people still dancing, all of them. They went dance mad."

Breaking the circle into a long line, the people danced east over the mountains, crossing the Trinity River, the Hayfork, and the McCloud before coming to the Pit, where they turned south, following it to its confluence with the Sacramento. Down to the foot of the valley they danced that summer, "through the marshes and swamps and among the water birds until there came to them the smell of salt on the air. Leaving the marshes behind, they danced down the Sacramento where it broadens at its mouth. And they stood and watched it empty into the sea.

"Wearied at last of watching, they danced again, this time on the lower rim of the earth where the river meets the sea. Keeping to the rim, they turned their backs to the river, dancing away . . . toward the north. The time of the dead leaves was past. The fog moon came and went, and it was already the time of the mud moon and of frosts. They saw all about them storms and rain and floods, but there on the lower rim of the earth there were no storms, and they continued to dance along its sometimes rocky, sometimes sandy shore.

"The season of storms and cold . . . came and went, blown away by the big winds of the awakening earth. And now the dancers turned inland, away from the sea, dancing and half blown toward home. They reached Swift Creek as the new clover was making a green mat over the earth, just as it had done . . . at the beginning of the dance journey. The dancers were home, and the dance madness was no longer on them. It had lasted through all the moons and seasons and had carried them all around the world."

Caught in the grip of the dance madness that is common to the folklore of most of the world's people, those legendary Wintu had encircled their universe, defining the bounds of their known world. For more than twenty-five years after World War II, Californians were caught up in another kind of dance. Like the dance of the Wintu, it was compulsive, impulsive, and irresistible; unlike the dance of the Wintu, it lacked even the direc-

*This is not Manhattan, nor even Chicago; it is San Francisco, California,* *looking south to the nearly complete Transamerica pyramid.*

*449*

tion of instinct that had led the people in their great earth-turning circle toward home. It was the dance of growth, and it was without known destination; yet its erratic, complex, and frequently exciting course was painstakingly charted by the rest of the country. The fascination with which America had always regarded the antics of her thirty-first star became obsession, for it was said, and believed, that California was the future. "So leap with joy, be blithe and gay, / Or weep my friends with sorrow," versifier Richard Armour once wrote; "What California is today, / The rest will be tomorrow." He was joking—but only just.

THE DANCE OF GROWTH: In 1940 the population of California was 6,907,387; in 1950 it was 10,586,223. In 1960 the population was 15,717,204; in 1970, it was 19,953,134. More than thirteen million people had been added to the state in thirty years; more than four million people every decade, four hundred thousand every year, 33,000 every month, 8,250 every week, 1,178 every day, 49 every hour. The game of statistics, like all games, has a threshold of absurdity; yet these population figures are a solid, sober, inescapable reality, one with which no other state in the country or region in the world has ever had to deal.

It is not to be supposed that Californians, released from the tensions and obstacles of war, suddenly fell to begetting like warm rabbits. As in the past, the bulk of the state's swelling population came, not from natural increase, but from immigration—although for a short period after the war it seemed that the tide of immigration was going to reverse itself. On the day following Japanese surrender, the Arizona border station at Yuma counted 417 automobiles rattling east on their way back to Oklahoma, Arkansas, Texas, Kansas, and other parts of the South- and Midwest. The stream continued the next day, and the next, and through most of August 1945. The *Los Angeles Times* was delighted: "The 'Grapes of Wrath' Folks have reversed their field with the sudden advent of peace and there is now an ever-growing exodus from Southern California." But the Folks were not leaving for good; with pockets full of wartime pay, they were simply taking advantage of the end of the war to make long-overdue visits to their families. By the end of the year, they were coming back

—and bringing friends and relatives with them. In August 1946, one year after the "exodus" began, the border station at Yuma reported that no less than 130,000 people had *entered* the state that month, some of them returnees, but thousands of them brand-new residents.

Many of the new immigrants were former servicemen. It has been estimated that as many as seven hundred thousand soldiers, sailors, marines, and airmen had some contact with California every year during the war—either passing through the state to and from the Pacific theater, being "laid over" during periods of shore leave, or being stationed at one or another of the state's bases and camps. Thousands of these hundreds of thousands liked what they saw, and after the war they returned with their families. They also told their friends and relatives of what they had seen, and thousands of these, in turn, packed up to come west.

Old patterns were given new life by this postwar surge, and the process continued, particularly in the decade of the 1950s. By 1960 there were 2,300,000 people living in California who had *not* been in California five years earlier. Of the population increase of more than five million in this decade, immigration accounted for 61 percent; and while a few points were shaved off this percentage in the decade of the 1960s, immigration continued to dominate the state's population growth.

Whatever their origins, the majority of these immigrants became city dwellers once they settled in California, and of this majority the greater percentage gravitated toward Southern California, drawn by climate, space, jobs, glamour, and several decades of propaganda. The population of the seven southern counties (Santa Barbara, Ventura, Los Angeles, San Bernardino, Riverside, Orange, and San Diego) rose from a little over three-and-one-half million in 1940 to a little over five-and-one-half million in 1950, from almost nine million in 1960 to more than eleven million by 1970. In the process was created the phenomenon called "urban sprawl," as the metropolitan centers of Southern California, like so many amoebas, gradually coalesced to become one vast megalopolitan ooze, spreading from the northern reaches of the San Fernando Valley to the former citrus groves of Orange County, and from Long Beach to San Bernardino. On a much reduced scale, a similar metropolitan expansion

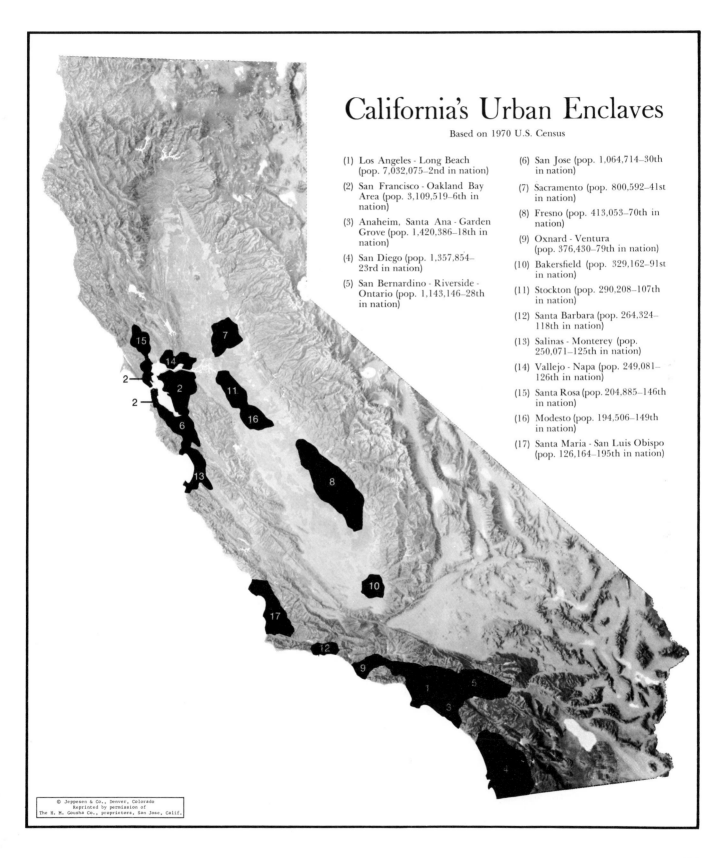

# California's Urban Enclaves

Based on 1970 U.S. Census

(1) Los Angeles - Long Beach (pop. 7,032,075–2nd in nation)

(2) San Francisco - Oakland Bay Area (pop. 3,109,519–6th in nation)

(3) Anaheim, Santa Ana - Garden Grove (pop. 1,420,386–18th in nation)

(4) San Diego (pop. 1,357,854–23rd in nation)

(5) San Bernardino - Riverside - Ontario (pop. 1,143,146–28th in nation)

(6) San Jose (pop. 1,064,714–30th in nation)

(7) Sacramento (pop. 800,592–41st in nation)

(8) Fresno (pop. 413,053–70th in nation)

(9) Oxnard - Ventura (pop. 376,430–79th in nation)

(10) Bakersfield (pop. 329,162–91st in nation)

(11) Stockton (pop. 290,208–107th in nation)

(12) Santa Barbara (pop. 264,324–118th in nation)

(13) Salinas - Monterey (pop. 250,071–125th in nation)

(14) Vallejo - Napa (pop. 249,081–126th in nation)

(15) Santa Rosa (pop. 204,885–146th in nation)

(16) Modesto (pop. 194,506–149th in nation)

(17) Santa Maria - San Luis Obispo (pop. 126,164–195th in nation)

spread through the valleys and the plains of the San Francisco Bay Area—filling up major chunks of San Mateo, Santa Clara, Alameda, Contra Costa, and Marin counties, as well as such other municipal regions as Fresno, Sacramento, Stockton-Modesto, and Bakersfield. In 1970, with 90.9 percent of her population officially classified as metropolitan, California was not only the urban state she had always been, she was the most urban state in the nation (as well as the most populous).

For the most part, this urbanized growth was accomplished with as much controlled direction as a rockslide. For the first few years after the war, in fact, it was almost as if the state's older settlers (those who had arrived before or even during the war) simply resisted the very idea of planning, as Carey McWilliams wrote in 1949: "Californians, of course, are fascinated by facts and figures showing the state's phenomenal growth and yet, on another side of their minds, they are disturbed and even repelled by these same figures. . . . They like the idea of growth and expansion, but withdraw from the practical implications. . . . This astonishing ambivalence, so amusing to watch, consistently undercuts any attempt to plan for the well-being of Californians, present and future. . . . Formerly Californians believed in attracting migrants; but the initiative has long since passed to the migrants. It is the migrants who are planning to come to California; not California that is planning to receive them."

With or without planning, they came, and having come, they bought houses, any kind of houses they could find. The variety of choices was not large, for the decade of the 1950s saw the first major boom of what poet Malvina Reynolds called "ticky-tacky." As neat and as identical as pins in a paper, hundreds of thousands of pastel-colored boxes were built in enormous, sterile, and thoroughly unimaginative housing tracts that spread across the land like treeless islands of gypsum, concrete, and asphalt. Constructed at, and sometimes considerably below, the minimum building standards, these developments could claim at least that they were there when they were needed.

The speed and machine-like efficiency of construction were startling. On a 3,375-acre tract called Lakewood Park near Los Angeles, for example, a developer laid out a potential community of 17,000 homes for a population of 70,000. Within a few weeks, street-paving crews had installed 133 miles of roads. Specialized machinery could scoop out a foundation trench in fifteen minutes. Precut lumber was stacked on building sites, and in a matter of hours building crews could erect the frame of a one-, two-, or even three-story house, complete with standardized wiring and plumbing. Within days, these same crews could have the place roofed, walled, windowed, doored, painted, and ready for occupancy. To eliminate bottlenecks, expediters with walkie-talkies cruised from house to house, ordering men and materials as they seemed necessary. As many as a hundred houses a day were started, and in two years ten thousand were completed and sold. It was not difficult to buy. With financing through the Federal Housing Authority and the Veterans Administration, a man could purchase his own $7,000 quarter-acre of Eden quite often for nothing down and at monthly payments that made any kind of rent seem like extortion.

Growth simply outstripped not only available conveniences but the most basic of municipal services. For instance, in the San Fernando Valley—whose population had bloated from 170,000 in 1940 to more than 850,000 in 1950—the shortage of schools kept 38,000 schoolchildren on half-day sessions until the middle of the 1950s. Sewer systems were so woefully inadequate that many developers were forced to install cesspools, and in at least one development, where the earth was too friable for the safe use of cesspools, sewage actually ran down the gutters of the streets until lines were finally installed. The Southern California subsidiary of the Bell Telephone System found itself more than a year behind in fulfilling orders for telephones. Roads not maintained by the developers themselves crumbled and rutted with neglect and the weight of many times more traffic than they had been designed to carry. Because water mains could not be built fast enough, shortages occurred in various areas; conversely, drains were so inadequate even as late as 1958 that winter floods closed two-thirds of the valley's schools.

Although the San Fernando Valley was the most dramatic illustration of growth without planning, in many other areas as well it would be nearly two decades before

*Making do on a grand scale: the model of a planned trailer community in Arcadia, 1949.*

*Home, sweet Sphinx, 1947. Amusing, yes—but the chances are this strange abode found a quick renter.*

such basic problems as schools and sewers would be solved to anyone's satisfaction. However, by the early 1960s the sporelike proliferation of the purely functional housing tracts had begun to slow. The land was being used up; and as it was used up, its value rose, making it more and more difficult for developers to buy up large sweeps of former farmland, lay out the serried rows of cheapjack houses, and sell them off at prices designed for a quick turnover. Moreover, people wanted, and many could now afford, more than the simple basics of four walls, a roof, a front lawn, and a backyard; they wanted *homes,* and they wanted them in an environment that was redolent of more than concrete and asphalt. Quite often they wanted trees; sometimes they even wanted hills.

Developers began to build communities, not housing tracts. Instead of shaving hills into flatland, they built on and around them; instead of cutting down every tree in sight, they started leaving them alone, frequently making them a part of the purchasable environment. One of the most successful of the community developments in the San Ramon Valley southeast of San Francisco, for example, featured not one but *two* oak trees for every lot, the fitting accompaniment to your basic, three-bedroom, two-bath, $40,000 home. More than convenience, ease of purchase, or the simple necessity of having a roof over one's head, developers began selling a way of life. Consider a sales pamphlet for Foster City, a planned community on filled land in San Francisco Bay: "In the age of many miracles wouldn't it be infinitely better to dream-build a new city than to redesign and over-extend an old one? . . . Can a dream like this become a reality? Yes, indeed! At this very moment the dream of a perfect city is being translated into steel and wood, concrete and glass. This is Foster City, a daring concept of an all-inclusive, self-supporting urban community. This is Foster City where a man may build his castle and raise his family in the finest of all possible worlds! . . . Foster City—a need fulfilled, a dream come true. . . ."

Like signposts to a brave new world, amenity-conscious developments like Foster City sprouted in elegant contrast to the gimcrackery of the 1950s, among them Valencia, Lake Forest, Westlake, and the most ambitious of them all, Irvine, the municipal adjunct to the University of California's Irvine campus on the south coast near Newport Beach; originally designed to accommodate a population of 100,000, Irvine was soon revised upward, some estimates calculating that it could handle as many as 500,000 people, although it would be decades before anyone would know for certain.

Varying in size, design, and geographic location, these new communities had one thing in common: the perpetuation of what had become known, quite self-consciously, as "California living." As a life-style, California living was affluent, consumptive, credit-oriented, extremely mobile, and leisurely self-indulgent in a kind of minor-league sybaritism. Above all, it was a life-style wedded to the out-of-doors—not to the wilderness or the woods particularly (although it included a great fondness for local, state, and national parklands), but to the *immediate* out-of-doors, that portion encountered by literally stepping out the back door on a balmy week-

*If there was a need in Los Angeles, there was always someone willing to meet it.*
*In 1946 one promoter converted abandoned streetcars into houses — and sold them.*

end afternoon. It had to do with covered patios and swimming pools, redwood furniture and grape-stake fences, sweet-smelling, freshly cut Sunday morning lawns and neatly clipped shrubbery, banks of brilliant, unlikely flowers and plants. Its finest moment might be said to be illustrated by the picture of a man standing on his patio on a Saturday evening, a drink of good Scotch in one hand and a spatula in the other, barbecuing a few two-dollar steaks while his wife prepares a cool green California salad, his children cavort on the lawn with the dog, and the patio lights dance on the chlorine blue surface of his kidney-shaped swimming pool. All the sharp edges of life are softened, and the stresses of twentieth-century living seem eons removed.

Too perfect an image, one supposes, and even if completely true, one not invulnerable to charges of shallow materialism. Was it for this, social critics could and frequently did ask, that man endured the long centuries of his pilgrimage? Yet here was a way of life that in its purest physical comforts surpassed anything man had ever before enjoyed, and for millions of Californians, who were no more given to dark, cosmic broodings than any other people, it was enough.*

---

*If this lifeway could be likened to a religion of sorts, then its bible was a thick, slick monthly called *Sunset: The Magazine of Western Living*. Filled from cover to cover with articles on food, fashions, gardening, home improvements, and travel—and a mass of advertising to support these and similar offshoots of California living—*Sunset* was a kind of "how-to" magazine that both reflected and defined a way of life. Moreover, even as *Playboy* proselytized for *its* philosophy, *Sunset* broadcast the delights of California living with enormous zeal and measurable success: with a circulation that approached one million and an assumed readership that approached five, it was one of the country's mass-circulation magazines, the only regional magazine to achieve such status.

*Doubtless posed for effect, this photograph documented the wretched
living conditions of much of the San Fernando Valley in the 1940s.*

T HE DANCE OF GROWTH: Between 1940 and 1970, California became the most advanced civilization-upon-wheels in the history of the world. In no other state of the Union was America's long-standing love affair with the automobile so torrid a passion, and in no other part of the state was that passion so reckless and all-consuming as in Southern California. By 1970, Californians possessed 11,900,896 registered automobiles, almost twice the number of any other state and more than one automobile for every two people. In Southern California, the ratio of people to cars was even greater: 1.3:1 —which, as Richard Lillard has written, "is getting close to the 1.0 ratio of a man to his epidermis." More than 80 percent of all Southern California households owned at least one automobile, and nearly nine hundred thousand households boasted two or more.

California living, in all its ramifications, had become unthinkable without the automobile. Without wheels a man would have been forced to choose his home at a reasonably short distance from his source of income; with them he could choose job opportunities scattered in a 360-degree circle over hundreds of square miles, his decision governed only by how far he cared to drive each day to and from work. Without wheels the elbow room

*Lest there be any uncertainty as to the meaning of the term "urban sprawl,"*
*the reader should peruse this aerial photograph of the Bay Area carefully.*

provided by California's horizontal urbanization would have been impossible; with them the region enjoyed one of the lowest urban density rates in the nation—5,638 per square mile in the Los Angeles–Long Beach region, for example, as compared to 23,321 in the New York–Northeastern New Jersey region. Without wheels a family's recreational opportunities would have been limited to areas accessible by walking or public transportation; with them a family could go anywhere it had time to go—and families did, traveling an estimated twenty-four *billion* miles every year in one-day recreational excursions, not including the billions of additional miles driven on weekend jaunts and annual vacations.

The automobile spawned a new economic and social culture. Three-fifths of the downtown sections of every major California city were given over to the asphalt of parking lots. Outside the central cities, a new urban form called the shopping center—90 percent parking lot and 10 percent shops—became manifest. Service stations sprouted like neon mushrooms on the four corners of thousands of major intersections all over the state. Drive-in movies, drive-in banks, drive-in laundries, drive-in restaurants, and at least one drive-in church (the Valley Community Church of Los Angeles, appropriately non-denominational) reflected an almost absolute dependence upon the automobile. "In California," Neil Morgan wrote in *The California Syndrome*, "the automobile assumes tribal significance. . . . When traffic slows toward the stop-and-go commuter rush hours, the student can be seen grasping his slide rule or turning to an anatomy chart. Businessmen are dictating into tape recorders. Others are plugged into tutor tapes, learning languages. Women are applying lipstick, brushing their hair, hooking their dresses. The automobile serves as office, bedroom and signboard. . . . Since there is now relatively little rapid mass transit in California cities, every man's car is his mobile castle."

Even though they were less personally involved with them, Californians were equally dependent upon trucks, for these vehicles handled the delivery of more than 90 percent of all goods—including automobiles—circulated in the state. California's 1970 truck population of 1,894,444 amounted to more than 10 percent of all trucks in the United States, and her annual trucking payroll of nearly eight billion dollars was more than

twice that of any other state and one of the largest single-industry payrolls in California.

These millions of automobiles and trucks sped over 162,223 miles of road—one mile of road for every square mile in the state—more than three thousand miles of which comprised the most ambitious freeway network in the country, a monument to the work of California's monolithic State Division of Highways. Those three thousand miles were only the beginning. With financing from a gasoline tax of seven cents a gallon (which went directly to the highway division without review by the state legislature) and additional funds from the federal government (90 percent of cost in the case of interstate freeways, 50 percent for all others), the division in 1957 committed itself to the construction of a total of 12,500 miles of freeways by 1980.* Every major metropolitan area in the state, from Sacramento to San Diego, was serviced by one or more freeways, and each of these regions was linked to all the others in a web of concrete. It was theoretically possible to drive in a great semicircle nine hundred miles from Truckee on the Nevada border near Lake Tahoe through Sacramento, the Bay Area, San Jose, Bakersfield, Los Angeles, and San Diego to Yuma, on the Arizona border—all of it without making a single stop for anything but gasoline, food, or purposes of personal hygiene.

In Southern California freeways covered the land like latticework crust on a pie: the Ventura Freeway, the Hollywood Freeway, the Golden State Freeway, the Harbor Freeway, the Santa Ana Freeway, the San Bernardino Freeway, the Santa Monica Freeway, the San Diego Freeway. . . . Enough freeway concrete had been poured in Southern California to pave the state of Rhode Island. Rhode Island would have objected; Southern California loved it. Each day, any given point would see scores of thousands of automobiles pass by, and at Los Angeles' famous four-level Civic Center Interchange (called the "Mixmaster" by local citizens), as many as five hundred thousand cars shuttled from one freeway to another in a bewildering and fascinating dis-

*Since California consumed more than nine billion gallons of fuel every year, the gas tax fund amounted to no small piece of change. In 1970 a bond issue designed to siphon off a portion of this money for development of rapid transit systems was defeated by the voters—much to the relief of the Division of Highways.

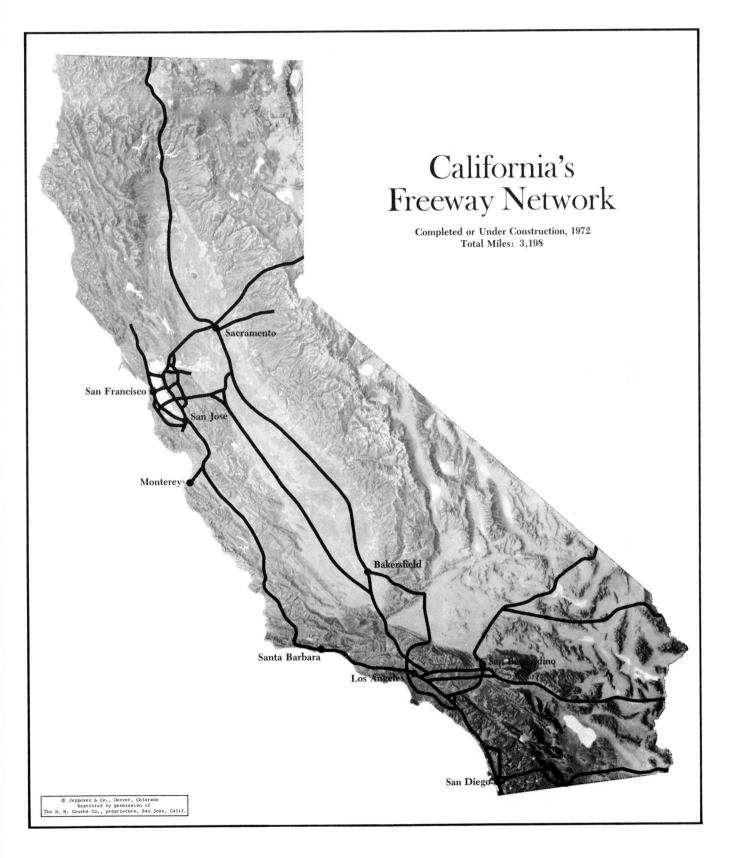

## California's Freeway Network

**Completed or Under Construction, 1972**
**Total Miles: 3,198**

Sacramento

San Francisco

San Jose

Monterey

Bakersfield

Santa Barbara

Los Angeles

San Bernardino

San Diego

*Looking like pieces in some outlandish game of giant chess, concrete studs await the roadbed of another freeway.*

play of transportation roulette. And even though maintenance, fuel, and insurance costs ate away as much as 7 percent of his income, even though one accident during commuting hours could tie up traffic for miles and hours, even though a foggy day could produce domino-like rear-end collisions involving scores of cars, and even though more than 4,000 people were killed and another 12,000 to 15,000 permanently maimed every year, the average Southern Californian refused to relinquish either his automobile or the freeway on which he sometimes drove it at the pace of a garden slug. Like a coffee-table copy of *Sunset* or the portable barbecue in his backyard, the freeway was something he recognized and accepted as an inseparable part of California living. With a demented, yet almost admirable stubbornness, he consistently ignored the persuasions of city planners

and traffic engineers that the only workable solution to the worsening congestion was the development of a mass-transit system to augment the freeways; only once in Los Angeles County, for example, did the question of mass transit ever get as far as a bond issue, which was soundly defeated. Angelenos did not want mass transit; they wanted more freeways.

The freeway fever was less virulent in the north. For one example, the citizens of San Francisco in 1967 refused to accept $180,000,000 of federal money for the construction of a "cross-town" freeway that would have carved up a part of Golden Gate Park, and resisted all

*Like scuttling ants, automobiles attack downtown Los Angeles. Count the parking lots.*

*A BART train on its maiden run from Oakland to Fremont, 1972.*

THE DANCE OF GROWTH: California's economic development in the postwar year matched her population growth statistic for statistic, a litany of progress that was marked most dramatically by the continuing exploitation of a traditional resource, together with the startling development of one more boom in the state's long history of economic booms.

The traditional resource was agriculture. As noted in chapter 20, by 1940 California's agricultural production outranked that of any other state; during and after the war, the trend not only continued but accelerated. By 1945 agricultural output topped two-and-one-half billion dollars a year. By 1950 it reached nearly three billion. By 1960 it approached four billion. And by 1970 it was on its way toward five billion—to be precise, California's agricultural product in that year was $4,588,025,000, more than four hundred million dollars above that of its nearest rival, Iowa.

The traditional drift toward bigness kept pace with the industry's economic gains. By a combination of urban sprawl and industrial consolidation, the total number of farms (including ranches and dairy farms) in California was inexorably reduced from year to year, while the average size of the individual farm grew larger. In 1940, 133,000 farms averaged 230 acres in size; in 1960, 99,000 farms averaged 372 acres; in 1970, 56,000 farms averaged 654 acres—and of this last number, more than ten thousand were classified as "noncommercial" farms (i.e., part-time operations earning less than $2,500 a year). The larger the farm, the more likely it was to be part of a corporate entity, and by 1970 some forty-five individual companies controlled more than 60 percent of the state's twelve million acres of cultivated land. With bigness came more of the industrialization and mechanization that had characterized agriculture for more than a century. Airplanes broadcast seed and sprayed pesticides. Automatic tree-shakers agitated fruit trees, spilling the harvest onto great canvas nets. Hydraulic lifts thrust pickers to the topmost branches of fruit trees too delicate to be shaken. Throughout the state huge, ungainly monsters crept up and down the geometric rows of one product or another, cutting, chopping, plucking, sorting, and packing.

Even with mechanization, the industry's need for its migrant labor force continued. In 1942 it prevailed upon the federal government to meet the wartime labor

efforts on the part of the Division of Highways to extend the Embarcadero Freeway all the way to the Golden Gate Bridge. For another, in 1962 the San Francisco Bay Area counties of Contra Costa, Alameda, and San Francisco approved the creation of a Bay Area Rapid Transit (BART) District, and construction on an extensive rail network to link the cities of the three counties began in 1965. In 1972 the first section—between Fremont, near San Jose, and Oakland—began daily service, and the entire system was scheduled for completion by the fall of 1973. BART was the first major rapid transit system in California since the demise of Henry E. Huntington's "Big Red Cars," and many believed—many hoped—that it would prove the ultimate solution to the accelerating conflict between cities and automobiles.

shortage by importing large numbers of Mexican workers. By contract with the Mexican government, the Department of Agriculture took on the responsibility of recruiting, transporting, housing, and feeding thousands of seasonal Mexican laborers—*braceros* ("the strong-armed ones"), as they came to be called. After the war, the bracero program continued as a year-to-year arrangement until 1951, when Public Law 78 broadened and formalized it—much to the delight of California's growers (as well as those in other parts of the West) who saw the program as the ultimate answer to their ancient quest: a cheap, convenient, and disposable labor force the responsibility for which rested entirely in the hands of the federal government (the Department of Labor after 1948). In the peak year of 1957, California utilized nearly 200,000 braceros, and for most normal years, 100,000 or more—comprising one-fourth of the total migrant labor force—were at work in the state's fields. It was not until 1963 that Congress finally balked at continuing to subsidize the labor needs of the agri-industrialists; ignoring the industry's dread predictions of economic collapse, Congress refused to extend the program beyond 1964. Collapse did not ensue.*

Agriculture remained secure in its traditions of gigantism, but in the 1950s and 1960s it was challenged, then surpassed as the central fact in California's economic life by a development light-years removed from such earthy concerns: the technological explosion in the aircraft, weapons systems, nuclear, aerospace, and electronics industries—industries pursued, as usual, on a scale unmatched by any other state in the nation.

California had enjoyed a respectable background in both pure and applied science even before World War II. On its purest level, that background had been established in part by the creation of three of the most renowned astronomical centers in the country: the Lick Observatory atop Mount Hamilton, the Mount Wilson

---

*What *did* ensue was the first clear opportunity for the unionization of farm labor. As will be seen in chapter 23, for California's postwar agri-business it was more of the same—with a difference whose name was Cesar Chavez.

*Tomorrow the stars: in the 1960s, California threw herself wholeheartedly into the lucrative space race.*

Observatory, and the Mount Palomar Observatory. On the more practical level, it had been furthered by the development of scores of advances in the fields of mechanical and structural engineering and, most especially, the horticultural sciences. At the University of California at Berkeley, Stanford University, and the California Institute of Technology, scientific communities comparable to any in the country had been established.

Even the more esoteric forms of applied science found expression at an early date in California. In the 1930s, Ernest O. Lawrence had built the world's first cyclotron, on the University of California campus at Berkeley. Experiments at the cyclotron, in turn, led to the production of plutonium in 1941, and plutonium made possible the first nuclear fission bomb in history, constructed and tested at Los Alamos Scientific Laboratory in New Mexico under the aegis of the Berkeley Radiation Laboratory (moved to a new location at Livermore, it later became the Lawrence Radiation Laboratory.)* Similarly, at Caltech in the 1930s, Theodore von Karman promoted research into both aerodynamics and rocket propulsion, which led to the creation of the Jet-Propulsion Laboratory in 1942, and, as a spinoff the Aerojet-General Corporation, the first private rocket-building firm in the nation.

The stimulus of war simply broadened California's scientific base, as it broadened her manufacturing capability, and by 1945 the state was in an excellent position to take full advantage of government largesse: it had climate, space, established factories, a scientific establishment, and a large body of skilled labor. The largesse was not long in coming, spurred on by the exigencies of the Cold War—or what Winston Churchill called "the peace of mutual terror." Billions of dollars every year began to be filtered through the Department of Defense for the development and construction of nuclear-armed Intercontinental Ballistic Missiles (ICBMs), air-to-ground and ground-to-air missiles, armed rockets for ground forces, new aircraft like the B-58 tactical bomber and the F-104 fighter bomber, and new varieties of nonnuclear bombs, together with all the electronic gadg-

---

*On a more positive note, the Lawrence Radiation Laboratory also designed the two-mile-long Stanford Linear Accelerator in the late 1960s, which unit serves as a testing station for pure and applied research in many fields, including medicine.

*Ernest O. Lawrence, whose laboratory harbored the seeds of an astonishing new world.*

etry necessary to make them swoop, whirr, click, buzz, roar, and explode.

By 1960 the Defense Department was dispensing more than twenty-five billion dollars a year for the research and development of such devices, and out of this total California received 40.1 percent of all research contracts and 23.7 percent of all production contracts—amounting to more than five billion dollars every year. University science departments swelled magnificently with new research programs, and old California companies like Lockheed, Douglas, Northrup, Convair, Hughes, and Ryan Aeronautical expanded their existing factories and built subsidiaries, while new companies like Rocketdyne, the Aerospace Corporation, and Litton Industries blossomed in the compost of federal money. Scores of smaller companies flourished on a diet of subcontracts from the larger corporations, and a non-profit "think tank" calling itself the RAND Corporation waxed fat while considering such rarefied matters as the tactics of nuclear warfare.

After 1957, the year of the Russian Sputnik satellite, the United States entered the so-called "space race" in earnest, and the newly created National Aeronautics & Space Administration funneled its own billions into the California economy in the development of its various satellite and space-exploration projects, including the Mercury, Gemini, and Apollo manned flights that culminated in Neil Armstrong's first moon-step in July 1969. Less nobly, perhaps, but no less significantly, the country's increasing involvement in the Vietnam War in the latter half of the 1960s also fattened California's technological pockets.

By 1970 more than one hundred billion dollars had been paid out to the state's defense and aerospace industries, which supported a total employment force of nearly six hundred thousand people—more than one-third of California's total manufacturing labor force. A new technocratic society had been established on the western edge of the continent. "Think of the astonishing constellation of talent," British novelist and scientist C. P. Snow wrote, "particularly in the physical sciences, all down the California coast, from Berkeley and Stanford to Pasadena and Los Angeles. There is nothing like that concentration of talent anywhere in the world."

As the decade of the 1970s opened, bringing with it a slowdown in the Vietnam War and major cutbacks in the national space program, thousands of engineers and scientists suddenly found themselves out of work, the luckier ones taking jobs in service stations and supermarkets to make ends approximately meet. Yet there was a world to be remade, and it was difficult to believe that California's "constellation of talent" would not soon be applying its energies to that task. "Our business is the management and processing of innovation," one aerospace executive said in the middle 1960s. "It is the committing of human, fiscal, and physical resources to complicated undertakings—the doing of difficult things for substantial rewards at considerable risk." And that, after all, was what Californians had been doing for more than a century.

T HE DANCE OF GROWTH: like an echo that would not die, the demand for water—more water—punctuated California's postwar years. As early as 1945, Southern California's astounding wartime population boom

*The Dos Amigos Pumping Plant of the State Water Project, south of Tracy.*

had given rise to concern over how long the Colorado River could continue to supply the region's water needs, and in that year a State Water Resources Board had been created to investigate present and future water demands. After issuing bulletins on the subject in 1951 and 1955, the board was supplanted by the Department of Water Resources in July 1956. Consulting its population projection charts, which determined that Southern California would contain twenty-eight million people by the year 2020, and giving ear to the desires of agri-industrialists in the San Joaquin Valley, who earnestly yearned for an alternative to Central Valley Project water (see chapter 19), the new department decided that California should enter the water business on a gargantuan scale.

The Department of Water Resources articulated its conclusions in the "California Water Plan" of 1957, a most remarkable document that not only examined the present and future status of the Central Valley Project, but related it to an enterprise of its own making: the

California Water Project, a plan that sought to meet the flood-control needs of northern California, the future urban needs of the area south of San Francisco Bay, the irrigation needs of the Central Valley not satisfied by the Central Valley Project, the future urban needs of the central coastal region, and most cosmic of all, the future urban needs of Southern California. The project's essential components included a large storage, flood-control, and power-producing dam on the Feather River in the vicinity of Oroville, which would regulate the delivery of water into the Sacramento River and ultimately to the "pool" of the Sacramento–San Joaquin Delta. Aqueducts would deliver water north of the delta, to a terminus in Marin County, and south of the delta, to a terminus in Santa Clara County, and a major aqueduct would take water south along the west side of the San Joaquin Valley. Near the border between Kings and Kern counties, a branch would deliver water to the central coastal region; after crossing the Tehachapi Range, the main aqueduct would branch again, a western section carrying water to a terminus south of the San Fernando Valley and an eastern section transporting it across the Antelope and Mojave plateaus, through the San Bernardino Mountains, and finally to a terminus near the city of Riverside—a total distance of more than six hundred miles. From the eastern terminus, connections would ultimately be made to the Coachella Valley and the Colorado River Aqueduct systems. When completed, the project would deliver up to eight million acre-feet of water annually.

The estimated cost of the project would be $2,500,-000,000. The department proposed that this amount be raised by the issuance and sale of state bonds, which would then be repaid (including interest at 5 percent, the maximum allowed by state law) from monies received from water districts using project water and from the sale of electrical power. In 1959, at the department's urging, the state legislature passed the California Water Resources Development Bond Act—more simply known as the Burns-Porter Act—which authorized the issuance of $1,750,000,000 in general-obligation bonds (not enough to complete the project, but all that the legislature determined it could reasonably allocate at the time and more than enough to begin it); it gave the project official articulation and placed the proposition on the ballot for the general election in November 1960.

Unsurprisingly—just because the bill dealt with water—the Burns-Porter proposition received warm opposition, most of it from the northern section of the state (the Feather River was *its* river) and much of it expressed by the *San Francisco Chronicle*, which described it as a "hoax," a "desperate plunge into the unknown," and "a blank check to irresponsibility, a compound of unfulfillable promises." Most irritating to the *Chronicle* and other opponents were the considerations that the funds authorized were not going to be enough to finish the project (where was the rest of the money to come from?), that 5 percent bonds were non-competitive with those from most other states (and therefore might never be sold), and that both the presumed need and the projected sale of water were based on population figures cast sixty years into the nearly unimaginable future (what if the department was wrong—how then would the project pay for itself?).

Such arguments were impressive, but not impressive enough to reverse the traditional response to California's water needs: on November 8, the voters approved the bond issue by a vote of 3,008,328 to 2,814,384. Construction on Oroville Dam—at 770 feet the tallest in the nation—began in July 1962 and was "topped out" in 1967; by July 1969 its reservoir was filled to the capacity of 3,537,577 acre-feet. By the end of 1970, most of the main elements of the project were complete or well on their way to completion, including most of the California Aqueduct, the massive A. D. Edmonston Pumping Plant to lift water over the Tehachapi Range, parts of the South Bay and Central Coast branches of the aqueduct, and most of some twenty miles of tunnels.

The Department of Water Resources called the 1960s its "action decade," but not all of the action had been good. Among other obstacles, more than $650,000,000 worth of the 5 percent bonds *did* remain unsold by 1969, a problem solved only by another election in June 1970 that authorized raising the interest rate to a competitive 7 percent. Still there was not enough money, and the department was forced to dip into the California Water Fund, a $200,000,000 reserve created by transferring monies received from Long Beach oil revenues from the state Investment Fund. Yet another fiduciary bandage was applied from the state's General Fund, but it was a tight squeeze in spite of such improvisations. Moreover, the end of the decade saw a concerted

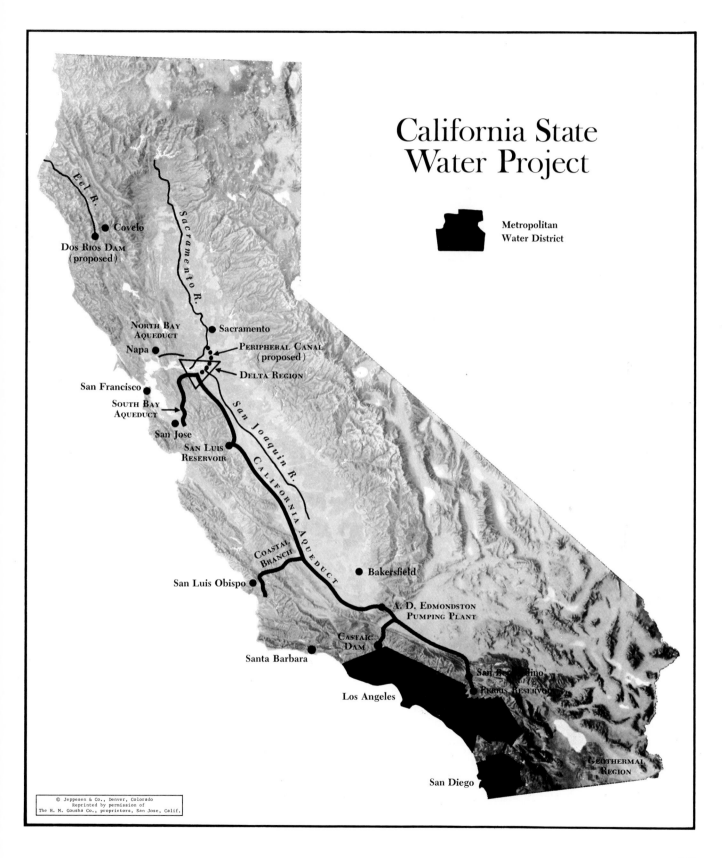

# California State Water Project

Metropolitan
Water District

© Jeppesen & Co., Denver, Colorado
Reprinted by permission of
The H. M. Gousha Co., proprietors, San Jose, Calif.

*The moderate's moderate: Governor Earl Warren tips his hat on V-J Day, 1945.*

*The conservative's moderate: Governor Goodwin J. Knight peers out from his official portrait.*

attack on the project from what DWR Director William R. Gianelli called "Chicken Little environmentalists" (see chapter 24).

Ignoring the "I told you so" jibes of the project's financial opponents and the surprisingly effective attack by conservationists, the department doggedly went on to finish the largest water-moving project in the history of the western world. Finally, in September 1971, Director Gianelli, Governor Ronald Reagan, other state officials, and hundreds of spectators gathered at the A. D. Edmonston Pumping Plant in the withering summer heat of the southern San Joaquin Valley to commemorate the first transfer of Northern California water across the mountains into Southern California. After a few appropriate remarks by a few appropriate officials, Governor Reagan solemnly raised a telephone to his lips. "Gentlemen," he said, "start the motors."

Nothing happened. He spoke again. Still, nothing happened. Finally, after a delay of several moments, the great pumps hummed, and in a matter of seconds the first trickle of water was sucked across the mountains into the southern section of the California Aqueduct. Had it not been said before—in 1913 by William Mulholland—Reagan might well have turned to someone on the podium from Southern California to remark: "There it is; take it."*

THE DANCE OF GROWTH: If politics is, indeed, the art of the possible, then nowhere was it more so than in postwar California—where *anything* seemed possible, even probable. Loose, amorphous, inconsistent, and unpredictable, California politics was an almost perfect reflection of the character and quality of the state's postwar life. Only two generalizations can be offered with security: first, in the sense in which the people of

*Simultaneously in San Francisco, conservationists held a press conference (a "wake," they called it) and with glasses of champagne toasted a "farewell to the sweet waters." Not too long thereafter—probably by coincidence—a portion of the Mojave Plateau section of the aqueduct ruptured, spilling thousands of gallons of water into the desert.

*The liberal's moderate: Governor Edmund G. Brown during his second gubernatorial campaign in 1962, flanked by Jesse ("Big Daddy") Unruh and President John F. Kennedy.*

any other state would have understood the term, "party politics" in California was almost meaningless; second, for most of the postwar years, politics and politicians embraced the growth ethic and all its works with the unquestioning fealty of acolytes in some obscure Eastern religion.

Party structure of the monolithic, controlled, and deep-rooted character that could be seen in such states as New York or Illinois simply did not exist in California. Outwardly, many of the same qualities were apparent; both the Democrats and the Republicans possessed the proper contingent of state, county, and municipal organizations that presumably directed the course of their actions, and each featured a large, if unofficial, "policy-making" body—the California Republican Assembly (CRA) and the California Democratic Council (CDC). Beneath this veneer of organization, however, lay a veritable stewpot of factionalism that ranged from almost unchartable degrees of right-wing opinion through moderate inclinations to left-wing radicalism. California's political parties, in the view of

Democratic Party leader Jesse Unruh, were less coherent bodies than expedient alliances of almost completely independent "duchies," each of which had its own acknowledged leader with his own set of principles, policies, and goals.

There were two main reasons for this curious state of affairs. The most obvious was the nature of California's voting population, 60 percent of which—like the population at large—had come to California from somewhere else. People with the gumption to sever all ties to the communities in which they had been born and raised and to seek a new life halfway across a continent, were not inclined to profess unthinking loyalty to any party or any party's representative, simply for the sake of loyalty. They comprised a shifting, drifting, ever-seeking population whose needs and wants changed not only from generation to generation, but often from year to year and even week to week. Their "party loyalty" was, at best, a nominal thing, and it frequently disintegrated at the polls. With this marginally dependable body of voters, California's political parties found

*The paradox of 1970: voters approved conservative Republican Reagan over liberal Democrat Unruh . . .*

*. . . while electing the liberal Democrat Tunney over the conservative Republican Murphy.*

it increasingly difficult to structure anything close to a solid base of power.

The second principal reason for the incoherency of California's party politics was a phenomenon called "cross-filing," which allowed a candidate to run on the ballots of *both* parties in primary elections without requiring him to state his political affiliation. Passed into law during the years of the Progressives (see chapter 14), cross-filing had been designed to sap the influence of political parties, thus reducing the possibility of one interest-group or another (such as, for instance, the Southern Pacific Railroad) gaining control of a party, and hence state politics. Unlike many reform measures passed by the Progressives (or anyone else), cross-filing accomplished its aims, but with side effects that proved more pernicious than its goal had been admirable.

For one thing, the procedure encouraged a candidate to cloak himself in respectable mediocrity, offend as few people as possible, and stay clear of exposing himself to any issue that might require a strong opinion; all he need wish for was to be warmly remembered at

the proper time, as Senator Alan Cranston has written: "Typically, a candidate, particularly an incumbent, campaigned without revealing his partisan identity. His literature usually described his political beliefs in safe generalities, extolled his professional abilities, listed his community affiliations, displayed his family (especially if attractive), and neatly avoided reference to his party. When the unsophisticated voter went to the polls at primary time, he assumed that all the candidates on his party ballot were members of his own party. He tended to vote for the most familiar name for each office, or the one on top of the list, or the one with the most impressive title. This benefited the incumbent." (Under California's Election Code, the incumbent's name was always placed at the top of the list for any given office.) Quite often, providing his party affiliation was sufficiently vague, his name sufficiently well known, or his general appeal sufficiently broad, a candidate managed to capture the nomination of *both* major parties in a primary election (in effect, winning the election before the election), particularly in the lower-echelon

*Democratic Senator Cranston, a moderate liberal,
defeated hardline conservative Max Rafferty in 1968.*

statewide offices. In 1942, however, running against the avowed Democrat and often-described "radical," Culbert Olson, Earl Warren, an appealingly moderate man, crossed over and captured the gubernatorial nomination of both parties—the only time cross-filing succeeded in eliminating one candidate for so high an office.

By the early 1950s, the inadequacies of the cross-filing procedure were becoming more and more apparent—particularly to Democrats, who maintained that the built-in advantage to incumbents was the major reason Republicans had enjoyed an almost uncontested reign over most of the state's higher offices for more than thirty years. Republicans, unsurprisingly, countered that their dominance was due to nothing more under-handed than their having served the best interests of the state's citizens, as Caspar W. Weinberger, former chairman of the Republican State Central Committee, stated in 1965: "The Republican administrations, which governed the state with only two short interruptions from the founding of the Party to 1958, were good for the people and for the state." Nevertheless, increas-

ing pressure for change inspired the state legislature to revise the procedure in 1952; while the revision still allowed a candidate to file with both parties in primary elections, it required that he identify his affiliation with the abbreviation "Rep." or "Dem." The revision was effective: in 1952, before it went into effect, 79 of the 100 contests for legislative seats were settled in the primary elections, but in 1954 only 33 candidates cross-filed successfully. Still, it was far from perfect, and when the Democrats finally gained control of the state legislature in 1958, cross-filing was abolished.*

Yet cross-filing, in combination with California's population mix, had done its work, shaping the character of the state's politics into patterns that were apparently destined to continue. "It seems clear," Caspar Weinberger wrote in 1965, "that both California's political parties lose when they nominate candidates on whom the label of 'extremist' can be successfully pinned. It does not matter whether the label is justified. The important fact is that California's voters will not support a candidate who, for valid reasons or otherwise, appears to them to be something other than a moderate, sensible, and generally safe person. Either party virtually guarantees defeat for itself if it nominates such a candidate." Thus, Governor Earl Warren, the moderate's moderate, easily won a second term in 1946, a third term in 1950, and might have gone on to a fourth term had he not been appointed to the United States Supreme Court (where he came to earn, ironically enough, the reputation of a radical, at least in some circles)—and his Republican successor, Lieutenant-Governor Goodwin J. Knight, successfully assumed the mantle of Warren's moderation in the election of 1954. Similarly, Democrat Edmund G. Brown billed himself as a middle-of-the-road man, labeled former Senator William F. Knowland an "extremist" for his advocacy of a right-to-work law, and managed to capture the governorship in 1958. Enough of that image remained for Brown to defeat Richard M. Nixon in 1962 (albeit

---

*Alan Cranston tells the story of one atypical but enterprising Republican congressman who made the best he could of the revised cross-filing law of 1952: "In a preliminary mailing to Democrats, he used the customary visual device of showing his name as it would appear on the ballot with a large X in the box beside it. He boldly included the "Rep." after his name, but with an asterisk. The footnote explained: 'Representative in Congress.'"

narrowly, for Nixon was then building the image of a moderate, experienced, and reasonable man that would ultimately carry him to the White House), but by 1966 Brown's opposition to the death penalty and his refusal to take hard action to suppress student riots (see chapter 23) were two of the major factors that enabled actor Ronald Reagan to win the governorship as a moderate conservative. Over the next four years, Reagan worked diligently to improve that image, and in 1970 defeated the gubernatorial bid of Assembly Speaker Jesse Unruh, who was accused of leftward inclinations.

And so it went. The key to the success of any candidate for a statewide office was the existence of approximately one million voters who were capable of swinging from one side to the other of any given issue or candidate. About all that could with any certainty be said of this "capricious million," as political analyst Gladwin Hill described them, was that they avoided radicals of whatever stripe. Beyond that, their voting patterns were unpredictable, frequently paradoxical, and sometimes inexplicable. In 1964, for example, the unfathomable million soundly rejected conservative Republican Barry Goldwater for president while supporting Democrat Lyndon B. Johnson—yet in the senatorial race defeated Democrat Pierre Salinger in favor of conservative Republican George Murphy. In 1968 they gave Republican Richard Nixon the edge that enabled him to carry the state over Democrat Hubert Humphrey in the presidential race—at the same time they were turning back conservative Republican Max Rafferty for senator while endorsing Democrat Alan Cranston. And in 1970 they defeated George Murphy in his bid for reelection, giving the senatorship to Democrat John Tunney—while reelecting Governor Ronald Reagan over Jesse Unruh.

Observers of the political scene in postwar California might have been tempted to echo the words of Lewis Carroll's *Alice in Wonderland:* "The only thing that makes sense is that nothing really makes any sense."

They might also have found wisdom in Alan Cranston's remarks: "What it adds up to, I think, is simply this: there is no longer a sure thing, Republican or Democrat, in California politics, from a statewide perspective. And this means that California politics, Republican and Democratic, is always challenging, ever uncertain, and never dull."

THIS, THEN, was the state of the art of life in California's most bumptious and progressive era: a civilization bursting with people, culturally confused, economically improvisational, immensely mobile, affluent, politically inconsistent, and almost directionless, although instinctively convinced that movement was, somehow, progress. To many it was still a kind of Eden. Listen to actress Julie Andrews on the delights of Los Angeles, for example: "The beauty of Los Angeles is what I would call 'pulse'—that wonderful steady beat of energy. You feel it in the early morning, when the sun is barely up, the air is cool and quiet, yet there is already a hint of excitement. Then you drive down into that busy life, and you can't help thinking—'It's going to be another wonderful day!' What more can anyone ask of a city?"

Many could ask a great deal more of the city—and the state. Many did. Some pointed to the affluence of the suburbs and then to the poverty of the cities and questioned whether a society that tolerated such inequities could survive. Others catalogued the ecological consequences of rampant technology—the pollution of air, water, and land, the sheer *ugliness* of many of man's works—and wondered aloud whether Enterprise and Progress were not agents of destruction. Still others took to the streets, as Americans had done before when dreams failed them, embracing blind violence to articulate frustration. And children challenged the faith of their fathers. . . .

Missteps in the thirty-year dance of growth.

*Sculptured fountain in the Ferry Building Plaza, San Francisco.*

# *California Mirror:*
# *Patterns of Culture*

*Culture relic: Presbyterian church, Mendocino, completed in 1867.*

"In the old days," Wallace Stegner once wrote, "in blizzardly weather, we used to tie a string of lariats from house to barn so as to make it from shelter to responsibility and back again. With personal, family, and cultural chores to do, I think we had better rig up such a line between past and present."

And future. The Presbyterian church shown above has been in almost continual use and under loving care since 1867. Its simple beauty speaks to us of pride, identity, and hope, and against that statement we can measure ourselves. That is one of its values, as it is the value of all art. Translated into steel beams and molded concrete, the same value reappears in San Francisco's St. Mary's Cathedral (right), constructed almost precisely one century after Mendocino's little church. And a century from now, it will more than likely be translated once again, thus completing the line from past to present to future.

*Culture relic: St. Mary's Cathedral, San Francisco, completed in 1971.*

Much is wrong with urban California, but one of the things right with it is that it has both the energy and the talent to build beautifully when it wants to—and it sometimes does. Fresno wanted to, and it created its splendid mall, a place for people rather than machines. Oakland wanted to, and it voted a $6 million bond issue to build a structure (right) that Arthur Drexler of the New York Museum of Modern Art described as "the most brilliant concept of an urban museum in America." Even Los Angeles, an accelerated society usually too busy building to build beautifully, wanted to, and so it created two of the most exciting complexes ever constructed by any civilization anywhere: the Los Angeles County Museum of Art on Wilshire Boulevard and the Music Center for the Performing Arts on the edge of Civic Center Plaza (see overleaf).

As it was for the congregation that fashioned the Mendocino church, the building of such monuments was an act of self-definition—a definition gained from the past and bequeathed to the future, one strand in the patterns of culture that bind us to what we were and what we might become.

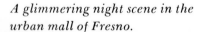
*A glimmering night scene in the urban mall of Fresno.*

*Designed by Kevin Roche and opened in 1969, the garden-hung Oakland Museum sprawls over much of the southeastern edge of the city.*

*The Los Angeles County Museum of Art, designed by William Pereira,*
*was completed and opened to the public in April 1965.*

*The Los Angeles Civic Center Plaza looking toward the Dorothy Chandler Pavilion,*
*part of the Music Center for the Performing Arts and designed by Welton Becket.*

# CHAPTER 23

# THE POLITICS OF CONFRONTATION

*Professors defy an oath; students, blacks, and Chicanos defy law and order; and violence and retribution punctuate a decade*

T HE FIRST PORTENT of what might be called California's Era of Sporadic Rebellion was felt not long after the end of World War II. Like the state's burgeoning aerospace and defense industries, the rebellion was a product of the Cold War. Unlike most of the revolts to follow, its violence was intellectual, not physical, and its drama correspondingly less intense—even though its implications were felt across the country and its legacy of bitterness lingered for more than twenty years.

California, like the rest of the United States, entered the postwar years hamstrung by an unreasoning terror of communism. "Americanism" and "un-Americanism" —terms vague enough to be interpreted however one chose—became the issues of the day, and were fully and cheerfully exploited by politicians. Nationally, Senator Joseph McCarthy announced his intention to ferret out Communists wherever he found them, and the House Un-American Activities Committee, founded in 1941, became the most powerful committee in the Congress.

In California a young Richard M. Nixon began his long and distinguished political career by defeating liberal Jerry Voorhis in the congressional race of 1946, largely on the strength of his charge that Voorhis was "one of those who front for un-American elements, wittingly or otherwise," and then went on to defeat Congresswoman Helen Gahagan Douglas (wife of actor Melvyn Douglas) in the senate race of 1950—again, by charging that the lady's voting record in Congress had followed, point by point, "wittingly or otherwise," the Communist Party line. And the state's own Committee

on Un-American Activities, headed by Assemblyman Jack B. Tenney and later state Senator Hugh M. Burns, began looking for any Communist influences Nixon might have missed.

Early in 1949 the committee focused its attention on the University of California, whose students and faculty had been known to engage suspicious speakers from time to time. Moreover, the committee was not certain that the university was doing all it should to screen out subversive elements among its employees. Chairman Tenney proposed a state constitutional amendment that would take the responsibility of insuring the loyalty of university employees out of the hands of the State Board of Regents and give it to the legislature. To counter this move, the university responded by offering to devise a more thorough loyalty oath than that required of all state employees. The offer was accepted by the committee, and after a closed board of regents meeting in March, which authorized the action, university president Robert G. Sproul announced in May that all employees on all eight of the university's campuses—from janitors to department heads—would be required to sign a new loyalty oath by July 1 or face dismissal or, in the case of faculty, non-renewal of teaching contracts. The oath was thorough and specific, requiring the signer to declare that he did not "support any party or organization that believes in, advocates, or teaches the overthrow of the United States government, by force or by any illegal or unconstitutional methods," and was later amended to include the statement that "I am not a member of the Communist Party."

*Political reflections: a night view of the capitol dome, Sacramento.*

*Free Speech, 1964: freedom's ferment reduced to a quiet simmer,*
*a student "sleeps in" at the administration building, UC Berkeley.*

Vigorous protest immediately ensued, based on four major objections: (1) coming so late in the school year, the new requirement made it virtually impossible for teachers to find new jobs if they chose not to sign; (2) the dismissal clause in the proposal destroyed the concept of tenure; (3) the new oath was an unwarranted duplication of the state oath that university employees had already taken; and (4) the requirement singled out one group of state employees unfairly. Reaction within

and without the university was so vehement that President Sproul soon reversed himself, asking the regents to invalidate their decision. He found support from Governor Earl Warren, who pointed out that any Communist worthy of the label would "take the oath and

*Free Speech, 1964: microphone in hand, leader*
*Mario Savio (upper right) addresses student crowd.*

laugh." Nevertheless, the regents refused to change their stand, led by John Francis Neylan (who, it will be remembered, had engineered a compromise during the General Strike of 1934) and Lawrence Mario Giannini, president of the Bank of America.

Debate continued for more than a year, as many professors fought the requirement. Finally, in August 1950, the regents dismissed thirty-two non-signing employees. Still, the employees fought back, taking their case to the State Supreme Court, which in 1952 ordered them reinstated—not on the grounds of academic freedom but because the statewide Levering Oath (passed by the legislature in 1950 and containing much of the language of the university oath) superseded the oath required by the university regents. Even though they had won their point, more or less, only sixteen of the non-signers returned to teach at the university, where they discovered that they had lost tenure and would have to start over to qualify for sabbaticals and other such seniority rewards. They sued the regents for redress, and the case was settled out of court in 1956.

Thus ended the first major academic rebellion in United States history. As the decade of the 1950s drew to a close, the fearfully intense emotions that had given birth to the affair had generally dissipated, yet a residue of doubt remained, as historian John Caughey—himself one of the non-signers—wrote in 1967: "Within the university the oath controversy certainly left resentments and scars. It may be questioned whether faculty voice in crucial determinations is as effective as it was from 1925 to 1949. The larger imponderable is what would have resulted from complete and quiet submission to the oath requirement."

AMONG SOCIAL HISTORIANS the period from 1950 to about 1960 is usually described as "the age of conformity," a by-product of the years of postwar prosperity and a time when social, political, and economic attitudes generally followed the cautious dictum laid down by an ancient phrase: "Don't rock the boat." The concept was quite as vulnerable to pointed exceptions

*People's Park, 1969: members of the Alameda County Tactical Squad reconnoiter a bulletin board.*

as any other generalization, yet it remained a fairly accurate description of the nation's overall mood in those years.

Nowhere was that mood reflected with greater fidelity than on the campuses of the country's colleges, where most students applied themselves with admirable diligence to the hard question of getting on in the world. They were encouraged in this direction by a rapidly expanding corporate world hungry for executive and technological talent. Corporation recruiters offered a variety of lures to potential graduates, including on-the-job training at generous salaries, broad insurance programs, profit-sharing and retirement programs to encourage employment longevity, as well as the security of being accepted as part of the corporate family.

The process appalled some social critics (including educators), who questioned whether this was what education was all about. What had happened to healthy inquiry, they asked, the testing of old ideas and the promulgation of new ones, the questing, the doubt, and the dreams of youth? Had the American student sold his intellectual birthright for a mess of security? The critics need not have worried, for the condition was no more permanent than most other social phenomena. By the end of the decade, the pendulum was beginning to swing in the other direction—ultimately too *far* in the other direction, according to many (including some of those critics of the 1950s). Not surprisingly, one of the first signs of that new direction was revealed in California as the new decade opened.

In 1960 the House Un-American Activities Committee, on one of its occasional countrywide tours, elected to hold closed sessions in the chambers of San Francisco's city hall. In the lexicon of the committee, the sessions were purely routine, but to its great surprise—and the surprise of city officials—scores of short-haired, neatly dressed students, most of them from the University of California at Berkeley, demanded access to the hearings, crowding the halls of the dome-capped building and giving out with cries of "Witch-hunt!" or "Inquisition!" or, among the better read, "Star-chamber proceedings!" A flabbergasted city government, devoid of experience in handling any kind of student disorder that did not have to do with feminine underclothes, sent in the police department with fire hoses and nightsticks. Many students, themselves inexperienced in such

*People's Park, 1969: wading through a fog of irritant gas,
highway patrolmen launch an attack.*

matters, resisted; many were washed, beaten, and dragged out of the elegant marble surroundings of San Francisco's magnificent city hall, thrown into paddy wagons, and hauled off to jail. One policeman suffered a heart attack.

City, state, and even national reaction to the city hall riot of 1960 ranged from stunned disbelief to charges that the incident had been a Communist plot to discredit and frustrate the efforts of the House Committee on Un-American Activities. More reasoned observations saw it for what it was: apathy was giving way to militant conviction among many of the student young, who were now ready not only to question old values but to challenge them directly, as hundreds did over the next few years in the southern states, staging sit-in demonstrations, freedom rides, and marches in an effort to end black segregation and all its works. Such students had grown hungry for causes; their hair grew longer, their clothing began to symbolize their disdain for the care-

ful goals of the larger society; their political and social beliefs became a confused amalgam of Jeffersonian Democracy, Marxist-Leninism, and good old-fashioned American anarchy, with touches of Transcendentalism, Zen Buddhism, and Gandhian fervency thrown in.

They comprised only a minority, but a vocal and militant one, and among them California was represented handsomely. Filled with a myriad of causes and the need to promulgate them (what good is a cause if it is not a crusade?), student organizers set up booths and tables on a narrow strip of land on the southern edge of the University of California's Berkeley campus at the beginning of the fall semester, 1964. Responding to a number of complaints from Berkeley citizens, the university administration decided to enforce an old rule that prohibited political recruitment on the campus. The students rebelled, labeled their rebellion the "Free Speech Movement," and engaged the "system" head on. In a move reminiscent of the IWW's "Free

Speech" fight of 1913 (see chapter 14), more than eight hundred students retaliated by crowding into Sproul Hall, the university's administrative center, sitting down, and refusing to move. Governor Edmund Brown then ordered state, local, and campus police to move them out. And so they did; nearly every one of the eight hundred was picked up, carried out, and arrested —the largest mass arrest in the state's history. The conviction rate was equally impressive: in a later mass trial, 578 of the students were convicted of trespassing and a number of resisting arrest.

The sit-in tactic may have been reprehensible, but the cause—that the largest university in the world should *encourage* rather than suppress the free expression of ideas—was closer to respectability, an idea given support when the university's faculty passed resolutions that the administration should not attempt to hamper political advocacy or regulate its content, and given further support by the administration itself, which relaxed its rules. Thereafter, the Berkeley campus and its environs became a kind of "free-thought" center for the dissemination of student opinion across the state and, to a remarkable degree, across the nation. Gradually, drawing a mixed bag of types, this and similar centers—most of them connected with college campuses—began to develop a kind of subculture (or "counterculture," as it called itself), with its own set of mores (particularly sexual mores), its own music,* its own public press (the *Los Angeles Free Press,* the *Berkeley Barb,* and so forth), and even a kind of language of its own. Confused and confusing, strident and exuberant, fragmented and deeply—too deeply—involved with the drug "scene," it was a culture whose participants were united mainly in their varying degrees of contempt for the world their fathers had produced, much of it expressed in violence and disruption.

Action bred reaction, beginning a chain of violence that sped through the rest of the decade. In the guber-

natorial campaign of 1966, Ronald Reagan successfully utilized the "campus unrest" issue, characterizing it as the direct and inescapable result of a generation of permissiveness. He intended, as one of the main points in his program, he said, to crack down hard; and among his first moves were forcing the dismissal of University of California president Clark Kerr in January 1967 and instituting sweeping budget cuts in the university's annual appropriations, although some critics of his administration wondered precisely what such actions had to do with quelling student violence—which continued. In December 1966, fully involved by now in the growing sentiment against the Vietnam War, Berkeley students crowded into the Student Union to protest the "preferred" treatment given navy recruiters over an anti-draft group. The usual contingent of police was called in, and the following day 8,000 of the university's 27,000 students went on a twenty-four-hour strike. Throughout the school year periodic incidents—including the burning of a part of the school's ROTC department— shattered the peace of the Berkeley campus.

The following year was quieter, but during the spring semester, 1969, the agony reappeared. Late in April a number of "street people," students and non-students alike, appropriated a parcel of university land and converted it into an extemporaneous playground and living area called "People's Park." Again responding to citizen complaints, the university administration ordered the people out of People's Park, surrounded it with a Cyclone fence, and posted campus and city police to guard it. On May 15 three thousand or more demonstrators marched on the park, throwing rocks, bottles, lengths of pipe, and apparently intent on tearing the fence down. The police, hopelessly outnumbered, responded with tear gas and buckshot. Three people on a rooftop were wounded; one of them, James Rector, later died, the first casualty of the student wars.

By nightfall the city of Berkeley was occupied by more than five hundred police (including members of the California Highway Patrol and Alameda County's Tactical Squad), Governor Reagan had declared a curfew, and units of the National Guard had been stationed just outside the city limits. For the next two weeks, Berkeley displayed the characteristics of an occupied city. Police helicopters circled overhead for hour after hour; patrol cars roamed the streets in tandem;

---

*Called in its various forms "acid rock," "hard rock," "soft rock," or "noise," this music, much of it developed and refined in San Francisco, was exerting a profound influence on the patterns of popular music in the country by the end of the decade. It was, according to many, the state's first significant contribution to the cultural life of America, since she had yet to develop a distinctive art or literature. Others would demur, pointing out the contribution of motion pictures, both as art and as industry.

*Watts, 1965: several of the more than six hundred buildings destroyed in the rioting go up in flames along Central Avenue.*

National Guard troops surrounded city hall. The days were broken into a series of seemingly climactic events: On May 19 National Guardsmen wandered through the city in army trucks, invaded the university, broke off gatherings with fixed bayonets, and arrested people. On May 20 a gathering on campus was dispersed by irritant gas sprayed from a helicopter. On May 22, 482 marchers in the downtown area were herded into a parking lot, arrested, and carried away in trucks. That weekend police were led on a chase all over the city by groups of protesters, some of them smashing windows, others planting "instant gardens" in vacant lots, city streets, and parking lots—gardens which the police patiently ripped up.

The climax came on May 30 as nearly twenty-five thousand people, representing a broad spectrum of the city's population, marched through Berkeley to Peo-

ple's Park to register their opinion about the occupation of the city. They marched peacefully, and no arrests were made. Shortly thereafter, police and National Guard units were withdrawn, and Berkeley was left with its scores of broken windows, its littered streets, its ruined businesses, its sky-high insurance rates, and its memory of what war could be like.

It seemed that violence on the part of the young was on its way toward becoming a kind of tradition, an unwelcome and possibly insoluble fact of life. In February 1970, students of the University of California's Santa Barbara campus ran amok in the nearby community of Isla Vista, violently "trashing" at random and burning the local branch of the Bank of America. In April a second riot swept through the community, and in June a third. Hundreds were arrested, scores injured, and one killed. It was not to be understood.

*Watts, 1965: business goes on more or less as usual at Tony's Shoe Shine Stand, August 17.*

Santa Barbara was the land of sunshine and surfboards. What did these young people want? Were they out to change society—or destroy it?

THE ONE POINT that frustrated observers of student revolt perhaps more than any other was that their grievances were not "real" in the material sense—they were children of the Affluent Society, after all—but had to do with such abstractions as morality, purpose, life goals, and even ethics, all of which were susceptible to the consistent inconsistencies of human interpretation. That could not be said of another source of the challenge and violence that characterized the 1960s: California's racial minorities, whose complaint could be summed up in a single phrase: they were on the outside looking in.

The two largest of these minorities were the blacks and the Mexicans, who between them comprised nearly 20 percent of the state's population. As noted earlier, California did not possess a significant Negro population until the beginning of World War II, but from that point forward it grew at a rate that more than matched that of the population at large. By 1970 there were 1,400,143 black people in California, more than in any of the southern states except Texas. Like the rest of the population, the black contingent was principally urban, although much of it—perhaps most of it—derived from rural sections of the South.

The largest concentration was in Los Angeles County, whose Negro population had grown from a little over 25,000 in 1940 to nearly 650,000 by the middle of the 1960s. Almost 90 percent of this population lived in a forty-six-square-mile area of south-central Los Angeles, the chief single sub-community of which was Watts. It was not a ghetto in the standardized, eastern sense of the term, an area of piled-up tenements, narrow city streets, and dirty little alleys where the sun never seemed to shine. In Watts the sun shone democratically, for it was a community of bungalows and yards, wide streets (some of them lined with palm trees), and the same quality of horizontal space as most of the rest of Southern California. Yet in all other respects, it was a slum— a horizontal slum. It was 99 percent black. Most of its bungalows were rented, not owned, most were old and in dismal repair, and most were overcrowded. The per capita income of Watts was $2,370, more than a thou-

sand dollars below the California average, and wide streets were meaningless to people who could not afford automobiles. Much of the population, driven from the rural areas of the Southeast by farm mechanization, was almost completely illiterate, and 40 percent of it had never been schooled beyond the eighth grade. These people, like millions before them, had sought the promise of California, but found themselves trapped— trapped by a lack of education and training, a lack of transportation, a lack of simple opportunity.

Even for those few who could afford it, escape was rendered difficult by Southern California's particularly virulent patterns of housing discrimination. In 1960,

*Watts, 1965: a National Guard trooper escorts a lady across the littered street and (presumably) out of the line of fire.*

according to the Los Angeles County Commission on Human Relations, the city of Los Angeles was more segregated than any city in the American South. Some hope might have been found in the passage of the Unruh Civil Rights Act of 1959, which prohibited racial discrimination in the practice of any business and provided for the recovery of damages from the courts. Yet in 1960, Remi Nadeau could still report that the "confinement of minority citizens to segregated districts has been deliberately created and scrupulously maintained by elements controlling property ownership and finance. Developers of new tracts generally exclude Negroes and often other minority people. . . . Many private lending institutions apparently adhere to this established custom by refusing loans to Negroes buying in white neighborhoods. Practically all owners of apartments in white districts will not rent to Negroes. Almost all real estate brokers will not be party to a transfer of property in a white neighborhood to a Negro family."

In 1963 the legislature passed the Rumford Act, which forbade racial discrimination in the sale or rental of residential property that included more than four units or was in part or whole financed through public assistance (e.g., the FHA). The California Real Estate Association responded to what it described as "forced housing" by securing enough signatures on an initiative petition to have Proposition 14 placed on the ballot for the November 1964 elections. This measure—the only such ever considered by any state in the nation—sought to invalidate any past, present, or *future* law that limited an individual's "right" to "sell, lease, or rent any part or all of his real property . . . to such person or persons as he in his absolute discretion chooses." California's voters approved this proposition by a margin of more than two-to-one.*

That vote, interpreted by the black community as the visible expression of outright bigotry, must be considered at least one cause for the sound of mutual gunfire that too often rang in the streets of California's cities over the next several years. Violence began in Watts on the evening of August 11, 1965, after a day of miserable heat. A highway patrolman attempted to

*In 1966 the State Supreme Court declared Proposition 14 to be unconstitutional, a decision upheld by the United States Supreme Court in 1967.

*Sacramento, 1969: coolly armed Black Panthers put their demands before the state legislature.*

arrest a young black man for drunken driving; he resisted, aided by his mother and another black woman. A crowd formed and soon swelled to more than a thousand. The patrolman radioed for help, and answering units of Los Angeles police were pelted with rocks and bottles. Over the next several hours, the incident became a major disruption, then a full-scale riot, and finally what could only be described as municipal warfare, with widespread looting, burning, and sniper fire. Frustration, rage, envy, and greed—all the darker elements of man's nature—seemed to have welled up in one explosive burst, whose destructive energy could not be contained for more than six days, as outlined in the *Report* of the McCone Commission, appointed by Governor Brown after the riot: "They looted stores, set fires, beat up white passers-by whom they hauled from their stopped cars, many of which were turned upside down and burned, exchanged shots with law enforcement officers, and stoned and shot at firemen. . . . Ultimately an area covering 465 square miles had to be controlled with the aid of military authority before public order was restored. . . . When the spasm passed, thirty-four persons were dead [three of them white people], and the wounded and hurt numbered 1,032 more. Property damage was about $40,000,000. Arrested for one crime or another were 3,952 persons." It was the longest, deadliest, and most destructive riot in the country's twentieth-century history.

And it was echoed, if never duplicated: again in Watts in 1966, in San Francisco in 1966 and 1967, in Fresno in 1967, and in several northern cities in 1968 after the assassination of Martin Luther King (and across the nation in Chicago, Washington, Detroit, Newark, and others). A sense of militant urgency and sudden pride was enveloped in a drive for "Black Power." Anger was translated into Movement, and the Movement thrust itself at the state's social structure. At its worst, the movement resulted in only more violence; at its best, it dramatized traditional inequities and accelerated the development of programs to help relieve them.

On college and university campuses, Black Studies departments were demanded and, for the most part, received (although not always without trouble, as at San Francisco State College in 1969 and 1970). Federal and state money for self-help and other assistance programs was demanded and received, and many of the programs became staffed largely by black people.

The new unity of purpose found political expression in the election of black candidates, like Congressman Ronald Dellums, formerly a radical city councilman from Berkeley. On the Los Angeles campus of the University of California, black professor Angela Davis, an avowed Communist (and as such a *rara avis* among black people), was fired by the university regents and had the audacity to challenge the dismissal.

In Oakland, Bobby Seale, Huey Newton, and Eldridge Cleaver—thugs or culture heroes, depending upon one's vantage point—formed the Black Panthers, a secretive, paramilitary organization, verbally aggressive in its conviction that black was not only beautiful but better, and would prevail.

Even prison inmates felt the new mood, organizing for penal reforms and engaging in their own kind of murderous violence, the most noteworthy example of which occurred in Marin County's magnificent Frank Lloyd Wright–designed courthouse, when three convicts under trial for the murder of a prison guard produced guns, kidnapped the judge in an escape attempt, and killed him before they were stopped—after which

*Salinas Valley, 1939: a Mexican-American migrant worker is captured by photographer Dorothea Lange.*

Angela Davis was accused, tried, and acquitted on the charge of having knowingly furnished the guns.

Progress and savagery: By the end of the decade, the black movement remained quite as directionless as the society it was challenging on so many levels. Yet it *was* a movement, and not without nobility and hope for the challengers themselves and for the society. For black Americans were by the very nature of their predicament more intensely "driven by a sense of what it is possible for human life to be in this society," in the words of black novelist Ralph Ellison. "The nation could not survive being deprived of their presence because, by the irony implicit in the dynamics of American democracy, they symbolize both its most stringent testing and the possibility of its greatest human freedom."

CALIFORNIA'S Mexican-American community shared much with her black community in the way of frustration, yet there were significant differences both in the nature of the problems involved and in the approaches to overcoming them.

Like the black population, the Mexican-American was overwhelmingly urban, and most of it was centered in Southern California; nearly one million lived in Los Angeles County alone, the majority in the sprawling *barrio* of East Los Angeles. Like the black population, the Mexican-American lived closer to poverty than the average Californian, was poorly educated, and encountered much of the same discrimination and institutionalized bigotry.

The principal difference between the two groups was one of cultural identity. Black Californians, however deprived and alienated they may have been, were inescapably part of the larger society; its culture was theirs, simply because three hundred years of slavery and systematic oppression had left them with no other. Mexican-American Californians, on the other hand, possessed a distinct and definable culture, and a history that could be traced back to the days of the Spanish Conquest and beyond. Welded together by membership in the Roman Catholic Church, powerful family traditions, and geographic proximity to Mexico, it was a culture that provided a long-standing pride of race such as the black community had only begun to discover.

But cultural pride could be a two-edged sword; if it

*San Francisco, 1969: "flower children" ritualize the death of "hip" in the Haight-Ashbury district.*

gave the Mexican-American a sense of community and emotional security, it also slowed his fair participation in the larger society. For most *barrio* children, Spanish was the *first*, not the second language of their lives, a circumstance that profoundly impeded their progress in a school system inexorably geared to English as the only teaching language. Tradition held, too, that a child's first responsibility was to his family, and if it became necessary for him to drop out of school to help in his family's support, he was expected to do so without complaint. Even *machismo,* that exuberant masculinity that was so much a part of the Mexican character, played a role, since it held that book-learning and all that went with it was somehow unworthy of a true man. All these cultural attitudes threw obstacles in the way of education—and without education in a society that demanded it, the Mexican-American was nearly helpless.

As a result, California's Mexican-Americans actually lagged behind black Californians in areas of education, employment, and income, a gap that grew wider and more obvious as black assertiveness gradually opened doors that had been closed. For this, black people were resented, envied, and finally emulated, particularly among impatient young Mexican-Americans. These began to form newer, more aggressive organizations to supplement (and, their organizers hoped, supplant)

such older, gentler groups as the Community Services Organization or the Mexican-American Political Association; chief among these was the Brown Berets (not to be confused with the Black Berets, a relatively insignificant group whose attitudes and format were patterned after the Black Panthers). The Brown Berets organized marches and staged demonstrations. In March 1968, 15,000 high school students struck and marched to protest what they called the bigotry of the Los Angeles school system, and when the strike leaders were arrested, students "sat in" the downtown office of the Board of Education for a week. In August 1970 a march to protest the deaths of Mexican-Americans in Vietnam degenerated into a riot that gave the movement its first martyr: newspaperman Rueben Salazar, accidentally killed by a stray tear-gas projectile.

Ironically, however, the most significant expression of "Chicano Power" occurred not in the urban *barrios* where most Mexican-Americans lived but in the fields of the Central Valley, where less than a tenth of them worked. It began in 1962, when Cesar Chavez left his job with the Community Services Organization to try to create out of whole cloth a farm labor union. "I thought I had a 2 percent chance of success," he later recalled (as quoted in Michael Davies' *California: The Vanishing Dream*). "I came to Delano, where I knew I could get people together. I thought: I have got to see this valley once more. So I started traveling, in my old car; I began up in the Tehachapis, then went from Bakersfield to Fresno, just looking at the topography and the system. I went east and west and all the way up north to Chico, and I would stop at all the chambers of commerce and pick up the histories of the little towns, and at night I would read them. Finally I came back to Delano. I got here at two in the morning, and my wife wanted to know all about my journey. . . . And I said 'You know, it's damn big. It's frighteningly big. But,' I said, 'it's got to be done.' And so we started."

With the patient energy of the true zealot, Chavez patched together the beginnings of the National Farm Workers Association (NFWA), which by 1965 had gained a membership of 2,000 and had won its first, albeit minor, strike, against a group of Delano rose growers. A bigger test came in the spring of 1965 when the Agricultural Workers Organizing Committee (AWOC), which had been formed under the aegis of the AFL-CIO in 1959, came to Chavez and asked for the support of the NFWA in its strike against ten of the largest grape growers in the San Joaquin Valley. Chavez put it to a vote; the response was *"Huelga!"* ("Strike!"), and the two unions began the first major challenge to California's agribusiness since the 1930s.

Shrewdly, Chavez courted the attention of the press and the public, particularly in the East, dramatizing the spectacle of a small group of oppressed Mexican workers taking on the largest agricultural empire in the country, and asking for a nationwide boycott of the growers' products. The tactic worked, and the resulting pressure forced the growers to sign contracts in 1966 for increased wages and fringe benefits in exchange for a promise not to strike during the harvest season. The two unions then merged to form a new organization, the United Farm Workers Organizing Committee (UFWOC), with Chavez as director; staged a secret-ballot election in the fields of the Di Giorgio Corporation to demonstrate worker support (winning by a margin of nearly two to one); and in 1967 launched another assault, this one directed against the Giumarra Vineyards near Delano, the world's largest grower of table grapes. Again, Chavez asked for a national boycott, and again the public responded. When other growers allowed the Giumarra company to ship its grapes under their labels, the union expanded the strike to cover the offending growers. This strike-boycott ground on for three years before Giumarra and the other growers succumbed, finally signing contracts in the summer of 1970 that included, for the first time in American farm labor history, health insurance programs.

Inspired by this success, the union continued the struggle, taking the growers on singly and in groups, constantly expanding, surviving jurisdictional disputes with the powerful Teamsters Union and even the hardened resistance of employers in such traditional centers of anti-union sentiment as the Salinas Valley. It was a grinding, uphill fight, but for the first time in history it *was* a fight, and it seemed inevitable, given time and patience enough, that California's farm labor would be successfully unionized. Equally inevitable was the prospect that the ultimate victory would be meaningless, for the accelerating pace of agricultural mechanization appeared almost certain to eliminate the need for significant numbers of farm workers.

Yet UFWOC was something more than a union, and Chavez was more than a labor leader. Together they were a symbol, the cultural focus for the aspirations of a people, and many believed their function would not end so long as those aspirations remained unsatisfied. Chavez himself was one: "Someday," he said, "we'll take the city on, and that day things are going to change."

THE DECADE of violent confrontation ended on a note of irresolution in the winter of 1970, when the United States Coast Guard removed the last Indian from the abandoned federal prison on Alcatraz Island in San Francisco Bay. The year before, a contingent of enthusiastic California Indians, filled with their own racial pride and with the example of the blacks and the chicanos before them, had occupied the site, christening it "Indian Land" and demanding that it be turned over to them for development as an Indian cultural center. The problems they sought to dramatize were real—even if the gesture itself bordered on fantasy—for California's estimated Indian population of eighty thousand (only half of which was native to the state, the rest coming from various other western reservations) was the most depressed and voiceless of the state's minority groups.

For a time, the occupation served its purposes. The island's new population swelled to more than a hundred; regular news conferences on the mainland were well attended; sympathetic public support came in the form of donated food and water; television cameras focused on the island night and day, recording film reports for use across the nation; and everyone—Indians and spectators alike—waited for that climactic, potentially violent moment when the government would choose to evict its unlikely tenants.

But the authorities, perhaps wiser by now in such matters, simply waited. In a matter of weeks, public interest waned; in a matter of months, it had nearly disappeared. Discouraged and no less destitute than they had been on the mainland, the island's Indians drifted away in chunks and driblets, until by the end of a year there were only a stubborn handful left—and when the government finally chose to evict these, they left without incident. It was a pointless and sad conclusion.

Sad and perhaps symptomatic, for as the new decade opened it became obvious that some fundamental change in attitude and approach had taken place, in both California and the nation. The student violence that was expected to erupt once again in the 1970–71 school year did not—nor did it in all of 1972, except for a brief, infinitely milder "People's Park" incident in the spring. Even the more strident militancy of the black movement seemed to have abated. The Black Panther Party, riven by internal dissension, seemed doomed, and in Oakland Bobby Seale announced his candidacy for mayor. The Chicano movement appeared to be in limbo, waiting for Cesar Chavez or his equivalent to lead it on to the next plateau. Conflict as an ideological tool seemed to have been set aside. "The movement," Father Daniel Berrigan had written in late 1970, "shows how constantly we are seduced by violence, not only as method but as an end in itself." Perhaps someone in California had been listening.

The unexpected lull, some said, was merely one more example of America's traditional ability to absorb its rebellions—and California was, after all, "the most American of all the American states." Still, there were indications, slight and ill-defined to be sure, that something more complicated was taking place. For the years of periodic violence had shaken California's society more deeply than it could know, or admit if it did know. It had been judged and found wanting by some of its own, a state of affairs that had to demand a profound self-analysis of any society not in a state of inexorable decay—and no one was willing to admit *that*. The so-called hippies (a loosely applied term at best) had pointed the way. Disdaining both traditional values and the blind activism and occasional depravity of the world of the counterculture, they had set out in the mid-1960s to find, or create, what they called "alternative" lifestyles, setting up idyllic communes in the finest California manner. Dipping into whatever poorly understood mysticism seemed handy, most were a chaos of garbled thinking that was consistent on only one point:

that in order to know oneself and others, it was far more important to *feel* than to think, and that the search for feeling was an inward journey.

Most of the communes died aborning, but by the end of the decade the central core of their thinking was reflected on a more refined and respectable level throughout much of the state. Immensely popular "sensitivity training" centers like Big Sur's Esalen Institute, San Diego's Kairos, or Palo Alto's Center for Creativity and Growth utilized varying combinations of Oriental mysticism, Jungian symbology, Gestalt therapy, and direct-encounter techniques in an effort to bring thousands of Californians in closer touch with themselves and others. Corporations sponsored "sensitivity clinics" for their executives; police departments set up encounter sessions between white policemen and black citizens; church groups organized their own clinics; and thousands of people who might have scoffed at the idea of traditional psychoanalysis spent hundreds of dollars and their entire vacations groping in the dark of their interior landscape.

A new direction? Some thought so. "Deprived of anything external in which to believe," Michael Davies wrote in 1973, "people in California are plunging inward in the hope that the search for themselves will somehow provide a new code of values to live by." Others more skeptical confidently awaited the day when this intellectual fashion, like phrenology or Fourierism, would be shoveled into the dustbin of history. Time would make the choice.

In the meantime, there was another landscape to be considered—the real, the visible one, whose mortal danger, many people said, rendered such issues as Black Power, Brown Power, Red Power, Student Power, or Enlightenment Power largely irrelevant. For the machinery of California's civilization, they said, was trampling the complicated web of existence, threatening the desperate fragility of life—all life.

*The Campanile at sundown, University of California at Berkeley.*

# California Mirror:
# The Knowledge Boom

*Woodbridge Elementary School, Woodbridge.*

Whatever else may be said of California's educational system, it must first be said that it is big—the biggest in the nation, and one of the biggest in the world. This immensity, like so many other characteristics of the state as it turned the middle corner of the twentieth century, was the direct result of a wartime leaning toward fecundity among young married people, coupled with the postwar immigration boom. By the early 1950s, elementary schools were receiving an unprecedented flood of children, and by the end of the decade, public school enrollment had increased more than 100 percent over the previous ten years. The state simply could not keep

*El Portal Elementary School, Escalon.*

*Chinese Camp Elementary School.*

*School under construction in the San Joaquin Valley.*

up with the demand, finding it increasingly difficult to provide even basic educational necessities, as historian Walton Bean has written: "The schools were chronically short of money, of classroom space, of teachers—of everything, in fact, except pupils." Fumbling with various funding plans and proposals, while property taxes continued to rise, the state never did catch up with its lower-level educational responsibilities, and it was not expected that any relief would be felt until the full impact of the dramatically declining birthrate of the latter 1960s and early 1970s manifested itself.

Inevitably, great pressure began to be felt on the

*Eaton Elementary School, Fresno.*

*Fresno High School, Fresno.*

institutions of higher education by the middle of the 1950s. City after city petitioned the state legislature to authorize the creation of local junior (two-year) colleges, most of whose funding was to come from the communities themselves. Enrollment at the twenty-one state college campuses leaped to more than one hundred thousand by 1960, and was expected to increase to two hundred thousand or more by 1970. The University of California had swollen to a total of eight campuses by 1960, with an enrollment of more than seventy thousand. In an effort to control the further growth of the higher educational system, the state legislature passed in 1960 the Donohoe Higher Education Act, or Master Plan for Higher Education.

*De Anza Community College, Cupertino.*

*Foothill College, Los Altos Hills.*

*Right: Leland Stanford, Jr., University, founded in 1891 by former Governor Leland Stanford in memory of his son.*

The master plan created a Coordinating Council for Higher Education whose function was to regulate expansion, enrollment, curriculum, and admission standards of the junior and state colleges and the University of California. It also required the state to begin paying 45 percent of the operating costs of the junior colleges by 1975, and divided state monies between the state and university systems. Under the council's aegis, the University of California was authorized to expand to three additional campuses: Santa Cruz, Irvine, and San Diego —making it the largest university in the world.

Altogether, the system deserved newsman Mel Wax's description of it as "a massive program of democratic higher education on a scale never before attempted by any state or nation." This was not surprising; it was, after all, a California institution.

*Aerial view of the privately funded Claremont Colleges near Ontario.*

*Administrative building of the University of
Southern California, founded in 1880.*

*Cowell Hall, University of California
at Santa Cruz.*

# CHAPTER 24

# THE WORLD-SAVERS

*A century of California conservation, in which a sentiment becomes a cause,*

*a cause becomes a movement, and growth itself is challenged*

Tʜᴇ ʟᴀsᴛ ʜᴀʟғ of the 1960s was replete with an agony of concern for the state of the Union's environment. Television documentaries, news reports, and late-night talk shows repeated the message that man's relation to his environment was less than symbiotic most of the time and downright lethal much of the time; enough books, magazine articles, and newspaper stories to rebuild whole forests were printed elaborating upon the theme; and *ecology* became a word that dropped sweetly from the lips of matrons at suburban cocktail parties. "Ecology," one anonymous cynic wrote, "is the last fad."

The environmental bandwagon was loaded, and much of what went on in its name was indeed faddish. Yet this popularity should not be allowed to obscure the fact that much of the expressed concern—however strident and repetitive it sometimes may have been— was utterly genuine, committed, and predicated on the reasonable assumption that time was running out, both for man and for the land he chose to call home.

It was entirely fitting that California should have been at the center of environmental concern, for she was the most advanced state in the most advanced nation in a world whose material growth was propelled by the twin machines of urbanization and technology. As such, she was uncommonly susceptible to the implications of Leo Tolstoy's nineteenth-century observation: "Each step we make today toward material progress not only does not advance us toward the general well-being, but shows us, on the contrary, that all these technical improvements only increase our miseries." The

pollution of air and water, the mistreatment of forests, the loss of wilderness and parklands, the exploitation of natural beauty, the nearly uncontrolled megalopolitan growth, the stair-step techniques of water development—all of the causes that moved the conservation movement on a national scale were found in brilliant profusion in the Golden State. In some cases, they were not only found there; it was there they were for the first time seen and *presented* as causes—another reason that helped to explain her leading role in the swelling tide of conservation sentiment.

If California was the first state to achieve the Technocratic Society, she was also the first to develop a cohesive body of conservation opinion whose impact could be materially felt outside her own borders. As it grew, this body of opinion acquired many shoots and branches, but its roots derived from the Sierra Club—and its tap root, so to speak, lay in the mind of one remarkable man: John Muir.

In 1868 the thirty-year-old, Scottish-born Muir stepped ashore in San Francisco and immediately asked a Market Street passerby how to get out of town.

"But where do you want to go?"

"Anywhere that is wild."

"He seemed to fear," Muir later said, "that I might be crazy, and . . . the sooner I got out of town the better, so he directed me to the Oakland Ferry."

Muir was a walker by inclination. The previous year he had hiked from Indiana to Florida, so not even California's sweep of land could intimidate him. He started walking from Oakland, through the Santa Clara Valley,

*Ironstone ridges pattern the shore of Drake's Bay,*
*Point Reyes National Seashore.*

*John Muir, the father of modern conservation, at the height of his fame and personal beauty.*

*From the beginning, Sierra clubbers were a vigorous, tree-climbing bunch; in 1905, this group tested the scale of a giant among the Big Basin redwoods.*

across Pacheco Pass, through the wild flowers of the San Joaquin Valley, up the canyon of the Merced River, and into Yosemite Valley, where he remained for the most part of the next five years. And for the rest of his life, Yosemite remained his spiritual base as he wandered over most, if not all, of the Sierra Nevada range, exploring its myriad details and bathing his eyes, mind, and heart in its beauty. And writing: between 1870 and 1890, Muir produced sixty-five separate magazine and newspaper articles broadcasting the delights of the

mountains he had come to love, many of them appearing in such substantial and influential national journals as *Scribner's Monthly, Harper's Weekly, Century, Atlantic,* and the *New York Tribune.*

By his early fifties, Muir had become one of the major voices in the country for the protection and preservation of wild places—particularly his beloved Yosemite; it was through his influence and that of *Century*'s associate editor, Robert Underwood Johnson, that Congress was persuaded in 1890 to create the 1,500-square-mile

Yosemite National Park to completely surround Yosemite Valley State Park. With the establishment later that same year of Sequoia National Park and General Grant National Park (later part of Kings Canyon National Park), engineered by George W. Stewart, editor of the *Visalia Delta,* and Daniel Zumwalt, land agent for the Southern Pacific Railroad*—both of whom were less interested in protecting beauty than in preserving the source of the San Joaquin Valley's water—California possessed three of the four national parks in the country (the other being Wyoming's Yellowstone).

It seemed obvious to Muir and others that some sort of formal organization would be helpful in protecting the new national park from exploitation; this sentiment, combined with a long-standing desire among several nature-lovers for some kind of alpine club, ultimately led to the gathering of Muir and twenty-six other men in San Francisco in 1892 to form the Sierra Club (with Muir as president), whose articles of incorporation neatly met both desires: "The purposes for which this Corporation is formed are as follows, to wit: To explore, enjoy and render accessible the mountain regions of the Pacific Coast; to publish authentic information concerning them; to enlist the support and co-operation of the people and the government in preserving the forests and other natural features of the Sierra Nevada Mountains. . . ."

The key phrase in the articles of incorporation was "to enlist the support and co-operation of the people and the government." From the beginning, one of the club's principal functions was to watchdog the environment, a role originally confined to the Sierra Nevada but later expanded to include the whole state, the whole country, and even, from time to time, the whole world. To do so, it had to become a political force, a kind of lobby representing the interests of mute nature; that this function was recognized by the club was illustrated barely six months after its founding. When a bill was

introduced in Congress that would have opened part of Yosemite National Park to stockmen for grazing and lumbermen for timber, the club drafted a resolution "directing the Board of Directors . . . to prepare a memorial to Congress against the bill and to use every effort to defeat it." It was the first, but by no means the last, time the club would take such action. (The bill, incidentally, was defeated.)

Over the next several years, the Sierra Club pursued its goals with vigor and considerable success, continuing to help stave off proposed alterations of Yosemite Park's boundaries, encouraging the establishment of various forest reserves, exploring and recommending sites for additional national parks along the Pacific Coast, helping to implement the transfer of Yosemite Valley State Park to federal control in Yosemite National Park, and earning an accolade from President Theodore Roosevelt: "California has for years . . . taken a more sensible, a more intelligent interest in forest preservation than any other state. It early appointed a Forest Commission; later on some of the functions of that Commission were replaced by the Sierra Club, a club which has done much on the Pacific Coast to perpetuate the spirit of the explorer and pioneer."

The organization was quite pleased with itself. "There is not the slightest question," recording secretary William Colby wrote in 1903, "but that the Sierra Club is destined to be one of the greatest clubs of its kind. . . ." Five years later it came dead up against its first major controversy.

As noted in chapter 15, in 1908 the city of San Francisco petitioned the Department of the Interior to grant it a reservoir site in the Hetch Hetchy Valley within the bounds of Yosemite National Park, a valley that Muir and many others considered second only to Yosemite in its beauty. Secretary of the Interior James Garfield granted the petition in May, setting off a furor that was to last for more than five years. John Muir's reaction was immediate and bitterly eloquent: "Dam Hetch Hetchy! As well dam for water-tanks the people's cathedrals and churches, for no holier temple has ever been consecrated by the hearts of men." He and the club's board of directors quickly set about organizing the group's opposition apparatus.

To their dismay, they discovered that there was significant opposition to their opposition *within* the Sierra

---

*Given the Southern Pacific's reputation during the nineteenth century, it seems only fair to point out that it always vigorously supported such park legislation. Not without self-interest, however: parks meant tourists, and tourists meant railroad fares; and in the case of the Sequoia and General Grant parks, the protection of watershed was important to the sales value of Southern Pacific's San Joaquin Valley land. Nevertheless, the importance of the railroad's influence on park legislation was immeasurable.

*Smog obliterates all of the San Bernardino Range and reveals only a sliver
of Mount Baldy in this view of the San Bernardino Valley of Southern California.*

Club, particularly among its San Francisco members, for the Hetch Hetchy issue lay like a fence between two ideologies: one holding that the use of natural resources should always be based on the concept of the greatest material good for the greatest number, at whatever cost to such abstract uses as the enjoyment of beauty, however uplifting; the other, that no matter how vital the intelligent use of resources was to the well-being of society, natural beauty of the scope represented by Hetch Hetchy was, in and of itself, a resource that must be protected.

Since San Francisco was indisputably going to need an additional water supply and since of all the available sources the Hetch Hetchy Valley was the cheapest,

*The attrition: little by little, thirty acres here and forty acres there, the rich orchard
land of the Santa Clara Valley of the north disappeared in the 1960s.*

it neatly satisfied the "greatest good" concept. Its advantages were outlined by Secretary Garfield: "The City . . . would have one of the finest and purest water supplies in the world; the irrigable land in the Tuolumne and San Joaquin valleys would be helped out by the use of the excess stored water and by using the electrical power not needed by the City for municipal purposes, to pump subterranean water for the irrigation of additional areas, the City would have a cheap and bountiful supply of electrical energy for pumping its water supply and lighting the City and its municipal buildings." Cheap water, cheap electricity—who, San Franciscans (including some Sierra Club members) wondered, could possibly challenge the primacy of these two obvious facts?

The board of directors of the Sierra Club could, secretary William Colby proclaimed in a letter to Gifford Pinchot in 1909: "Let me assure you that we have only begun our fight, and we are not going to rest until we have established the principle 'that our National Parks shall be held forever inviolate', and until we have demonstrated to the satisfaction of every one . . . that the American people stand for that principle. We are going to keep up the good fight without fear or favor, 'if it shall take until doomsday'."

The "good fight" lasted until 1913, beset all along the way by almost constant friction within the organization and cluttered with mounds of testimony before one congressional committee after another, scores of minor and major meetings, and reams of resolutions, memorials, proclamations, newspaper advertisements, and mailings for public support across the state and the nation. It was a good fight, and a long one, but finally in vain: On December 6, 1913, Congress confirmed the

Department of Interior's grant, and on December 19, President Woodrow Wilson signed the confirmation. After five years of almost constant work, Muir was exhausted, brutally disappointed, but irrepressibly optimistic in spite of everything: "The destruction of the charming groves and gardens, the finest in all California, goes to my heart. But in spite of Satan & Co. some sort of compensation must surely come out of this dark damn-dam-damnation." On Christmas Eve 1914, just one year after the Hetch Hetchy defeat, he died.

N EITHER MUIR nor the Hetch Hetchy Valley survived the conflict of ideologies that had surrounded them; the Sierra Club did, but it would be many years before the scars of dissension would heal, and many years beyond that before it regained the cutting edge of purpose and whole-souled evangelism that had made it a major force for the rescue of wild places in an age when the concept of preservation rarely stirred the imaginations of people infatuated with growth as an inherent good.

In the years before World War II, the conservation movement was hardly a movement at all; rather, it was a relatively unsophisticated and generally disorganized attempt by a few individual organizations to rescue bits and pieces of the environment. Chief among these, in addition to the Sierra Club, were the Save the Redwoods League and the Sequoia Sempervirens Club (each of which was instrumental in the preservation of thousands of acres of redwood trees), together with local branches of the Audubon Society and the Wilderness Society. As dedicated and diligent as they certainly were, such organizations could hardly claim that they commanded wide public support. The simple fact was that California's civilization was just not ready to doubt seriously whether the patterns of the past could be carried into the indefinite future. More had always been better, had it not?

After the war that faith could not be held with quite so much assurance, for Californians began to be assaulted from too many directions by some of the more noxious products of growth. The reddish-gray pall of smog began to hang over too many of the state's metropolitan centers too often, eating the paint off houses, killing plants, irritating eyes, noses, and throats, and aggravating respiratory conditions among too many people. Too many factories, cities, towns, and farms were pumping effluents that ranged from deadly poisons to raw sewage into too many rivers, streams, and bays, and even the ocean. Too many people were living in too many houses that sprawled over too many acres of farmland, open space, and coastline. Too many freeways were plunging through too many cities and parks with too much disregard for either destruction or simple aesthetics. And too many people were crowding into too few parks.

The evidence threatened to become overwhelming and public reaction began an evolution from mild concern, through anxiety, to agitated demands for someone, somewhere, to *do* something about it. Samuel E. Wood and Alfred Heller's *California, Going, Going . . .* (1962), Raymond F. Dassman's *The Destruction of California* (1965), Richard G. Lillard's *Eden in Jeopardy* (1967), and William Bronson's *How to Kill a Golden State* (1968) outlined the past, the present, and the potential future of the state's environmental failings. In San Francisco, Alfred Heller founded California Tomorrow in 1961 to bring to the public "a greater awareness of the problems we must face to maintain a beautiful and productive California," and *Cry California*, its quarterly journal under the editorship of William Bronson, launched an all-out assault on the "land-wreckers," ranging from the State Division of Highways to the United States Army Corps of Engineers. In Berkeley, a group of environmentally concerned young people got together in 1969 to establish an ecology center for the dissemination of information and to function as a base for direct action against environmental problems; by the end of 1973, forty-five such centers had been established across the country, from Los Angeles to Washington, D.C., and had been tied together under the aegis of the Ecology Center Communications Council. Political leaders, responding to the upwelling of public concern, took hold of the environmental issue and shook it down into committees, bills, debates, and investigations.

Like waves from a storm, the energy of what had become known as the Ecology Movement ("Green Power!") spread throughout the state, making itself felt in nearly every part—even Southern California, whose century-old love affair with growth was rudely

*The antagonists: the battle lines are clearly drawn in this view of orange groves and freeway near Santa Ana in Orange County.*

challenged by a growing and eminently vocal minority who pointed to the region's massive environmental problems and proclaimed them the nation's leading example of the mess man was capable of creating in the name of progress. At the forefront of the movement was the Sierra Club once again, by now the single most influential conservation organization in the world, with a membership that had grown from a little over 20,000 in 1960 to more than 100,000 in 1973—a kind of conservation monolith whose fulminations, requests, and even mild observations were listened to by senators and congressmen with the sort of deference normally reserved for majority stockholders in automobile companies. Much of this change in image could be ascribed to the leadership of four men: successive presidents William Siri and Edgar Wayburn, conservation director Michael McCloskey, and most particularly, executive director David Brower, who was called the "knight errant to nature's rescue" by *Life* magazine in 1966 and "the last Druid" by himself some years later. Perhaps Brower's most important contribution was the Exhibit Format Series of picture-books-with-a-message, beginning with *This Is the American Earth* in 1960—outsized, beautifully designed, and elegantly printed books that not only spread the name of the Sierra Club but stood as eloquent reminders of the club's major contention: "In wilderness, the world gets put to its own music again," as Brower put it. "Wipe out wilderness and the world's a cage." (Brower departed the organization in 1969 after an internal dispute reminiscent of the Hetch Hetchy hassle, taking the Exhibit Format idea with him and forming Friends of the Earth; but under his successor Michael McCloskey both the club's conservation action and its book publishing program continued with unabashed vigor.).

The conservation movement of the 1960s was unique in the state's history, for the environmental issue, unlike any other, crossed all political lines, incorporated all classes of people, and found support among all ages. It was the one issue—possibly the only issue—on which, say, a retired policeman from Coalinga and a long-haired sophomore from the university at Berkeley could unite. That breadth of support was of profound importance, for no matter how vigorous and dedicated the movement's leadership may have been, no matter how many books and magazines may have been published, no matter how many engineering reports or governmental studies may have been issued—and no matter how *right* all of this may have been—it would have been meaningless without the committed support of people who could set aside ideological differences long enough to agree that their physical world was in trouble.*

---

*This is not to suggest that the conservation movement was without internal disagreements. A case in point was Proposition 9 of 1971, which would have established stringent controls and corrective measures on nearly every imaginable area of environmental concern. Called by many a "blanket indictment" of progress, the measure was defeated. Still, it should be noted that it was the proposition's *methods* that were found objectionable—not its goals.

The result was a decade and more of environmental reforms of far-reaching effect: the creation of a number of state agencies devoted to various aspects of the environment; the establishment of Redwood National Park, Point Reyes National Seashore, and Golden Gate National Recreation Area; the enforcement of the most stringent anti-smog laws in the country; the so-called "Freeway Revolt," which blocked proposed freeways in San Francisco, Santa Monica, and several other cities; the killing of a proposal by the Department of Water Resources and the Army Corps of Engineers for a high dam on the Eel River and the postponement of a "peripheral canal" to divert 80 percent of the Sacramento River's flow around the Delta for delivery to the State Water Project; the creation of a San Francisco Bay Conservation and Development Commission to regulate all aspects of development in and around the bay, and a Tahoe Regional Council to do the same for Lake Tahoe; and the passage of a startling number of environmental measures the most important of which was Proposition 20 on the November 1972 ballot—the so-called "Coastline Initiative," which authorized the creation of a commission to regulate *all* development, federal, state, or private, along the California Coast.

Not enough, some said, not enough simply because California's problems were too complex, too entangled in a web of interrelationships, and finally too broad ever to be solved by fragmented and sometimes conflicting government agencies, or by occasional legislation. What was needed was a *plan,* an overall plan that outlined what had to be done to correct present problems and prevent problems in the future.

THE STATE OFFICE OF PLANNING, an agency presumably capable of developing such a plan, had been established during the first administration of Edmund G. Brown. After several years of research, the office issued a report in 1968 that outlined the state's problems and concluded that some sort of plan was, indeed, necessary. The Reagan administration, however, did not believe that the state should become extensively involved in the planning process, contending that local and regional agencies should be left to develop their own outlines for the future. "The state's role," wrote Director of Finance Caspar Weinberger, "should be

*Tahoe Paradise? There were those who looked upon this sort
of thing as a kind of hell.*

limited primarily to furnishing such assistance as local
or regional agencies may request, to the development
of certain broad guidelines or general principles, and
the transmission, to local agencies, of general information." The office's successor, the State Office of Planning and Research (established in 1970), continued in
those traditions, issuing occasional reports, dispensing
information when called upon, and making general
recommendations—none of these actions binding, none
of them comprehensive.

Such an approach was piecemeal planning, many
critics maintained, planning without purpose or power.
Among them was California Tomorrow, which in 1970
decided that if the State Office of Planning and Research
was not going to make a plan, it would. Gathering

together a "task force" of planning consultants, architects, economists, and environmentalists, the conservation organization set about the task and in March 1971
issued a detailed "preliminary sketch" of its conclusions
and recommendations. Much revised and expanded,
the sketch was published in the summer of 1972 as
*The California Tomorrow Plan,* a book whose three
principal sections divided the state into "California
Zero," which summarized the major social and environmental problems facing the state and outlined the traditional approach to solving them; "California One,"
which painted a rather dismal picture of what California would be like in the future if the California Zero
way of doing things continued; and "California Two,"
which outlined alternative proposals, what it would

*A view of what many San Francisco citizens dubbed the "city-wrecker,"*
*a whiplike ribbon of steel and concrete called the Embarcadero Freeway.*

take to implement them, and what California might be like under such planning.

Reaction to the California Tomorrow Plan was widespread, drawing responses from planning experts and agencies across the country—and not a little newspaper ink. Not all of those reactions were complimentary, however. Many felt that adherence to the plan's concept of statewide control would create a "Big Brother" kind of institutional monolith whose dead hand would limit the freedom of every individual in the state. Others, principally the State Office of Planning and Research, remarked that it was a nice try, but still a simplistic and unrealistic approach to problems the plan's authors were not equipped to understand fully —mainly because they were not tied into the govern-

mental structure through which any kind of plan would have to be implemented. People not in power, they said, do not understand the uses of power. Still others pointed out that the plan was utopian, simply because it called for a major shift in attitudes on all levels of California's society, from workingman to businessman, from schoolteacher to construction engineer—a shift that the weight of all history made impossible.

The defenders of the California Tomorrow Plan countered such criticisms by emphasizing the fact that, whatever its shortcomings may or may not be, it was the only guidebook to the future California had or was ever likely to have. Writing in the *Sierra Club Bulletin* in January 1973, historian and conservation writer Roger Olmsted gave it the imprimatur of the world-savers: " 'Are you making a better plan?' is the challenge that Alfred Heller throws at the people of California. ... Well, the state of California has already spent several million dollars to come up with a report that suggests that we *need* a plan. The California Tomorrow task force spent nickles and dimes to come up with a plan concept sufficient to make us *think*.... That is why the plan was made: to help us think our way to a better future. It may be the most important document ever published in California."

I F THE WORLD-SAVERS could have chosen one villain to which most of California's ills could have been attributed, it would have been the growth ethic. "If only the population growth during and following World War II had not been so rapid," Robert W. Durrenberger wrote in *California: Its People, Its Problems, Its Prospects* (1971), "better choices would have been available and better decisions might have been made. The great demand for homes and jobs permitted unscrupulous politicians and land developers to consummate the rape of one of the most beautiful landscapes in the world and replace it with a monotonous urban montage. Where are the open spaces within the cities that are so necessary for those of all ages to enjoy life to the fullest? Where are those bright clear days so that one can enjoy the view of the mountains? And in the mountains, where are the unpolluted streams along which to walk and fish and dream?"

Both the concept and the effects of growth had been challenged—sometimes successfully—by the environmental movement. Some even suggested that the very reality of growth be challenged by the establishment of population limitations of one kind or another. Yet what few people expected was that growth, the one constant dynamic in the state's history, would slow of its own accord. But that was exactly what seemed to be happening by the early 1970s. For the first time California's annual growth rate dropped—only a bare fraction, but a significant fraction—below that of the nation at large in 1971. Her birthrate, too, fell below that of the rest of the country. Even immigration, that flow of people extending clear back to the gold rush years, was falling off. In 1972, according to the State Department of Finance, an estimated 350,000 people left California while some 300,000 were entering.

It had to happen, as demographer Daniel P. Luten pointed out as early as 1964: "California cannot continue to grow forever, or even for a very long period, at a greater rate than the nation. Simple arithmetic shows that if California maintains its growth rate at the traditional 3.8 percent per year and the nation maintains its rate at the 1.6 percent of 1960, then in about 110 years, say 2070, the populations of both the United States and California would be about a billion. That is, all Americans would live in California. This seems unlikely."

Unlikely indeed, but the apparent end of California's traditional growth threw one more uncertainty into the state's grab bag of uncertainties, and the Golden State stumbled toward the last quarter of the twentieth century quite as confused as she had always been. Confused —and fully as eager to discover what the future held. Californians still carried the light of tomorrow in their eyes, which was only as it should have been in the land of the Sundown Sea.

*A 1790 Japanese buddha in Golden Gate Park, San Francisco.*

# *California Mirror:*
# *The Parkland Heritage*

*The varieties of life, Griffith Park, Los Angeles.*

One key characteristic of the city is variety: variety of
biological and cultural stocks, variety of wants, variety
of opportunities, variety of institutions, variety of
fulfillments. Where variety is absent, the city does not exist.
                                                    —Lewis Mumford, 1932

*Escape from the sun and the ungiving sharp edges of the
streets—Griffith Park, Los Angeles.*

*The five-roofed pagoda of the Japanese Tea Garden, Golden Gate Park, San Francisco.*

At last
I shall give myself to the desert again,
that I, in its golden dust,
may be blown from a barren peak,
broadcast over the sun-lands.
If you should desire some news of me,

go ask the little horned toad
whose home is the dust,
or seek it among the fragrant sage,
or question the mountain juniper,—
and they by their silence
will truly inform you.

—Maynard Dixon, 1935

*Ocotillo plants in Anza-Borrego State Park, Southern California.*

*Coal Mines Area Regional Park on the slopes of Mount Diablo, East Bay Regional Park District.*

*Del Valle Regional Park south of Livermore.*

Come away, you who are obsessed with your own importance
in the scheme of things, and have got nothing
you did not sweat for, come away by the brown valleys and
full-bosomed hills to the even-breathing days, to the
kindliness, earthiness, ease. . . .

— Mary Austin, 1903

*Point Pinole Regional Park on San Pablo Bay.*

*Golden Gate National Recreation Area: the Marin Headlands, looking south . . .*

*. . . and looking north to an attenuated Lighthouse Point.*

*Sand, sun, and naked hills: Death Valley National Monument.*

In this part of California man is no more than a tenacious
intruder. The desert draws some men almost irresistibly
by its challenging brutality, but when man is gone, the
desert blithely erases his mark. Like the sea,
but with more diversity, the desert
bespeaks the mystic strength of unseen power.

— Neil Morgan, 1969

*Pinnacle Rock, Point Lobos State Park, south of Carmel.*

I gazing at the boundaries of granite and spray, the
  established sea-marks, felt behind me
Mountain and plain, the immense breadth of the continent,
  before me the mass and doubled stretch of water. . . .
  —Robinson Jeffers, 1933

*The withered ghost of a cypress tree, Point Lobos.*

Climb the mountains and get their good tidings.
Nature's peace will flow into you as sunshine flows
into trees. The winds will blow their freshness
into you, the storms their energy, while cares will
drop off like the autumn leaves.

—John Muir, 1907

*Three views of Sequoia National Park:
the Parker Group of redwoods . . .*

*. . . the heavy white pall
of a Sierra winter . . .*

*. . . and bursting spring ceanothus, slickrock granite, and the
upthrust backbone of the high Sierra.*

Sleeping near the ocean, you
are dimly aware, at intervals
through the night, of the
rhythmic rising and falling
roar of the surf, surely
the most primeval sound on
this planet, taking you back
to all the beginnings, and
the beginnings before the
beginnings. . . .
　　　—Harold Gilliam, 1972

*The line of breakers at
Point Reyes National Seashore.*

# EPILOGUE

I T HAS BEEN TEN YEARS since this book was first written, so long ago that at times it seems to me that it might just as well have been a century. That is the California syndrome. Whatever else one may say about California, the speed of its history over the past one hundred and thirty-four years—from that morning in 1848 when James Marshall saw something glittering in a mill-race to 1982, when the state's voters for the first time rejected a water development proposal—has hardly diminished. In his Pulitzer Prize-winning novel *Angle of Repose,* Wallace Stegner addressed himself to the Doppler Effect of history. He posited it by imagining a man standing at the side of a railroad track. There is silence at first, then the distant wail of a locomotive's whistle and the barely discernible mutter of its engine. Both sounds intensify as the rushing train grows closer, reaching a thundering crescendo as it passes, then swiftly fading, soon becoming no more than a memory—until the next train. California.

California will not, perhaps cannot, remain static. From time to time, this comes home to us who were born there. As the dedication of this book suggests, I am a native Californian, a condition of life that once was as rare as the Furbish lousewort. I spent the first twenty-four years of my life in the Mormon-founded town of San Bernardino, seventy miles east of Los Angeles, then lived for sixteen years in the San Francisco Bay Area before moving on to New York City, and from there to Washington, D.C., where I now rest my bones. Since my departure from the state in 1976, I have made a number of homecoming pilgrimages, learning to my discomfort that Thomas Wolfe was more right than he knew: I couldn't go home again because home was no longer there. San Bernardino, for example.

When I lived there, San Bernardino was a community of about 100,000, surrounded by the sea of orange trees described in Chapter 20 of this book. When I last saw it, the orange trees had all but disappeared, having succumbed to the concrete of freeways and the spreading gypsum board of housing developments. The lyrical sweetness of orange blossoms had been replaced by the stench of photochemical smog creeping east from Los Angeles, obscuring the escarpment of the San Bernardino Mountains that had once been the region's most treasured landmark. The several houses I had lived in had long since been razed. The downtown section of the city—where I had once been on a first-name basis with the proprietors of coffee shops, movie houses, pizza parlors, and dime stores—had been obliterated. In its place were the impersonal ramparts of urban redevelopment: enclosed shopping malls, a lot of glass, that sort of thing. My high school, the center of my life for four years, had been torn down and on the site rose a ten-story apartment complex for senior citizens. Even McDonald's drive-in two blocks from the last San Bernardino house I lived in, the original McDonald's, the first of the chain that has since spread across the country, had been ripped away by bulldozers; only the skeleton of its foundation was left, looking like the gums of a toothless old man.

There was an ineffable sadness in all this for me, but no surprise. I had learned by then that the stability of California life was that of a sand dune in Death Valley—a finely sculpted thing whose appearance alters with the breath of passing winds. What it was yesterday is not what it is today; what it is today is not what it will be tomorrow. There is nothing in the state's history to suggest otherwise.

Consider even the briefest scenario of the past ten years. Politically, the great mass of California voters remain as serenely unpredictable as they ever have been, casting their ballots as their hearts or pocketbooks dictate with only marginal allegiance to either the Democratic or Republican parties. These voters gave Republican Ronald Reagan a second term as governor then helped to send him on to the White House as President of the United States in 1980. In his stead, in 1974 they elected as governor Edmund G. ("Jerry") Brown, Jr., a man only a little over half the age of Reagan, son of the former Democratic governor, and a politician whose private and public attitudes could not have been further removed than those of his predecessor if he had been born on the moon. (His sympathy with various elements of what was still known as the "counterculture," in fact, earned him the nickname of "Governor Moonbeam.") These same voters retained

Democratic liberal Alan Cranston as one of their two senators while rejecting Democratic liberal John Tunney and electing in his place Republican S. I. Hayakawa, the semanticist and former president of San Francisco State College, whom a critic once described as "being a little to the right of Genghis Khan." As this printing of *California: An Illustrated History* goes to press in late 1982, the political scene continues on its merry way. Senator Hayakawa is retiring and Governor Brown is seeking his seat. Democrat Tom Bradley, the first black mayor of Los Angeles, is in turn running for governor. Both are running against staunch conservatives. Given the past performance of the California electorate, to predict the outcome of either election would require the optimism of a poker player drawing for an inside straight.

Who, for example, could have predicted the overwhelming success of Proposition 13 in 1978, the first major amendment to the California state constitution since the days of the Progressives? This measure was the brainchild of Howard Jarvis, a grassroots activist reminiscent of Francis Townsend in the Depression years (see Chapter 18), who stumped up and down the state with a zealot's fervor in order to get enough signatures for it to be placed upon the 1978 ballot. He did it; it was; it passed. It stipulated that property taxes be calculated on only 40 percent of the assessed value of a person's home, an enormous saving to individual homeowners and a great cost to state government. Its long-term economic ramifications will not be fully understood for years, but it is clear that the "taxpayer's revolt" that it represents is one more instance in which California presaged much of the nation; since 1978, seven other states have passed similar measures.

Another, even more astonishing, revolt took place in June 1982, when the state's voters for the first time rejected a major water development project. This was Proposition 9, which would have authorized construction of the Peripheral Canal to divert Northern California water around the Sacramento–San Francisco Bay Delta and plug it into the California State Water Project for delivery to San Joaquin Valley farmers and Los Angeles municipal water users (see Chapter 20) While the motivation for this particular revolt can also largely be laid to economic reasons (Californians, like the rest of the nation, were feeling the bitter pinch of the worst slump since the Depression), much of it was the work of the environmental movement, which had capitalized on the clout it had achieved in the frenetic 1960s and early 1970s (see Chapter 22). By the middle of 1982, for instance, the San Francisco–based Sierra Club had swollen to a membership of more than 300,000, and it was by no means reluctant to let its continuing opposition to the Peripheral Canal be known. Neither were others, among them California Tomorrow, whose California Plan (Chapter 22) has yet to be matched by the state government.

These rebellions were substantially middle class in character, filled with burning rhetoric but not much given to violence. Violence, in fact—at least on the scale of the riots and demonstrations that had punctuated the previous decade (see Chapter 21)—was notably absent from California life through most of the 1970s, although a gay rights demonstration in San Francisco in 1979 did get out of hand and anti-nuclear activists did some fence-pulling and rock-throwing at the site of the nuclear power plant under construction in Diablo Canyon, south of Monterey. The counterculture, too, slipped out of the mainstream of public awareness, many of its members quietly entering middle-class life. (Some retired to become successful, though illegal, businessmen by growing marijuana in the rainforest fields of Northern California, an illicit crop that now is estimated to be worth more than one billion dollars a year.)

During the Gold Rush, journalist Bayard Taylor looked about him and characterized California in a poem. "O panther of the splendid hide!" he wrote, and the comparison was more than apt. Like a cat, California obviously is still a creature whose innermost workings remain much of a mystery even to those who know her intimately. Mysterious, independent—and forever unpredictable.

*T. H. Watkins*

*Washington, D. C.*
*1982*

# APPENDIX
## A CALIFORNIA CHRONOLOGY

**1539:** Surveying the shores of the Sea of Cortés (Gulf of California), Francisco de Ulloa discovers that Baja California is a peninsula.

**1540:** Hernán de Alarcón discovers the Colorado River; Melchior Díaz crosses the Colorado near Yuma on his trek across Arizona, to become the first European in Alta California.

**1542,** *Sept. 28*—Into San Diego Bay (which he calls San Miguel) sails João Rodrigues Cabrillo (Cabrilho).

**1579,** *June 15*—Francis Drake sails into unknown northern California bay and claims "Nova Albion" for Queen Elizabeth.

**1602,** *Nov. 10*—Sebastián Vizcaíno sails into San Miguel Bay, which he renames San Diego de Alcalá. *Dec. 16:* He enters Monterey Bay.

**1701:** Jesuit Father Eusebio Francisco Kino crosses southeast corner of California. Works among Indians of Pimería Alta.

**1769,** *April*—Two vessels arrive in San Diego Bay with supplies for the colony there; *May-June:* Led by Gov. Gaspar de Portolá, Capt. Fernando de Rivera y Moncada and Father Junípero Serra, settlers and soldiers come overland from Baja California with cattle; *July 16:* Father Serra blesses site of Mission San Diego de Alcalá, first of twenty-one to be built in California; *Aug. 2:* Portolá camps at site of Los Angeles. Heads north looking for Monterey Bay but passes it unnoticed on *Oct. 2; Nov. 2:* Advance guard José Artego sights San Francisco Bay; expedition turns back and reaches San Diego on *Jan. 24, 1770.*

**1774,** *March 22*—Arriving from Sonora by overland route, Juan Bautista de Anza reaches Mission San Gabriel.

**1776,** *March 28*—With 247 colonists, Anza reaches site of San Francisco; *Sept. 17:* He founds presidio of San Francisco. Missions San Francisco de Asís (Dolores) and San Juan Capistrano follow.

**1777,** *Nov. 29*—California's first pueblo—San José de Guadalupe—founded.

**1781,** *Sept. 4*—Los Angeles founded.

**1812:** Less than 100 miles north of San Francisco, Russians build a trading post at Fort Ross.

**1821,** *February*—Agustín de Iturbide leads rebel army into Mexico City and becomes the ruler; *October:* Luis Arguello explores the Sacramento Valley.

**1825,** *March 26*—California becomes a territory of the Mexican Republic.

**1826,** *Nov. 27*—Jedediah S. Smith and trappers arrive at Mission San Gabriel, the first Americans to trip overland to California.

**1831,** *Nov. 29*—Pío Pico, Juan Bandini, and José Antonio Carrillo lead revolt against Gov. Manuel Victoria, who resigns.

**1833,** *Aug. 17*—Mexican Congress votes to secularize missions. Task is completed four years later.

**1839,** *July 1*—Johann August Sutter arrives in San Francisco from Switzerland. Establishes New Helvetia and builds Sutter's Fort in the Sacramento Valley; in 1841 acquires Fort Ross and ends Russian encroachment in California.

**1842,** *March 9*—Placer gold discovered in Santa Feliciana Canyon, San Fernando Valley; *Oct. 19:* Thomas ap Catesby Jones, USN, seizes Monterey and raises American flag, believing America and Mexico are at war. Two days later he apologizes, returns Monterey, and departs in haste.

**1843,** *May 1*—First and only U.S. consul to California, Thomas Larkin, is appointed.

**1844,** *March 8*—Capt. John Charles Frémont, U.S. Army, reaches Sutter's Fort; *Nov. 14:* Californios revolt, forcing abdication of Governor Micheltorena; *Dec. 13:* First wagon train reaches Sutter's Fort over Truckee-Donner Lake route.

**1846,** *March 6*—Frémont raises American flag on Gavilan Peak near Monterey. Retreats to Sutter's Fort when ordered to leave California; *May 13:* War between U.S. and Mexico declared; *June 14:* Bear Flag raised at Sonoma; *July 5:* Frémont takes command of revolt and declares California's independence; *July 7:* Comdr. John D. Sloat raises American flag over Monterey; California declared a U.S. possession.

**1847,** *Jan. 9*—U.S. forces win last battle of rebellion. Articles of capitulation signed four days later at Rancho Cahuenga.

**1848,** *Jan. 24*—While building sawmill on American River, James Wilson Marshall discovers the gold which starts the rush; *Feb. 2:* Treaty of Guadalupe Hidalgo ends war with Mexico; U.S. gets California, New Mexico, Utah, Nevada, much of Arizona, and a piece of Colorado.

**1849,** *Feb. 28*—First steamer to bring gold rush passengers to San Francisco, the *California* arrives with 365 passengers; *Sept. 1:* Delegates draft State Constitution in Colton Hall, Monterey. It is adopted on *Oct. 10,* signed *Oct. 13,* and ratified *Nov. 13.*

**1850,** *Sept. 9*—President Fillmore signs act admitting California into the Union.

**1851,** *March 3*—Land commission appointed; *June 9:* Under Sam Brannan, San Francisco Vigilantes organize.

**1853,** *March 3*—Congress okays railroad survey from Mississippi River to Pacific.

**1854:** Sacramento becomes state capital.

**1855,** *Feb. 22*—Financial panic begins with run on Page, Bacon, and Co.; hard times last for two years.

**1859,** *Sept. 13*—Senator David C. Broderick and Judge David S. Terry duel; Broderick is killed.

**1861,** *June 28*—Central Pacific Railroad Co. of California is organized.

**1869,** *May 10*—Central Pacific and Union Pacific are joined by final spike at Promontory, Utah, to complete the first continental railroad.

**1871,** *Oct. 24*—Chinese massacre in Los Angeles.

**1886,** *Feb. 14*—First trainload of oranges—a big citrus valentine—leaves for the East from Los Angeles.

**1890:** Congress creates Yosemite National Park.

**1892:** Conservationist John Muir founds Sierra Club.

**1900,** *April 3*—Greening of Imperial Valley through irrigation begins.

**1906,** *April 18*—Earth shakes, sky burns in San Francisco.

**1910,** *Oct. 1*—*Los Angeles Times* building dynamited. Labor leaders J. B. and J. J. McNamara are later convicted.

**1911,** *Jan. 3*—Hiram W. Johnson becomes governor for two terms (serves as U.S. senator for four successive terms from 1917); *April 3:* Initiative, Referendum, and Recall Act approved.

**1913,** *May 19*—California Land Act prohibits alien Japanese ownership of agricultural land. Congress approves Hetch Hetchy Dam.

**1915:** Panama-Pacific International Exposition opens in San Francisco. Panama-California Exposition opens in San Diego.

**1916,** *July 22*—Preparedness Day parade in San Francisco bombed. Warren K. Billings and Thomas Mooney are convicted.

**1934,** *Dec. 16*—Work begins on All-American Canal from Colorado River to west of Calexico.

**1935,** *Feb. 1*—Gates close at Boulder Dam and storage of Colorado River water for California begins.

**1936,** *November*—San Francisco-Oakland Bay Bridge opens.

**1937,** *May*—Golden Gate Bridge opens.

**1939,** *Feb. 18*—Golden Gate International Exposition opens on Treasure Island in San Francisco Bay.

**1941,** *Dec. 7*—Japanese attack Pearl Harbor. United States declares war.

**1942:** Under Executive Order 9066 Japanese-Americans removed to relocation centers; Earl Warren wins first of three gubernatorial elections.

**1943:** "Zoot Suit" riots in Los Angeles.

**1949:** All employees of University of California required to sign loyalty oath or face dismissal.

**1957:** Department of Water Resources sires California Water Plan.

**1958:** Edmund G. Brown elected governor.

**1959:** State legislature passes California Water Resources Development Bond Act (Burns-Porter Act).

**1960:** Closed sessions of the House Un-American Activities Committee in San Francisco trigger student riots.

**1962:** San Francisco, Alameda, and Contra Costa counties approve creation of Bay Area Rapid Transit system.

**1963:** Rumford Act forbids discrimination in sale or rental of residential property.

**1964:** Proposition 14 repeals Rumford Act of 1963; Free Speech Movement sit-in at University of California, Berkeley, leads to largest mass arrests in California history.

**1965:** Thirty-two die in Watts Riot—longest, most destructive in twentieth century; Cesar Chavez's National Farm Workers Association wins its first strike; later joins Agricultural Workers Organizing Committee and the two unions merge as United Farm Workers Organizing Committee.

**1966:** Ronald Reagan elected governor.

**1969,** *May*—"People's Park" conflict results in first casualty of student wars and transforms Berkeley into an occupied city.

**1970:** California becomes most urban state in nation as well as most populous. Governor Reagan re-elected. Students riot at University of California in Santa Barbara. Chicano protest over Mexican-American Vietnam casualties generates riot in Los Angeles—one dead. Grape growers end farm worker boycott and sign contracts including health insurance programs for first time in U.S. farm labor history. Coast Guard removes last protesting Indian from occupied Alcatraz.

**1971:** Governor Reagan sets in motion first transfer of water by State Water Project from Northern California across the mountains to Southern California.

**1972:** "Coastline Initiative" (Proposition 20) authorizes a commission to regulate all coast development—the most significant conservation development in California history.

**1974:** Edmund G. ("Jerry") Brown, Jr., is elected to serve as governor. As the son of the former Governor Brown, this is the first gubernatorial dynasty evidenced in the state. After his second term, Brown decides to run for the Senate in 1978 in an attempt to replace the retiring Senator S. I. Hayakawa.

**1976:** BART—the Bay Area Rapid Transit system—goes into service, with lines connecting Oakland and San Francisco with Concord on the west and Fremont and Daly City on the south. It is the first large-scale rapid transit system in California since the days of the "Big Red Cars." In the meantime, Southern California voters turn down one mass-transit bond issue after another, retaining their half-century love affair with automobile and the everlasting freeway system.

**1978:** Proposition 13—the so-called "Jarvis Amendment"—is approved by the voters of the state. It is the first major amendment to the 1879 California state constitution since the passage of Referendum and Recall in 1911, and stipulates that no home can be taxed at more than 40 percent of its assessed valuation. Similar measures in other states soon follow.

**1982:** Rejection of Proposition 9 marks the first time in California history that the state's voters have turned down a major water development project. The Proposition would have authorized construction of the Peripheral Canal around the Sacramento River–San Francisco Bay Delta in Northern California; it would have delivered water to the southern San Joaquin Valley and the Metropolitan Water District of Southern California through the facilities of the California State Water Project.

# SUGGESTED READING

There is no shortage of books about California. There *definitely* is no shortage of books about California. One glance at the bibliography of any general history might convince the uninformed observer that California was an elderly national power with approximately twelve centuries of history to recall, not a mere American state with hardly more than two hundred years of a recognizable past. The following listing, then, is highly selective and purely arbitrary, but I believe it will give the general reader, should he wish to explore the subject further, a solid grasp of the major factors that have gone into the formation of the Golden State. Most of the books are either still in print or available from any public or college library of respectable dimensions.

**Geology, Geography, and Prehistory:** *Earth Song: A Prologue to History* by Charles Camp (Palo Alto, 1970); *California Through the Ages: The Geological Story of a Great State* by William J. Miller (Berkeley, 1957); *California, Land of Contrast* by David W. Lantis, Rodney Steiner, and Arthur E. Karinen (New York, 1963); *An Island Called California: An Ecological Introduction to Its Natural Communities* by Elna Bakker (Berkeley, 1970).

**General Histories:** *California: An Interpretative History* (Revised Edition) by Walton Bean (Berkeley, 1972); *California* (Revised Edition) by John Caughey (Los Angeles, 1970); *Everyman's Eden* by Ralph J. Roske (New York, 1968); *California: A History* by Andrew F. Rolle (New York, 1963); *California: Two Centuries of Man, Land, and Growth in the Golden State* by W. H. Hutchinson (Palo Alto, 1969); *California: The Great Exception* by Carey McWilliams (New York, 1949); *California: A History of the Golden State* by Warren Beck and David A. Williams (New York, 1972); *California: Land of New Beginnings* by David Lavender (New York, 1972); *Historic Spots in California* by Mildred B. Hoover, Hero E. Rensch, and Ethel Rensch, revised by Rev. William N. Abeloe (Berkeley, 1966).

**Anthologies:** *West of the West: Witnesses to the California Experience, 1542-1906* by Robert Kirsch and William S. Murphy (New York, 1967); *California Heritage: An Anthology of History and Literature* by John and Laree Caughey (Itasca, Ill., 1971); *Readings in California History* by N. Ray and Gladys Gilmore (New York, 1968).

**The California Indians:** *Handbook of the Indians of California* by Alfred L. Kroeber (Washington, D.C., 1925; reprinted, 1953); *The California Indians: A Source Book* by Robert F. Heizer and Mary Ann Whipple (Berkeley and Los Angeles, 1953); *Ishi in Two Worlds: A Biography of the Last Wild Indian in America* by Theodora Kroeber (Berkeley and Los Angeles, 1961); *The Inland Whale* by Theodora Kroeber (Berkeley, 1959).

**Pre-American Settlement and Development:** *Spanish Voyages to the Northwest Coast of America in the Sixteenth Century* by Henry R. Wagner (San Francisco, 1929); *A History of California: The Spanish Period* by Charles E. Chapman (New York, 1921); *Outposts of Empire* by Herbert E. Bolton (New York, 1931); *California Under Spain and Mexico, 1535-1847* by Irving B. Richman (New York, 1911); *The History of California, Volume I, 1542-1800, Volume II, 1800-1824, Volume III, 1824-1846* by Hubert Howe Bancroft (written by Henry L. Oak, San Francisco, 1884-1888).

**Expansionism and American Acquisition:** *Manifest Destiny and Mission in American History* by Frederick Merk (New York, 1963);

*Exploration and Empire* by William H. Goetzmann (New York, 1966); *James K. Polk: Continentalist* by Charles Sellers (New York, 1968); *The Year of Decision, 1846* by Bernard DeVoto (Boston, 1943); *A History of California, Volume IV, 1846-1848* by H. H. Bancroft (written by Henry L. Oak, San Francisco, 1888); *This Reckless Breed of Men* by Robert G. Cleland (New York, 1950); *Jedediah Smith and the Opening of the West* by Dale L. Morgan (Indianapolis and New York, 1953); *The California Trail* by George R. Stewart (New York, 1962); *Men to Match My Mountains: The Opening of the Far West* by Irving Stone (New York, 1956); *Fremont: Pathmarker of the West* by Allen Nevins (New York, 1932).

**The Gold Rush and the Golden Era:** *Gold Is the Cornerstone* by John Caughey (Berkeley, 1948); *Anybody's Gold* by Joseph Henry Jackson (San Francisco, 1970); *California Gold* by Rodman Paul (Cambridge, Mass., 1947); *The California Gold Discovery* by Rodman Paul (Georgetown, California, 1966); *Mining Frontiers of the Far West* by Rodman Paul (New York, 1963); *Gold and Silver in the West: The Illustrated History of an American Dream* by T. H. Watkins (Palo Alto, 1971); *The Gold Mines of California* by Jack R. Wagner (Berkeley, 1970); *The El Dorado Trail* by Ferol Egan (New York, 1970); *Fool's Gold: A Biography of John Sutter* by Richard H. Dillon (New York, 1967); *William Tecumseh Sherman, Gold Rush Banker* by Dwight L. Clarke (San Francisco, 1969); *Sea Routes to the Gold Fields* by Oscar Lewis (New York, 1949); *California from the Conquest in 1846 to the Second Vigilance Committee* by Josiah Royce (New York, 1949); *Express and Stagecoach Days in California* by Oscar O. Winther (Stanford, 1946); *David C. Broderick: A Political Portrait* by David A. Williams (San Marino, California, 1969); *Committee of Vigilance* by George R. Stewart (Boston, 1964).

**The Comstock Lode and Its Impact:** *The Big Bonanza* by Dan de Quille (New York, 1947); *The Saga of the Comstock* by George D. Lyman (New York, 1934); *Ralston's Ring* by George D. Lyman (New York, 1937); *History of the Comstock Lode* by Grant H. Smith (New York, 1943); *The Silver Kings* by Oscar Lewis (New York, 1947); *Comstock Mines and Miners* by Eliot Lord (Berkeley, 1964).

**Land Monopoly, Railroad Monopoly, and Reaction:** *California Ranchos and Farms, 1846-1862* by Paul W. Gates (Madison, Wisc., 1967); *Land in California* by W. W. Robinson (Los Angeles, 1948); *The Cattle King* by Edward F. Treadwell (New York, 1931); *Henry George* by Charles A. Barker (New York, 1955); *The Big Four* by Oscar Lewis (New York, 1935); *The Great Persuader* by David Lavender (New York, 1970); *Leland Stanford: Man of Many Careers* by Norman E. Tutorow (Stanford, 1970); *Chapters in the History of the Southern Pacific* by Stuart Daggett (New York, 1922); *High Road to Promontory: The Building of the Central Pacific* by George Kraus (Palo Alto, 1969); *Westward to Promontory: The Building of the Union Pacific Across the Plains and Mountains* by Barry B. Combs (Palo Alto, 1969); *The Mussel Slough Tragedy* by J. L. Brown (Fresno, 1958).

**The Growth of Southern California:** *The Cattle on a Thousand Hills* by Robert G. Cleland (New York, 1951); *The City-Makers, 1868-1876* by Remi Nadeau (New York, 1948); *Los Angeles: From Mission to Modern City* by Remi Nadeau (New York, 1960); *The Boom of the Eighties in Southern California* by Glenn S. Dumke (San Marino, California, 1944); *Sixty Years in Southern California* by Harris Newmark (edited by W. W. Robinson; Los Angeles,

1970); *The Free Harbor Contest in Los Angeles* by Charles D. Willard (Los Angeles, 1899); *Southern California Country* by Carey McWilliams (New York, 1946).

**Corruption, Reform, and Labor Strife:** *Boss Ruef's San Francisco* by Walton Bean (Berkeley and Los Angeles, 1952); *The California Progressives* by George E. Mowry (Berkeley and Los Angeles, 1951); *California's Prodigal Sons: Hiram Johnson and the Progressives, 1911-1917* by Spencer C. Olin, Jr. (Berkeley and Los Angeles, 1968); *Oil, Land, and Politics: The California Career of Thomas R. Bard* by W. H. Hutchinson (Norman, Oklahoma, 1966); *We Shall Be All: A History of the I.W.W.* by Melvin Dubofsky (Chicago, 1969); *Frame-Up: The Incredible Case of Tom Mooney and Warren Billings* by Curt Gentry (New York, 1967).

**Oil Discoveries and Development:** *Oil, Land, and Politics* by W. H. Hutchinson (Norman, Oklahoma, 1966); *Scientists in Conflict: The Beginnings of the Oil Industry in California* by Gerald White (San Marino, California, 1968); *Formative Years in the Far West: A History of Standard Oil Company of California and Predecessors through 1919* by Gerald White (New York, 1962); *Little Giant of Signal Hill* by Walker A. Tompkins (New York, 1967); *Economics of the Pacific Coast Petroleum Industry* by Joe S. Bain (Berkeley, 1944-1947).

**Water Projects and Problems:** *The Water-Seekers* by Remi Nadeau (New York, 1950); "Triumph and Failure in the Imperial Valley" by Helen Hosmer, "The Desert Shall Rejoice. . . ." by Paul S. Taylor, and "Making an Empire to Order" by T. H. Watkins, in *The Grand Colorado: The Story of a River and Its Canyons* (edited by T. H. Watkins; Palo Alto, 1969); *The Colorado* by Frank Waters (New York, 1946); *The Thirsty Land* by Robert W. De Roos (Stanford, 1948); *California Water: A Study in Resource Management* by David Seckler (Berkeley, 1971); *The Water Hustlers* by John Graves, T. H. Watkins, and Robert H. Boyle (Sierra Club, New York, 1971); *Aqueduct Empire* by Erwin Cooper (Glendale, California, 1968).

**Agriculture and Agricultural Labor:** *California Agriculture* edited by Claude V. Hutchinson (Berkeley, 1946); *Garden of the Sun* by Wallace Smith (Los Angeles, 1953); *History of the Sacramento Valley* by Joseph A. McGowan (New York, 1961); *Factories in the Field: The Story of Migratory Farm Labor in California* by Carey McWilliams (New York, 1939); *Ill Fares the Land: Migratory Labor in the United States* by Carey McWilliams (New York, 1942); *Mexican Labor in the United States: Imperial Valley, California* by Paul S. Taylor (Berkeley, 1928); *An American Exodus: A Record of Human Erosion* by Paul S. Taylor (with Dorothea Lange; New Haven, 1969); *Labor Relations in Agriculture* by Varden Fuller (New York, 1955); *Delano: The Story of the California Grape Strike* by John Gregory Dunn (New York, 1971).

**The Depression Years:** *The Politics of Upheaval* by Arthur M. Schlesinger, Jr. (New York, 1960); *Glory Roads: The Psychological State of California* by Luther Whiteman and Samuel L. Lewis (New York, 1936); *The Autobiography of Upton Sinclair* (New York, 1962); *Old Age Politics in California: From Richardson to Reagan* by Jackson K. Putnam (Berkeley, 1970).

**The Movies:** *The Movies: The Sixty-Year Story of the World of Hollywood and Its Effect on America. . . .* by Richard Griffith and Arthur Mayer (New York, 1971); *Hollywood: The Movie Colony, The Movie Makers* by Leo C. Rosten (New York, 1939); *The Lion's Share: A History of Metro-Goldwyn-Mayer* by Bosley Crowther (New York, 1957); *Hollywood Rajah: The Life and Times of Louis B. Mayer* by Bosley Crowther (New York, 1960).

**Politics:** *The Dancing Bear: An Informal History of California Politics* by Gladwin Hill (Cleveland, Ohio, 1968); *The Rumble of California Politics, 1848-1970* edited by Royce D. Delmatier, Clarence F. McIntosh, and Earl G. Waters (New York, 1970); *California Politics and Policies* edited by Eugene P. Dvorin and Arthur J. Misner (Palo Alto, 1966); *Political Change in California: Critical Elections and Social Movements, 1890-1966* by Michael Paul Rogin and John L. Shover (Westport, Conn., 1970).

**Minority Relations:** *The Other Californians* by Robert F. Heizer and Alan F. Almquist (Berkeley and Los Angeles, 1971); *Ethnic Conflict in California History* edited by Charles Wollenberg (Berkeley, 1970); *The Conflict Between the California Indian and the White Civilization* by Sherbourne F. Cook (Berkeley and Los Angeles, 1943); *The Decline of the Californios: A Social History of the Spanish-Speaking Californians, 1846-1900* by Leonard M. Pitt (Berkeley and Los Angeles, 1966); *Archy Lee* by Rudolph M. Lapp (San Francisco, 1969); *The Anti-Chinese Movement in California* by Elmer C. Sande-Meyer (Berkeley, 1939); *Bitter Strength* by Gunther Barth (New York, 1964); *The Indispensable Enemy* by A. P. Saxton (Berkeley and Los Angeles, 1971); *Americans Betrayed: Politics and the Japanese Evacuation* by Morton Grodzins (New York, 1949); *Concentration Camps USA: Japanese Americans and World War II* by Roger Daniels (New York, 1971); *Executive Order 9066: The Internment of 110,000 Japanese Americans* by Masie and Richard Conrat (San Francisco, 1972).

**The Dynamics of Growth:** *California: Its People, Its Problems, Its Prospects* edited by Robert W. Durrenberger (Palo Alto, 1971); *The California Revolution* edited by Carey McWilliams (New York, 1968); *California: The New Society* by Remi Nadeau (New York, 1963); *Westward Tilt* by Neil Morgan (New York, 1963); *The California Syndrome* by Neil Morgan (New York, 1969); *California: The Vanishing Dream* by Michael Davies (New York, 1973); *California: The Paradox of Plenty* by T. H. Watkins (New York and Toronto, 1970); *Los Angeles: The Ultimate City* by Christopher Rand (New York, 1967).

**Sundry Riots:** *Burn, Baby, Burn: The Los Angeles Race Riot, August, 1965* by Jerry Cohen and William J. Murphy (New York, 1966); *Violence in the City: An End or a Beginning?* by the Governor's Commission on the Los Angeles Riots (Los Angeles, 1965); *We Are the People Our Parents Warned Us Against* by Nicholas Von Hoffman (New York, 1969); *The Berkeley Student Revolt: Facts and Interpretations* edited by Seymour M. Lipset and Sheldon S. Wolin (Berkeley, 1965); *The Campus War* by John Searle (New York, 1971); *The Report of the President's Commission on Campus Unrest* (Washington, D.C., 1970).

**The Conservation Movement:** *John Muir and the Sierra Club* by Holway R. Jones (San Francisco, 1965); *California, Going, Going. . . .* by Samuel E. Wood (San Francisco, 1962); *The Phantom Cities of California* by Samuel E. Wood (with Alfred Heller; San Francisco, 1963); *The Destruction of California* by Raymond F. Dassman (New York, 1965); *Eden in Jeopardy* by Richard G. Lillard (New York, 1966); *How to Kill a Golden State* by William Bronson (New York, 1968); *Between the Devil and the Deep Blue Bay: The Struggle to Save San Francisco Bay* by Harold Gilliam (San Francisco, 1969).

# CHRONICLERS OF THE GOLDEN STATE

The following list, like the list of suggested readings above, is both selective and arbitrary. It incorporates those writers and those works which seem to me to most effectively re-create the California experience in strictly literary terms—even for those titles listed which are largely reportorial or reminiscent in nature. With all deference to the fact that one man's literary standards are another man's object of laughter, I believe the following selection will provide the interested reader with the sense of having participated in, as well as observed, some rather important moments and moods of California history.

Richard Henry Dana (1815–1882): *Two Years Before the Mast* (1840), an account of his adventures in the brig *Pilgrim*, out of Salem, in the years 1834–1836. The *Pilgrim* was a hide-and-tallow trader for the Boston firm of Bryant & Sturgis, and Dana's description of life in Mexican California is surpassed only by his persuasive and evocative rendition of life aboard a Cape Horner in the glory days of sail.

Bayard Taylor (1825–1878): One of the most prolific travel writers in an age that crawled with them, Taylor came to California in 1849 and set down his impressions in *Eldorado, or, Adventures in the Path of Empire. . . .* (1850), an account particularly descriptive of the trip across the Isthmus of Panama and of a San Francisco painfully building itself upon sand dunes and water-lots.

Louisa Smith Clapp (1819–1908): As "Dame Shirley," this young bride wrote regularly from a tiny mining community on a branch of the Feather River to her sister "Molly" in Amherst, Massachusetts, giving us the finest single treatment of life in the California mines in the early 1850s. The letters were first published in the short-lived San Francisco periodical, *The Pioneer*, and were later anthologized in several editions as *The Shirley Letters*.

Bret Harte (1836–1902): Primarily an editor and short-story writer, Harte so effectively mythologized the period of the Gold Rush during the three years of his editorship of the *Overland Monthly* that neither he nor the Gold Rush were ever fully able to escape what he had done. The best of his stories are "The Luck of Roaring Camp" (1868) and "The Outcasts of Poker Flat" (1869); both have been collected in various anthologies, including *The Luck of Roaring Camp and Other Sketches* (New York, 1928) and *The Outcasts of Poker Flat and Other Tales* (New York, 1964).

Samuel Clemens (Mark Twain; 1835–1910): Although California's claim on the greatest humorist of American literature is somewhat anemic, *Roughing It* (1872), one of his earliest and best books, limns the peculiarities of life on the Comstock Lode with a flair and perception no other writer was able to match.

Frank Norris (1870–1902): In *The Octopus* (1901) Norris laid bare the excesses of the Southern Pacific Railroad in a novel that possessed all the subtlety of an axe-blow at the base of a redwood tree—but powerful and moving withal. In *McTeague: A Story of San Francisco* (1899), by far the lesser-known work, he achieved equal power with greater grace, in a study of greed and ambition and gothic tragedy.

Gertrude Atherton (1857–1948): The three best books of California's most renowned woman writer were *The Splendid Idle Forties* (1902), a consciously romantic view of California in the days before the Americans, *The Adventures of a Novelist* (1932),

an autobiography, and *My San Francisco: A Wayward Biography* (1946), a fond look at a well-loved city.

Jack London (1876–1915): London, California's first native-born writer to achieve national stature, produced two books directly relating to California: *Martin Eden* (1909), a heavily-autobiographical account of the struggle, rise, and ultimate downfall of a young writer, and the much lesser work, *The Valley of the Moon* (1913), which waxes eloquent about the California landscape in the region in which London found his final home.

Lincoln Steffens (1866–1936): Although he acquired his public image as a muckraker of large dimensions (*The Shame of the Cities*), his most finely-honed and lasting work was *Boy on Horseback* (1935), the reminiscence of a youth spent in the Sacramento Valley.

Upton Sinclair (1878–1968): *Oil!*, published in 1927, captured the hysteria, boom-and-bust psychology, and waste of the oil boom years of Southern California; it was just one of the scores of books produced by California's full-time socialist, sometime politician, and prolific disturber of the peace.

Robinson Jeffers (1887–1962): Sometimes excessively bitter over the works of man and sometimes awkward in their phrasing, the poems of Jeffers are never without an awesome power and a sure sense of the shape and mood and feel of the California landscape, particularly in the Big Sur region, which he loved above all others. It can quite safely be said that he is the only California poet to produce work of an importance for future generations; his best narratives were *Roan Stallion* (1925), *The Women at Point Sur* (1927), and *Give Your Heart to the Hawks* (1933).

John Steinbeck (1902–1968): Steinbeck is considered California's "great" writer, and not without reason: with *The Pastures of Heaven* (1932), *To a God Unknown* (1933), *Tortilla Flat* (1935), *In Dubious Battle* (1936), *Of Mice and Men* (1938), *The Long Valley* (1938), *The Grapes of Wrath* (1939), *Cannery Row* (1945), and *East of Eden* (1952), Steinbeck achieved a body of work of a general quality that no California novelist has ever matched, or is ever likely to match. Little needs to be said for his Pulitzer Prize–winning *The Grapes of Wrath*, but personal prejudice enjoins me to single out *To a God Unknown* and *The Long Valley* as two of the most moving interpretations of the nearly mystical love that men can have for the land on which they live and work that exist in our literature.

Other works of more than passing merit *The Human Comedy* (1943) by William Saroyan, *East of the Giants* (1938) by George Stewart, *South of the Angels* (1958) by Jessamyn West, *The Postman Always Rings Twice* (1945) by James M. Cain, *What Makes Sammy Run?* (1941) by Budd Schulberg, *The Day of the Locust* (1939) by Nathanael West, *The Last Tycoon* (1941) by F. Scott Fitzgerald, *The Deer Park* (1954) by Norman Mailer, *The Ninth Wave* (1956) by Eugene F. Burdick, *On the Road* (1956) by Jack Kerouac, *The Maltese Falcon* (1944) by Dashiell Hammett, *Farewell, My Lovely* (1940) by Raymond Chandler, and *The Goodbye Look* (1971) by Ross Macdonald (Kenneth Millar).

Franklin Walker's *San Francisco's Literary Frontier* (1939) is still the major study of California literature, although it has been amply reinforced by Lawrence Clark Powell's recent *California Classics: The Creative Literature of the Golden State* (1971).

# ACKNOWLEDGMENTS AND PICTURE CREDITS

Portions of this book appeared in the following publications and are used with permission: *Laughing in the Jungle* by Louis Adamic (Harper & Row, 1925); "California: After 19 Million, What?" by Robert C. Cook (in *Population Bulletin*, June 1966); *California: The Vanishing Dream* by Michael Davie (Dodd, Mead & Co., 1973); *California: Its People, Its Problems, Its Prospects* by Robert W. Durrenberger (National Press Books, 1971); *The San Francisco Experience* by Harold Gilliam (Doubleday, 1972); *The Inland Whale* by Theodora Kroeber (Indiana University Press, 1959); *California: The Great Exception* by Carey McWilliams (Current Books, 1949); *The California Syndrome* by Neil Morgan (Prentice-Hall, 1971); *Los Angeles: From Mission to Modern City* by Remi Nadeau (Longmans, Green & Co., 1960); "Is California Civilized?" by Robert Whitaker (in *The Nation*, April 1931).

Aero Photographers, Sausalito: Page 457. Automobile Club of Southern California: Page 330. Bancroft Library, University of California, Berkeley: Pages 2-3, 18, 21, 34, 37, 41, 42, 43, 50, 52, 54, 55, 71, 76, 80, 86, 87 (left), 89, 97-107, 109-111, 114-115, 121-122, 124-127, 130-134, 138-139, 142-143, 150, 154, 170, 176-177, 178, 181-187, 190-202, 210, 215 (bottom), 220, 222-228, 231, 234, 238-239, 280-286, 290-291, 303-304, 313, 320-321, 323, 325 (courtesy of Standard Oil of California), 366 (Dorothea Lange photo), 372-373, 413 (Dorothea Lange photo), 437, 463-464, 468 (left), 469, 492 (Dorothea Lange photo), 506-507. William Bronson: Pages 509, 514. Bureau of Reclamation, Department of the Interior: Pages 388, 391-392. California Department of Education: Pages 498, 499 (top, middle). California Historical Society: Pages 4, 78, 87 (right), 90-91, 113, 116-119, 140-141, 153, 165 (bottom), 174, 205, 207, 233, 235 (bottom), 289, 292-293, 428-429 (from paintings in a traveling exhibit: "Months of Waiting"). California State Archives: Page 235 (top). California State Library: Page 468 (right). Eloise Carter: Pages 524, 530-531. Mark Chamberlain: Pages 402-403. Claremont Colleges: Page 502 (top). Richard Conrat: Page 510. Ed Cooper: Pages 146-147, 383, 421, 444 (bottom), 447 (top), 446-447 (bottom), 448, 473-474. E. B. Crocker Art Gallery: Pages 44-45, 94-95. Department of Water Resources: Page 465. Division of Highways: Pages 461, 512, 515. East Bay Regional Park District: Pages 522, 523. George Eastman House: Page 123. C. E. Erickson map: Page 84. Foothill Community College District: Page 500. Gerald French: Pages 443 (top left), 462. Fresno Unified School District: Page 499 (bottom). George Hall: Page 384. History Division, Los Angeles County Museum of Natural History: Pages 28, 74-75, 188-189, 216-217, 221 (top), 229-230, 260, 268-269, 311, 318, 322, 331 (bottom), 338 (top), 340, 341 (top), 396. Mrs. Mary Hood and Yosemite Park Museum: Page 331 (bottom). Imperial Valley District Association: Pages 334, 335 (top). Kaiser Industries: Page 436. Library of Congress: Page 412 (Dorothea Lange photo). Los Angeles Recreation and Parks Department: Pages 518, 519. *Los Angeles Times:* Pages 299, 300, 301. David Muench: Pages 7-8, 12-16, 144-145, 168, 240, 294-295, 377-380 (top), 381 (top), 422-424, 441, 446 (top), 478-480, 497, 503-504, 517, 520-521, 525-529. Josef Muench: Page 404. Tom Myers: Pages 11, 48, 96, 148, 380 (bottom), 381 (bottom), 382, 442, 443 (right). Oakland Museum: Pages 137, 172, 236-237. Office of Senator Alan Cranston: Page 471. Office of Governor Ronald Reagan: Page 420 (left). Office of Senator John Tunney: Page 470 (right). Walter Sanders: Page 401 (photo in *Life* magazine, May 22, 1970; copyright Time, Inc., 1970). San Francisco Public Library, Special Collections: Pages 108, 287, 315-316, 347-349, 354-356, 360-365, 367-371, 374, 386, 390-391, 393, 397, 409-410, 415-420, 430, 432, 434-435, 438-439, 453-456, 482-483, 488-490. Security Pacific National Bank, Los Angeles: Pages 189 (bottom), 244, 247-248, 250, 306, 324, 344-345, 352, 358, 407, 426, 432. Southern Pacific Railroad: Pages 157-158, 163. Southwest Museum: Page 29. Stanford University: Page 501. Title Insurance and Trust Company, Los Angeles: Pages 27, 30-33, 128, 216, 221 (bottom), 243, 246, 254-255, 257-259, 308, 314, 332-333, 339, 353, 395. Title Insurance and Trust Company, San Diego: Pages 209, 211-215 (top), 218-219, 245, 249, 251-253, 256, 261-263, 266-267, 271-272, 302, 308, 327-329, 335 (bottom), 337, 338 (bottom), 342-343, 346, 350, 357, 408, 431. Tom Tracy: Pages 120, 296, 444 (top), 445, 475, 476 (courtesy of Pacific Telephone & Telegraph Co.), 477. United States Geological Survey: Page 9 (NASA photo). University of California at Santa Cruz: Page 502 (bottom). United Press International: Pages 491, 494. Union Pacific Railroad: Pages 159-162, 164-165 (top). Collection of Robert Weinstein: Pages 69, 70, 72, 73. Warren Yee: Page 486 (from *People's Park*, Alan Copeland and Nikki Aria, 1969). De Young Museum: Page 166-167. James Yudleson: Page 484 (from *People's Park*, Alan Copeland and Nikki Aria, 1969). Except for that on p. 84, all the maps in this book are through the courtesy of the A. M. Goushá Company. Mechanical overlays are by Owen Welsh, San Francisco.

As the picture credits list above makes perfectly clear, the source from which the largest single bloc of illustrations for this book were obtained was the Bancroft Library of the University of California, Berkeley. This seems as good a time and place as any to express deep thanks to the staff of the library, which for more than ten years has been rendering service above and beyond the call of duty (or even friendship) not only to the author but to the American West Publishing Company in general. Special thanks in this regard must go to Robert Becker, assistant to the director, John Barr Tompkins, director of public services, and Mrs. Alma Compton, who has been faithfully deciphering the author's semi-legible picture-orders for years without a single mishap. *Selah!*

The Bancroft Library is not alone. In any book of this size and complexity, a veritable army of people have been of service in one regard or another. Here are just a few of them: Peter Evans, Craig Perrin, and J. S. Holliday, director of the California Historical Society; William Mason of the History Division, Los Angeles County Museum of Natural History; Gladys Hansen of the Special Collections Department, San Francisco Public Library; Victor Plukas of the Security Pacific National Bank, Los Angeles; Therese Heyman of the Art Division, Oakland Museum; David Shapiro of the Title Insurance and Trust Company, Los Angeles; Larry Booth of the Title Insurance and Trust Company, San Diego; and Robert Weinstein, who devoted materials, time, and energy to this project.

Finally, a very special thanks must go to two men. To Roger Olmsted, who has for years been cheerfully allowing the author to borrow his mind when his own seemed moribund and decrepit, and never more so than on this project. And to W. H. Hutchinson, not only for reading the book in manuscript and challenging some of the author's more visible failings, but for being the teacher and friend he has been for ten years. Neither he, Olmsted, or any other individual, of course, should be held responsible for any errors of fact or interpretation this book may contain; these are the sole and exclusive property of the author.

And of course there was always Joan, without whom nothing would be possible.

542